Occupational Therapy and Activities Health: Toward Health Through Activities

Occupational Therapy and Activities Health: Toward Health Through Activities

Simme Cynkin, M.S., O.T.R., F.A.O.T.A.
Consultant in Private Practice,
New Rochelle, New York

Anne Mazur Robinson, M.A., O.T.R., C.R.C.
Chief, Therapeutic Activities and Vocational Rehabilitation Service, Department of
Psychiatry, St. Vincent's Hospital and Medical Center of New York;
Associate in Clinical Occupational Therapy, College of Physicians and Surgeons,
Columbia University, New York, New York

Little, Brown and Company
Boston/Toronto/London

Library of Congress Catalog Card No. 89-85554

ISBN 0-316-16611-1

Printed in the United States of America

To our husbands
  To our mothers
    To our fathers, in memory

CONTENTS

PREFACE

The preface to a previous book, *Occupational Therapy: Toward Health Through Activities*, ended with a challenge to the reader: "Your testing and attempts at validation will be the addendum to this book, whether they come in the guise of an article in a learned journal, a dissertation, an independent study, a paper read at a conference or, best of all, excellent service to the patient/client . . . ." Some ten years later, questions, suggestions, reactions and actions of students, educators, and practitioners alike have contributed to an addendum that has almost outstripped the original in expansion of ideas.

Hence this successor. The concept of *activities health* is alive and well, nurtured in particular by those students who have plunged into a novel and not altogether risk-free educational experience; those educators who have ventured into relatively unknown territory, willing to shed for a while the more comfortable and familiar role of "teacher" as they have explored the world of human activities in a "community of learning"; and those practitioners excited enough by the therapeutic potential of activities to test the concepts, connections, and conclusions that now appear, fully fledged, as Part I.

The Educational Model, presented in Part II, has also come to full maturity. Based on the premises offered in that previous book, it first saw the light of day in 1981 at Columbia University, where Barbara Neuhaus, Ed.D., O.T.R., as acting director of the occupational therapy program, sponsored and supported what was then a largely experimental approach to the teaching of activities. A wonderful thing happened to the Educational Model along the way. In 1984, Anne Mazur Robinson spent a full academic year as observer/participant in this unusually focused activities course. She then consented to take on responsibility for the entire program of coursework. Her enthusiasm, creativity, intellectual curiosity, and devotion have led to a remarkable acceleration in the growth and development of the Educational Model. Hence the writing partnership, which has resulted in a perfect situation for *reciprocity* in Bruner's [15] sense, as well as in the exchange of ideas that have imbued this book.

Part III, on clinical application, is both the culmination of these ideas and the source of further insights supporting the concepts, connections, and conclusions of Part I and the theoretical base, objectives, and methods of the Educational Model presented in Part II. The promise of our profession—excellent service to the patient/client—is highlighted by means of two complete case studies presented by Patricia

A. Miller, M.Ed., M.A., O.T.R., F.A.O.T.A., and Anne Spencer, M.A., O.T.R., F.A.O.T.A., who have made *activities health* an attainable reality for many. Their examples serve as a spur to others, while the "how-tos," part and parcel of the clinical application section, help to make the promise come true.

Despite the expansion of the text, the original challenge to the reader still holds good. Yet another addendum is awaited!

S. C.

ACKNOWLEDGMENTS

Those who contributed the seminal ideas on which this book is based have already been acknowledged in *Occupational Therapy: Toward Health Through Activities*. We add our thanks to the many colleagues, students, family members, friends, and others, without whose involvement this expanded and revised version could not have come into being.

We begin, in chronological order, with Barbara Neuhaus, O.T.R., Chairperson of the Occupational Therapy Program at Columbia University, whose commitment to the study of activities led to the introduction of the Educational Model, which is presented in this book. With the enthusiastic participation of a succession of students, this model has since burgeoned and solidified. We are indebted to Dr. Neuhaus and many of these students for permitting us to use material from course assignments as illustrations of the beauty, infinite variety, and power of activities as tools for learning and living. Their names appear in the last paragraph of this section as well as in Part II.

The questions, suggestions, and discussions arising from the coursework and later from ongoing presentations to colleagues and students in other settings—both educational and clinical—have enabled us to rethink, refine, and in some instances reshape the concepts, connections, and conclusions relating to *activities health*, which serve as the theoretical basis for the Educational Model as well as for the application to practice. For their contributions to our education, we thank Josephine Cohen, O.T.R., and her dedicated faculty at Elizabethtown College in Elizabethtown, Pennsylvania, who succeeded in adapting coursework for graduate students in an urban medical school setting to meet the needs of baccalaureate students at a small liberal arts college in a rural setting; Deborah Labovitz, O.T.R., Chairperson, and Rosalie Miller, O.T.R., of the Occupational Therapy Program at New York University, both of whom provided a forum for the teaching of activities to a variety of students differing in sociocultural background, life experience, age, and educational history; our colleagues at meetings and in-services, too numerous to mention individually; and the many clinicians who tested our ideas in practice and gave us valuable comments and suggestions in so doing. In particular, we say a heartfelt "thank you" to each of those clinicians who contributed to the development of the *Activities Health Assessment* during its trial runs and subsequent revisions, and to those who provided the case materials that have enriched Part III, whose names appear in the last paragraph of this section.

We wish to thank those who helped, directly or indirectly, to illuminate and clarify our ideas—Herb Robinson, of the Herb Robinson Studio, who, with his infinite capacity for taking pains and his artistic sensibility, has created photographic essays that bring the student activities contributions strikingly to life; Gene Gordon, of Eugene Gordon, Inc., whose array of perceptive cross-cultural photographic studies made it almost impossible for us to narrow down our choices; Sherry Bruck, of *Fresh Concepts*, describing accurately the perspective from which she has created crystal-clear graphic images to make intelligible such complexities as the links between *activities health* and occupational therapy (the Activities Health Model), the process of clinical problem-solving, and the intricate activities connections related to cooking in natural and clinical settings (we also thank her for advice on how best to present the student contributions); Bill Russell, for the workmanlike and faithful rendering of the activities "pie" and adapted macrame project, both of which appeared previously in *Occupational Therapy*; Hester Kinsey, who with patience and undiminished interest, typed and retyped many of the tables and appendixes as we sought clarity in terminology and presentation; Nancy Coon, formerly of Little, Brown, whose enthusiasm and advocacy at the earliest stages gave shape, form, and even size to our planned project; Shana Wagger, Editor for Development at Little, Brown, whose ongoing support and encouragement gave that prospectus a body and identity; and Marie Linvill, Editor, and Jonathan Sarner, Production Editor, who have moved us toward a real book at last!

We thank those who helped us, at times unwittingly, by their example—Gordon Williamson, for instance, a former student to one of us, a teacher to the other, a clear, rigorously honest and independent thinker, a constructive and sensitive critic, a loyal colleague, and a fine occupational therapist. Some have contributed by sharing their experiences with us, like Jean Seymour, who offered her personal and professional insights in the development of a course assignment devoted to the *Activities Health Interview*, along with her unwavering support during the writing of this book. Still others have actively shared in the testing and development of our ideas—the most current and comprehensive involvement yet has come from the members of the Department of Psychiatry at St. Vincent's Hospital in New York City, under the leadership of Joseph T. English, M.D. Thus, we also express our appreciation to Ralph A. O'Connell, M.D., for his ongoing interest in our ideas and his commitment to our profession; Linda Silber, O.T.R., for her inspiration as both admired colleague and devoted friend and for a good laugh when needed most; Joan Avallone, O.T.R., who has incorporated the concept of *activities health* into her store of knowledge and wealth of experience with enthusiasm and discrimination; Jacqueline Carbone Turbert, O.T.R., and Janet Fink, O.T.R., for their skilled leadership and creativity in incorporating an *activities health* approach into the development of exciting clinical programs; and to all the Therapeutic Activities and Vocational Rehabilitation Service staff for their openness and eagerness to examine activities in new and different ways, including help in piloting the *Activities Health Assessment*.

Our gratitude is due to Jerome Bruner and Alexander Szalai, whose writings have materially influenced the direction in which our ideas about activities have moved. In their beautifully expressed and intellectually challenging thoughts, we have found the key to a deeper understanding of human activities—as phenomena worthy of study in themselves and as links to health and well-being. For permission to quote from their work and from the works of others, we thank the authors and their publishers.

Last but not least, we thank those family members and friends who stood by us throughout and put up with us while their activities configurations had to be modified and adjusted to accommodate to our physical and mental absence. Deserving of particular mention are Christopher Robinson, Fran and Lloyd Bowers, and Michael Smartt, each of whom has provided nurturance to the heart and soul at precisely the right moments, thus ensuring that one of our two sources of energy was constantly replenished. Being in the direct line of fire, so to speak, since their respective fields of action were taken over by foreign objects such as reams of paper, computers, and reference books, our husbands, Norman Klebanow and Herb Robinson, deserve a special accolade. They continue to fit to perfection our blueprints for life partners.

Contributors to this volume were numerous. Student contributors from Columbia University (whose graduation dates appear in parentheses) include Lisa Aikens ('87), Joan Augustine ('89), Susanna Cobb ('85), Ellen Fine ('87), Rhonda Fisher ('87), Helen Fogarty ('89), Diane Heimer ('86), Monica Huang ('89), Julie Lowy ('89), Melanie Klein ('87), Kate Jacob McKay ('87), Christine D. Momich ('88), Victoria Pearlman ('84), Rozanne Pelosi ('88), Sharla Perel ('88), Andrea Redlich ('83), Robin Ellen Reece ('89), Lauren Robertson ('87), Jean Rohleder ('89), Peter D. Ruopp ('89), Darlene Halvorsen Sarchino ('90), Nadia Shivack ('89), Karen Van Den Heuvel ('89), and Jennifer Winsor ('88). Occupational therapists who contributed case material include Joan Avallone, Mary Buxton, Sophie Chiotellis and the staff of the Institute of Rehabilitation Medicine (from the previous book), Janet Fink, Elnora Gilfoyle (from previous book), Susan R. Goldberg, Cheryl L. Jagow, Patricia A. Miller, Victoria Schindler, Linda Silber, Anne Spencer, and Jacqueline Carbone Turbert.

S. C.
A. M. R.

Notes to the Reader Before Using the Text

No one chapter or section of this text should be studied alone. Full comprehension of the concepts, connections, and conclusions in Part I requires a steady progression from chapter to chapter, with a pause for the assignments at the end of each chapter to reinforce learning and to prepare for the next step.

Without Part I, neither Parts II nor III makes sense. With Part I fully understood, it is possible to move on to clinical application in Part III, but it will be necessary to refer to Part II many times both for illustration and elaboration of the ideas advanced in Part I and for help in completing many of the assignments, including clinical problem-solving, in Part III. You will find a number of cross-references in the text, but we urge you to dip more frequently into the treasury of student projects in Part II while learning about activities as natural human phenomena and the connections between *activities health* and occupational therapy in Part I and while practicing the principles underlying clinical application in Part III. The Educational Model in Part II, while also serving as a contextual two-way bridge between Parts I and III, stands as an invitation to educators to look at activities in a new and different way.

Notice that to cover all eventualities we use the term *patient/client* generally to designate the recipient of occupational therapy care, but that, in the case histories, the terminology varies in accordance with the usage by those providing the clinical material. Similarly, we use *activities*, not *activity* (except in the case of *activity-centered analysis* in which a single entity is being considered in depth), since neither in its generic sense nor when used to indicate a discrete entity does the singular form of the word convey the essence of the multiple series of manifest operations permeating the fabric of everyday living in an endless variety of patterns. In addition, note that gender-specific terms are used only in direct quotes, or for grammatical consistency with those quotes. It is obvious from the context that "man," for instance, refers to all humankind.

We wish you a joyous and satisfying learning experience.

Occupational Therapy and Activities Health: Toward Health Through Activities

PART ONE

Concepts, Connections, and Conclusions

CHAPTER 1

Occupational Therapy and Activities: A Natural Bond

The pervasive importance of everyday activities to the well-being of humankind was a notion recognized and captured by our occupational therapy forebears some 70 years ago. Today, we still affirm, in our professional documents [3], our theoretical and philosophical speculations [2, 34, 70, 87, 90, 91], and our legal definitions*, that activities are the distinctive hallmark of occupational therapy.

For the most part, the activities of everyday living are as ordinary and homespun as blueberry pie. There is little that is dramatic or glamorous for the individual in making a bed, fixing a faucet, threading a loom, taking a shower, washing clothes in a stream, programming a computer, milking a cow, piloting an airplane, pounding corn, wrestling with an algebra problem, playing Marabaraba (an African board game), cuddling a doll, modeling a designer gown, braiding hair, skipping rope, writing a letter, chopping vegetables, bringing in the catch, decorating a ceramic pot, chanting a nursery rhyme, harvesting rice, playing football, or playing the flute—if the activity is woven into the fabric of day-to-day living.

Many activities are so routine that they are performed automatically. Others are accompanied by dissatisfaction, boredom, or distaste and may be engaged in reluctantly, if at all. Still others generate anticipation and enthusiasm. But most of the activities that form the pattern of one's life are taken for granted, until some form of dysfunction intervenes.

Early occupational therapy was founded on the belief that being engaged in activities promotes mental and physical well-being and that, conversely, absence of activity leads at best to mischief and at worst to deterioration or loss of mental and physical functioning. And with that belief came a commitment to the use of activities as therapeutic media for individuals suffering from mental and/or physical dysfunction, a commitment that implicitly assumes that *dysfunction is reversible through engagement in activities*. At first, "activities" consisted of a circumscribed

---

* States' definitions of occupational therapy for licensure.

range of crafts, which became augmented over time, however, by categories variously labeled A.D.L. (activities of daily living), games and hobbies, social activities, and work-related activities.

The specific activities and associated events that can be listed in each of these categories and the everyday activities of any one person at any stage in the life span are numerous and varied. In other places, other societies, and other cultures, specific activities, and indeed even categories of activities, are often different from our own, thus adding even greater number and variety to the gamut of day-to-day activities engaged in by people.

We may well ask why occupational therapy began only with crafts. And of all the crafts in the world, why in particular did we inherit basketry, woodworking, leatherwork, and needlecrafts? It is true that basketry and pottery appeared on the scene many thousands of years ago and are found as activities in most parts of the globe. But are they, and other handicrafts, doomed like the dinosaur to extinction—this time by the Electronic Age? Or do they all have a significance that transcends a passing utility and expedience? How do we account for the resurgence of the "handmade" look in our society right now? So highly valued is it that designers are putting together exclusive kits for hand-knits and chic little boutiques are snapping up baskets and handwoven stoles to be sold at outrageous prices. What sets in motion these fads, fancies, and fashions? And what do they have to do with occupational therapy and our patients? With our classifications such as leisure and work? With health and ill-health?

It is essential to ask and seek answers to these kinds of questions. In this way we begin to view the activities that form the fabric of everyday living as *natural human phenomena*. As phenomena, activities are observable, and as natural phenomena, they are subject to study by the methods of natural science. From this vantage point it becomes possible to describe and order, to seek and find classification schemes, perhaps typologies—already a reality presented by Allen [2]—and even a taxonomy, and certainly patterns and configurations with their boundaries, variations, continuities, and discontinuities. It also becomes possible to delve into history and even prehistory and to examine activities in the context of field-of-action and behavior habitat. In the following chapters, these concepts will appear again, clarified and discussed in relation to the phenomenology of activities, to activities analysis, and to the links between activities and health.

When we know more of what activities are all about, we can generate hypotheses about the links between activities and health and find indices of meaning and relevance of activities to individuals and groups. Already, we have one occupational therapy hypothesis that links health, not directly with activities, but with specific functional components of the actor. Reilly [71] states "that Man, through the use of his hands as they are energized by mind and will can influence the state of his own health." Within this hypothesis lies a brilliant but also deceptively simple pointer to a definition of activities for occupational therapy—*activities are the observable results of the use of the hands as they are energized by the mind and will*. In elaborating on her hypothesis. Reilly reveals the underlying assumption on which it stands, ". . . that the mind and will of man are occupied through central nervous system action, and that man *can and should* [emphasis added] be involved consciously in problem-solving and creative activity."

This powerful assumption leads inevitably to the conclusion that [71]:

1. Every human being has the potential to be "involved consciously in problem-solving and creative activity"
2. For attainment of optimal function (or health) it is imperative that every human being "be involved consciously in problem-solving and creative activity".

And, returning to the hypothesis, problem-solving and creative activity are also linked with the use of the hands. Thus, it follows that activities, to foster health, require the following of the actor:

1. The use of the hands
2. Conscious problem-solving
3. Creative activity

At first glance, these criteria seem to demand an impossibly high level of functioning from the ordinary individual who goes about the business of carrying out the activities of day-to-day living. How many individuals claim that they are "no good" with their hands? How many individuals are creative in the sense of producing original works of art or literature? How many individuals are problem-solvers wrestling with complicated issues in physics and mathematics? It is necessary, therefore, to take a closer look at these criteria.

The Use of the Hands

It is important to keep in mind that the hands, those finely tuned instruments for the reception of stimuli, for expression and communication, and for skilled performance, are linked structurally and functionally with the neck, head, trunk, and the lower limbs, and all are exquisitely coordinated and synchronized by the brain (which also has something to do with the mind and will). In a description of a young woman who is making a pie, Cynkin makes these connections:

She must have good neuromuscular control and coordination to pour and cut to exact specifications. She must also have integrated the concepts of size, weight, pressure, and coldness and thus be able to transmit her knowledge of the size of a small pea to her hands and eyes as they obediently cut and assess to the required dimensions. The dough reaches a perfect consistency and is accurately shaped, not only because of the coordination and dexterity in her arms and hands, but also because the gentle pressure called for is monitored by the messages from her sensitive hands and fingers to her brain, which directs the strength of the muscular response. The control of her movements is dependent also on the stability of her head, neck, and trunk and, if she is standing, on the stability of her lower limbs as well.

If one were to describe a day's typical activities for one person in terms of the use of the hands only, it would be found that practically all activities devoted to self-care and the care of one's environment require involvement of the hands. (See

Assignment 1 at the end of this chapter.) This is also true of a large proportion of activities related to work and leisure.

Conscious Problem-Solving

To dispel the popular notion that problem-solving is somehow the domain of the intellectually-gifted few, it is useful to return to dictionary definitions. A *problem* is defined as "any question or matter involving doubt, uncertainty, or difficulty" and to *solve* is "to work out an answer" (*Random House Dictionary of English*, 1987). Thus, problem-solving may be defined as "the process of working out an answer to any question or matter involving doubt, uncertainty, or difficulty." This definition makes it clear that, as Asimov [6] aptly puts it, "everyone must solve a problem of some sort at almost every moment of his life or her life—even if it is a simple one, such as 'where did I put my glasses?'" The "conscious" part of problem-solving is not in an awareness of the process by which the problem gets solved but in the realization that a situation involving doubt, uncertainty, or difficulty *exists* and that some definite way is to be found that resolves the situation. The very first activity in Assignment 1—getting out of bed—offers an illustration of the kind of problem-solving that necessitates decision-making. The question is—"To get out of bed or not?" You worked very late last night, your bed is snug and warm on a cold morning, the radio predicts massive traffic jams on your route. On the other hand, the work is piling up in your office, you want to ask for a few days off to go skiing next month, you'll have to call your department head to explain your absence. What do you do? Other day-to-day problem-solving situations can be elicited from Assignment 2.

Creative Activity

The *Random House Dictionary of English* (1987) gives several definitions of *to create*, all of which are pertinent to the carrying out of those activities that are woven into the fabric of everyday life:

1. To evolve from one's thought or imagination.
2. To give rise to.
3. To cause to happen, bring about, arrange.
4. To do that which is constructive.

Creativity is defined as "originative or productive." *Creative activity*, therefore, can be defined as that activity that evolves from one's thought or imagination and/or that causes things to happen and/or is constructive and is either originative or productive. As with problem-solving, creative activity is part of the ordinary business of everyday living, though most people may not recognize it as such. An example of creative activity relates to one of the routines in the "getting-up-in-the-morning" constellation (Assignment 1). Half asleep, you turn on the faucets to splash your face with water, and nothing happens. Before you leave for work you have to observe the rudiments of hygiene, including rinsing after you brush your teeth. What do you do? A creative solution is offered by the individual who remembers a six-pack of club soda stored in the kitchen. Poured into a pan, warmed over the gas flame while the "fizz" subsides, the liquid provides an acceptable though unconventional alternative for washing the face and a palatable rinse for the mouth. Further opportunities to explore "creative activity" are offered in Assignment 3.

It is quite apparent that creative activity is related intimately to problem-solving. Indeed, DeBono [22] has identified two kinds of thinking—*vertical*, which is based on "dominant ideas" or rules that people rigidly hold on to, or *lateral*, which allows one, after trying prescribed ways of solving a problem, to "try elsewhere." DeBono [22] contends that this kind of creative thinking has been stifled by overemphasis on vertical thinking in our culture. "Creativity thus continues to be viewed too often as a rare and mysterious gift, rather than as a part of the standard equipment of the human mind" [22]. That creative activity is the most human of human attributes is confirmed by Bronowski [12], who traces the cultural evolution of humankind:

[Man] has what no other animal possesses, a jig-saw of faculties, which alone over three thousand million years of life, make him creative. Every animal leaves traces of what it was; man alone leaves traces of what he created.

The close links between problem-solving and creative activity and the implication that they are an intrinsic part of human potential is summarized in Buckminster Fuller's [18] provocative statement, "I think that all humans are born artists-scientists-inventors" (see Assignment 4). The central nervous system connection with these forms of functioning that is alluded to by Reilly in unfolding the assumption on which the occupational therapy hypothesis is based will be discussed in later chapters, as we examine in greater detail the links between activities and health and the ways in which engagement in activities can help reverse dysfunction in the direction of function.

Assumptions About Activities

Underlying the general proposition that engagement in activities can produce change from dysfunction toward function, which implies applicability to all kinds of individuals of all ages in all kinds of cultures and societies, are a number of assumptions about the nature of activities, the nature of humankind, and the nature of change.

ASSUMPTION 1
ACTIVITIES OF MANY KINDS ARE CHARACTERISTIC OF AND
DEFINE A HUMAN EXISTENCE

This assumption carries with it the implication that a large number and a variety of activities are inherently important to the individual, fulfilling basic human needs and wants. Activities of the human world are first directed to survival, subsistence, and coexistence. Further, they mediate in the multiple and complex interactions of individual and environment and are essential to physical and mental growth and development, acquisition of social skills, and the achievement of steps toward ultimate fulfillment, self-realization, and mastery, whether this ultimate state is called self-actualization [56], competence [89], generativity [27], insight [39], or any other designation.

Acknowledgment of the pervasive importance of activities comes from a number of respected sources. Piaget's [67] theorizing points to the conclusion that all knowledge of the world comes from an individual's engagement in activities, even those as simple and apparently spontaneous as thumb-sucking. To Kluckhohn and Murray [46], the personality is "both the ground and the product of activity—physical, social and mental." Our humanness is real and visible through the products of human skill and endeavor, which become the means of recording forever the activities of humankind. In the distant past [88], our remote ancestors in Europe left us a legacy that emanates from their characteristically human attributes—the use of the hands, mind, and will—evident in the figurines, tools, cave paintings, personal adornments, and shelters that have survived to become part of a museum exhibit today (Museum of Natural History, New York City.)

In another place and time, the skilled hands and creative mind of a Chinese artist produced a scroll that brings to life the human activities of a rural village in seventeenth-century China [80]. As we traverse the great length of the scroll, we see individuals, sometimes in clusters, sometimes alone, some men, some women, engaged in one or other of the activities that form the fabric of their daily routine—playing music, dyeing fabric, weaving, drinking tea, yoking bullocks to a cart, wielding brush for calligraphy, feeding chickens, repairing a roof, carrying water, going fishing, boating, cooking, carrying bundles of grain, planting seedlings, folding cloth. Another scroll depicts the village children at play—swimming, climbing trees, gathering blossoms, throwing a ball, fishing, flying kites, walking on stilts, playing games that look like tag, blindman's bluff, and tug-of-war, riding piggyback. One cluster is intent on a cockfight, two individuals play a game with a cup and a shuttlecock, and a solitary individual is absorbed in calligraphy.

Through picture research, Fox [36] has brought to light the activities of women in medieval Europe (1300–1550). Manuscript illuminations and woodcuts from the first printed books (in themselves a complex of activities that unite the hands, mind, and will in doing) show women engaged in a wide range of activities, including sweeping, spinning, carding and weaving, milking, churning butter, nursing the sick, drawing water, carrying a sack of wheat to the mill, mining, haying, writing a manuscript, selling leeks, dispensing medicine, designing a fresco, sculpting, breeding silkworms, building a wall, working at a forge, performing surgery, and defending a castle with a crossbow.

The first settlers in the New World in Florida (1562–1565) and Virginia (1585–1590) have left us a graphic picture of the everyday activities of the aboriginal inhabitants, through narrative, watercolors, and etchings [55]. We see Indian youths at exercise, training for strenuous running races, practicing with bow and arrow, and playing "a game in which they cast a ball at a square target placed on top of a high tree." Groups of men hunt alligators, deer, and smaller animals, catch fish, dry and smoke meat and fish, ferry (with women and children in tow) supplies to public granaries, paddling canoes that hold as many as six people at a time, go to war, till the soil; women make earthen pots and baskets, plant beans and corn, tend children. Whole families go on pleasure jaunts, taking supplies in baskets, swimming or wading to get to a suitable spot. Men and women together prepare meals, including great feasts at special times of the year, and gather round a fire with rattles to "sing and make merry." Only men participate in ritual dances.

Descriptions of everyday life abound in art and literature, ethnographic and sociological studies, historical records, history books, explorer's notes, and personal diaries. What would appear in a depiction of day-to-day activities in any one segment of our society today? In the briefest of surveys, for instance, of an entering class of occupational therapy students—nine women and one man, ages 21 to 36, from a mostly urban background—a composite list of "activities" (not defined for the students in any way) produced 84 separate and distinct items. Some, such as grooming, eating, cleaning, and doing laundry, were common to everyone in the group. More than half the class listed exercise, dancing, and cooking. Shared by at least two people were child-care, grocery shopping, household budgeting, gardening, camping, typing, skiing, and swimming. The rest of the activities appeared only once in any one person's list—examples are piano-playing, reading, photography, furniture finishing, belly-dancing, folk-dancing, sand art, candle-making, botanical drawing, playing backgammon, fishing, cycling, sewing, traveling, caring for houseplants, theater technology, play-reading, bowling, writing words for songs, playing the guitar. (See p. 102 for another example of a class listing.) Any informal and/or formal observation of a playground, a park, a side street, a small-town fishing harbor, one's own neighborhood or farther afield, or the daily routines of family and friends would likewise produce pictures of human activities that in some respects would be similar to and yet, in other respects, different from our own (see Assignment 5).

Throughout the developmental cycle, beginning with the thumb-sucking that Piaget [67] refers to, humans engage in activities that are characteristically human. The best-loved games of childhood appear, sometimes in different guises, all over the world, and many seem to "happen" spontaneously and perhaps intuitively [64]. Theories of play (35, 72, 77) have variously emphasized its usefulness in the transformation of reality to allow for symbolic representation of the world, as an aid in the development of creativity, as an aid to practice and master activities necessary for the endeavors of adulthood, and as an aid to catharsis in development. None of these theories appears to be mutually exclusive; all relate to the inextricable connection between activities and development of humanness.

The endeavors of adulthood continue to include forms of play that in many respects are strikingly similar in many parts of the world, activities that relate to the earnest business of survival, and expressive activities that, ubiquitous and inevitable as they are, may not always have an economic use, but nevertheless are part of the human imperative—"the artist-scientist-inventor [who] was born with human history [18]."

Reilly [71] adheres to two basic postulates to explain the nature of man:". . . The first duty of an organism is to be alive" and ". . . the second duty of an organism is to grow and be productive." The outcome of being productive, which entails "using the equipment that makes man human" [71] is an infinite number and variety of characteristic activities, which in turn help man "to master his environment, to alter and improve it" [71]. It is therefore reasonable to assume that a number of specific kinds of activities are indeed characteristic of a state of humanness and that engagement in these kinds of activities contributes to the development and maintenance of a physically sound and well-integrated personality, capable of reacting to, acting upon, and interacting with the environment in the activities of survival, subsistence, and coexistence—and of attaining a sense of mastery and well-being in the process.

ASSUMPTION 2
ACTIVITIES ARE SOCIOCULTURALLY REGULATED BY A SYSTEM OF VALUES, BELIEFS, AND CUSTOMS AND ARE THUS DEFINED BY AND IN TURN DEFINE ACCEPTABLE NORMS OF BEHAVIOR

Common experience and observation show us that people belonging to groups different from our own (another religion, ethnic background, nationality, tribe, or part of the world) carry out their activities—often different in outward forms too—in ways different from ours. In every culture and society some activities are regarded as proper, some inappropriate, and others unacceptable for specific ages, social status, economic class, men or women, times of day, days of week, or seasons of the year. The ways of "doing things," what Kroeber [50] has called "the learned and transmitted motor reactions, habits and techniques. . ." are so deeply ingrained that there is no conscious awareness of the underlying values and beliefs that shape the characteristic life-style of the individual from day to day. Yet everyone is familiar with the kind of activities-based description of an individual that reveals the observer's prevailing values and expectations of desirable behavior. To the question, "But why do you think he's peculiar?" the reply may be, "Well, he's strange. Look at the way he dresses. I don't think he's washed his hair in weeks. He's been drifting in and out of all kinds of odd jobs since he quit college. Reads philosophy—for fun! Doesn't go out, even for a beer with us, and doesn't date—at 24!" Here we have a set of standard expectations, which in this instance are not being met, for a young adult male coming from the upper middle class. He should be dressing within prescribed bounds, conforming to the rudiments of hygiene, and after completion of his studies, capitalizing on his brain and social connections to acquire a well-paying and prestigious job. The complex of activities related to working has its own set of expected behaviors, which include regularity of attendance, diligence, and emphasis on career advancement. He is expected to pursue leisure-time activities suitable to his age and station, such as sports perhaps (but in no way reading philosophy for fun!), and to live up to group expectations of social behaviors, as exemplified by going to parties, dating, and drinking beer. In many groups, activities are strictly allocated and circumscribed by age, sex, caste, class, or occupation. A man of an isolated tribe in South Africa would be mortally offended if asked to carry a heavy pot of water, an activity that is culturally defined as "women's work"! In India, even today, individuals are locked into specific occupations determined by caste. Our own technologically advanced, complex, pluralistic society, in which there is a relative blurring of prescribed limits, still imposes constraints on individuals, classifying them by socioeconomic status, ethnic background, age group, and sex. The young man mentioned above who does not conform to expectations is a case in point, although he also illustrates the fact that deviations from the norm are tolerated, if not completely accepted.

One example of a group whose deviant activities patterns have percolated into the mainstream of our society (although not necessarily universally accepted) is the "hippie" subculture. Within the space of two decades, it has shaken the very foundations of the work ethic by questioning the value of routine, regular (and often monotonous and dehumanizing) work as an integral, respectable, essential activity. With the advent of the "hippie" subculture, handicrafts, hitherto occupying a lowly place in a society that offers its highest rewards for activities associated with science and technology, became elevated as symbols of humankind's return to individuality, creativity, and oneness with the natural world. In passing, it is interesting to note that since that time, the valuation of handicrafts has shifted from the idealistic to the materialistic; economic gain and fashionable appearance in clothes and furnishings are the predominant themes today.

Today, we are also in the midst of the consequences of a conscious rebellion against a series of socioculturally prescribed activities that were for many years taken as the norm. Sex-allocated roles and their associated activities patterns, challenged by feminist ideas, have produced changes that are already apparent. "House-husband" has entered our vocabulary side-by-side with the "housewife." Women function as police, garbage collectors, construction workers, corporation presidents. A whole revolution is epitomized in the picture (although it relates to a not so dramatic activity) of a husky young man, as liberated from stereotyping as his female counterpart, unconcernedly working on a piece of needlepoint as he rides to work by subway. Medieval women's occupations (see Assumption 1) would not have surfaced as a distinct collection without the current interest in "women's place." Our astonishment at the number and variety of activities engaged in by women of different classes of that time reveals our socioculturally-colored preconceptions of medieval women, either as ethereal creatures of romantic fancy, drifting through days of delicate needlework and playing of the harp, or ground-down drudges, without any choices in between. In every society, whether permissible limits are tightly drawn or stretched to accommodate a number of individual and group variations, there is a point at which deviations from expected norms in activities patterns are deemed unacceptable, labeled in various ways, and dealt with according to the mores of the group. Activities patterns themselves, being readily apparent, in turn define the borders between acceptable and unacceptable.

ASSUMPTION 3
CHANGE IN ACTIVITIES-RELATED BEHAVIOR CAN MOVE IN A DIRECTION FROM DYSFUNCTIONAL TO FUNCTIONAL

Closely associated with this assumption is one other fundamental assumption about the nature of humankind—that the individual can change and indeed desires change. That the individual can change is axiomatic if one adheres to the two basic postulates that explain the nature of humankind: ". . . the first duty of an organism is to be alive," and "the second duty of an organism is to grow and be productive" [71]. It follows that to be alive the organism must adapt to changing conditions; that is, it must change, and to grow and be productive, the organism must change too. Inherent in the human organism, therefore, is the capacity to change. That humankind also *desires* change is a reasonable conclusion to draw from studies of human motivation, including those of White [89] and others, that stress the drive for competence, the need to explore and master the environment, and the attraction to novel situations. The ultimate condition toward which desired change is directed is the subject of much debate by theologians, philosophers, psychologists, psychoanalysts, and other students of humankind. That the individual is by nature more likely to reach for function, acceptance, and well-being rather than submit to dysfunction, nonacceptance, pain, and discomfort is an article of faith, acknowledged or not, that governs the very reason for existence of a number of so-called helping professions. There is no reason to think that activities-related behavior is exempt from this article of faith.

ASSUMPTION 4
CHANGE IN ACTIVITIES-RELATED BEHAVIOR FROM DYSFUNCTIONAL TO FUNCTIONAL TAKES PLACE THROUGH MOTOR, COGNITIVE, AND SOCIAL LEARNING

Besides the innate adaptive mechanisms that are humankind's biological inheritance, human beings have the unique capacity to pass on adaptive information through learning. This kind of adaptive information, as it relates to the carrying out of everyday activities in socioculturally acceptable ways, is passed on ultimately through learning by doing—"What we have to do, we learn through doing" [5]. With activities, learning by doing entails practicing a series of motor acts, as well as a "thinking through" process, remembering, organizing information, sequencing, conceptualizing, and transferring learned skills to a variety of different situations, and if relationships with others are part of the learning process, social modeling as well.

Now that these assumptions have been made explicit, it is possible to move toward a closer look at activities as natural human phenomena—to examine their properties, their socioculturally acquired characteristics, their meaning to individuals and groups, their potential as instruments of change, and their role as functional ends in themselves.

Assignment 1 _____

Observe "the use of the hands" in everyday activities:

A. Write down everything you do, in careful detail*, from the time you wake up in the morning until you are fully dressed. Note the points at which

* In our everyday actions we usually tend to disregard a number of important steps because they are so much taken for granted. Be sure to include them in your listing.

"the use of the hands" (see The Use of the Hands) is involved. An example of the detail required follows: "Wake up, rub eyes, stretch, switch on bedside lamp, turn bedcovers down, sit up, shuffle into slippers, stand up, walk to bathroom, open door of bathroom, switch on light, walk to sink, turn on faucets, check water temperature, pick up soap, wet washcloth, soap washcloth, replace soap, wash and rinse face and hands, rinse and wring out washcloth, spread washcloth to dry, pick up towel, dry hands and face, replace towel, open door of medicine chest, take out toothpaste, screw top off tube, put down top, pick up toothbrush, replace top on tube, brush teeth, turn on faucet, fill tumbler with water, turn on faucet, rinse brush in running water, shake out water from brush, turn off faucet, return brush to stand," and so on.

B.   Ask someone you know to do the same thing. Compare.

Assignment 2

Observe "problem-solving" in everyday activities:

A.   Write down everything you do *in detail* (as illustrated by the example in Assignment 1, A) from the time you are ready to go to work to your first work break (coffee, lunch, or other meal, exercises, shopping—anything that interrupts work for more than 20 minutes; going to class counts as work, moving from class to class is part of work, not a break). Make a note every time "problem-solving" (see Conscious Problem-Solving) is involved.

Suggested method: Keep a small notebook and pencil handy. If your routine is regular, write down what you do from recall. This can be done a day or two before you complete the assignment. Then note the problem-solving situations as they occur.

B.   Ask someone you know to do the same thing. Compare.

Assignment 3

Observe "creative activity" in everyday activities:

A.   Write down everything you do in detail (as illustrated by the example in Assignment 1, A) from your first work break to a second work break (or end of the workday). The same method applies as for Assignment 2, A, and Assignment 3, A except that you are to make a note at every point where "creative activity" (see Creative Activity) is involved.

B.   Go over *all* activities you have described as required in A in Assignments 1, 2, and 3. List those that require use of the hands *and* problem-solving *and* creative activity.

Assignment 4

Find the "artist-scientist-inventor" in everyday activities (see p. 7): Obviously, Buckminster Fuller [18] believes that everyone has the potential to create, solve problems, and come up with ingenious ideas.

A. In what ways can you see yourself as artist-scientist-inventor as you think about your daily routine of ordinary activities now? In the past?

B. In what ways do you see a selected member of your family, or a close friend, as an artist-scientist-inventor in the daily routine of ordinary activities now? In the past?

C. In what ways can you see a person who is known to you and has less formal education than you (e.g., someone who has not finished high school or who has never gone to college) as an artist-scientist-inventor?

Assignment 5

Observe similarities and differences in activities of different groups: Are some activities universal? Do children in all societies play games? Do all cultures have expressive activities? Can we identify them as such, even though they may be different from our own? Are there parallels between play and the activities of adulthood in all groups? In what ways are activities in other groups similar to our own? In what ways are they different? Start trying to answer these questions by observing and interviewing people and groups you are most familiar with, such as your family, classmates (colleagues), and their families. Then compare and contrast the information with information obtained from a less familiar group, such as a family from a different ethnic group or a family from a different socioeconomic class. Begin to look at groups of people other than families. Lastly, read what anthropologists and other behavioral scientists have to say about activities in other parts of the world. Keep an open mind, and keep looking!

CHAPTER 2

Activities as Natural Human Phenomena

From the many, although necessarily restricted examples in Chapter 1, it is clear that the activities of everyday living can be regarded as external representations of a state of humanness. It is also clear, even from this small sampling, that these activities, numerous and diverse, have some connection to historical time, geographical setting, social structure, and cultural influences.

The activities, or products of activities, that are enumerated in Chapter 1 appear in no particular order or grouping according to kind, yet we can recognize most of them even across the most distant span of years. Referring to the exhibit of Ice Age art (see Chapter 1, Assumption 1) as the documentation of previously unparalleled creativity, Goelet [41] adds, "Daily life is not forgotten, however, and we can equally discern the roots of the common humanity that unites us all, everywhere, in the humbler productions of these earlier people." That this commonality has survived over time and space is emphasized by Bronowski [12], as he traces the cultural evolution of humankind:

The basic devices of the *nimble-fingered mind* [emphasis added] lie about, unregarded, in any village anywhere in the world. Their cornucopia of small and subtle artifices is as ingenious and in a deep sense as important in the ascent of man as any apparatus in nuclear physics: the needle, the awl, the pot, the brazier, the spade, the nail and the screw, the bellows, the string, the knot, the loom, the harness, the hook, the button, the shoe—one could name a hundred and not stop for breath.

Each of these devices is an "amplifier of human action" [14], enabling humankind to fulfill the biological imperative of survival by adapting to and sometimes altering a puzzling, inhospitable, or hostile environment. Buckminster Fuller [18]—who refused to be put into any professional category, but is a thinker on a broad humanistic scale—used his distinctively human gift of imagination to conjure up for us a scenario at the birth of one of these inventions that is still a part of our everyday world today:

Some hundreds of thousands of years ago the artist-scientist-inventor saw that man had been cupping his hands for endless years to pick up water and realized that by making a vessel of hollowed stone or wood or a tightly woven basket or clay bowl or sewn skin, this repetitive job could be done much more successfully. Next he saw that he could make a large vessel, an enormous pair of "cupped hands" and could carry the water with him. . . .

To outward appearances at least, it seems that a large range of human activities transcend time and place, recognizable to us because they are extensions of our human nature. As we take a closer look, we also find differences—in outward form, in function, and in other ways that give us pause to question. For no listing of activities, however detailed, can convey in any but the most superficial sense the ways in which these activities have become woven into the fabric of everyday living and assume a pervasive role in the day-to-day existence of any individual in any place at any moment in time.

We may well ask, "So what was a typical day like for those far-away ancestors or our human kindred in other times and places; or what is it like for them in the there, here, and now?" For the activities in the here and now, such as the student list mentioned in Chapter 1 (p. 9) or our own everyday pursuits, we may feel that no such question is necessary, since these activities are so familiar and so much taken for granted that the answer is self-evident. But as we begin to elicit the patterns and configurations that distinguish a characteristic life-style for each and every one of us, we are struck with new insights and a different kind of awareness.

Patterns and Configurations

Although we are not generally conscious of it, all our activities are carried out in distinct patterns that are influenced by our socioculturally shaped world view, values, and beliefs (see Chapter 1, Assumption 2) and, within this framework, by our own preferences and emphases. A *pattern* may be defined as a "combination of qualities, acts, tendencies, etc., forming a consistent or characteristic arrangement" (*Random House Dictionary of English*, 1987). One such arrangement, in this instance a formal one externally imposed, is the familiar class schedule, which is a list of activities relating to a special and definite end goal encapsulated in a framework of time. Similarly, each individual operates within a daily timetable, which, while governing the sequence and flow of activities, tends to be less than formal, less deliberate, more automatic, and subject to periodic fluctuations in timing and content and is not directed consciously to a single and definite end goal. Within that timetable, each individual has, often below the level of awareness, a distinctive set of routines and a specific repertoire of activities, which, if recorded in time bands for a day, a week, a month at any point in the life span, reveal an *idiosyncratic activities pattern* for that individual at that point in time.

The *idiosyncratic activities pattern* is a graphic representation of the daily use of time by one individual at one specific period of the life span and is thus limited to a static and fleeting depiction of the fabric of everyday living. It does, however, serve as an admirable point of departure for delving deeper. To come closer to that "typical" day, other questions have to be addressed, relating to continuity, regularity, balance and classification of activities, and the "personal equation" that includes the individual's feelings, learning history, preferences, sense of autonomy, and the social and spatial environment in which the activities take place. From the answers to such questions, together with the *idiosyncratic activities pattern* that serves as the springboard for these questions, comes an *idiosyncratic activities configuration*, to provide a picture of the distinctive life-style of one person at one particular point in the life span.

It will be noted that *time* serves as the point of departure from which the activities pattern and configuration unfold. "Time-budget" studies have long been part of the techniques of social science research, providing "fairly adequate itemized and measured accounts of how people spend their time within the bounds of a working day, a weekend or seven-day week, or other relevant period" [81]. In the introduction to a monumental cross-cultural survey of the use of time, Szalai [81] points out:

The use of time consists, of course, in doing some kind of activity; *even loafing or resting are to be understood as activities* [emphasis added] in this kind of context. Studies on the use of time, conventionally called time-budget studies, are thus in effect concerned with the day-long activities of people. . .

The day-long activities of *one* person are depicted in the *idiosyncratic activities pattern*, which shows, by virtue of its structure, three aspects of the temporal, or time-related, attributes of human activities:

1. *Timing:* at what specific time the activity is done.
2. *Duration:* how long each activity lasts over the day.
3. *Sequential order:* what comes before and after each activity.

Other temporal attributes of activities can be elicited from questions designed to reveal the *idiosyncratic activities configuration*:

1. *Frequency:* How often?
2. *Historical duration:* How long over the life span has the activity endured?

Also considered in the activities configuration are what Szalai [81] calls the

spatial or locational aspect of everyday activities . . . because people tend to *behave differently depending on where they are.* Even outwardly similar activities often mean something very different when carried out in different places. To meet friends at home is not the same as to meet them in a club or restaurant. . . . *Even the mere proportion of time spent during the day in various locations*—indoors and outdoors, at home and around home, in streets and public places, at the workplace, in various locales and establishments—*is highly characteristic of people's way of life* [emphasis added].

The *context* in which activities take place, which encompasses the *field of action* (spatial/locational aspects already discussed), *sequential order*, and the *behavior habitat* (sociocultural aspects), is all-important. Questions relating to all of these aspects will be found in Appendix A, which offers an example of an *Idiosyncratic Activities Configuration Questionnaire*. Szalai [81] comments on *sequential order* as follows:

We know from everyday experience that there is some "logic" in the way people carry out their activities, one after the other, during the day. We also know that the choice of what to do next is often strongly influenced by what one has done before and what one wants or has to do afterwards. We know, finally, that some rather interesting and culturally relevant habits may express themselves in such typical sequences of activities as doing exercises after jumping out of bed, taking a nap after lunch, playing with the children before dinner, or reading before going to sleep.

Already introducing "cultural relevance" in connection with *sequential order*, Szalai [81] also takes cognizance of another part of the *behavior habitat* as he refers to the social dimension of everyday activities. He feels that we need to learn

. . . how much of their [people's] time they spend with their family, with neighbors, with friends and colleagues, in the midst of anonymous crowds, or simply alone. It seems to be almost trivial to add that the character of persons interacting or even merely present determines to a very great extent what people can do and choose to do at any given time.

To summarize, the *idiosyncratic activities configuration* is a descriptive survey of one person's everyday activities at one point in the life span. It emanates from an idiosyncratic activities pattern and reveals the rhythm and flow of daily activities, the context in which the activities takes place, the "personal equation" relating to the activities, and continuities, regularities, and balance. We are able to draw reasonably accurate conclusions about the nature of a typical day from both objective information, "[who] does what (and what else simultaneously) during the day, for how long, how often, at what time, in what order, where and with whom. . ." [81], and subjective accounts relating to feelings, associations, opinions, and historical events affecting the individual involved in the activities.

So far in discussing activities and configurations, the emphasis has been on the individual. As mentioned before, however, the individual's distinctive patterns and configurations are influenced by a socioculturally shaped world view and values and beliefs. It is important, therefore, to take into consideration notions of time and space, definitions of social roles, customs, usages, and notions of the desirable that are prevalent in the societal group or groups to which the individual belongs. Theoretically at least, it should be possible to elicit a *sociocultural* (or group) *activities configuration* in parallel with an *idiosyncratic* (or individual) *activities configuration*, the latter congruent with the former, but reflecting individual variation in so far as it is permitted by the group. Sociocultural influences will be discussed further under other headings in this chapter.

Classification

To learn "who does what" requires a listing of every single activity as it occurs hour by hour throughout a 24-hour period or combination of 24-hour periods. In a society where existence is dependent on the vagaries of nature and technology is rudimentary, the gamut of activities is likely to be limited and relatively similar for different individuals at any period of time. At the other extreme, in a complex, stratified, and technologically advanced society such as ours, we have, beside the core of essential activities that are at the base of our humanness and those variants that are socioculturally prescribed, room for a great deal of personal choice (see Chapter 1, Assumption 2). A potentially inexhaustible pool of activities is available to us that shifts in content and emphasis with the fashions of the time. The list of activities for any individual therefore varies in a number of respects from person to person and group to group at any one point in time.

THE DILEMMAS OF CLASSIFICATION: A WORK/LEISURE CLASSIFICATION AND ITS LIMITATIONS

In our everyday discourse, we have inherited a way of categorizing activities as *work* or *leisure* (or play). Until the early 1970s, work represented more than a means of earning money. In our society and others like ours, work was invested with a deeply held set of values leading to the belief that the act of working is good in itself. Freud added a psychological explanation for the importance of work to man: "His work at least gives him a secure place in a portion of reality, in the human community." [83]. It is small wonder then that much of people's self-worth has depended, and to a large extent still does depend, on their image of themselves as workers. By the same token, leisure, as demarcated from work, tended to be regarded as a form of laziness, particularly if one were alone doing nothing overtly active, like daydreaming on a hot summer afternoon or waiting for hours for a fish to bite.

However, in the last 20 years or so there has been a change in commonly held ideas about work and leisure, the signs of which are becoming apparent in a number of ways. In the world of work, a new term, "flextime," reflects a nudging of the hitherto firmly held 5-day, 9-to-5 norm by which all other time patterns are judged. While these temporal accommodations—3 days a week, 12 hours a day or half-days for 6 days a week, for example—have not always been successful in practice, they have to some extent invaded and modified current ways of thinking about work patterns.

In a number of instances, the home, which had tended increasingly to be separated from the workplace, is once again becoming the center for remunerative occupation—the professional who works at home, an arrangement designed to accommodate both job and shared homemaking responsibilities with spouse (besides having financial advantages); the housewife who turns her leisure-time occupation of knitting into work by making saleable items for a neighborhood store; the couple who market authentic homemade cookies from their home kitchen after the principal wage-earner lost his job—the examples are many and continue to proliferate.

These patterns of change also bring with them questions about the seemingly clear-cut demarcation between work and leisure. The example of the housewife/knitter who turns a hobby into self-employment is a case in point. If she were to record her activities configuration, would she separate knitting for profit from knitting for love, if she continues to provide family and friends with gifts? What about others, like the sculptor who labors in his loft for many hours a day, hoping for recognition of his talent, but who works as a bartender to "pay the rent and keep body and soul together"? Or the retired railroad worker who spends a great deal of time fishing from a small bridge near home and occasionally barters his catch for supplies at his friend's country store? Since he receives some remuneration (in kind, in this case) could we call his fishing work—sometimes? Then there is the single parent who juggles her time between a career as a computer programmer and homemaking and child-care responsibilities. How do we classify the seemingly endless list of activities that are part of homemaking, like doing the laundry, taking out the garbage, preparing meals, shopping at the supermarket, driving the children to the dentist, or reading them a bedtime story? Do these activities fit into work or leisure? This is a question that affects every one of us, since care of oneself and one's environment (including other people in it) is a basic requirement dictated by our socioculturally shared values and beliefs.

The situation of the growing population of the aged and aging in our society most graphically highlights the blurring of the lines between work and leisure. Forced to leave the world of work by the "planned obsolescence of people"* [83], these individuals, granted a longer life span by the miracles of science, must often seek from the pool of so-called leisure activities for a replacement that will have equivalent meaning in the years to come.

The neat separation of work and leisure is further complicated by a number of activities that do not fit quite comfortably into either category. One example is driving to work. Is this work or leisure? Some say, "Work—because it's not enjoyable, the traffic is terrible, and I wouldn't do it if I didn't have to get to work." Others say, "Leisure—because I enjoy the beautiful scenery along the way, and it gives me time to relax and organize my thoughts before I start on the daily grind." Another example is grooming and dressing. The answers in this instance also go either way. "Work—I hate to shave in a hurry and spend a lot of time getting into formal clothes. The weekends are different though; I can lounge around in sloppy jeans, and I don't have to shave unless I go out—but yes, it's still work!" Or, "Leisure—I allow myself plenty of time, it's fun to plan what outfit I'm going to wear, even if it's just a blouse and shorts, and I love what make-up does for me." Or, a third possibility, "Neither, I just go through the motions and try to get it over with in a hurry."

It is obvious from these examples that each individual is likely to have a different rationalization for choice of category, much of which relates to feelings of pleasure, displeasure, or indifference and which then may shift according to mood. On the other hand, there may be a general trend that connects work with displeasure and leisure with pleasure. If that is the case, then there is some substantiation of Terkel's [83] observation that

there is a sacrilegious question being asked these days. To earn one's bread by the sweat of one's brow has always been the lot of mankind. . . . The scriptural precept was never doubted, not out loud. . . . Lately there has been a questioning of this "work ethic," especially by the young. Strangely enough, it has touched off profound grievances in others hitherto devout, silent and anonymous.

The recognition of ambiguities and changing trends is important, since activities

---

* A 1987 Act of Congress virtually ends compulsory retirement, but the effects of this legislation are not likely to be noticeable for some time.

as natural human phenomena have to be studied from the viewpoint of natural science, which "needs a combination of observable features to attract attention" [47]. The work/leisure grouping expressed in ordinary conversation has a practical value for communication about everyday activities in our society and others like ours. But as a classification it has obvious shortcomings. It is neither exhaustive (accounting for all possible human activities) nor exclusive (separating out what does not belong).

OTHER CLASSIFICATION SYSTEMS

To be truly universal, a classification would have to begin from a frame of reference that takes into account the basic postulate referred to in Chapter 1 (Assumption 3)—the first duty of an organism is to survive—and the commonalities in our human condition. Thus a *sociobiological classification* would begin to define the activities that help us survive, in the recognition that all humans have to take care of their bodily needs but also have to band together and live with others for pro-creation and support. A *sociocultural classification*, on the other hand, would focus on the extragenetic factors that impinge on the human organism and that relate to the groups to which it belongs. Culture, a distinctively human phenomenon, gives direction to the ways in which activities are carried out, who carries out which activities, when these activities are carried out, and which activities predominate at which times.

Assignments at the end of this chapter provide an opportunity to explore the classification of activities further, while Appendixes B and C elaborate on the two kinds of classification that have been suggested.

A sociocultural classification such as the one outlined in Appendix C brings the realization that in the life of the individual some activities may be passed on from generation to generation virtually unchanged, a strong thread of connection throughout the life span. Other activities, also passed on from generation to generation, appear only periodically in the life span and relate to specific developmental stages, rites of passage, and personal needs for attachment to the past. Still other activities appear periodically in the life span, as choices for personal satisfaction at the time or imposed by the pressures of external events. And there are also activities that appear only fleetingly in the life span in response to current fads and fancies. As we know, our own society is particularly susceptible to short-lived "crazes," like the hula hoop, encounter groups, video games, chocolate chip cookies, macrame bracelets, and "The Hustle."

This constellation of activities, this ". . . way of life we inherit, practice and pass on to our descendents . . . the everyday world around us" [13], has now become the focus of study. The *Journal of Popular Culture* provides us with a publication that examines activities with a history as well as contemporary activities in a number of different social and cultural contexts. Thus, for example, we find "Family Art: Domestic and Eternal Bliss" [65], "Baseball in Cuba" [86], and "Bingo: The Whys and Wherefores of a Popular Pastime" [24] side by side with "Social Science Research on Video Games" [68] and research on "The Party Behaviors of a Small

Community" [23]—all of which look at the connections between the actors and their activities in everyday life.

Contexts

As has become abundantly clear, the nature of everyday activities emerges only from the context in which they are embedded. Context has already been mentioned, particularly in relation to patterns and configurations (see Patterns and Configurations), where field of action (situational/locational aspects) and behavior habitat (sociocultural aspects—transactions and interactions) together identify the immediate matrix in which the activities take place. Also mentioned is sequential order, which identifies not only which activities come before and after, but also the antecedents to and consequences of each particular activity at any one time. This will be explored further in subsequent chapters.

There are other ways of viewing context that move away from the immediate connections among the activity, the actor, and the environment in which the action takes place. In the most general sense, historical time and geographical place provide the outer layer, as it were, as it is apparent from the discussion of everyday activities in other times and places (see Chapter 1). Another view, coming from a general sociocultural perspective that gives coloration, pattern, and direction to everyday activities of distinctive groups, also impinges on the more intimate connections between the individual and the activity. Thus notions of the desirable, do's and don'ts, classifications (formal and informal), popularly held beliefs, and practices that relate to a society and/or subgroups of that society strongly influence who does what, when, where, how, with whom, and for how long.

Summary

So far we have glimpsed prehistory and history, a sprinkling of places around the globe, and the here and now. We have learned something of our biological inheritance, which includes the propensity to learn extragenetically through culture. And in seeking to know the nature of everyday activities we have examined the connections between our human nature, the societies and cultures we have fashioned and that fashion us, and the activities patterns that distinguish both our shared humanness and our individuality. Thus we are now able to identify a number of distinctive features of activities:

1. They are a series of manifest operations, carried out as part of the procedures of day-to-day living.
2. They involve a process of doing.
3. They are characteristic of and necessary to a human existence.
4. They are socioculturally regulated.
5. They can be learned.

In the next chapter, we look at the links between activities and health and the reason for being of occupational therapy.

Assignment 1 ───────────────────────────────

    A.   Use the *Idiosyncratic Activities Configuration Questionnaire* (Appendix A) to obtain information about one week's activities (Monday through Sunday):
        1.   for yourself.
        2.   for someone you know well.
        3.   for someone who is different from you in terms of age, gender, socio-economic status, country of origin, religious affiliation, ethnic background (all or some, but at least four).
    B.   With the three of you together, compare and contrast your configurations:
        1.   What did you find different?
        2.   What did you find similar?

Assignment 2

    A.   Using the suggested frameworks for classification (Appendixes B and C) as guides, classify all the activities appearing in all three configurations in terms of
        1.   a sociobiological classification.
        2.   a sociocultural classification.
    B.   Compare your findings with those of your classmates (colleagues). With your group, construct a third classification that will be *universal* and *exclusive* for *all* the activities encompassed in the group's findings.

Assignment 3

Using the list of activities obtained from the combined findings of the three configurations in Assignment 2, tabulate them in three columns: The first column should read *Requiring Devices or Equipment* (e.g., needles and thread, TV set, knife, fork, hammer, pliers, sneakers, stove, tennis racquet, toothbrush, computer, shoelaces, frying pan, reading light, playing cards); the second column should read *Requiring no Devices or Equipment* (e.g., talking, taking a stroll, singing—a cappella, of course—daydreaming); the third should read *Requiring Special Environment* (e.g., restaurant, office, bathroom).

Assignment 4

Select *five* different activities from the list you have obtained for Assignment 3. Describe each activity in terms of *context*, looking at *field of action* (location/situation), *behavior habitat* (people, interactions, and transactions), and *sequential order* (which activity comes before and after, what leads up to the activity, and what results from the activity).

Assignment 5

In Chapter 1 (p. 3), there is a long, random list of activities of everyday living. With each activity in turn, answer the following questions to the extent that you are able (do this in a group, assigning five activities to each person):

A. Who does this kind of activity (e.g., age, gender, sociocultural background, geographical area)?

B. When is this activity done (e.g., time of day, day[s] of week, time of year)?

C. With whom is this kind of activity done?

D. How is this kind of activity classified (e.g., work, leisure, hobby, social activity, ritual)?

E. Describe the field of action for this activity to the extent that you are able.

F. For those activities that you have never done, but for which you are able to answer at least some of the questions, how did you learn about them?

CHAPTER 3

The Concept of Activities Health: Links Between Activities and Health

Imagine—and we think imagination is unique to the human brain—the information processed by the ten billion neurons for a *simple activity like playing basketball* [emphasis added] in the yard with a few friends. Without your really thinking about it, you coordinate your muscles so that they move feet and arms. You keep your eye on the ball, on the hoop, and on other players. You make a long hook shot, and the ball falls neatly through the hoop. You smile and feel a surge of confidence, of well-being, and you don't think about all the muscles that make the smile. In your mind's eye you see yourself as a pro.

You see the dog leap off the porch and dart between two of the players as he chases the ball. You manage to avoid tripping over the dog as you yell at him. You hear the radio playing in the house, and recognize the music, which makes you think of a dance next week and wonder whom you'll go with. A mosquito lands on your arm, stings, and absently you swat at it. Reacting to the heat, you sweat and wipe your forehead without much thought. You squint in the sunlight and perhaps remember where you left your sunglasses.

The phone rings. You hear it and wonder if it's for you. And during all these fleeting thoughts and reactions, you are talking with your friends, hearing their words, sorting and storing information. One day in the future you will remember this game and joke about the dog trying to get the ball. You smell cookies baking, and suddenly you are aware of hunger. You keep breathing, your heart beats steadily, and all systems work together, every one of them coordinated by the brain. [30]

With the above description, we return to the central nervous system connection cited in Chapter 1 (pp. 4–5). It is readily apparent that even with a so-called simple activity, a multiplicity of events are taking place, some simultaneously, others concurrently, and yet others in sequence with the central complex of actions and interactions that are characteristic of this game of basketball. The actor is responding to numerous and different stimuli in the environment, many of which are below the level of consciousness. Some are intrinsic to the game; others, like the playful dog and annoying mosquito, the ring of the phone, or the smell of the freshly-baked cookies, are peripheral to the action but release in each case a train of associations and feelings and, in some cases, physical responses.

These stimuli are received, sorted, and selectively attended to, and appropriate responses are produced, actions are synchronized and sequenced, even as subtle internal adjustments are made in response to messages relayed from the organism as it responds. The entire elaborate process is set in motion, regulated, and co-ordinated by the busy brain. In the basketball game, the actor *moves*—jumping, grasping, throwing, running, dodging, tossing, talking, yelling, slapping—*plans* strategy, *remembers* the rules, *registers* peripheral sounds, smells, sights, *recalls* previous experiences, *looks forward* to events in the future—*feels* elation, annoy-ance, pleasure—all within a relatively short time, while completely unaware of the exquisitely orchestrated workings of his body and brain.

Besides the conclusions we are able to draw about the nature of these complex processes because we have knowledge of the structure and function of the central nervous system, we can also make inferences about the relationship between the actor and the activity. For example, from the description of the game in progress, we may conclude that the actor is quite familiar with the rules of the game and is sufficiently skillful as a player to be able to attend to peripheral matters even while the game is proceeding. This means that he has stored up and is able to call upon previous learning, which enables him to behave appropriately and perform com-petently without the need for continuous attention to what he is doing. Moreover, an array of memories, stored up from previous experience and released by stimuli from the activity environment, can be responded to without detracting from full participation in the game.

This kind of complete immersion in the process and progress of activities—the mind, will, and hands (body) fully occupied—is what we commonly call *engagement*. There is, of course, a greater or lesser degree of involvement at any one time with any one activity, which depends on

1. The nature of each *activity*
2. The mood, attitude, physical state, and idiosyncratic style of the *actor*
3. The context (*behavior habitat/field of action*) in which the activity takes place

To illustrate with an example familiar to many a student, a lecture involving the recital of dry facts in the late afternoon in a hot and airless classroom is likely to produce in the student frequent yawning, fidgeting, lapses of concentration, and increasing awareness of the discomfort of a hard, unyielding seat. At the same time, counter activities to boredom may include doodling, taking a catnap, gazing out of the window, or planning a pleasurable outing when the day is over.

Gradations of engagement range from complete immersion to minimal partici-pation. For the most part, however, the activities of our everyday lives entail neither the high degree of excitement and "busyness" of the basketball game nor the deadly boredom of the afternoon lecture. But no matter how much or how little we engage, our ongoing involvement in the gamut of day-to-day activities necessitates the use of the hands (body), the mind, and the will, in varying degrees (see Chapter 1, pp. 4–5). It is reasonable to conclude, therefore, that there is an inextricable connection between the activities of everyday living and the optimal functioning of the human organism.

In the ideal conception of health, optimal function evokes a picture of intact physical structures and physiological mechanisms, well-developed cognitive and social skills, and emotional stability, all nicely balanced in a well-integrated ego. But formal definitions of health vary in emphasis depending on the point of view from which they arise. Thus a medical view may lead to the definition of health as freedom from disease or ailment, while a holistic view takes into account the total quality of life that is affected by every interrelated aspect of living. There are many other definitions of health, ranging from the relatively narrow perspective of personality development [28] to the all-encompassing universal view of the World Health Organization.

Defining *Activities Health*

In the context of an emphasis on human activities, *health* (and its practical correlate *function*) is manifested in the ability of the individual to participate in socioculturally regulated activities with satisfaction and comfort.

Thus, an individual may be said to be in a state of *activities health* when able to carry out the activities of everyday living with satisfaction and comfort in ways that are socioculturally approved (Figure 3-1). Both from Figure 3-1 and from discussion of the assumptions in Chapter 1 (pp. 7–12), it becomes clear that *activities health* not only is *expressed* through activities (in patterns and configurations)

Figure 3-1. Summary diagram of the links between activities and health.

but also is *attained* through activities. The human organism, impelled to be active, grows and develops physically, intellectually, and emotionally through engagement in activities, and is socialized—by means of activities carried out in distinctively patterned ways—to become an individual who is capable of attaining a state of *activities health.*

To exist, subsist, and coexist, every individual engages in a considerable number of different activities each day, the patterns of which vary from culture to culture. It is highly unlikely that any individual in an ideal state of *activities health* would be satisfied with the same few activities day after day. As Fromm [40] has said, "Man is the only animal that can be bored."

An example from the mainstream of our society, in this case a day in the life of a waitress, shows a count of 38 different activities in one day from waking up to going to bed. This number does not include the breakdown of each general activity into component activities (e.g., preparing breakfast for self and family includes slicing and toasting bread, buttering toast, breaking eggs, beating eggs, cooking eggs, dishing out eggs, placing toast on plates, measuring water, measuring coffee, brewing coffee, pouring coffee—an addition of 12 component activities to a single activity).

It goes without saying, however, that *number of activities by itself* cannot be regarded as an index of *activities health*. But we have already been introduced to the notions of *balance* and *context* (see Chapter 2), which allow us to determine from the enumeration of specific activities the proportion of time spent

1.   With different kinds and categories of activities
2.   With other people or alone
3.   At home and out of the home
4.   Indoors and outdoors
5.   With activities liked and activities disliked
6.   With activities chosen and activities imposed on one

This quantitative determination of *balance* of activities, itself a socioculturally derived notion of what is good, enables a qualitative criterion to be added—that of a *sense of balance* perceived by the individual, which meshes with an *overall sense of comfort and satisfaction.* Comfort with one's activities refers to a feeling of being able, in general, to cope despite problems—which is akin to an overall feeling of *mastery* or *competence* as described by White [90]. By the same token, a *sense of satisfaction* with one's patterns of everyday activities relates to an overall feeling of well-being, despite periods or areas of dissatisfaction, boredom, and/or disinterest.

With these special connotations of *comfort* and *satisfaction* in mind, the definition of *activities health* can now be expanded as follows: *a state of well-being in which the individual is able to carry out the activities of everyday living with satisfaction and comfort, in patterns and configurations that reflect sociocultural norms and idiosyncratic variation in number, variety, balance, and context of activities.* (Look at Figure 3-1 again in light of this new definition.)

Activities health, in common with other states of health that are looked on as more than freedom from illness, is ". . . like love or happiness . . . a quality of life that is difficult to define and impossible to measure" [25]. There are, however, a number of interrelated factors that serve as reasonably accurate indicators of a state of *activities health*:

1. *Number* and *variety* of activities of everyday living that are *appropriate*
2. *Number* and *variety* of activities of everyday living that are *balanced*
3. *Overall feeling of comfort* with the activities of everyday living
4. *Overall feeling of satisfaction* with the activities of everyday living

Indicators of Activities Health

NUMBER AND VARIETY OF ACTIVITIES

As has been mentioned previously, the *number* of activities alone cannot be regarded as an adequate indicator of *activities health*. The determination of the *kinds* of activities and the *mix* of activities, in other words, the *variety* of activities found in any numerical listing, is a more accurate pointer to a state of *activities health*. However, even number expressed in terms of *variety* is incomplete unless the activities enumerated are qualified as both *appropriate* and *balanced*.

We know that humans, even as far back as the Ice Age, engaged in many more activities than were needed just to stay alive. And through the ages and in different parts of the world, including ours, there are records showing the diversity of activities that seem to constitute the norm for the daily life of the individual (see Chapter 2). It appears to be human nature for the individual to stretch beyond fulfilling basic needs for survival—to explore the unknown, take up the challenges of a risk-filled environment, seek new experiences, and express the self through creative endeavor. Certainly psychologists such as White [90] and others give credence to this belief as they talk about effectance or competence. Thus we can say that *variety* and diversity (qualified by appropriateness and balance) are indicators of a state of health in which the individual is fully engaged in reacting to, interacting with, and acting upon the environment, attaining a sense of mastery and competence in the process.

All these varied and diverse activities do not occur randomly in the everyday life of the individual; they are given direction and shaped in patterns by the sociocultural group or groups to which the individual belongs. Every society, and subgroup of society, has a set of beliefs and values that govern notions of what is *appropriate* to do or not do for each individual who is distinguished and separated from other individuals by age, gender, social and economic status, ethnic background, or other culturally selected criteria (see Chapter 1, Assumption 2). It is these notions of *appropriateness* that are greatly influential in determining the activities patterns of each individual.

APPROPRIATENESS

As has just been mentioned, appropriateness of activities is socioculturally determined. In our own society, even though we like to think we have a great deal of personal choice, we are subtly and pervasively influenced by sociocultural expectations with regard to what we do and how, when, where, for how long, and with whom we do it.

Even our most intimate and personally distinctive activities—like washing, grooming and dressing—are given direction by our society, which places a high value on cleanliness and attractive personal appearance. Indeed, so firmly held are these values that a permanently dirty, disheveled appearance is often seen as a clue to some sort of pathological condition. The numerous and different activities that are connected with personal hygiene, grooming, and dressing are "musts" in every individual's configuration, even though there are choices within these categories that allow for individual variation. Thus everyone must be clean, but how one gets clean—tub, shower, sponge-wash, soaps, lotions—can be a matter of personal preference. (It is important to mention here that other variations can be due to such factors as habit passed on from generation to generation or economic circumstances that do not allow one the luxury of hot and cold running water).

The *amount of time* it is appropriate to spend on keeping oneself clean is also socioculturally regulated. While a range of times—to accommodate individual differences—is allowed as appropriate, an excessive allocation of time each day to keeping oneself clean is regarded as strange, unacceptable, or in extreme cases, pathological. *When* it is appropriate to carry out the activities associated with personal hygiene is also socioculturally directed. Whether it is to be morning or evening, or both, is left for the individual to decide, but other times of the day are deemed unusual, if not odd. *How often* it is appropriate for the activities to be done allows for variation, the most desirable being "every day," while "once a week" seems to be reaching beyond the outer limits of what is acceptable.

With whom one does the activities is also socioculturally determined. Thus, while it is expected that adults bathe their children until they can manage by themselves with comfort and safety, and it is quite acceptable for young children to bathe together, bathing and other activities relating to personal cleanliness are regarded by our society as private and therefore properly done alone. By contrast, in certain segments of Japanese society, communal bathing may be invested with carefully prescribed rituals for a highly valued social and sensually pleasing activity.

Appropriateness in our society, and others like ours, also relates to the proportion of time it is considered good and proper to spend with different kinds of activities. Thus we are expected to use our time for working, attending to our physiological needs, attending to our environment (including the people in it), and playing (leisure-time pursuits), apportioning amounts of time that are neither too limited nor excessive for any one category. A wide range of variation is tolerated to accommodate to individual differences, both in selection of representative activities and allocation of time. Yet there are a number of "musts"—care of one's self and environment (including the people in it), work (or its analog), and sleep—that take a large portion of our daily time and are generally carried out regularly, despite possible periods of discontent, reluctance, and a desire to do other, more appealing things, like the "electives" permitted in that category of activities we call leisure.

For example, at the end of the day, an unwanted but compulsory chore, part of care of one's environment, awaits some member of the family. A favorite television program is beckoning for the two teenagers at home, while dad is sitting in the car, waiting for mom to join him for the ride to a meeting. The garbage has to be taken out for collection soon, packaged in a specified manner. In this case, the obligation is very clear and enforced by legal penalties for noncompliance. Similarly, there are many activities in our daily routine where prescriptions and proscriptions are quite clear, most times unwritten but sometimes contractual, as at work. Thus, for example, there is a loss of job as a consequence of chronic unpunctuality, a failing grade for cutting too many classes, suspension of privileges for staying out too late at night and forgetting homework, avoidance by peers for looking different from the "group."

In many other instances, however, the "musts" are not so obvious. Indeed, they are hardly perceived as such, since there appear to be no direct penalties for noncompliance. And yet we continue doing these socioculturally prescribed activities, day after day, sometimes reluctantly, but impelled somehow to go on, for the most part unaware of how tightly intertwined they are in our activities configurations. A familiar example is bed-making. What impels so many individuals to go through this daily ritual despite, very often, negative feelings and sometimes physical strain? (See Assignment 2 at the end of this chapter for a look at other examples.)

By the same token, what impels us to attend traditional celebrations with relatives with whom we do not have much in common? And how do we know that we are expected to dress appropriately, perhaps against our personal inclinations, for a job interview? Even the activities over which we think we have complete freedom of choice, such as hobbies, are selected from a repertoire that is deemed appropriate by our culture. Moreover, the very word *hobbies* is fraught with socioculturally derived associations—"leisure," for instance, or specific pastimes such as collecting stamps, flying a kite, growing indoor plants, collecting recipes, reading mysteries, fishing, or repairing dolls (see Chapter 8, Assignment 5). The list seems endless, but it is nevertheless ultimately circumscribed by socioculturally shaped notions of what is to be properly fitted into this category of activities, notions that may change periodically in response to the fashions and technology of the times.* Though not necessarily aware of what these notions are, we are able to recognize that all the activities that have been enumerated fit appropriately into the category of "hobbies," just as we tend to be jarred by a sense of inappropriateness when the young man cited in Chapter 1 says he reads philosophy for fun.

Our sense of what "feels right" about our activities is socioculturally learned. We are all subject to subliminal but pervasive sociocultural influences that color our perceptions, conceptions, and actions relating to everyday activities. Work/play balance, leisure, 5-day workweek, weekend break, adults' activities, children's activities, old people's activities, teenage activities, traditional activities, men's activities, women's activities, celebrations, rituals, getting up in the morning, bedtime, fashions, and individual choice are some of those socioculturally derived notions that affect the selections we make from the repertoire of activities available to us.

Whether the individual goes along totally with what is deemed appropriate or resists a pull toward conformity by questioning, revising, avoiding, omitting, re-

---

* Here is where a reference to the *Journal of Popular Culture* (see p. 21) helps to keep us abreast of changes as well as aware of those parts of our heritage that are carried into the present.

belling, or compromising, every personal choice is made within the framework of a socioculturally determined set of "do's" and "don'ts" and a range of variation kept within acceptable limits. Because our many-layered, complex society places a high value on individuality, a wide range of variation is acceptable in terms of *appropriateness*. Yet there is always a point, impossible to define exactly, where degree and extent of variation become unacceptable, and the individual is deemed odd, antisocial, or unhealthy and dealt with accordingly. For the most part, however, the individual in a state of *activities health* will have arrived at a kind of dynamic equilibrium in which idiosyncratic variation is sufficient to ensure a sense of satisfaction and comfort but also is within the boundaries of sociocultural acceptance and approval, another source of satisfaction and comfort to the individual.

BALANCE

Other than the proportion of time allocated to each socioculturally determined category of activities, which is sometimes defined as *balance* and was discussed under Appropriateness, it is possible to compute and compare the amount of time spent with a number of contrasted components of the activities context. There are people, places, feelings, and choices, as well as categories, to be considered in determining balance, in itself a socioculturally derived notion of the desirable, and one that is congruent with well-being and wellness. As with *appropriateness*, there is a great deal of variation from individual to individual, so it is virtually impossible to arrive at an absolute formula for balance. For one individual, 50:50 may be the ideal proportion of time to spend in doing activities alone and with others. Another individual, much more given to solitary activities, may feel that 30:70 is a better balance. The first individual may concur, however, with the second in determining that the ideal proportion of time to spend at home as contrasted with outside the home is 70:30. The permutations for each individual, and from individual to individual, are so great that a preferred way of determining balance might be to elicit an *overall sense of balance* from the individual, who either "feels right" or does not "feel right" in terms of equilibrium of daily activities. Further probing may then be done by means of selected computations of proportionate time.

COMFORT

As has been mentioned before, a general sense of balance meshes with an *overall sense of comfort*, which in turn relates to a feeling of being able to cope with one's everyday activities in spite of problems and setbacks and is akin to an overall feeling of mastery or competence. One factor that defines *positive wellness* is "adaptability to cope with and overcome all types of stress in everyday living." Another is "feelings of accomplishment and personal growth" [25]. Both these factors are close to our definition of *comfort*, which stands well as an indicator of *activities health*.

SATISFACTION

As has also been mentioned before, an *overall sense of satisfaction* with one's everyday activities relates to a general feeling of well-being, despite periods or areas of dissatisfaction, boredom, or disinterest. This *sense of satisfaction* is close to "feelings of contentment and happiness" [25], which appears as yet another factor in the definition of positive well-being but is also related to *sense of balance* and *sense of mastery* and hence also to a sense of *comfort* with one's everyday activities.

All the indicators of *activities health* are found in or can be derived from the Idiosyncratic Activities Configuration (see Chapter 2, Patterns and Configurations, and Appendix A), which encapsulates individual variation in a sociocultural framework and provides simple rating scales for both *overall sense of comfort and overall sense of satisfaction, as well as overall sense of "fit" with sociocultural patterns.*

Summary

In this chapter, the links between activities and health have been examined, leading to the presentation of an activities-based definition of health. Indicators of *activities health* have been analyzed and discussed, and attention has been drawn to the Idiosyncratic Activities Configuration as an instrument from which these indicators can be derived. We can now move to the connections between *activities health* and occupational therapy and begin to look at the implications of this theoretical construct for clinical practice.

Assignment 1

Select any individual whom you consider to be in a state of *activities health*.

A. Ask this individual to complete an Idiosyncratic Activities Configuration Questionnaire (Appendix A).
B. Compare this completed questionnaire with those you obtained from Assignment 1 in Chapter 2 in terms of
 1. number and variety of activities.
 2. appropriateness of activities (you will need background data like age, gender, socioeconomic status, and cultural background for this).
 3. balance of activities.
 4. overall sense of comfort.
 5. overall sense of satisfaction.
C. From this comparison, rate the individual's *activities health*, using the following scale:

very low	moderately low	moderately high	very high

D. List the criteria you used to select the individual in an ideal state of *activities health*. Compare
 1. your rating of this individual.
 2. this individual's rating on the scale in C.
 3. this individual's rating of himself/herself.

Assignment 2

In looking at your own completed Idiosyncratic Activities Configuration, identify the activities that

A. you do regularly; you find burdensome most of the time; you are made to do because of regulations or fear of sanctions (see Appropriateness for elaboration on these kinds of activities).
B. you feel are an expression of you.
C. you feel you have to do because they are typical of
    1. your nationality.
    2. your ethnic group.
    3. your religious group.
    4. your peer group.
    5. your socioeconomic group (e.g., middle-class professional, blue-collar worker).
    6. your community (e.g., rural/urban/suburban/small town).

Assignment 3

You have already used the random listing on page 3 of Chapter 1 for Assignment 5 in Chapter 2. Read the paragraph again.

A. Classify the activities under the following headings: Appropriate for ages 1–3, 4–6, 6–12, 13–18, 19–25, 26–40, 41–60, 61–75, 75 on (some activities may fit into more than one heading).
B. Classify the activities as appropriate for individuals who belong to a rural/urban/suburban/small-town society.
C. List the activities that are different from those that you are familiar with in your own society. In what part of the world and in what kind of society are they found?
D. Use either the sociobiological or sociocultural classification suggested in Appendixes B and C to sort out the activities in yet another way.
E. Make a list of all the activities you have heard or read about, seen, or even participated in that are different from those in your own society.

CHAPTER 4

Activities Health and Occupational Therapy: The Activities Connection

In the preceding chapters, most of the emphasis has been on the exploration of activities as natural human phenomena and on the links between activities and health. Dysfunction and ill-health have scarcely been mentioned. Yet occupational therapy is a profession that is committed to working with those who have some kind of physical, emotional, and/or cognitive impairment, helping them to turn from dysfunction toward function. On the other hand, occupational therapy is also a profession that has recognized, from its earliest days, that engagement in activities has an important connection with physical, emotional, and mental well-being.

As already mentioned, in the context of an emphasis on activities, health (or its practical correlate, function) is manifested in the ability of the individual to participate in socioculturally delineated and directed activities with satisfaction and comfort. Conversely, ill-health (or dysfunction) is evinced (over and above clinically labeled signs, symptoms, and behaviors) in the inability of the individual to carry out with satisfaction and comfort the activities of everyday living in those patterns that are socioculturally designed and approved. As beacons of health, and indeed determinants of a state of *activities health*, activities are therefore the ends to which the efforts of occupational therapy are directed. But activities are also the means to those ends. Justification for the instrumental role of activities comes with a simple statement: There is no better introduction to activities than these very same activities themselves. It is unlikely that some magical leap occurs between attainment of an improved physical or psychological state—such as increase of muscle strength, normalization of tone, appropriate expression of feelings—and the integration of activities in ways that are personally satisfying and socioculturally acceptable, particularly if the dysfunction is severe or of long duration. However, even with a less severe problem, the integrating function of activities can be important to full recovery. This is well illustrated in the case of the puzzled orthopedic surgeon, working with a well-known football team, who began to see that there was a missing component in an otherwise excellent program to restore physical function after meniscectomy. For, even with quadriceps strengthened to the maximum and a smooth and effortless gait, these healthy young men would come off the field time and again after their first practice session and complain, "Doc, I forgot how to run!"

Although perfect function—physical, emotional, social, and cognitive—is regarded as the ultimate determinant of an ideal state of health, there are countless individuals who, even with severe and permanent handicaps, are healthy in an activities sense. Thus, for occupational therapy, of necessity working with individuals whose condition seldom allows for a complete cure, it is important to bear in mind that ". . . often the most effective and vigorous human action is of a compensatory or substitute nature" [20]. A most telling exemplar of *activities health* is Mr. L., who had a bilateral shoulder disarticulation many years ago:

Mr. L. has earned a living as a demonstrator for, among others occupational therapy and physical therapy students, traveling from place to place to show how a person without his own upper limbs is able to carry out his everyday activities in ways that fall within the range of sociocultural approval. The demonstration begins with undressing, so that Mr. L. can show his daily routine in chronological order. With double prosthesis, harness, and protective underclothes laid out on the bed in careful order by means of teeth and jaw, head, neck, and scapular muscles, he literally dives into each piece of equipment, and then uses shrugging motions and head and trunk rotation to get all of them on. Once his prostheses are properly aligned, he is ready to go through (by demonstrating or describing) the gamut of his everyday activities, which are balanced to his satisfaction among care of self and environment, work, and leisure. Although independent in most of his activities, he has come to recognize that he needs help from other persons for activities like driving from place to place and carrying all his gear, as well as for cutting down on the length of time it takes him to do some chores. Formally dressed in a dark suit, button-down shirt, and tie, he lectures animatedly, punctuating his remarks by gesticulating with his prostheses. The unselfconscious use of his artificial limbs for expression is perhaps the best indicator of how comfortable Mr. L. feels (and hence how comfortable everyone else around him feels) about himself and his activities of everyday living.

Underlying the capacity to engage effectively in activities despite disability is the human will—the *will to change* and the *will to learn*, which will be discussed again later in this chapter. At this point it is appropriate to recall the two assumptions (3 and 4) in Chapter 1 that postulate that humankind has a tendency to desire change in a direction from dysfunction toward function and that such change takes place through learning. As Bruner [15] points out, ". . . The single most characteristic thing about human beings is that they learn. Learning is so deeply ingrained in man that it is almost involuntary, and thoughtful students of human behavior have even speculated that our specialization as a species is a specialization for learning." Our assumption that learning is the vehicle for change from dysfunction toward function is supported by this view. But what kind of learning are we, as occupational therapists, talking about? How did Mr. L. learn to do his everyday activities in patterns that are still socioculturally acceptable, despite his disability? Indeed, how do we all, with our shared human heritage, learn to carry out our daily schedule of activities in ways that are characteristic of the groups to which we belong, in patterns that are individually distinctive and socioculturally acceptable?

To attempt to answer this question, we need to look not only at the formal learning that takes place as a prominent part of any complex society such as ours, but also at how, as Bruner [14] says, "the 'uninstructed' portion of our . . . culture gets passed on." It is this "uninstructed" portion of our culture that gives us our characteristic styles of doing activities and our distinctive activities patterns that are shaped by culturally transmitted time perspectives, perceptions, values, and world view. Unfortunately as Bruner [14] points out,

> . . . There has been little enough effort expended in trying to understand in some decently detailed way, how a young man, say, learns not only to hunt but to recognize the necessary blend of technique and ritual—learns the pattern of sharing as well as of hunting. The Bushman,* for example, knows extraordinarily exquisite rules about how meat is to be shared after a hunt—what is his own share, what belongs to the owner of the arrow that was "lent" to him as a gift, what belongs to this kinsman and that, and so forth. The politesse is as functional as it is subtle. Little is known of how it is transmitted.

We, too, as members of a complex, technologically advanced society learn to recognize the necessary blend of "technique and ritual" required to carry out our activities in socioculturally acceptable ways—even though the "rituals" may be far less formal (and therefore not recognized as such) than those described by Bruner. A case in point is the young woman who obviously sets great store by dressing fashionably. She is poised and ready for her job interview (she has learned the techniques—some formally by reading "how-to" books, some from previous experience, and some by applying social rules learned from other situations). While she is waiting, she engages in conversation about the latest craze—above-the-knee skirts—and she says she loves them but will only wear them for "going out." For business, she thinks that a mid-calf skirt is more appropriate, especially for this interview, where she wants to make a good impression as a potential vice-president of a bank. While seemingly quite independent in her decisions, this young woman has in fact chosen between two outward symbols (styles of clothing, each laden with a number of socioculturally derived connotations) of a socioculturally patterned ritual—presenting oneself for a specific occasion. In addition, she has made a judgment, based on the "uninstructed" part of her learning, about appropriateness. (As a contrast in appropriateness of dress for work, see Figure 4-2.)

There are any number of subtle ways in which our activities of everyday living are socioculturally influenced and directed. We are usually completely unaware of them as we go about our daily business of doing, and seldom, if ever, do we wonder how we got to do what we do in the particular ways that we do it. As occupational therapists, however, it becomes incumbent on us to find out more about how these "uninstructed portions of our culture," which include many of our everyday activities, are learned. As Bruner has indicated, we do not know very much in the way of detail about how portions of our culture are passed on in all their subtle

---

* Bruner is referring here to the !Kung Bushman of the Kalahari, who has been the subject of a number of anthropological and psychological studies.

nuances. But we do have some idea of how the activities of everyday living are learned—by any one individual at any one particular time. As we look at the answers to some of the questions asked in the Idiosyncratic Activities Configuration (Appendix A)—such as, from whom and how long ago did you learn this activity?—we begin to get glimpses of how the activities might become woven into the fabric of everyday living.

In passing, it is interesting to note that when the answers to these questions were tabulated for three consecutive sets of first-year occupational therapy students, it was strikingly obvious that by far the greatest number of activities for the combined group, derived from a week's activities for each person, were learned either from family or peers, while learning from teachers or by oneself hardly counted—for every single individual in the group. "Learning by watching and copying" or "just learning because I was around" outnumbered "learning by being told" or "finding out for myself" just as strikingly. To draw any conclusions at all from a small, select, and circumscribed group that is scarcely representative of the total population would be premature, to say the least. However, this line of questioning appears to have potential for delving deeper in systematic ways into how the culturally shaped portions of our everyday activities are "conserved and transmitted." To know about how, and also from whom and when, the individual has learned to do all those activities that make up distinctive socioculturally delineated patterns can only add ultimately to the effectiveness with which activities are incorporated as therapeutic tools in directing change from dysfunction toward function.

The Will to Learn

For activities to become therapeutic or, in other words, instrumental in producing the kind of change that leads to a state of *activities health* (or function), it is important to arouse and sustain in the individual the *will to learn*. This concept, offered by Bruner [15] in the context of education, is equally applicable to occupational therapy because the human being "is born into a culture that has as one of its principal functions the conservation and transmission of past learning" [15], which, of course, includes the distinctive ways and patterns in which the activities of everyday living are carried out.

In invoking the will to learn, Bruner, while not altogether negating the usefulness of extrinsic rewards, dwells on the *intrinsic motives* for learning. The idea of such motives for learning tacitly underlies most occupational therapy practice. In effect, occupational therapy assumes that in the doing comes the reward, either in the process itself or in the attainment of a successful end result, much as Bruner [15] defines the will to learn as ". . . an intrinsic motive, one that finds both its source and its reward in its own exercise." Arousing and sustaining the will to learn depends, according to Bruner [15], on the enlistment of ". . . the natural energies that sustain spontaneous learning—curiosity, a desire for competence, aspiration to emulate a model, and a deep-seated commitment to the web of social reciprocity." We will look more closely at these intrinsic motives in Chapter 5.

Each of these "natural energies" inheres in the interactions between the individual and the environment, which also includes the activities environment. As has been amply discussed in Chapter 2, the natural environment in which activities take place has a great deal of bearing on how activities are carried out, how they are perceived, and how they are learned in the first place. Indeed, activities are so intimately bound up with their context that they lose a great deal of their meaning and relevance to the individual when they are extracted from a familiar field of action or extrapolated into a greatly different one. On the other hand, in the ordinary course of our everyday lives, we find that some basic activities can be classified in a number of different ways depending on the setting in which they occur and the rules that govern their operation. Therefore, for occupational therapy, the field of action is a crucial determinant in structuring activities experiences so that they simulate as nearly as possible conditions in the real world and thus have meaning and relevance to the individual.

A perfect illustration of the ramifications of one activity in different fields of action is eating. The intake of food is obviously directed to self-care. Since a certain amount of sustenance is also necessary for survival, eating in this instance may be further classified as a primary and universal activity. On the other hand, the secondary activities of eating vary from culture to culture. Eating as a social activity encompasses a variety of attendant rituals and customs, from using a fork and knife properly to the complexities of family and other group celebrations. In many segments of our society, eating out is associated with leisure-time pursuits, as a pleasurable end in itself or an accompaniment to outings designed for pleasure. Again in our society, mostly in the executive or professional class, eating is sometimes related to work, as expense-account dinners and conference breakfasts testify. In addition, in affluent and relatively sophisticated societies, the derivatives of eating ramify into a vast array of associated activities. These range from leisure-time pursuits such as collecting cookbooks or recipes, embroidering tablecloths and napkins, and fashioning table decorations to work-connected activities exemplified by dishwashing, waiting on tables, writing a food column for a newspaper, or running a specialty food store or a series of cooking classes (see Chapter 2, Classification).

Field of Action

The field of action encompasses not only the physical environment in which a specific activity takes place but also the objects and people in the environment and all the rules that govern the conduct of each activity. We have already cited rules as they relate to subtle sociocultural rituals. These are part of the implicit rules that give direction and pattern to each activity and have been absorbed from the "uninstructed" part of our culture. Other implicit rules for conduct have been learned and integrated from past experience (including previously stated explicit rules) or past formal instruction and are triggered by subliminal messages received from the field of action and responded to accordingly. There are also explicit rules, which are specific directives that are communicated verbally or by other means either before or during the event. In most situations, there is a combination of both kinds of rules. Bruner [15] has pointed out that situations have a "demand value" in themselves—"A child in a baseball game behaves baseball; in the drugstore the same child behaves drugstore." In other words, the field of action may be said to create a behavior habitat, in which expectations for the right kinds of reactions, interactions, and transactions are relayed by virtue of the nature of the total context in which the action takes place. The right kinds of responses are governed by the rules, which are not only directives but indicators of expectation for appropriate behavior.

Activities Analysis

Activities can be analyzed not only in terms of their field of action but also from the points of reference of the actor and the activity itself. It goes without saying that there can be no activity without an actor, just as there can be no activity without its field of action.

Each way of approaching activities analysis elicits different kinds of information that sometimes mesh with and at other times diverge from the others. Each kind of information contributes to a more comprehensive understanding of the potential of activities as therapeutic ends and means. Each of the three approaches to activities analysis—field of action-centered, actor-centered, and activity-centered—provides a convenient point of reference for processing complex and often interwoven strands of information. It is therefore inevitable that there will be some degree of overlap whenever the information about the actor, the activity, and the field of action meshes at focal points. This overlap is a distinct advantage in cross-comparison between idiosyncratic variation and generic characteristics in activities, allowing ultimately for determination of the degree to which dysfunction relating to performance components interferes with the *activities health* of the individual. It is important to read, concurrently with this discussion of activities analysis, of the educational model (see Chapter 9, Step 2: Activities Analysis), which provides additional discussion, guidelines for analysis, and specific examples of all three approaches. Keeping the possibilities of overlap in mind, we return to a separate discussion of each of the three approaches to analysis.

THE FIELD OF ACTION

To an observer analyzing the *field of action* for any one activity or concomitant multiple activities (as in Figure 4-1), the *environment* and the *objects* (both human and nonhuman) can be enumerated and described reasonably accurately. The *explicit rules* are obvious and can be recorded exactly. The *implicit rules*, however, are not quite as readily apparent. Mostly they derive from inferences made by the observer on the basis of events and actions that are familiar to the observer because of shared knowledge (e.g., the rules of baseball and expected behaviors are familiar to a great number of people) or parallel experience. For those from the same or similar culture, the implicit rules are tacitly understood and therefore relatively easier to elicit. Using eating again as an example, two different fields of action can be analyzed and compared for the same activity—a business lunch and a family picnic, both of which are familiar to, if not actually experienced by, any observer from cultures similar to ours. A complete analysis will be found in Appendix D.

On the other hand, even within our own complex society, there are subgroups whose activities may be unfamiliar and therefore somewhat puzzling, despite numerous cues available to the observer from the field of action and its behavior habitat. However, even from a photograph, which has frozen the activity in a field of action in a brief moment of time, it is possible to arrive at a reasonable approximation of what is happening, even to the implicit rules that govern the conduct of the "happening." Figure 4-1 depicts a New York art auction. At first glance, the picture appears impossibly confusing. Yet, as we look closer, we find two main foci of activity: (1) the bidder, with a number raised, looking toward someone who is out of the picture (we can infer it is the auctioneer taking the bid) among a group of interested onlookers, some of whom have catalogs and others who seem to be present merely as spectators, and (2) the demonstrator, who holds up a piece of art for viewers. It is likely that this is the object being offered for auction, but we cannot be sure until we know more about how art auctions are run.

The physical space, although apparently large, consisting of a main room and balcony, is crammed with objects, both human and nonhuman. The behavior hab-

Figure 4-1. An art auction at the Phillips Auction Gallery in New York City.

itat seems to call forth involvement of people in different ways and to different degrees. The most active individuals are the bidder, who is interacting with someone not seen in the picture, and the demonstrator, who seems happy to be interacting with a group of individuals, who seem equally pleased. Other individuals seem to be greatly interested in watching the action, and a few may be getting ready to offer a counter-bid. One man, standing with his arms behind his back in line with the bidder's number, may not be an onlooker but a security guard and thus may be responding to the behavior habitat in a different way from the spectators. No one seems to be removed from the transactions and interactions in this field of action, although the young man in the left foreground is intent on something other than the art work or the bidder—perhaps a catalog. Obviously, art auctions attract individuals of different ages and demand a certain decorum in appearance—all the men wear jackets and the women are well-groomed and rather formally dressed.

An extreme contrast is provided by Figure 4-2. Here we are in Bourkina Fasso (formerly Upper Volta in Africa) in a small village where the Chief looks on as his wives bring in the harvest. The physical environment is defined by rough stone

Figure 4-2. In Bourkina Fasso (formerly Upper Volta), a Koumi village chief looks on as his wives bring in the harvest.

dwellings on either side of a sandy pathway. The objects and people are sparse in number. The clothing, both for the Chief and his wives, is greatly different from what we expect of a high-ranking male and working females in our own society. For the children, clothing is practically nonexistent, again strange to our eyes, attuned as we are to being "properly dressed" and to the range of clothing and styles of dress available to both boys and girls. The women swing along the street carrying the harvest in great baskets on their heads, while the men and children look on. The behavior habitat does not seem to call forth any interaction between the two actors or among them and the onlookers. Perhaps the photographer has distracted the Chief and the others, so in the more usual course of events there may be more communication than is apparent in the picture.

We obviously need to find out more about the techniques, rituals, and patterns that underlie the activities of everyday living in this remote village. Yet we already have at least one implicit rule (in this case expectations for behavior) emerging from the situation. Wives (the Chief has more than one wife) do the heavy work, while it is perfectly appropriate for the husband to stand by and watch. We may perhaps conclude that the status of Chief allows for this division of labor (so to speak), but on the other hand, there are two other men in the picture, also watching, so we might infer—until more information is available, for a more generally applicable rule—that women do the heavy work of carrying, men and children (male and female?) may watch but do not get involved in this kind of work. Assignments described later on allow for an analysis of different fields of action in greater detail.

The importance of analyzing the field of action in which specific activities take place cannot be emphasized enough. As already mentioned, for occupational therapy this kind of analysis has a direct bearing on the structuring of activities situations—environments, interpersonal transactions, rules for conduct—so that they retain meaning and relevance to the individual who is moving step-by-step toward a state of *activities health* (function), even when adaptations for special needs have to be made. Indeed, pointers to modifications of the activity also come from the analysis of the field of action.

THE ACTOR

The actor is the individual who is engaged in the activity. To carry out each of the activities of everyday living with satisfaction and comfort in socioculturally acceptable ways, the actor has to have a number of prerequisite abilities, which Mosey [62] has identified as "performance components." These, in her words, include the following [62]:

1. sensory integration—. . . the ability to receive, differentiate, perceive, and use sensory stimuli for planned interaction with one's external environment.
2. neuromuscular function—. . . the ability to use one's body to act effectively relative to the environment. This includes reflex integration, coordination, range of motion, strength, and endurance.
3. cognitive function—. . . the ability to
   a. learn at a rate comparable to one's peers in chronological age;
   b. comprehend one's past, present and anticipated future environment relative to time, place, and significant individuals;

    c. conceptualize, establish abstract relationships, and solve problems within the logical system of one's culture.
4. psychological function—. . . the ability to process information currently available from the environment in such a way as to perceive oneself and others realistically. It also includes the ability to experience, identify, and express emotions in a manner acceptable to oneself and others.
5. social interaction—. . . involves a close sustained relationship with other individuals; friendship, love, nurturing; and the ability to engage in a variety of groups of meaningful and significant others.

Besides the kind of social interaction described by Mosey that involves close relationships, there is also what Bruner [15] calls *reciprocity*.

Where joint action is needed, where reciprocity is required for the group to attain an objective, then there seem to be processes that carry the individual along into learning, sweep him into competence that is required of the group. . . . Human beings . . . fall into a pattern that is required by the goals and activities of the social group in which they find themselves.

To analyze activities from the point of reference of the actor, it becomes necessary to examine each activity in terms of (1) the performance components required of the actor, (2) the meaning and relevance of the activity to the actor, (3) the sociocultural norms that influence the actor, and (4) the place of the activity in the idiosyncratic patterns and configurations that distinguish, have distinguished, and may continue to distinguish the actor's everyday activities.

The actor-centered approach to activities analysis ultimately provides information that helps to determine the state of *activities health* of the individual—particularly highlighting the extent to which any of the performance components fail to meet the requirements of specific activities situations and so interfere with the attainment of a desired state of *activities health* (see Chapter 9, An Actor-centered Approach to Activities Analysis). Also from the actor-centered approach come indicators of meaning and relevance of the activity to the individual, providing pointers to appropriate selection of activities for therapeutic purposes.

THE ACTIVITY

Each activity as an entity can be analyzed in terms of

1. *Intrinsic properties and characteristics*: These are the attributes of the activity by virtue of what it is in terms of procedures, processes, material, equipment, end products, and interpersonal field and built-in time dimensions.
2. *Acquired characteristics*: Since there is no activity without an actor, the physical and intellectual capacities called for in performing the activity as well as the actor's responses become part of the activity's characteristics, as do the socioculturally colored perceptions of the activity based on its classification and valuation. Because these properties are attributed to the activity by the actor as an individual or as a member of a sociocultural group or other designated group of actors, they frequently vary among individuals.
3. *Relationship to the real world*: A determination of where the activity (with all

of its socioculturally acceptable variations) fits into socioculturally designed activities patterns and configurations.

A comprehensive analysis of each activity as an entity, emphasizing descriptive detail relating to properties and characteristics, allows for comparison of similarities and differences among a number of different activities and for sorting them into types of activities as they relate to patterns and configurations. The indexing of activities by means of a classification that takes into consideration both distinctive and interchangeable attributes ensures that a wide repertoire of activities is available for therapeutic purposes. This becomes vital when, because of institutional or other constraints, simulations of activities situations have to be considered as alternatives to the real thing. In the best of worlds, this information would be readily accessible by pressing a button. But pending the availability of a data bank from which such information can be retrieved, it becomes incumbent on the occupational therapist to analyze the properties and characteristics of a wide range of activities, comparing and contrasting for similarities and differences.

Determination of where and how the activity fits into the real world of sociocultural patterns and configurations provides indicators of how relevant that activity is for the individual. Moreover, examination of the range of possible variations of the activity that are socioculturally acceptable provides pointers to appropriate adaptations of the activity for therapeutic purposes.

These approaches are by no means the be-all and end-all of activities analysis. There are any number of other ways of analyzing activities that stem from different points of reference and different theoretical emphases. One important perspective coming from an emphasis on time is of overriding importance to all other analyses and is therefore discussed in some detail.

TIME AND ACTIVITIES ANALYSIS

A long-standing and cherished notion held in our culture, and cultures like ours, is that time is a valuable commodity. Our everyday language, replete with allusions to time in terms of economics—save time, waste time, spend time, time is money—reveals the importance attached to using one's time profitably. Thus, amount of time spent is an important determinant of the relative value attached to different kinds of activities and to activity and nonactivity in general.

Activities Patterns and Configurations

As has been shown in Chapter 2, the use of time offers a convenient framework for encompassing the activities of everyday living in recognizable and distinctive patterns. These patterns serve as a basis for activities configurations that reveal, again with the use of time as an underlying determinant, not only the organization of activities in specific concentrations of time, but also the relationships between different categories of activities—including the relative importance of each, general group expectations for the proper use of time and approved individual variations, and consistencies and irregularities in patterns. An activities clock (Figure 4-3) is a useful device for representing relative time allocated to broad categories of ac-

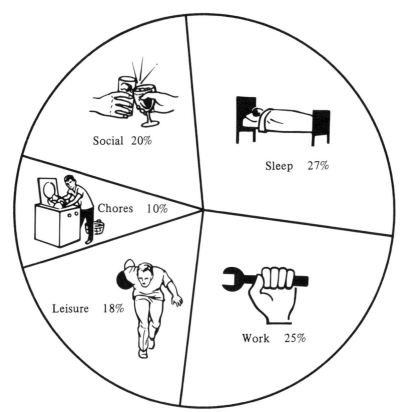

Figure 4-3. Activities clock. This clock shows the relative number of hours per week spent by a 24-year-old construction worker on the indicated categories of activities.

tivities over a designated period. A collection of individual activities clocks from representatives of the same sociocultural group may reveal common group expectations and may also be used for cross-cultural comparison.

Activities configurations determine the relevance of activities to the real world in which the individual is expected to function. Idiosyncratic (individual) activities configurations provide indexes of meaning as well as relevance. The idiosyncratic activities configuration also serves as the basis for determining the state of *activities health* of the individual at any one point in time of the life span of that individual (see Parts II and III).

Because of the importance attached to the use of time, the temporal attributes of activities occurring in patterns can be teased out and examined separately from other characteristics. Thus, as already discussed in another context in Chapter 2, one may concentrate on (1) timing, (2) duration, (3) sequential order, (4) frequency, and (5) historical duration—individually or in differing combinations.

Analysis from this particular perspective provides information about the individual's distinctive ways of organizing activities within a time frame. This includes balancing of activities and adhering to schedules, which reveal regularity/irregularity, consistency/inconsistency, and congruence with/deviation from sociocultural prescriptions for appropriate time allocations to selected categories of activities. Because temporal regulation of activities is to some extent also governed by the inner mechanisms of the individual, psychological time as presented by Kielhofner [44] and the workings of biological time [19] are other important perspectives that can be incorporated into activities analysis related to the use of time.

OTHER PERSPECTIVES ON ACTIVITIES ANALYSIS

There are a number of other perspectives from which activities analysis emanate, such as the analysis that Llorens [53] advocates based on a cognitive-perceptual-motor developmental approach, Fidler's [33] predominantly psychodynamic approach to analysis, and Allen's [1] task analysis, which is related primarily to levels of cognitive functioning and is based on a matrix of *task attributes* and hierarchical *levels of action*. Each provides an ordered means of entering into the complexities of the connections between the individual—sometimes described in terms of a clinical dysfunction model—and the activities that distinguish daily existence. Each comes from a different vantage point toward the same focus of attention—those activities that are woven into the fabric of our everyday lives and ultimately express and define function.

Summary

This chapter has established the connection between *activities health* and occupational therapy, which leads to the conclusion that activities are both the ends (*activities health*/function) and means (therapeutic media) of occupational therapy. In helping the individual to change from dysfunction toward function through learning, both formal learning and the "uninstructed" portions of learning (i.e., technique and ritual) have to be considered in relation to the distinctive ways in which activities of everyday living are carried out. For activities to become instrumental in producing the kind of change that leads to a state of *activities health*, it is important to arouse and sustain the will to learn. Activities analysis is an essential prerequisite to understanding the potential of activities as therapeutic tools and as determinants of a state of *activities health*. Since there is no activity without an actor, just as there is no activity without a field of action, all three serve as points of reference for analysis. Other approaches to activities analysis emanating from different emphases and theoretical perspectives are mentioned, and one, the use of time, is more fully discussed.

Assignment 1 ——————————————————————

Select one of the cases from Part III that describes an individual with a chronic condition.

  a. Based on the information provided, describe an ideal state of *activities health* that is attainable by this individual despite the continued presence of a clinical condition.
  b. List all the activities included in the ideal pattern that will need to be done in a compensatory manner because of limitations imposed by the clinical condition(s).

Assignment 2

List all the activities that you have done so far today. Mark an *I* next to each of the activities that you learned through formal instruction; mark those activities that you learned through "uninstructed" means (as defined by Bruner) with a *U*. Compare your findings with those of others, and discuss as a group the degree to which the pool of all activities was learned through formal, as contrasted with informal, learning experiences.

Assignment 3

Select an activity that you have engaged in both in a work situation and as a leisure pursuit. List the implicit and explicit rules for each of these activity experiences.

Assignment 4

Describe any activity that is a regular part of your activities pattern in terms of the time dimensions discussed in this chapter (i.e., timing, duration, sequential order, frequency, historical duration).

Note: For additional assignments, consult the Education Model, which includes more comprehensive assignments related to activities analysis. They appear as follows: (1) Actor-Centered Approach, p. 149; (2) Activity-Centered Approach, p. 144; (3) Field of Action–Centered Approach, p. 151.

CHAPTER 5

Occupational Therapy: Activities as Ends and Means

With the connections between *activities health* and occupational therapy established, it is now possible to examine in detail the ways in which the activities of everyday living serve as both *ends* and *means* in the practice of occupational therapy. If consulted frequently as the discussion proceeds (Figure 5-1), the *Activities Health Model* will serve to clarify the dynamics of the relationships among occupational therapy, activities, and *activities health*. But first, it is important to make explicit the underlying beliefs that guide and direct this approach to practice. The uniqueness of occupational therapy rests with activities in the belief that

1. Activities of everyday living are characteristic of and define a human existence.
2. Culturally specific activities patterns and configurations can be detected and described by studying manifest activities, values, and norms of different sociocultural groups.
3. Acceptable or unacceptable idiosyncratic variations can be found and described by studying activities patterns and configurations of individuals in these groups.
4. The individual leads a most satisfying way of life if able to carry out the activities of everyday living in patterns and configurations that are acceptable to the group and also fulfill personal needs and wants.
5. Such activities patterns and configurations delineate a state of activities health, which can be equated with function.
6. Activities themselves, systematically selected and combined in patterns and configurations tailored to each individual, are means for the development of and/or restoration of function.

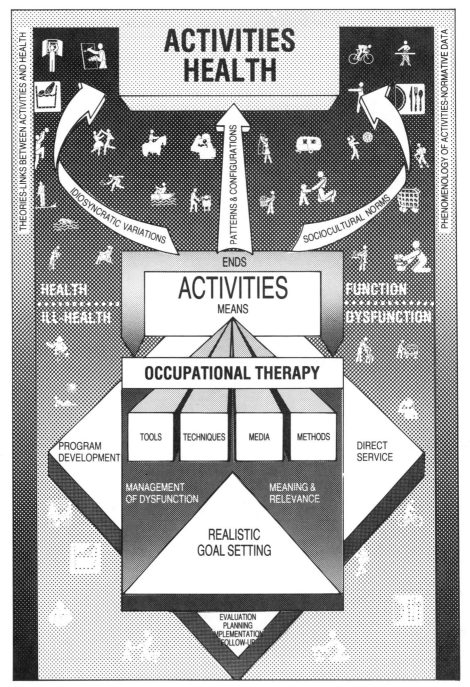

Figure 5-1. *Activities Health Model*, depicting the relationships that link activities and occupational therapy within the framework of *activities health*.

Activities as Ends

Activities health is the end to which occupational therapy directs its efforts. The concept of *activities health* has been discussed at length in Chapter 3, but the definition bears repeating in the context of this particular discussion: *Activities health is a state of well-being in which the individual is able to carry out the activities of everyday living with satisfaction and comfort, in patterns and configurations that reflect sociocultural norms and idiosyncratic variation in number, variety, balance, and context of activities.*

By nature of its focus, *activities health* delineates a state of well-being with regard to the activities of everyday living for only *one* individual at any one particular point in the life span of that individual. Thus the *activities health* profile for any individual will differ in many respects from that of any other individual. Similarly, the *activities health* profile for any individual will at any one time differ from the profile at other points in the life span of that individual. There is no absolute point that separates *activities health* from a state of ill health (or absence of *activities health*). Whether an individual is in a state of *activities health*, or whether steps are required to move an individual toward *activities health* is ultimately determined by a clinical judgment that takes into account the information obtained from the Idiosyncratic Activities Configuration (Appendix A) and its congruence with the individual's subjective rating of overall satisfaction, comfort, and "fit" with sociocultural patterns.

As mentioned before, the idiosyncratic activities configuration (see Chapters 2, 3, and Appendix A) is the means for eliciting a picture of the activities of everyday living that the individual carries out in idiosyncratically characteristic and socioculturally shaped ways at any one point in the life span of that individual. But, to accommodate to the special needs and problems of each individual suffering from dysfunction, and to ensure consistent and systematic gathering of information, the Idiosyncratic Activities Configuration is modified to serve as a clinical tool, entitled *the Activities Health Assessment* (see Chapter 6).

The *Activities Health Assessment* is designed to obtain information that

1. Is characteristic of one individual at one particular point in the life span of that individual.
2. Derives from both objective facts and subjective judgments made by the individual (or when needed, also from information obtained from other sources such as family, friends, professionals of other disciplines).
3. Is elicited by means of procedures adjusted to the pace and level of functioning of the individual.
4. Serves as a basis for
    a. Assessing the state of *activities health* of the individual.
    b. Determining the ways in which clinically labeled dysfunction interferes with the attainment of a state of *activities health*.
    c. Determining the needs of the individual who can be helped to change from dysfunction toward a state of *activities health* (function).
    d. Determining the step-by-step progression toward a state of *activities health*.

The *Activities Health Assessment* provides the basis for delineating the ultimate state of well-being possible for and desired by an individual, in terms of carrying out the activities of everyday living. Whether or not this "ideal" state is ever attained, it serves as the end goal to which all other goals are directed. Each goal (or subsidiary end) leading toward that end goal may be perceived both as a stepping-stone to *activities health* and as a contribution to the mosaic of activities that will ultimately delineate a desirable activities configuration.

Activities as Means

Recalling Aristotle's precept that we learn to do by doing (see p. 12) [5], it is reasonable to conclude that activities somehow are the natural means toward attaining a state of *activities health*, which is delineated, to a large degree, by characteristic ways of doing. From the discussion of activities as natural human phenomena in preceding chapters, it is clear that each activity is inextricably embedded in its own context (see Chapter 2, Contexts) and linked to other activities in patterns that are socioculturally directed and individually distinctive. There is therefore no such thing as a simple activity, nor can any one part of the activity serve as a representative for the total activity, complete with its actor, field of action, and antecedent and consequent activities.

To illustrate the complexity of the chaining and interweaving of day-to-day activities, we begin with a focus on *cooking*, which happens to appear often in activities schedules in a number of different clinical situations for a number of different clinical reasons.

In the real world, as exemplified, for instance, by a mother of five, living in a small town (see Figure 5-2), whose primary work is homemaking, *cooking* takes its place among a complex of activities more accurately labeled *meal preparation*. A number of preparatory steps are necessary before *cooking* can begin. These antecedent activities may encompass *budgeting, shopping for supplies, planning a menu, selecting a recipe* for a special dessert, and *setting the table. Cooking* itself is a complex series of steps and procedures that can only be revealed by the analysis of the *activity,* the *actor,* and the *field of action.* Cooking is also linked to a number of consequent activities, which may include *washing up utensils and equipment, tidying and cleaning the kitchen, serving the meal, eating the meal, cleaning up after the meal, washing up, and stacking away dishes and utensils.*

This particular pattern of chaining and interweaving of activities, practically unnoticed as we go about our daily business, is characteristic of all activities configurations that come from cultures like ours. But, the number and kind of antecedent and consequent activities and the sequencing and frequency of these activities vary from individual to individual (see Figure 5-2—"natural setting" for examples), as do the products, processes, and field of action for *cooking* itself. Thus, one homemaker may shop for supplies only once a week and may then have an extra antecedent activity to *cooking—organizing and storing supplies.* Another may run out to the neighborhood store each day to shop for the main ingredients necessary for preparing dinner. Similarly, one homemaker may have a menu plan that scarcely varies from week to week, while, at the other extreme, another may put together meals as the fancy strikes. Washing up after *cooking* may be deferred to general washing up after the meal. Meal preparation may consist of heating a TV dinner or opening cans, may be omitted in favor of eating out, or as in the case of the mother of five (see Figure 5-2—"natural setting"), may be directed to producing a three-course, nourishing, and filling meal. Each *cooking* session is different in a number of respects for the same individual—different meals of the day, different menus related to freshness of produce of basic supplies and many other variations in the state of the environment and the individual—and of course, variations from individual to individual are even more numerous.

Not only is *cooking* part of an interlocking pattern of antecedent and consequent activities ultimately directed to a very important and universal human activity—*eating*—but the whole chain of events entailed in the process is interwoven in different ways amidst the flow of those many other activities of everyday living that are characteristic of each individual's activities configuration. For example, a glance at the use of time by the mother of five shows gaps between some of the successive steps in the process of meal preparation (see Figure 5-2). Before the first step, *shopping for supplies*, she has already attended to her own self-care activities, supervised those of the younger children, prepared and served breakfast for the family, prepared and packed lunches for four (husband and three older children), cleaned up the kitchen, stacked the dishwasher, and delivered the younger children to nursery school. She returns from shopping, during which the menu for the *main meal* (dinner) evolves, to *unpack and store supplies*, have a quick lunch, pick up the younger children after their nap and lunch at nursery school and take them to the local pool for a swimming class, sew buttons on children's clothes, and toss a load of laundry in the machine. Only then does she begin to *prepare dinner for seven*, while keeping an eye on children and laundry. After dinner, one of the older children helps to bathe the little ones and get them ready for bed, while the others help with *clearing the table*, and *stacking the dishes* in the dishwasher.

The working couple, on the other hand, have compressed the process of meal preparation into late afternoon and evening by using travel time allocated to driving home from work also for *menu planning* (wife), limiting *shopping for supplies* to a once-weekly procedure (husband), and also sharing the remaining sequential steps of the process each day. Except on weekends, they do not worry about preparing other meals, which consist of coffee-shop breakfasts and lunch at desk-side or business lunches at restaurants. All other activities are just as carefully demarcated and organized for maximum efficiency in coping with the numerous tasks entailed in demanding work, care of self and environment, and leisure-time pursuits on weekends.

By contrast, the young, single construction worker's activities relating to meal preparation follow a sequential order directed to minimal expenditure of effort. At one point the sequence is interrupted by attention to another activity—watching TV, which is also simultaneous with parts of the process, such as *eating*. This "meal preparation" pattern appears only sporadically in the total configuration—at most three times a week. For other main meals he eats out, either at his girlfriend's apartment or at a favorite bar where he drops in for a beer with co-workers, or with his girlfriend at a restaurant on Friday or Saturday nights. The only regular and unchanging mealtime is Sunday dinner at his mother's house. A similarly erratic pattern appears with all other activities except work, where he has to "clock-in" and "clock-out." As far as meals are concerned, breakfast is often skipped in favor of a coffee-break snack at work, purchased at a local delicatessen, and lunch consists of a sandwich or pizza, eaten in or out. Further opportunities to explore other variations in the interlocking activities that form the matrix for cooking will be found in the assignments at the end of the chapter.

Given the extraordinarily complex context in which it is embedded, how can an activity called *cooking* in the clinic have meaning and relevance to the individual, whose patterns of cooking in the real world are so intricately meshed with other activities and also distinctively different from those of anyone else? How can such an activity, which seemingly is so far removed from the individual's real world of activities in terms of time, place, and context, arouse the will to learn, which, as shown in Chapter 4, is the key to helping the individual move from dysfunction toward function through activities? These are questions crucial to understanding the role of activities as means for movement toward a desirable state of *activities health*. Before these questions can be addressed, however, it is important to clarify *meaning and relevance* and continue with the discussion of the *will to learn* begun in Chapter 4.

MEANING AND RELEVANCE OF ACTIVITIES

Both *meaning* and *relevance* are emotionally charged terms colored by bias and misapprehension. As such, they are likely to be glossed over in discussions centering on the question of what makes activities therapeutic. Generally, and somewhat loosely, activities have been considered to have meaning to an individual if they are familiar to the individual, arouse positive associations, and tend to elicit approval from others who are respected and admired. Inferences such as these about the meaning of specific activities to an individual are usually made from items of information about the individual's background and general style of living. Included are age, educational history, socioeconomic status, family history and work history, and a listing of hobbies and interests. Without necessarily going into a philosophical discussion of meaning or making an extensive analysis of the underlying psychodynamics or symbolism, it is possible to probe beyond these inferences to arrive at some nearer approximation of the meaning of activities to an individual.

As has been amply shown in Chapters 2 and 3, the Idiosyncratic Activities Configuration, (Appendix A), and, in its clinical form, the *Activities Health Assessment* (Chapter 6) is a way of revealing the nuances of meaning in the activities life of the individual. Information is elicited about feelings, associations, characteristic styles of dealing with choices, problems, failures, and successes; activities voluntarily chosen and those required by others; the amounts of time allocated to each and the duration of the activity through the life span; activities carried out alone or with others; and the overall sense of satisfaction, comfort with one's activities, and sense of "fit" with one's culture. The newly discovered awareness aroused in the process of examining activities can be tapped to encourage the individual to take both a retrospective and prospective view—to weigh, speculate, plan ahead, examine courses of future action, and list preferences in order of priority.

There are also a number of exploratory tools that probe into specific activities constituents of the fabric of everyday living. Thus the *activities inventory* produces a chronological listing of specific activities that have helped to form the patterns of the individual's everyday life from the earliest remembrance to the present. Another, the *object history*, uncovers feelings and associations about the significant objects, human and nonhuman, that have been connected with activities. These objects may be toys, games, tokens, collections, books, clothes, pets, parents, teachers, friends, or mates. Several different aspects of the activities history are discussed, and the instrument used in each case is described by Matsutsuyu [57], Moorehead [60], and Takata [82].

Other than the deeply personal vicissitudes that reveal underlying values and endow activities with meaning for the individual, there has to be a yardstick for assessing *relevance*—the relationship of activities to the real world to which the individual has to return and belong. It is true that, as Sharrott [79] declares, "the world of everyday life is the paramount reality . . . [and is]. . . the realm of existence we can manipulate and change through bodily activities." However, the world of everyday life as perceived by the helping professional may only partially coincide with the world of everyday life as perceived by individuals belonging to groups differentiated by such socioculturally determined divisions as gender, age, religious belief, ethnic background, or socioeconomic status. In a complex society such as ours, relevance becomes even more relative for those belonging to groups that do not wish (e.g., religious cults) or have no way (e.g., the homeless) to enter the mainstream of society. It is here that the sociocultural activities configuration mentioned in Chapter 2 can be helpful in revealing the activities patterns—and values attached to the activities—of the group to which the individual belongs and also the extent of individual deviation from the norm that is tolerated by the group.

The following vignette serves to stress how important it is to be attuned to the individual's activities background, not only in its outward trappings but in the nuances that give it significance. For graphic illustration, an extreme case of cultural variation has been chosen, although the sensitivity and awareness required of the occupational therapist are not less even when the differences are not so obvious.

He is wheeled into the occupational therapy department, a thin small figure, slumped to one side, head lolling, a trickle of saliva at the corner of his drooping mouth, right arm hanging flaccidly. His eyes are dull, his furrowed skin ashy gray.

Newly recruited from his tribal home to work in the mines near the big city, he has awakened, after weeks of unconsciousness caused by a blow on the head, to a terrifyingly unfamiliar world. All attempts to communicate with him have failed. He seems to be quite unaware of the returning function in his right lower limb and trunk, so physical therapy has had to continue solely with its program of passive exercise. There is no objective way to determine whether he is aphasic or has deteriorated mentally, although he is regarded as a half-wit, probably bewitched, by his compatriots.

In the occupational therapy department his bewilderment is compounded by the strange apparatus and yet another white-coated "nurse" who gesticulates incomprehensibly and moves him as if he were a stuffed doll. The attendant with him, attempting to translate, shrugs his shoulders and rolls his eyes upward to indicate that the case is hopeless.

Outside on the lawn in the bright sunshine a group of other white-coated attendants on their lunch break and outpatients waiting their turn in the clinic are clustered around two players intent on outmaneuvering each other on a makeshift board (a discarded box lid) with "men" represented by soda bottle caps beaten flat. Loud chatter and frequent outbursts of laughter indicate that the bystanders are an essential element in this game of marabaraba, an African pastime so popular that it is played with improvised equipment in any available city spot during any break in the day's work.

One of the bystanders is an attendant, one foot encased in a walking cast, who is hopping about excitedly. The light dawns on the occupational therapist—a tribal game . . . a handicapped opponent . . . lower limb motion . . . adapted checkers . . . improvisation . . . an African way of life . . . time enough to enlist the ready-made crowd of spectators. Checkers adapted for lower limb exercises are available at the large general hospital across the road. A messenger, hastily dispatched, returns with 4-inch square wooden blocks, to which wire hoops are affixed for slipping over the ankle. A greatly enlarged board is marked out in chalk on the paved path outside the occupational therapy department. The patient is transferred from his clumsy wheelchair to an office chair with armrests and smoothly gliding castors. The puzzled attendant with the cast is coaxed into a similar chair. The opponents are wheeled into place, facing each other. Slowly the attendant slips the wire hoop, adjusted to accommodate to the size of the cast, over his foot. He flexes his hip, knee extended, lifting the block in the process; he pauses, surveys the board, extends his hip, and drops his "man" onto the appointed place. The bystanders, their curiosity aroused, crowd around, clicking tongues and shaking heads in pity and disbelief. Now it is the patient's turn. The block is slipped over his right ankle. With gentle pressure over the patient's hip joint the therapist draws the chair and extended leg back and forth alongside the board, then waits for a sign. The patient's eyes brighten, his head straightens, he focuses on the board, moves his hip independently, hovers over the board, frowns in concentration, and then, with visible effort, drops the block onto the exact spot he has selected. A roar of approval from the bystanders brings a crooked smile, a gleam in his eyes, a renewed frown of concentration, and the game is on . . .

In this instance it happened to be an inspired guess on the part of the occupational therapist that made the connection between a form of activity observed halfconsciously each day and its meaning and relevance to an individual with whom no form of communication seemed possible. Not only was the game familiar to the patient and associated with pleasure, but the concomitant, vociferous involvement of the bystanders contributed to the arousal of his interest. The support from a group of his peers was strong enough, in combination with the explicit rules of the game and its predictable outcome, to make tolerable the novelty of the adaptations and the unfamiliar setting.

It is appropriate here to emphasize once again the importance of the field of action, which, if structured to fit situations in the real world as closely as possible, gives the activity its relevance. In this game, although it was adapted to fit the requirements of a very special situation, the essential components of the field of action remained the same. The explicit and implicit rules were unchanged; the essential persons, opponents, and spectators (the latter adding their seal of approval) were there; and the therapist, who remained a shadowy figure once the game had been set in motion, did not materially affect the progress of the activity. The objects (the equipment used for the game), though substantially modified, retained enough of their original characteristics to ensure that they were not distorted or unusable, while the introduction of the chairs made sense in view of the patient's disability. And the setting contained enough familiar elements to ensure that it was recognizable and therefore acceptable.

THE WILL TO LEARN

Besides having meaning and relevance to the individual, this activity, by virtue of its inherent characteristics as a game, had a known beginning and end and built-in ways of assessing progress. It also demanded of the individual the exertion of effort. The attendant with the cast, pressed into the game as an opponent, served as a competence model, as he interacted with the patient to demonstrate that the game could be played effectively even with physical limitations and as he risked participation in a strange version of a known activity, which could just as easily have called forth ridicule as support from peers. The patient rose to the demands of the give-and-take situation, "behaving marabaraba" as typically as his fellow participants. The conditions for arousing the *will to learn* were inherent in the situation and the processes of the game, as well as the preparations, which aroused everyone's curiosity.

As mentioned in Chapter 4 (see The Will to Learn), arousing and sustaining the *will to learn* depends, according to Bruner [15], on the enlistment of ". . . the natural energies that sustain spontaneous learning—curiosity, a desire for competence, aspiration to emulate a model and a deep-seated commitment to the web of social reciprocity."

In discussing these "natural energies," Bruner [15], as he elaborates on each, provides us with guideposts for facilitating learning of activities:

1. *Curiosity*: Curiosity, one of the most basic of intrinsic motives, needs to be channeled, since at first attention is held by something that is "unclear, unfinished, or uncertain." This is well illustrated in the example of the head-injured patient, where the strange preparations for the game of marabaraba aroused the curiosity of all. To channel curiosity from the "passive, receptive episodic form" to the "sustained and active form" requires that the activity have a sustained sequence, a habitual routine, so that attention can be held by shutting off irrelevant impressions. This is certainly true in the case of the adapted version of marabaraba, where all participants, their curiosity aroused, remained interested to the end in the sustained sequences of the game.

2. *A desire for competence*: Robert White [89] discussed *competence* in connection with *motivation*, describing *competence motivation* in terms of behavior that is ". . . directed, selective, and persistent, and it continues not because it serves primary drives . . . but because it satisfies an intrinsic need to deal with the environment." To achieve a sense of accomplishment or competence requires, according to Bruner, a task that has some beginning and some distinct end. The drive to completion is enhanced by tasks that are interrupted; those that have been completed without interruption are less likely to be remembered. "*But the drive to completion does not hold true if the tasks are 'silly,' in the sense of being meaningless, arbitrary, and without visible means for checking*

progress" [15]. It is interesting to note that the game of marabaraba as it was set up for the head-injured patient has all the qualities that enhance the drive to completion. In Bruner's [15] terms, an activity *(provided that it is "approved"—that is, appropriate for a given age group, class, or gender)* is meaningful if it requires skill that is beyond that now possessed by the individual— in other words, if it necessitates learning by the exercise of effort, again, a built-in characteristic of the game of marabaraba described earlier.

3. *Aspiration to emulate a model:* Since there is a strong human tendency to model oneself and one's aspirations on some other person, there is also a tendency to seek out "competence models," who offer some desired competence attainable by interaction. Thus the "teacher" of activities serves as a "day-to-day working model with whom to *interact*, not to *imitate*" [15]. In the game of marabaraba discussed earlier, the nursing attendant served as competence model by interacting with the patient, not only demonstrating the first moves and showing that it is possible to perform despite a physical disability, but also, by his attitude, transmitting the idea that it is safe to risk the unknown.

4. *Commitment to reciprocity:* Bruner [15] defines *reciprocity* as "a deep human need to respond to others and to operate jointly with them toward an objective." The *situations* of everyday activities call for patterns of behavior from the individual required by the "goals and activities of the social group." Thus situations have a demand value that requires not so much conforming as *"fitting one's efforts into an enterprise"* [15]. Once again, the game of marabaraba illustrates perfectly how the activities situation—complete with actors, activity, and field of action—is designed in order to enlist reciprocity as yet another form of "natural energy" for arousing and sustaining the will to learn (see Assignment 2).

We now return to the question of how activities (in this chapter exemplified by one activity—cooking), seemingly detached from their context in the real world of the individual's activities life, can serve as the means toward attaining a desirable state of *activities health* (function). All discussions so far point to the fact that activities can only serve effectively as means, thus enabling change to take place in a direction from dysfunctional toward functional, if they

1. Have meaning and relevance to the individual who is to change.
2. Fulfill the conditions for arousing and sustaining the will to learn.

As we start to compare *cooking* as an activity in several natural settings with cooking in a variety of clinical settings (Figure 5-2), it is strikingly obvious that there is a tilt in the use of time in the clinic toward the middle of the day, when the main meal is eaten, in accordance with institutional practice. On the other hand, the random sampling of cooking in natural settings shows in all three cases that the main meal is eaten in the evening. That this small number is scarcely representative is quite evident, but there is a strong suggestion that in our culture the main evening meal is accepted as the norm in the population at large, even though individual variations do exist. Support for this assumption comes from the diet sheets of the American Diabetes Association and a variety of other nationwide organizations directed to helping people lose weight or improve their nutritional habits. All refer to the three meals of the day as breakfast, lunch, and dinner, with the largest allowance of portions for the evening meal.

A closer look at the diagram shows that in most of the clinical settings, antecedent and consequent activities are truncated or absent, such as *shopping for supplies*, which appears only in one instance. Some time sequences are inverted, for example *menu planning* is done at the end of one cooking session for the next. Other differences will become apparent as the diagram is studied further (see Assignment 3, A).

Beyond these obvious differences, we know that there are other major differences between the natural and clinical settings in which activities are carried out. In all cases, the primary focus in clinical settings is management of clinically labeled dysfunctions. To that end, in by far the largest proportion of clinical settings, the individual is encapsulated in an institutional structure, in which the activities of everyday living are constricted and shaped by activities environments, rules, and regulations that are often far removed from those governing the activities patterns and configurations of the world outside. Under these conditions, activities, detached from their natural context, can easily become invested with special remedial properties and directed primarily, like medication and other therapeutic procedures, toward symptom reduction. Thus, to return to our specific example once again, in a psychiatric clinic, the primary objective of a cooking group may be to increase the ability to work cooperatively with others, while in a rehabilitation clinic, cooking in a simulated kitchen may serve to improve upper limb coordination.

While each of these objectives, and many others with a primary emphasis on remediation, may be perfectly legitimate in addressing specific aspects of clinical dysfunction, the activity of *cooking*, structured and directed solely in this way, can at best serve as a *point of entry* into the activities life of the individual. From this beginning, it is essential that a transition from *cooking as remedy* to *cooking as a component of the individual's everyday activities life* be made if this activity, and indeed any other activities, are to serve properly as means to the attainment of *activities health*.

It is obvious, therefore, that the occupational therapist has constantly to refer back to each individual's idiosyncratic activities configuration (as elicited by the *Activities Health Assessment*) and to the analysis of *cooking* (again, as an example) from each actor's point of view. This process not only keeps in perspective the meaning and relevance of the activity to each individual but allows for realistic planning of step-by-step progress toward *activities health*, while taking into consideration the multiple effects of clinical dysfunction on the performance components that are necessary for attaining a desirable state of *activities health*.

MANAGEMENT OF DYSFUNCTION

Obviously, with individuals suffering from physical and/or psychosocial problems, the measures taken for management of dysfunction have to be meshed with the conditions, already discussed, for ensuring that activities serve effectively as ther-

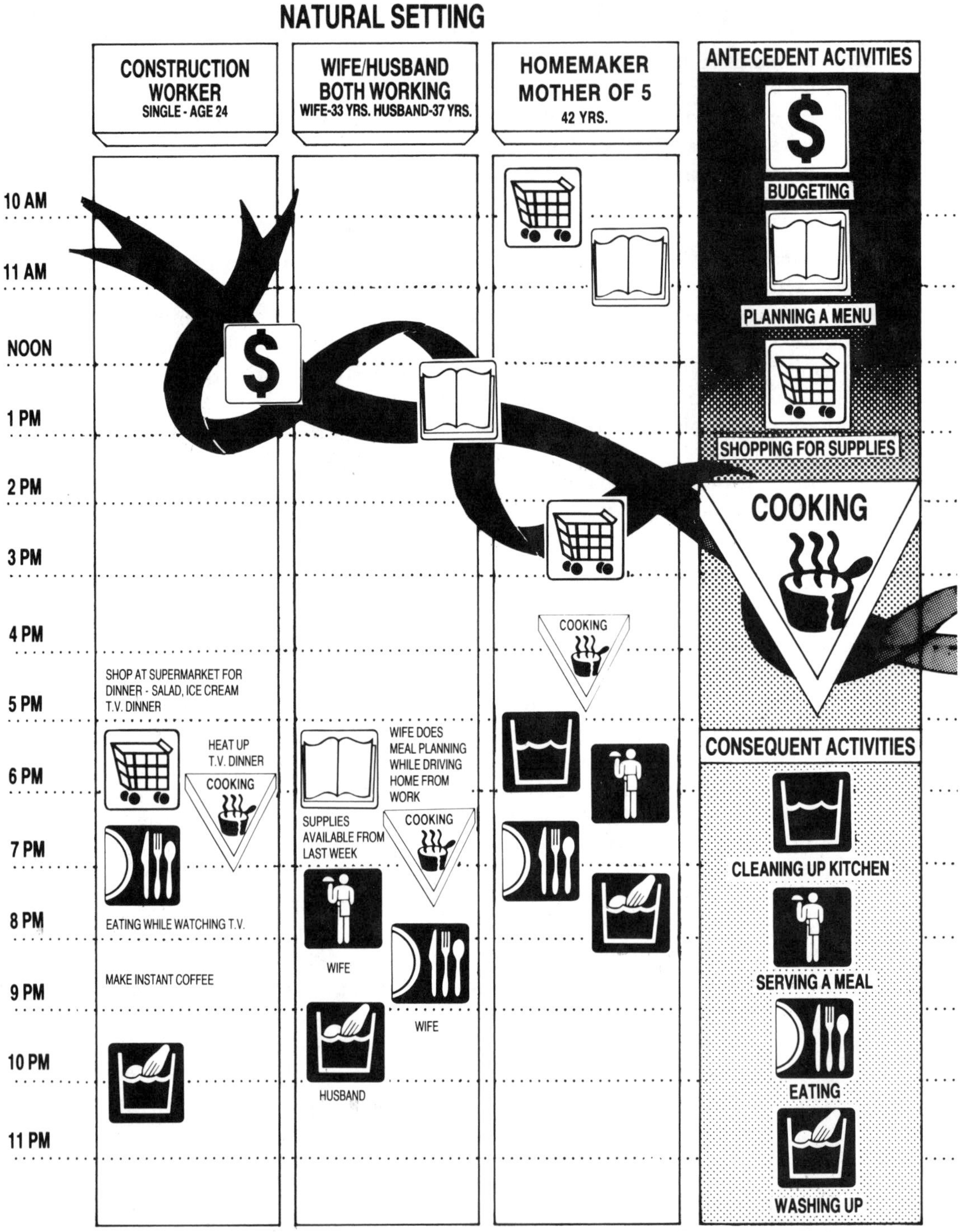

Figure 5-2. Diagram comparing the antecedent and consequent activities involved in cooking in both the natural and the clinical setting.

CLINICAL SETTING

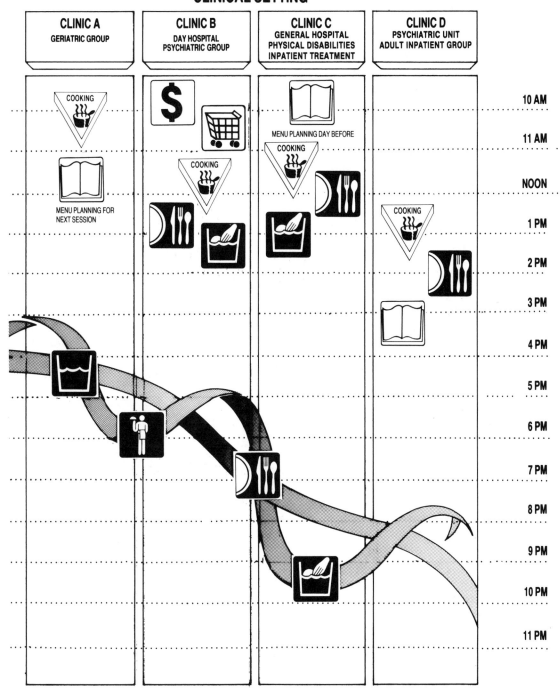

apeutic means. It goes without saying that each specific kind of clinical condition calls for specific and appropriate management measures. The principles of orthodox therapeutic exercise, for instance, take into consideration the fact that damaged tissues can tolerate only a certain amount of stress (hence graduated resistance and regulated frequency of effort), that gravity operates on humans as well as all other objects (hence emphasis on correct positioning to prevent deformity and a system for evaluating muscle strength based on positioning), and that fatigue occurs when muscles are overused (hence duration of treatment in graduated stages).

In other cases, guidelines for procedure derive from theoretical propositions about the nature of the human individual, the stages of development that lead to this kind of individual, the criteria that differentiate a functional from a dysfunctional individual, and in many instances and to varying degrees of specificity, the measures that can be taken to help the individual turn from dysfunction toward function. Numerous psychosocial theories are a case in point, exemplified in psychoanalysis by such exponents as Freud [38] and Erikson [27], in the client-centered approach of Rogers [73] and his followers, in the behaviorist school [29], and in countless offshoots and combinations of these approaches [9, 10, 37, 51].

In the neurobehavioral approaches to the management of dysfunction of Ayres [8], Brunnstrom [16, 17], Bobath and Bobath [11], Rood [76], and others, primary emphasis is given to the development and functioning of the nervous system, the effects of nervous system dysfunction on behavior, and proposals about ways to influence the nervous system so that dysfunction can turn in the direction of function. Whatever the approach, however, and whatever the kind of dysfunction to which the approach addresses itself, each offers directed and gradual change from dysfunction toward function, provided that the methods advocated are applied in a systematic and sustained fashion.

In occupational therapy, it is necessary to reconcile and integrate the rules for the learning of activities with those for dealing with physical and psychosocial dysfunction. In adopting a procedure or, more likely, a combination of procedures that provides a systematic approach to the management of dysfunction, the occupational therapist has to ask a number of crucial questions. How do these procedures relate to the conditions for the learning of activities? How do they fit in with an activities-centered base? Wholly, partially, not at all? In what ways? It is in the search for answers to these questions that the procedures, dovetailed with activities, assume their true perspective, not as ends in themselves, but as means to the ends of occupational therapy.

In light of this emphasis on the management of dysfunction, it is now time to reexamine and answer more completely the question of what makes activities effective as means toward attainment of *activities health*. Activities are effective (or therapeutic) when they enable change to take place in a direction from dysfunctional toward functional. But activities will only enable this kind of change to take place if

1. They have meaning and relevance to the individual who is to change.
2. They are systematically organized and specifically designed so that
   a. The conditions that arouse and sustain the will to learn are fulfilled.

b. A methodical approach to management of dysfunction, which is based on a theoretical rationale and/or empirical evidence is appropriately followed.

The next question is, how can activities be integrated as vital components of the occupational therapy process, so that they do indeed serve as effective means toward the attainment of a state of *activities health*? As occupational therapists, we have at our disposal a number of instrumental supports for designing appropriate activities situations and for adaptation of activities so that they meet clinical needs of the individual and overcome constraints of the clinical setting; these are *media, methods, tools,* and *techniques.* Not only are activities the *means* toward a desirable end state, but they serve as *media* when designed and adapted for therapeutic purposes. *Methods* are the procedures and processes by which activities are integrated into therapeutic intervention programs, while *tools* and *techniques* are at the disposal of the occupational therapist to facilitate the use of activities to meet specific patient needs. In Part III, each of these aids to design, adaptation, and integration of activities as therapeutic means will be defined and discussed in detail and the question of "how" addressed at length.

Summary

Activities of everyday living are the *means* for the individual to move toward attaining a desirable *end—activities health.* The *Activities Health Assessment* is a clinical adaptation of the Idiosyncratic Activities Configuration, serving: (1) to delineate the state of *activities health* of any one individual at any one point in the life span of that individual; and (2) as a basis for helping the individual to progress, step-by-step, toward *activities health.*

This progression is attained through the design, adaptation, and integration of activities into treatment so that they serve as therapeutic means. The conditions under which activities serve in this way depend on the meaning and relevance of activities to each individual, the conditions for arousing and sustaining the will to learn, and the appropriate measures taken in the management of the clinical dysfunction that interferes with attainment of a state of *activities health.* Instrumental supports—media, methods, tools, and techniques—enlisted by the occupational therapist to ensure that activities serve as means toward *activities health* are discussed in detail in Part III.

Assignment 1

A. Using your own completed Idiosyncratic Activities Configuration (Chapter 2, Assignment 1), describe the part *cooking* plays in your activities life as follows:
1. Use of time: specific times you cook (hours, days and times per week).
2. Place of cooking in process of meal preparation—antecedent and consequent activities in time sequence, your role in these activities, other people involved.

3. Place of meal preparation in your total configuration—proportion of time spent on meal preparation per week, connecting links with other activities.

B. Following the same steps with the Idiosyncratic Activities Configuration of someone similar to you (e.g., friend, colleague, fellow student) and compare. Note differences and similarities.

C. Follow the same steps with the Idiosyncratic Activities Configuration of someone whose life-style, in contrast to yours, does/does not include *meal preparation* as a primary activity. Compare with yours. For the person whose configuration does not include meal preparation as an activity, describe when and how he/she gets each meal per day of the week and what other activities take the place of those devoted to meal preparation.

Assignment 2

A. With a group of colleagues or classmates, make a list of four activities that are to be found in each one's idiosyncratic activities configuration (not necessarily common to everyone in the group) that, because of the activities situation, calls forth *reciprocity*. Remember what Bruner [15] said, "A child in a baseball game behaves baseball; in the drugstore the same child behaves drugstore."

B. Analyze *one* of the listed activities in terms of
1. the actor
2. the activity
3. the field of action

You may divide yourselves into three working sections, one for each part of the analysis. Then share findings at the end (more reciprocity!).

Assignment 3

A. As you study Figure 5-2, which compares natural settings and clinical settings with *cooking* as a point of entry, list the ways, other than those discussed in the chapter, in which cooking as an activity differs in the clinical settings from cooking in the natural settings. Consider
1. use of time
2. number and variety of antecedent and consequent activities
3. actors, field of action, and the activity in the clinical setting (Use your own observations/experience or ask others working in clinical settings such as those given in the example.)

B. From your own observations/experiences or from discussion with others working in clinical settings, describe the total activities context for one actor participating in *cooking* as an activity. Compare with the description of the context of *cooking* for the three individuals in natural settings on pages 60–61.

Assignment 4

As you learn or teach someone a new activity, check whether your teaching/
learning experience has aroused and sustained the *will to learn* by considering
whether, and how, the following were built into the situation:

A. A sustained routine.
B. A known beginning and end.
C. Interruption of the task.
D. A task that
   1. has meaning.
   2. was not arbitrarily chosen.
   3. has visible means for checking progress.
   4. is appropriate for a given age, class, or gender.
   5. requires the exercise of effort (i.e., is a little beyond the skill now pos-
      sessed).
E. A competence model with whom to interact.
F. Reciprocity.

Assignment 5

Analyze, under the headings outlined in the worksheet (Appendix E), a number
of theoretical approaches to physical and psychosocial dysfunction that you
have learned about or that are familiar to you. Read the chapter "Integration
of Information" in *Development of Sensory Integrative Theory and Practice*
by A. J. Ayres [7] for a model of how to analyze theoretical concepts for clinical
implications and also "Integrating Play in Neurodevelopmental Treatment" by
Anderson, Hinojosa, and Strauch [4]. What Miller [59] has said about theories
for the practice of occupational therapy is equally applicable here: "One must
be certain when using multiple theories that they are based on compatible
assumptions and that their concepts fit together logically."

CHAPTER 6

The Activities Health Assessment: An Organizer for Enlisting Activities as Therapeutic Means and Ends

The formal purposes of the *Activities Health Assessment* are discussed in Chapter 5 and enumerated in the instrument itself. However, besides fulfilling these purposes, the *Activities Health Assessment* serves to encapsulate the concepts, connections, and conclusions presented in the preceding chapters in a working document. This document not only helps the occupational therapist to organize diverse activities under the umbrella of *activities health* but also clarifies for the patient/client the relationship of very personal and seemingly ordinary activities of everyday living to health and well-being (see therapist's note in the case of Mr. D. in Detailed Case Histories in Chapter 12).

This chapter is therefore allocated to the *Activities Health Assessment.* The fact that it appears in a chapter rather than as an appendix does not negate its usefulness as an information-gathering instrument, but it may also be "read," page by page, as an organizer for enlisting activities as therapeutic means and ends. A word of caution is in order. The *Activities Health Assessment* will not effectively fulfill its function unless the concepts, connections, and conclusions relating to occupational therapy and *activities health* are fully comprehended.

Activities Health: A Definition

In the context of an emphasis on human activities, *health* (and its practical correlate *function*) is manifested in the ability of the individual to participate in *socioculturally regulated* activities with *satisfaction* and *comfort.* Conversely, *ill-health* (or *dysfunction*) is evinced (*over and above clinically labeled signs, symp-*

toms, and behaviors) in the inability of the individual to carry out, with *satisfaction* and *comfort*, the activities of everyday living in patterns designed and *approved* by the culture(s) to which the individual belongs.

The Activities Health Assessment

The *Activities Health Assessment* is used for the examination of the patient/client's quality of life related to the activities of everyday living. The individual's *activities configuration* provides the point of departure for the assessment process.

   I. Purpose: The *Activities Health Assessment* is designed to obtain
     A. A graphic representation of patterns of activities at a selected point of the life span of the individual, encompassing
       1. Use of time
       2. Specific activities as arranged in categories (see *Activities Schedule Coding Key*, p. 74)
     B. The following information about the activities depicted in the diagram:
       1. Thoughts related to the classification of activities according to the Activities Schedule Coding Key
       2. The specific activities included in each category outlined in the Activities Schedule Coding Key
       3. Feelings about the specific activities included in each category outlined in the Activities Schedule Coding Key
       4. From whom and how the specific activities were learned
       5. Duration and frequency of the specific activities
       6. Comparison with past configurations
       7. Future projections
     C. Information regarding the patient/client's overall impressions and perceptions regarding his or her life-style and functioning as revealed by the configuration:
       1. Overall sense of satisfaction/dissatisfaction
       2. Overall sense of comfort/discomfort
       3. Overall sense of fitting in/not fitting in with one's sociocultural group
       4. Overall sense of autonomy in choice of activities
       5. Desired changes
       6. General observations
  II. Materials required
     A. Small notebook, pencil (for preconfiguration phase only; see *III. Procedure*)
     B. Blank Activities Schedule (see pp. 71–73) divided into 7 days of the week, intersected by 1-hour, 3-hour, or 6-hour bands.
     C. Activities Schedule Coding Key
     D. Colored pencils: green, red, purple, yellow, orange, and blue
     E. Interview Guidelines (see p. 74)
 III. Procedure: *The procedure offers general guidelines only and makes provisions for adjustments to be made according to the patient/client's unique needs and the constraints of the clinical situation* (such as limits on time).

Possible modifications are suggested for purposes of illustration. Since obtaining appropriate and adequate activities information is essential for this assessment, patients/clients should be given assistance whenever necessary to complete each step of the procedure.

A. STEP 1: PRE-CONFIGURATION
  1. Give patient/client a notebook and pencil and the following instructions (written if necessary):
     a. Keep this notebook and pencil with you at all times.
     b. Record what you do each day for one week, including the weekend (don't forget sleep!).
     Possible modifications:
     a. *Record only 3 days, including one weekend day.*
     b. *Omit pre-configuration step. Instead, ask patient/client to record activities of the past 2 or 3 days.*
     c. *Omit pre-configuration step. Instead, interview patient/client to obtain a picture of a typical day, using Activities Schedule 1, 2, or 3 to fill in information. Add further information as it emerges from subsequent contacts with patient/client or significant others.*

B. STEP 2: FILLING IN THE ACTIVITIES SCHEDULE
  1. Select the Activities Schedule form best suited to your patient/client's needs and abilities.
  2. Instruct the patient/client as follows:
     a. Fill in the specific activities that you recorded in your notebook in the appropriate space on the Activities Schedule.
     b. Here is the Activities Schedule Coding Key and a colored pencil for each category. Color in each activity according to the color code. Every activity you recorded must be fitted into one of the designated categories (e.g., if you recorded *eating* as an activity each day from 7–8 P.M., you should decide whether it is to fit into "leisure" [alone/with others], "work," or "self-care"). *Remember that there is no "correct answer" for how each activity should be categorized. In fact, even the same activity can be categorized differently at various times of the week.*
     Possible modifications:
     a. *Therapist provides the degree of assistance necessary for the activities to be filled in and coded.*
     b. *The form may be completed in stages over a period of time, due to the patient/client's limited concentration or time constraints in the setting.*

C. STEP 3: INTERVIEW
  1. Using the Interview Guidelines and the color-coded Activities Schedule (*activities pattern*) as the point of departure, discuss the pattern with the patient/client.
  2. Record responses.
     Possible modification: *Use a questionnaire to obtain answers to designated questions.*

D. STEP 4: INTERPRETATION: Summarize and discuss the results of the assessment with the patient/client.
IV. Time required: The time needed to complete this evaluation is highly variable, depending on the specific format selected and the individual's responses. However, for most individuals whose conditon does not severely interfere with the ability to participate, these guidelines can be used:

Step 2	1 hour (may be done independently)
Steps 3–4	1½ hour
Total time	2½ hours

Summary

To summarize, the *Activities Health Assessment* provides the following information for the patient/client, the occupational therapist, and ultimately the treatment team:

1. The meaning and relevance of specific activities and categories of activities of everyday living to the individual.
2. The characteristic life-style of the individual at a specific point in time, as defined by the activities pattern and configuration.

The information that the assessment yields can be useful in all phases of treatment, including treatment planning, implementation, and follow-up:

1. Treatment Planning
    a. Determining the patient/client's needs and wishes related to carrying out his or her activities of everyday living.
    b. Setting realistic short-term goals that will lead to the attainment of a greater degree of *activities health* (long-term goal).
    c. Selecting activities that are meaningful and relevant to the individual for incorporation into the treatment program.
2. Implementation
    a. Incorporating activities into the treatment plan in ways that approximate as closely as possible the patterns/configurations of the individual.
    b. Checking progress in terms of movement toward goals.
3. Follow-up: Comparing configuration while in treatment setting to post-discharge configuration at various intervals.

Activities Schedule 1

	MONDAY	TUESDAY	WEDNESDAY	THURSDAY	FRIDAY	SATURDAY	SUNDAY
12 Midnight to 1 A.M.							
1 A.M.-2 A.M.							
2 A.M.-3 A.M.							
3 A.M.-4 A.M.							
4 A.M.-5 A.M.							
5 A.M.-6 A.M.							
6 A.M.-7 A.M.							
7 A.M.-8 A.M.							
8 A.M.-9 A.M.							
9 A.M.-10 A.M.							
10 A.M.-11 A.M.							
11 A.M.-12 Noon							
Noon-1 P.M.							
1 P.M.-2 P.M.							
2 P.M.-3 P.M.							
3 P.M.-4 P.M.							
4 P.M.-5 P.M.							
5 P.M.-6 P.M.							
6 P.M.-7 P.M.							
7 P.M.-8 P.M.							
8 P.M.-9 P.M.							
9 P.M.-10 P.M.							
10 P.M.-11 P.M.							
11 P.M. to 12 Midnight							

Activities Schedule 2

	MONDAY	TUESDAY	WEDNESDAY	THURSDAY	FRIDAY	SATURDAY	SUNDAY
12 Midnight to 3 A.M.							
3 A.M. to 6 A.M.							
6 A.M. to 9 A.M.							
9 A.M. to 12 Noon							
12 Noon to 3 P.M.							
3 P.M. to 6 P.M.							
6 P.M. to 9 P.M.							
9 P.M. to 12 Midnight							

Activities Schedule 3

	MONDAY	TUESDAY	WEDNESDAY	THURSDAY	FRIDAY	SATURDAY	SUNDAY
12 Midnight to 6 A.M.							
6 A.M. to 12 Noon							
12 Noon to 6 P.M.							
6 P.M. to 12 Midnight							

Activities Schedule Coding Key

Sleep—green
Work—red
Chores—purple
Leisure
   Alone—yellow
   With others—orange
Self-care—blue

In this book, the typeface of which is in one color, textures are substituted for colors—see Figures 8-1 and 12-5.

Interview Guidelines*

I: ADDRESSING INFORMATION ABOUT SPECIFIC ACTIVITIES AND CATEGORIES OF ACTIVITIES

1. What other activities that are part of your everyday life do not appear on this schedule? Where do they fit in on this schedule?
2. Do you consider this to be a typical week for you? If not, what is unusual about it?
3. Which activities have you coded as chores? work? self-care? leisure? Where do each of these fit in on this schedule?
4. When you look at the completed schedule, does anything in particular strike you? If so, what, and why?
5. Did you have any problems fitting your activities into categories in the code? If yes, which gave you the most difficulty? Why? How did you eventually resolve the problem? (For example, is riding to work with a friend work or leisure? "I enjoy driving, and I work in the suburbs, so it's not like work—it's more like leisure, really.")
6. Which activities did you choose to do? Which just happened? Which did you have to do? Why?
7. Feelings about specific activities:

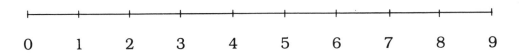

0   1   2   3   4   5   6   7   8   9

    a. This is is a 9-point scale: 9 means that you like the activity very much, 0 means that you do not like it at all—in fact, you dislike it very much. In between is a range between like and dislike—the higher the number, the more the activity is liked; the lower the number, the more the activity is disliked. Let's look at some of the activities we have already talked about. First choose one work, one leisure, and one chore activity, and give each

---

* To be used with completed Activities Schedule.

a number anywhere from 0 to 9 to indicate how you feel about the activity. Then I will pick a few more for you to rate (e.g., dusting—"I hate it, so 0."; fixing meals for myself—"So-so, number 4"; fixing meals for others— "That's different, number 8.").

b. Let us look at the activities you have rated low on the scale and check on how often you do them (e.g., "Look at that—dusting appears daily as a chore on your schedule. Why do you think you go on doing it, even though you hate it?").

c. *Possible modifications:*
   (1) Direct questioning instead of scale: Do you like/dislike/feel neutral about . . . (enumerate specific activities)?
   (2) Use columns headed "like," "dislike," "neutral." Put specific activities in the appropriate column.

8. From whom and how were the activities learned?
   a. I notice that you do a great deal of . . . (e.g., baking, knitting, repairs, fishing). When did you first learn this activity?
   b. Who taught you?
   c. How did you learn? Were you shown? Just watching? Picking it up? Special lessons? Other ways?
   d. Has anyone else learned this activity from you? If so, who, and how?

9. Frequency and duration of specific activities:
   a. I notice that some activities appear twice a week, others daily, and others five times a week. Is this typical, or does this frequency vary? If yes, explain.
   b. How long have you been . . . (e.g., working at this job, playing baseball, washing dishes)? Less than a year? 1–5 years? 5–10 years? More than 10 years?
   c. Have you done this activity regularly throughout that time, or have you dropped it sometimes? For how long? For what reason?

10. Comparison with past configurations:
    a. Is this configuration similar to your configuration(s) 1 year ago? 5 years ago? 5 to 10 years ago?
    b. In what ways are they the same? In what ways are they different?

11. Future projections:
    a. Which activities do you think you will still be doing 5 years from now?
    b. Which activities do you think you will drop?
    c. Which activities do you think you will add?

II: ADDRESSING THE INDIVIDUAL'S OVERALL IMPRESSIONS AND PERCEPTIONS REGARDING LIFE-STYLE AND FUNCTIONING

1. On a scale of 0 to 9, to what extent do you feel a sense of balance between the following?
   a. Work and leisure

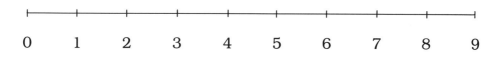

0   1   2   3   4   5   6   7   8   9

   b. Activities done alone and activities done with others

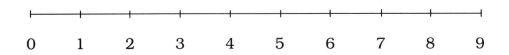

   c. Activities you must do and activities you want to do

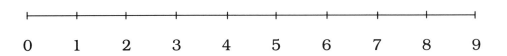

   Note: You may wish to precede these questions by calculating the proportion of time spent in each of the above categories.
   d. *Possible modification:* Instead of scale, list activities in columns headed
   "Good," "Fair," and "Poor," which indicate degrees of balance.
2. What changes would you like to see in your configuration in the future, related
   to specific activities or categories, time allocations, environments (including
   both objects and people), and so on?
3. Despite the fact that there are times when you wish you could do something
   different or differently, rate on a scale of 0 to 9 to what degree your activities
   as a whole provide you with a *sense of overall satisfaction.*

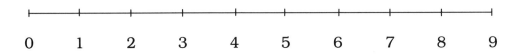

4. Despite problems (e.g., negative feelings, physical handicaps, general stress,
   aches and pains), rate on a scale of 0 to 9 to what degree you feel able to cope
   with your activities of everyday living, that is, *sense of overall comfort.*

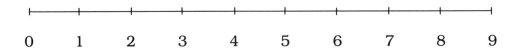

5. Overall, on a scale of 0 to 9, rate to what degree you feel that your activities

are *acceptable* to the people in the groups to which you belong (e.g., family, friends, nationality, religion), that is, *overall sense of sociocultural fit.*

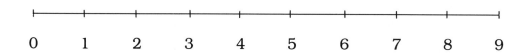

Further probing with individual who rates overall sociocultural fit as 5 or less:
a. In which particular ways do you feel different (i.e., what you do, when, how, and where you do it)?
b. From whom do you feel different?
c. To what degree does it bother you that you are different (i.e., not at all, a little, a lot)?

PART TWO

The Educational Model: A "Community of Learning"

CHAPTER 7

Introduction to the Educational Model

In the preceding chapters, you have been introduced to a model for occupational therapy practice that requires an understanding of and respect for the value of human activities. The following questions arise as one considers the way in which the ideas presented relating to activities can best be conveyed to occupational therapy students:

1. How do we incorporate into the education of the occupational therapist an understanding of and respect for the value of human activities?
2. How do we integrate understanding and knowledge of human activities, including their links to health, with the vast and varied knowledge in a broadly based curriculum?

The process of learning about the world of activities presents an opportunity for students to become aware of the central importance of activities in the lives of all people and to experience the power of activities as learning tools. In addition, the study of activities as natural human phenomena requires that the student make connections between what has been learned about normal physical and psychological development of human beings, pathological conditions that can develop, theoretical frames of reference that underlie the prevention, assessment, and treatment strategies for management of dysfunction, and the specific techniques that serve as tools for clinical practice. An integrated understanding of activities in relation to occupational therapy can be the link that is needed for students to view people in the holistic way to which the occupational therapy profession so often attests, since each human activity involves the orchestration of the *mind, body, and will* [7].

Part II describes an educational model for the teaching of activities in the occupational therapy curriculum consistent with the theoretical and philosophical ideas set forth in earlier chapters. *These ideas are applied here specifically to an educational context, which in many respects is similar to but in other respects is distinctly different from the context of practice.* These similarities and differences will become clear as you read further. However, it is important that both students and instructor always keep in mind that all activities-centered experiences discussed here are specifically directed toward the fulfillment of educational objectives.

The educational model will emerge as the following questions are addressed:

Who?—the characteristics of both instructor and learner and the nature of the *relationships* that facilitate the learning process.

Why?—the *assumptions* that underlie this model for learning and the *objectives* that follow from them.

Where and *when?*—the *field of action,* or environment that is most conducive to learning; and the *temporal considerations,* that is, how time can be most effectively used to facilitate learning and meet the specific objectives.

How?—the *methods* that are most effective to promote the attainment of the course objectives.

INSTRUCTORS AND LEARNERS: RELATIONSHIPS FOR LEARNING

Teaching, in my estimation, is a vastly over-rated function.

Carl Rogers [74]

This provocative assertion by Carl Rogers is echoed in the writings of other exponents of self-directed learning theories and strategies, such as Dewey [85] and Kolb [48]. Despite significant differences in the beliefs and approaches of these and other theorists, virtually all espouse the importance of the instructor as the *facilitator* of the learning process. One of the major sources of disagreement, however, relates to the degree to which the instructor should direct the course of the student's learning. While Rogers [74] states in *Freedom to Learn* that "too many have been guided, shown, and directed," Jerome Bruner [14] on the other hand contends, " . . . Direction (provided by the instructor) depends upon knowledge of the results of one's tests, and *instruction should have an edge over 'spontaneous learning' in providing more of such knowledge* [emphasis added]."

It is consistent with the underlying assumptions and goals of this educational model that the instructor assumes a facilitating role, rather than a solely directive one. The roles of instructors and learners are flexible and at times interchangeable, thereby fostering a partnership for learning. To avoid language that is too cumbersome, the terms *instructor* and *student* will be used for the purposes of this text. The reader should be aware, however, that all participants share in different ways the learning and instructing that are ongoing throughout this educational process.

Each instructor must decide on the degree to which learning experiences will be regulated and structured for the student, keeping in mind the importance of selecting educational techniques that are compatible with the individual style of the instructor and the particular characteristics of each student group. However, generally speaking, the guidelines provided by Bruner [14] are useful:

Since learning and problem-solving depend upon the exploration of alternatives, instruction must facilitate and regulate the exploration of alternatives on the part of the learner. There are three aspects to the exploration of alternatives, each of them related to the regulation of search behavior. They can be described in shorthand terms as activation, maintenance, and direction. To put it another way, exploration of alternatives requires something to get it started, something to keep it going, and something to keep it from being random.

Thus, the course instructor becomes both facilitator and resource person, who actively shapes and adjusts the learning experience as necessary to promote the achievement of the objectives.

It is assumed that in the learning process, all individuals, including instructor and students, are potential resources for the learning of activities, an assumption that will be presented and discussed later. From the start, the potential for sharing is tapped, and throughout the course, such interchanges are encouraged. Some of the assignments are geared toward the imparting of expertise in activities; students teach one another, students teach the instructor, the instructor teaches the students. Through this network of exchanges, the foundation for future colleagueship is laid. Students become aware of the opportunities for learning available through others while experiencing themselves as resources for the learning of others, which will eventually be extended to include patients/clients.

The Learning Contract: A Means for Negotiation

The learning contract is a tool that can be used as "a sort of transitional experience between complete freedom to learn whatever is of interest, and learning which is relatively free but which is within the limits of some institutional demand" [74]. Through the use of a learning contract, an example of which can be found in Appendix F, the student selects from a variety of options that will fulfill course requirements. Each student chooses the specific activities to be used in the exploration of activities as natural human phenomena. In the contract, each student is also given latitude in selecting the kinds of teaching/learning experiences to be pursued, while also participating in decisions about the number of course points to be allotted for.

1. The evaluation of a specifically selected "Constructive Project," with end product (see Chapter 8, Assignment 3).
2. The evaluation of the "Expressive Project" presentation (see Chapter 8, Assignment 4).
3. The teaching of selected activities to others (see Chapter 8, Assignment 2).

The learning contract communicates to the students the value of developing an awareness of preferred ways of learning and the importance of their input into the design of meaningful learning experiences. The *negotiation* that occurs during the initiation and implementation of the contract requires that both student and instructor clearly communicate expectations and plans and find ways to resolve differences through compromise and trade-offs. The contract provides a structure for working out conflicts that arise and reality-testing ideas ahead of time, thereby helping students to avoid excessive frustration in the learning process. This experience provides a foundation for handling of future contracts, both explicit and implicit, whether they are between student and fieldwork supervisor, therapist and supervisor, or therapist and client. The contract promotes the clear delineation of responsibilities and expectations, and facilitates the development of awareness and mutual respect for the needs of each of the parties involved.

Evaluation of the Learner

What type of evaluation process is consistent with this educational approach? Is evaluation merely a "necessary evil," to be carried out solely to achieve compliance with institutional requirements, or is it a meaningful exercise that is a useful part of the learning process? For many individuals, evaluation is an anxiety-producing process, often colored by previous experiences in which lines of authority have been clearly drawn between instructors and students and have left no room for student input into the evaluation of performance. Therefore, when evaluation methods are considered, educators face a situation that is associated with past experiences and potent feelings and attitudes about authority, achievement, competition, success, and failure. Also having an impact on the evaluation process is the context in which this particular learning takes place—the occupational therapy curriculum. Since curricula are almost always intense and demanding, imposing sanctions for in-adequate grades, there are external as well as internal pressures on the student to "do well'—that is, to receive good grades.

In this educational model, evaluation is conceptualized as a dynamic, ongoing process in which all individuals have the opportunity to engage in discussions about their satisfactions and dissatisfactions with their own learning, as well as the way in which the coursework is progressing. An important part of the process is the ongoing exploration of ways in which the prescribed learning sequence can be adjusted, so that learning can be enhanced.

In the evaluation of students, it is of utmost importance that they be aware of the criteria used for evaluation. This is especially true for those assignments that involve a degree of personal disclosure or risk-taking, as the evaluation of these kinds of assignments are likely to be experienced as more threatening. A specific instance in which the student is likely to perceive the instructor's judgment as subjective is the evaluation of end products. How, then, are end products to be fairly evaluated? The answer can be found in the real world of activities—that is, the way in which activities end products are evaluated in everyday living. In the world at large, standards for evaluation depend on the purpose of the activity and the context in which it takes place. Therefore, it is fitting that criteria for evaluation vary from one assignment to the next and are delineated according to the specific objectives. Variation will become evident as sample assignments are described in later pages. For each of these assignments, the criteria for evaluation are specified in a summary section, illustrating how appropriate standards can be determined.

Built into the evaluation process is the availability of a variety of avenues for communication after results have been shared. Students can *seek clarification* or even *challenge evaluation results* when they wish, in an atmosphere that supports an open exchange of ideas. This type of negotiation reinforces the students' active participation in every aspect of the educational process. In addition, students are given opportunities to *evaluate their own performance*, a skill that can be particularly valuable in fieldwork and clinical practice. When appropriate to the assignment and student group, *peer evaluation* may also be incorporated, providing the student with opportunities both to give and to receive feedback according to established criteria.

In summary, the evaluation process in this learning model presents a challenge to both students and instructor. If approached thoughtfully, evaluation can be much more than the fulfillment of an institutional requirement; the process can be of immediate and long-lasting benefit to the student. *Like the learning contract, this evaluation process provides a model for ways of handling evaluation in the clinical setting between student and supervisor, therapist and supervisor, therapist and colleague, and therapist and client.*

UNDERLYING ASSUMPTIONS AND COURSE OBJECTIVES

As in the conceptual framework, implicit in this educational model is a set of assumptions about the nature of activities, the nature of humankind, and the nature of change. In fact, the reader will recognize similarities between these assumptions and those presented in Chapter 1 that relate to the general proposition that engagement in activities can produce change from dysfunction toward function. Before the introduction of goals and methods, these assumptions will be made explicit, since they are the base from which this educational model emanates.

The Assumptions

1. *Everyone does activities and has an individually characteristic activities repertoire.*

   Recognizing that the things that people do are of central importance in the life and life-style of every human being, it can be assumed that each occupational therapy student comes to this educational endeavor with a lifetime of experience in doing. As information about some of the activities in each student's repertoire is shared, an image of the person behind the activities develops—the sports enthusiast, the craftsperson, the waitress, the person who likes to putter around the house, the gourmet cook, the "dare-devil" who enjoys skydiving and rock-climbing, the martial arts expert, the preschool teacher. In much the same way that people get to know one another in social or work situations, the instructor and students share information about the activities that they do. As they share interests, skills, and previous experiences, impressions are formed about the individual's family and other significant relationships, as well as values, attitudes, beliefs, likes, and dislikes. While it is fair to asume that each student will have an individually characteristic activities repertoire, it is also important to recognize that the conclusions that others draw from this information are no more than first impressions that may very well change over time. As long as those involved are mindful of the personal biases that influence the conclusions that are drawn, each individual's activities repertoire can be a source of valuable insight.

2. *Everyone's repertoire of activities includes both unique and shared activities:* "*In some ways man is like all other men, in some ways man is like some other men, in some ways man is like no other man.*"—Warren Bennis

   It is certain that through the process of sharing experiences with activities, students will discover both commonalities and differences, illustrating the universality of certain activities, and the idiosyncratic nature of others (see Chapter 2). Coming from each group of occupational therapy students is a wealth of data from which these similarities and differences can be examined. Intragroup commonalities in activities such as shopping, cooking, driving, showering, watching television, and reading are always found, but individual variations exist in the way that people do them. Discussions about the many ways in which any one activity is performed, how long it takes, what skills are entailed, and what feelings are evoked heighten awareness of the fact that although many of us do the same activities, they are not necessarily identical experiences. As discussions occur about activities personally chosen by each individual, students gain an appreciation for their own uniqueness as well as the uniqueness of others.

3. *In the natural doing of activities, all people have occasion to transmit what they know to others:* "*A culture in its very nature is a set of values, skills, and ways of life that no one member of society masters. Knowledge in this sense is like a rope, each strand of which extends no more than a few inches along its length, all being intertwined to give solidity to the whole*" [14].

   Jerome Bruner refers to this phenomenon as a "community of learning" [14] in which the enrichment of others occurs through a natural sharing of skills and ideas. In keeping with this recognition of an innate need both to learn and impart knowledge, it is vital that the learning environment foster what Bruner [15] calls "reciprocity," or "the deep human need to respond to others and to operate jointly with them toward an endeavor." Often, students claim that they "have never taught anyone anything." Perhaps in a formal sense, this is so. Upon closer examination, however, it becomes clear that the sharing of activities is commonplace for all people. Things that we do sometimes spark the interest of someone else—a hobby, a vocational pursuit, a new recipe. This is an everyday occurrence as a new fad is generated—a new hairstyle, the latest dance or fashion, the rise of a popular television show. Once the students become aware of the many overt and subtle ways in which activities are shared with others, they begin to recognize that they have the potential to participate in an exchange of activities skills.

4. *Throughout the developmental cycle, activities are agents for growth and learning:* "*Doing is a process of investigating, trying out, and gaining evidence of one's capacities for experiencing, responding, managing, creating, and controlling. It is through such action with feedback from both nonhuman and human objects that an individual comes to know the potential and limitations of self and the environment and achieve a sense of competence and intrinsic worth*" [32].

   This assumption leads to a belief that is central to the practice of occupational therapy and has been discussed in this context in Chapter 1. Developmental theorists such as Piaget [67], White [90], and Bruner [15] have posited the existence of an innate need to strive for learning and competence, which moves people to seek out experiences in the world that bring them closer to realizing their potential. If this assumption is to be applied to an educational situation, activities become prime media for learning. As we steep ourselves in learning about and through activities, the *hands, mind*, and *will* are all engaged in doing [71] (see Chapter 1, pp. 4–7). This, however, does not preclude the use of other traditional learning tools such as reading, writing, and discussion. Learning experiences encompass a well-balanced combination of doing, researching, reflecting, documenting, and sharing, all directed toward helping the student gain an understanding of activities as natural human phenomena and as valuable therapeutic tools.

The Course Objectives

Now that the assumptions that underlie this educational model have been articulated, specific objectives can be identified. The objectives are divided into two parts, the first relating to the study of *activities as natural human phenomena* and the second addressing *activities as therapeutic means toward activities health*.

The objectives are largely directed toward the development of knowledge about activities and skills needed for the structuring of relevant therapeutic activities. In addition, there is a third set of objectives that may not be as immediately apparent but is of equal importance, relating to the *"affective domain"* [49]. These objectives are focused on the acceptance of a set of attitudes and values, in this case about activities and the practice of occupational therapy. Krathwohl, Bloom, and Masia [49] contend that there are three distinct but closely related domains of learning—the *cognitive, affective*, and *psychomotor*. They point out the importance of identifying and evaluating the learner's achievement in each of the domains involved, since research shows that change in one area does not automatically produce change in another and that learning in all domains may not occur simultaneously or equally.

This threefold division is useful in understanding the educational model, since learning about and through activities is focused on the development of knowledge, psychomotor skills, attitudes, and values. Herein lies a striking parallel between the concepts guiding practice and education, that is, the recognition that integrated learning experiences, like all activities experiences, involve an intricate interplay between the *hands*, the *mind*, and the *will* [71].

ACTIVITIES AS NATURAL HUMAN PHENOMENA: PRODUCTS AND PROCESSES

1. *To demonstrate an understanding of activities as natural human phenomena.*
    This first and primary course objective forms a basis for all the others. The aim is for the student to understand activities from the perspective discussed in the earlier chapters of this book. Through a process of "consciousness-raising," the students are encouraged to develop a curiosity about human activities. As they become aware of the central importance of activities in everyday living,

they also discover the range and variety of activities thay they have in their own repertoires. Over time, students become able to recognize the many subtle ways in which activities are reflective of the life-style and personal characteristics of each individual and the culture(s) to which he or she belongs.

2. *To be able to analyze activities in relation to their natural context.*

   As you will recall from Chapter 2, this theoretical model emphasizes the importance of examining activities in the *natural context* of the *field of action* (spatial/locational components), *time* (temporal components), and *behavior habitat* (sociocultural components). The students' awareness of these external influences on activities performance can later be applied to the clinical situation, which calls for the therapist to choose and structure activities that are compatible with the individual's culture, physical environs, and activities patterns.

3. *To develop basic competence in selected new activities, involving the use of a variety of tools and materials.*

   Occupational therapists are required to engage in a variety of activities, which necessitate the use of a number of different tools and materials. Although it is unrealistic to expect that the student will develop expertise in a large number of activities, it is important that exposure to new activities be provided, so that the beginning therapist will feel confident enough to seek out the necessary resources to learn new activities skills in the future. Throughout the coursework, students are exposed to dozens of different activities from each aspect of everyday living, resulting in an expanded activities repertoire, as well as increased familiarity with a variety of tools and materials.

4. *To be able to provide instruction* in activities in a one-to-one or group setting.*

   In practice, occupational therapists are required to structure experiences that promote the patient/client's learning of new activities, or new ways to approach familiar activities, to enhance their ability to meet the demands of everyday living. This instruction is an interactive process, which occurs within the context of a one-to-one relationship at times and on other occasions is done in a group setting. Opportunities for instruction provide practice in the skills that are necessary for structuring activities experiences. Students are encouraged to experiment with various instructional styles and techniques within a variety of learning environments.

5. *To demonstrate the ability to plan and problem-solve in relation to activities experiences.*

   In the clinical setting, the designing of each therapeutic activities experience requires both *planning* and *problem-solving.* The occupational therapist must determine, obtain, and arrange the materials, tools, and space needed, select the methods to be used in implementation, budget time, and resolve problems that arise, often within limited time. Since the ability to plan and problem-solve is essential for the occupational therapist, the course includes opportunities for development of planning and problem-solving skills in a very practical and realistic way.

---

* We refer to the concept of "instruction," as presented by Bruner [14], as a social process by which knowledge is structured so that it can be grasped by the learner.

6. *To be able to analyze activities for their meaning and relevance to the individual.*

As discussed earlier, activities can best be understood in relation to the individual's life-style and sociocultural background, which are reflected in the idiosyncratic activities configuration. It is therefore of critical importance that activities be examined within such a context to determine their *meaning* and *relevance* to the individual as a member of a sociocultural group. As students analyze activities, they are required to consider the many ways in which various individuals and groups incorporate similar kinds of activities into their lives, and the diverse meanings ascribed to them by different cultures and individuals.

ACTIVITIES AS THERAPEUTIC MEANS TOWARD ACTIVITIES HEALTH

Follow the steps of the process of clinical problem-solving (reasoning) in order to be able to:

1. *Assess the individual's state of activities health.*

Activities health, presented in Chapter 3, has been described as *a state of being in which the individual is able to perform activities of everyday living in ways that are satisfying and comfortable and contribute to an overall sense of "fitting in" with one's sociocultural group or groups.* Occupational therapists are required to assess the needs of individuals who are limited in their ability to perform activities in ways that promote a sense of overall comfort, satisfaction, and sociocultural fit. Through the process of clinical reasoning described in Part III, the therapist uses knowledge and skills to determine the needs of the individual. Students are provided with opportunities to learn how to arrive at an *activities health* assessment, based on the individual's idiosyncratic activities configuration (see Chapter 5 Activities as Ends), in combination with other assessment findings and available information. This initial assessment is used as the basis from which needs can be determined and treatment goals established.

2. *Determine how a variety of clinical conditions affect one's state of activities health.*

A prerequisite to meeting this objective is the student's study of a variety of pathological conditions, each of which can affect one or more of the individual's physiological and psychological systems. To determine the ways in which various kinds of pathology can have an impact on the performance of everyday activities, it is necessary to integrate the understanding of clinical conditions with knowledge about human activities. Learning experiences are designed to help students learn to examine the relationship between the patient/client's clinical condition and activities functioning, with an appreciation for the variations in activities dysfunction that exist among individuals.

3. *Identify the individual's needs and resulting treatment goals that will support the attainment of a greater degree of activities health.*

The integrative process continues in this step of the clinical reasoning process that is dependent on the achievement of the two previous objectives. It is at this juncture that assessment findings are first incorporated into the occupational therapy treatment plan. Through the use of clinical case examples, the student learns to set meaningful and realistic treatment goals that are focused on the individual's state of *activities health.* Here the student encounters dilemmas commonly faced in the treatment situation; priorities must be considered when needs are many, and goals established that are compatible with the resources available in the clinical setting.

4. *Analyze activities as potential therapeutic tools that can help the individual achieve a more desirable state of activities health.*

    In addition to the assessment of the individual's needs, there is another type of analysis that is of critical importance to the practicing therapist. *Activities analysis* provides information about the performance components entailed in the nature of the *activity,* leading to specific requirements of the *actor,* in a particular *field of action,* and the *meaning* and *relevance* ascribed to the activity by various individuals and groups (see Chapter 4). Students analyze different kinds of activities from three distinct perspectives, all of which are ultimately used to explore the therapeutic potential of activities.

5. *Select meaningful and relevant therapeutic activities and to explore possibilities for adaptation and modification that will promote the patient/client's attainment of a greater degree of activities health.*

    This objective requires that the students have achieved basic mastery of the preceding objectives, since the selection and structuring of meaningful and relevant therapeutic activities experiences require the integrated use of skills in *activities health* assessment, activities analysis, and the establishment of occupational therapy goals. To this end, students are given assignments that require them to apply their newly developed clinical problem-solving skills by means of case examples that represent those encountered in practice. Students are guided in the selection of meaningful and relevant therapeutic activities and are then encouraged to use creative problem-solving as they explore possibilities for modification of the activity and/or field of action that will enhance the patient/client's performance of everyday activities.

6. *Select relevant theories and strategies for managing dysfunction.*

    As illustrated in the *Activities Health Model* (see Fig. 5-1), the occupational therapist makes use of a variety of theories, therapeutic techniques, and tools, in combination with meaningful and relevant activities, to help the individual achieve a more desirable state of *activities health.* Once the students have acquired an understanding of selected theoretical approaches (e.g., behavioral, occupational behavior, neuro-developmental), techniques (behavior modification, neurophysiological techniques, sensory integration), and tools (e.g., adaptive equipment, splints, computers, special environments), they are encouraged to explore how these theories, techniques, and tools fit into an *activities health* approach to clinical reasoning. Thus, they are helped to see how occupational therapy theories lead to *strategies for the management of dysfunction,* to be used to structure selected activities as therapeutic means. The incorporation of strategies to facilitate the carry-over of therapeutic gains into everyday living is specifically addressed.

7. *Formulate discharge plans.*

Discharge planning is a necessary step toward the ultimate attainment of greater *activities health.* Since for most patients/clients, change in day-to-day functioning often occurs over an extended period of time, occupational therapists are often rquired to become involved in planning for follow-up services. In preparation for their role in *discharge planning,* students are introduced to this step as a distinct part of the clinical reasoning process. They are asked to consider the kinds of services the patient/client may need to continue to make gains in everyday functioning, as well as some of the issues that often arise during the patient/client's *termination* and *transition* to a subsequent treatment setting.

8. *Reassess the individual's state of activities health at appropriate intervals.*

The occupational therapist's work with a client is incomplete without periodic assessment of the ways in which treatment efforts have resulted in changes in everyday living. Sometimes this is done within a formal reassessment session; other times the reassessment occurs in the form of a dialogue with the client and "thinking through" about the degree to which goals have been achieved. Regardless of how it is approached, reassessment in one form or another is part of clinical reasoning. Students are reminded to measure the relative success of treatment by finding out if interventions have made a difference in the patient/client's idiosyncratic activities configuration, rather than relying solely on observations of the patient/client's performance of activities in a treatment situation.

THE LEARNING ENVIRONMENT: FIELD OF ACTION AND TEMPORAL CONSIDERATIONS

In Chapter 2, the impact of spatial/locational, sociocultural, and temporal characteristics of the activities context was discussed. How do these concepts fit in with the educational model? Since the educational process consists of a sequence of activities, the field of action (consisting of both spatial/locational aspects and implicit and explicit rules), and temporal context selected by the instructor, all influence the learning experience. It is therefore important that the learning environment, which consists of physical, behavioral, and temporal components, be designed so that it will support the achievement of the learning objectives.

Spatial/Locational Aspects

What is the field of action, or environment, in which this learning takes place? The answer is implicit in the educational objectives. As the reader will recall, the first objective is for the student *to demonstrate an understanding of activities as natural human phenomena.* One of the ultimate objectives is for the student *to be able to select meaningful and relevant therapeutic activities and be able to explore possibilities for adaptation and modification that will promote the attainment of a greater degree of activities health.* The educational process is designed to promote the students' understanding of the relationship between these two objectives. By the time the students begin to explore the ways in which activities can be structured for therapeutic purposes, they have learned how to analyze the meaning and relevance of activities in the life-style of the individual—as done in their natural fields of action—thus providing a point of reference for the selection and design of simulated activities experiences in clinical practice. To attain these objectives, it is necessary to make use of a *variety* of fields of action, including the *natural environment* found in the world at large, the traditional *classroom/laboratory,* and the *clinical setting.*

THE NATURAL FIELD OF ACTION

In the early stages of the learning process, it is a priority for the student to gain an understanding of activities in their *natural context,* with an emphasis on the ways in which the field of action influences the doing of activities. Therefore, students are encouraged to work on their assignments in the very same environments in which they occur; doing needlework in front of the television or while traveling on the bus, for example, enables the student to experience and examine the activity in its natural form, with all of its accompanying sensory experiences. Later on, the students are required to observe the activities of other people, once again in their natural environments. The students' developing awareness of the significance of the natural field of action provides a basis for the acquisition of skills necessary for the designing of relevant therapeutic fields of action.

THE CLASSROOM/LABORATORY SETTING

The classroom and activities laboratory are also important fields of action during the learning process. Throughout the coursework, the students are encouraged to reflect on and share with one another what they have experienced. The classroom surroundings are used to facilitate this process by providing a neutral ground where students can step back and share their experiences, by means of discussions that promote the integration of knowledge already acquired through a variety of learning methods, which will be described later.

In addition, the classroom and laboratory setting, which is often relatively sterile in nature, provides practice in structuring activities experiences. Once the students have learned to analyze activities in terms of the natural fields of action in which they occur, the classroom or laboratory can be used to experiment with the modification of artificial fields of action so that they can serve as representations of real-life activities settings. Through such experiences, the student first encounters the challenge encountered by all occupational therapists—how to structure the therapeutic field of action so that it relates to the individual's everyday environment, in the hope that skills will be more readily carried over into daily living. To this end, assignments are developed that first require the student to analyze a specific activity's natural field of action in terms of the arrangements of people, furnishings, tools, and materials, and accompanying sounds, tastes, and tactile experiences, as well as the environmental rules that govern behavior. Following this examination, the student is asked to present the same activity in the more sterile classroom/

laboratory setting, designing the surroundings so that the characteristics of the natural field of action are incorporated as much as possible.

THE CLINICAL SETTING

The field of action in the traditional treatment setting offers the learner the opportunity to apply what has been learned in the fields of action already described to actual clinical practice. Despite its artificial nature and other commonly found limitations in space, equipment, tools, and materials, the clinic area is frequently the field of action for the practice of occupational therapy. While some clinical environments are more institutional in appearance than others, virtually all need some degree of modification to be relevant to the life-styles of patients/clients.

Since occupational therapy curricula universally include fieldwork experiences, there is ample opportunity for students to apply newly acquired skills in the settings where occupational therapy practice most frequently takes place. For example, assignments can be developed that require the student to analyze the elements of the clinical field of action and to adapt that physical environment to replicate the natural field of action more closely. In addition, the fieldwork setting offers students a place to apply systematically what has been learned about activities and their therapeutic potential—under the supervision of an occupational therapist.

In summary, the fields of action that support this entire educational experience require constant attention, as they influence the learner from beginning to end. Students learn to use the understanding of the natural field of action to design relevant therapeutic activities experiences and are provided with opportunities to make use of their understanding of activities and clinical reasoning skills—under supervision—in a practice setting.

Temporal Aspects

The relationship between time and human activities in general was discussed in Chapter 2; in this section, these ideas will be examined as they specifically apply to this educational process. The temporal context can be considered from these perspectives:

1. Relationship of the study of activities to the overall curriculum—at which point in time these learning experiences fit in with the curriculum as a whole; what the other learning experiences are that precede, follow, and accompany this learning process.
2. The learning sequence—the ordering of content and learning methods.
3. Duration—how much time is allotted for the coursework as a whole; the proportion of time devoted to seminars, labs, and assignments.

CURRICULUM SEQUENCE

Curriculum sequence is one of the first and most global concerns for the educator: Where in the total sequence and pattern of courses does this educational model belong? The study of activities as natural human phenomena is ideally introduced at the outset, since the knowledge thus acquired provides a foundation for the study of activities as therapeutic tools and the development of one's identity as an occupational therapist. As the student becomes ready to examine the therapeutic potential of activities, learning can take place within the context of a course introducing clinical reasoning based on an *activities health* framework, which can then be applied in a number of other courses of study. Clearly, the integration of this educational model into the study of occupational therapy theories and treatment strategies in all specialty areas strengthens the student's ability to apply what has been learned. Therefore, activities-related learning is best incorporated into the curriculum at intervals throughout the total sequence of courses, so that as the students learn about various theories, techniques, and tools used in the practice of occupational therapy, these too can be integrated with the understanding of activities as natural human phenomena and therapeutic means toward *activities health*. As with other learning, principles relating to activities are better understood and applied when they are reinforced in a variety of learning contexts (see Chapter 10, Postscript to the Educational Model, for further discussion).

THE LEARNING SEQUENCE

As discussed in Chapter 2, the sequential order in which activities are carried out affects the actor's experience. Likewise, the order in which the student engages in this series of learning experiences influences the acquisition and integration of knowledge about activities. How are these various learning activities sequenced to promote the achievement of the objectives? The following principles for sequencing address this question:

1. *Activities are studied as natural human phenomena before they are examined for their therapeutic potential.*

   From the start, students are involved in the exploration of activities as they naturally occur in the course of everyday living. Students examine time dimensions, some of the many ways of categorizing activities, fields of action, the impact of culture, the relative importance of different activities to the individual, and the symbolic meanings with which activities are invested. They grapple with questions about the existence of a desirable balance between work and play, time alone versus time with others, and the activities that one has to do versus those that one chooses to do. Through the exploration of these and many other related issues, students begin to develop an understanding of the many ways in which activities are woven into everyday living and the complex of other human phenomena that influence if, when, where, and how activities are done.

   It is only after this kind of understanding has been achieved that activities are examined for their therapeutic potential. Students then examine how a variety of clinical conditions affect the individual's performance of activities and how activities can be used as both means and ends to promote greater comfort and satisfaction in everyday living.

2. *The learning process begins with the students' examination of their own activities, followed by the study of activities of people with backgrounds similar to and different from their own.*

   The first of the assumptions that underlie this educational model emphasizes the resources for learning that are represented by the activities repertoire of each student. By using their own activities as a point of departure, students can immediately begin to view them in a way that is new and thought-provoking. At the same time, students begin to look at the ways in which personal values and biases—derived from their own sociocultural environments and individual perspectives—influence their perceptions about specific activities and categories of activities. Having developed a degree of awareness of their own activities, students can more effectively look beyond personal experience and study the activities of other individuals and groups.

3. *The learning experiences are structured so that the student first participates in, then observes others' participation in the doing of activities, and finally integrates (through the use of methods that will later be described) what has been learned through doing and observing in light of knowledge acquired through reading. Methods involving sharing and writing are incorporated throughout the learning sequence.*

Since the goals of this educational process include the simultaneous development of desirable attitudes, skills, and knowledge related to activities, a carefully ordered combination of doing, observing, reading, writing, and sharing is used. These learning methods are sequenced so that they focus the learners first on the study of activities as natural human phenomena (as described in Principle 1), beginning with the examination of their own activities lives (as described in Principle 2). Through the use of appropriately sequenced methods, students are gradually guided toward the study of activities as therapeutic means. Throughout the sequence, they are expected to read literature relevant to their learning, share knowledge and skills in a variety of ways, and engage in writing assignments used for purposes of reflection, examination, investigation, and documentation. The use of each of the methods identified will be discussed and illustrated in detail in Chapter 8.

DURATION

The amount of time that is available for learning about activities critically affects the planning of this learning experience. Once this is known, the instructor must decide on the way in which time will be allocated, determining the balance between experiencing, reflecting, and sharing most appropriate to each particular group of students.

It is important that the learning process include opportunities for students to learn to make optimal use of available time. The use of an "open lab"—a designated space available to students for a specific time period that can be used to carry out independent assignments, if the student so chooses—helps the students to acquire time management skills that are crucial in clinical practice.

OVERVIEW OF THE EDUCATIONAL METHODS AND COURSE ASSIGNMENTS

How are learning experiences designed to promote the achievement of the objectives? As each stage of learning is developed, the instructor must choose appropriate methods; the order in which these methods are introduced is partially governed by the prinicples regarding the learning sequence discussed under The Learning Sequence. As mentioned earlier, it is also important that methods be selected and structured in relation to learning needs of the particular student group, as well as the context in which this coursework takes place—the occupational therapy curriculum as a whole.* This assessment of needs and context includes consideration of the following:

1. The characteristics of the student group—educational level, age range, previous learning experiences, and nature and scope of their cumulative activities repertoire.
2. The overall philosophy of the occupational therapy curriculum, especially how it relates to activities and occupational therapy practice.
3. The relationship of these courses to the curriculum as a whole—time allotted and sequencing with other coursework.

The information obtained from this assessment enables the instructor to select and structure specific learning experiences that are appropriate for each unique learning situation. However, as will be discussed in some detail, there are learning methods that are particularly compatible with this approach to the study of activities.

The Learning Methods—An Overview

A review of the learning objectives in the first part of the educational model, focusing on activities as natural human phenomena, and the second part, which addresses the therapeutic use of activities, reveals basic differences in the nature of these learning experiences. Generally speaking, the first phase of learning is largely experiential and reflective; the second phase involves a great deal of theoretical learning and is thus directed in large part to understanding of concepts, although experiential learning is interwoven throughout. Since the learning methods are distinctly different for the two parts of the educational model, they will be discussed separately, in Chapters 8 and 9. For each part, the kinds of methods that lend themselves to the study of the particular subject matter at hand are described, followed by a set of assignments developed and used successfully in both baccalaureate and master's level occupational therapy curricula. Additional assignments can also be found at the end of each chapter in Part I of this book. It is not intended that these specific assignments be used prescriptively in all situations. They are offered *as examples* of opportunities for practicing principles from which other ideas can be generated and developed.

---

* Herein lies another parallel with an *activities health* approach to occupational therapy practice; the selection of learning methods and the means for incorporating them into actual assignments is based on the educator's assessment of the actor (learner), field of action (context), activity (assignment), and relevant strategies (learning methods).

CHAPTER 8

Activities as Natural Human Phenomena: Products and Processes

The Learning Methods

Before reading further about the methods that support the attainment of the objectives of the first part of this learning process, a review of the objectives listed in chapter 7 is suggested. The achievement of these objectives requires that the learner engage in experiences involving *doing, reading, reflecting, observing, sharing, writing, negotiating, and problem-solving.* Specific assignments are developed by the instructor (with input also provided by students when feasible), consisting of varying combinations of these methods used for learning and reinforcement. Like activities in general, these assignments are tools for learning, valuable not merely as the means to a greater understanding of and appreciation for everyday human activities, but also for the particular end products that they generate. As *means*, these assignments are used to promote the development of the student's awareness of activities as natural human phenomena, from a variety of perspectives. The *end products* are the skills and knowledge about activities that can later be drawn upon in clinical practice. The students' personal exploration of activities is accompanied by the study of the literature related to activities as natural human phenomena, thereby providing a basis from which personal experiences can be better understood.

The Assignments

In this chapter, examples of course assignments are presented. At the conclusion of each assignment is a summary section, indicating (1) how the assignment can be used as *means* of learning about activities as natural human phenomena, (2) how the assignment can result in *end products* (i.e., skills and knowledge that can be applied to the practice of occupational therapy), (3) *criteria for student evaluation,* and (4) *method used for evaluation.*

Following the presentation and discussion of course assignments are examples of student work contributed by some of the participants in this learning process. These examples provide the best illustration of the ways in which carefully designed assignments serve as vehicles for the acquisition of knowledge, skills, and the development of positive attitudes about activities and occupational therapy.

ASSIGNMENT 1: THE ACTIVITIES CONFIGURATION AND REPERTOIRE OF ACTIVITIES

During the month preceding the student's entry into the educational program, each student is sent a letter with the following instructions:

   A. Keep an hour-by-hour record of all your activities for one week, which you will bring to class.
   B. Mail to the instructor a list of the activities that you do, marking with a "T" those that you are able to teach.

Because activities are so much a part of our daily lives and are often done without our awareness, it is useful to begin this learning process through a look at activities in our own lives. Information gathered about one's own activities is used to begin to develop an *activities pattern* and *configuration,* as well as a listing of the repertoire of activities that already exists in the class as a whole.

The Configuration

During one of the first class sessions, the following instructions (adapted from Appendix A) are given:

   A. Fill in the weekly Activities Schedule (see Appendix A) with the activities that you recorded during the week. If more than one activity was done at the same time (e.g., watching TV and sewing), bracket both in the same time slot. If any activity does not occupy the full hour, fill in all the activities that occupy the time slot, in order.
   B. Code the activities by color according to the classification system delineated in Appendix A, Activities Schedule Coding Key. Every activity you recorded must be fitted into one of the designated categories (e.g., if you recorded eating as an activity each day from 7–8 P.M., you should decide whether it is to fit into leisure [alone/with others], work, or self-care). Remember that there is no "correct answer" for how any activity is categorized.

The completion of these steps results in an *activities pattern* (see Chapter 2, Patterns and Configurations, and p. 101 for a student example). The instructor then conducts a discussion that touches on some of the questions that are involved in translating the information from the activities pattern into an *activities configuration* (see Appendix A for discussion guidelines, p. 18 for a definition of an activities configuration).

By filling in their activities patterns and participating in the discussion that follows, the students personally test the validity of the assumptions that underlie this educational model. The students are able to arrive at the following truths about themselves in relation to activities, which echo the assumptions presented at the beginning of this chapter:

I do activities.

I have a repertoire of activities that I am willing and able to impart.

I have unique skills and skills that I share with others.

Many activities permeating my daily interactions and transactions are not in my
  immediate awareness.

The activities configuration can lead to insights about one's individual style of living (e.g., "I always alternate the things I hate to do with the things that I like— it makes it less painful.") and reality-testing of one's self-perception (e.g., "I always thought of myself as spending a lot of time alone, and there was only one hour in this week that I was alone."). This assignment frequently elicits nostalgia for old friends, hobbies, and places and provides an effective vehicle for students to learn about the interests, work experiences, and significant relationships of one another.

The activities configuration also requires that *classification systems* be considered. For example, what one person identifies as play is another's work, as was discussed in Chapter 2 (see example on p. 20). Early on, the students become aware that classification systems, while useful as tools for sorting, are in fact laden with seeming contradictions. The inconsistencies that become apparent as individuals categorize their activities can be very revealing, since the way in which individuals perceive their activities tells us something about their values, preferences, and lifestyles.

The Activities Repertoire

During the seminar, the students are asked to do the following:

> Using the list that you compiled prior to your entry into this course, share with other class members that list of activities, indicating those that you are able to teach.

At the same time, the instructor lists on the board the activities mentioned by each student. This list represents the class's activities repertoire at the start of this coursework.

The listing of a cumulative activities repertoire of class members (see example under Class Activities Repertoire), confirms the assumption that everyone does activities and graphically illustrates the *variety* and *number* of different activities done by class members. Talking about pursuits, interests, and areas of expertise helps students to view themselves and their peers as potential resources for learning and promotes the making of connections among students. Frequently, the listing of the comprehensive repertoire awaken interest in activities that students would like to learn from one another. The range and variety of skills available among students and instructor are always impressive and always generate enthusiasm about possibilities for sharing.

The review of student lists and activities configurations provides a forum for the discussion of features common to all activities (see Chapter 2, Summary) as well as activities classification. Since the list is requested prior to their introduction to the principles underlying the coursework, many students include nothing but leisure activities, some even to the extent of reporting only crafts. Others come in with a broader view, including work, household, and self-care activities, in addition to leisure pursuits. Regardless of how the listing has been approached, by the time of the discussion, students have already been introduced to the concept of activities as part of every aspect of daily living. This more far-reaching perspective on the scope of human activities can then be reinforced and thus challenge preconceived notions about the types of activities that are relevant in occupational therapy. The activities repertoire also provides a starting point for the sharing that later occurs in the teaching labs (see Assignment 2).

Summary

Assignment as means of: developing awareness of distinctive features of activities and significance of specific activities to self and others; identification of resources for the learning of activities; introducing systems for classifying activities.

End products: skills necessary for the development of an activities pattern and preliminary skills needed for the development of an activities configuration; awareness of activities repertoire of oneself and other class members.

Criteria for evaluation: ability to create an activities pattern and configuration at an introductory level; basic understanding of features common to all activities and an awareness of some of the methods of classifying them.

Method of evaluation: informal peer and self-evaluation.

A student example of a filled-out Activities Schedule is illustrated on the following page.

	MONDAY	TUESDAY	WEDNESDAY	THURSDAY	FRIDAY	SATURDAY	SUNDAY
12 Midnight to 1 A.M.	Sleep	Sleep	Sleep	Sleep	Late night snack with friends	Baby shower	Sleep
1 A.M.-2 A.M.					Driving Shower	Driving Shower	
2 A.M.-3 A.M.					Sleep	Sleep	
3 A.M.-4 A.M.							
4 A.M.-5 A.M.							
5 A.M.-6 A.M.							
6 A.M.-7 A.M.							
7 A.M.-8 A.M.	Grooming Breakfast	Grooming	Grooming	Grooming	Grooming	Sleep	Sleep
8 A.M.-9 A.M.	Read paper	Breakfast	Breakfast	Breakfast	Breakfast	Breakfast Shower	Church
9 A.M.-10 A.M.	Watched TV	Clean up	Clean up	Clean up	Clean up	Straightened up	Read Sunday paper
10 A.M.-11 A.M.	Shower	Read newspaper	Finished typing paper	MD appointment	Supervised children in playroom	Sewing a wedding gown	Cleaned house and planned meal
11 A.M.-12 Noon	Laundry	Typed paper	Mailed paper	Went to post office			
Noon-1 P.M.	Lunch	Lunch	Lunch	Driving Grocery shopping	Lunch	Driving	Shopping for groceries
1 P.M.-2 P.M.	Talked to people at previous job	Clean up	Cleaned up Talked to staff		Straightened up playroom	Lunch	Waiting in line
2 P.M.-3 P.M.		Conducted staff meeting	Cleaned cupboards	Cooking	Wrote letter	Clothes shopping	Cooking dinner
3 P.M.-4 P.M.	On phone Ran 3 1/2 miles		Meeting	Made phone calls	Driving	Sewing	↓
4 P.M.-5 P.M.	Shower Drove	Relaxed Ran 3 miles	Nap	Reading	Went to bank Shopping for gift		Set table Phone call
5 P.M.-6 P.M.	Cooking dinner	Played lottery	Ran 3 miles with friend				Last-minute cleaning
6 P.M.-7 P.M.	Eating dinner	Watched news	Grooming	Dinner	Visited friend	Talked on phone	Greeted guests Dinner
7 P.M.-8 P.M.	Clean-up	Grooming Driving	Talked on phone	Relaxed w/ boyfriend	Ran 3 miles	Ironing Grooming	
8 P.M.-9 P.M.	Driving	Dinner at restaurant	Dinner out w/ boyfriend		Watched news	Went to a baby shower	Clean up
9 P.M.-10 P.M.	Watched TV		Driving Read paper	Watched TV	Movie		Entertained guests
10 P.M.-11 P.M.		Out for ice cream	Laundry -- running up and down w/ laundry	Grooming			
11 P.M. to 12 Midnight		Driving Grooming	Sleep	Sleep	Late night snack w/ friends		Shower

Legend:

- Sleep
- Chores
- Leisure with others
- Work
- Leisure alone
- Self care

Class Activities Repertoire

The following list, in random order, represents the combined activities repertoire of one class of occupational therapy students prior to their entry into the educational program:

swimming
gymnastics
racewalking
bicycling
massage
baking
cooking
shopping
sewing
poetry writing
flute playing
gift-card making
waitressing
deli/counterperson work
macrame
weaving
yoga
dancing
cross-stitch
racquetball
backgammon
shotputting
salad making
doing arithmetic
speaking Spanish
wallpapering
skating

scrapbook making
sign-language communication
housekeeping
grooming
typing
film criticism
archery
basketball
teaching piano
teaching singing
music reading
autoharp playing
word processing
computer telecommunicating
embroidery
stenciling
jam making
aerobics
ballet
tap dancing
baton twirling
horseback riding
waterskiing
scuba diving
sailing
guitar playing
windsurfing

rowing

badminton

hiking

parenting

beading necklaces

mobile making

flower arranging

drawing

rug braiding

singing

driving

gardening

bed-making

skiing

furniture moving

painting

set designing

script writing

tutoring

puppet-show directing

decorating candy canes

making holiday ornaments

needlepoint

gift wrapping

stationery making

copper tooling

banner making

jogging

softball

field hockey

crocheting

calisthenics

ceramics

quilting

reading

filing

speaking Hebrew

cake decorating

home repair

bargain-hunting

traveling

weight lifting

wreath making

boating

photography

jumping rope

crewel

rug hooking

purchase ordering

games

leading discussions

speaking German

camping

rugby

ASSIGNMENT 2: THE TEACHING LABS

   A. Indicate on your Activities Lab Contract (see Appendix F) if you elect to earn credit by sharing one or more activities with member(s) of the class.
   B. If you choose to conduct one or more lab session(s) as part of your learning contract, develop a teaching plan according to the guidelines in Appendix G.
   C. After your plan has been approved by the instructor, make all necessary arrangements with interested class members, and carry out your teaching lab in the time and place that you have planned.

Earlier in this chapter, we discussed our assumption that each student comes to this learning process with an ability and willingness to teach specific activities. Through the use of a learning contract (see Chapter 7, The Learning Contract), students can elect to earn credit for sharing their skills with others in the class. In this way, the students' avenues for negotiating contracts extend beyond their relationship with the instructor; the course design includes opportunities for students to contract with one another to teach and learn about a variety of activities. Learners' interests are matched with skill resources available; activities such as bread baking, clogging, piano playing, weaving, word processing, and hair styling all become vehicles for a stimulating network of activities-sharing that benefits "learners" and "teachers" alike.

The development of the teaching plan requires that the student consider the level at which the activity will be taught, the objectives that are realistic, and the number of hours required. Anticipated needs for space, materials, and equipment are also documented. The submission of the plan enables the instructor to offer feedback on any of the elements included. Questions commonly arise about the feasibility of achieving the stated goals within the allotted time, the selection of teaching methods, and the class size that can be accommodated.

Once the teaching plan (which is analogous to the *group protocol* in the clinical setting) has been approved by the instructor, the student is expected to make all of the arrangements necessary for carrying it out. As was mentioned in the discussion of course objectives, such planning and problem-solving skills are important prerequisites for structuring activities experiences in the clinical setting. Negotiations for mutually convenient times and locations, the design of the field of action, and recruitment campaigns for participants are all examples of available opportunities for acquiring professional decision-making and communication skills.

The teaching labs also generate exchanges of skills and knowledge, thus expanding the students' activities repertoires. There are opportunities for exposure to new activities, as well as the chance to become reacquainted with activities done in the past that have since fallen by the wayside. Even skeptical students quickly become aware of their abilities both to learn and to teach, a principle that is fundamental to this coursework.

Summary

Assignment as means of: participating in learning contracts, both as "learner" and "teacher"; developing planning, problem-solving, decision-making, and communication skills necessary for the structuring of activities experiences; developing teaching skills.

End products: new activities skills (as "learner"); teaching skills (as "teacher").

Criteria for evaluation: the degree to which objectives identified in teaching plan were met; the degree to which the contract was carried out and/or re-negotiated as necessary.

Method of evaluation: written self-evaluation and peer evaluation.

ASSIGNMENT 3: THE CONSTRUCTIVE PROJECT

A. Choose a craft project in which you are interested. It may require either skills that are new or skills that are familiar to you. Decide on the degree to which you plan to become involved in the project, using 12 hours as the expected time allotment for maximal, 10 hours for moderate, and 8 hours for minimal level of engagement (see Appendix F for further clarification), indicating this on a written learning contract outlined in Appendix F. (Remember that these course points can be supplemented with other assignments—see Appendix F.)

B. As you engage in this activity, record your experiences in a journal. Make note of your experiences and reactions as you go along—the triumphs, the frustrations, the adjustments made along the way, the problems that arise.

c. Plan a 30-minute lab session, in which you will teach this activity to four to five classmates. When designing the teaching experience, consider the ways in which you can introduce elements of the natural field of action into the more artificial laboratory setting. You will need to decide how to make best use of the limited time available to introduce your participants to the activity, making sure to include a "doing" component.

The only way to make the [student] conscious of his social heritage is to enable him to perform these fundamental types of activity which make civilization what it is. . . . In the so-called *expressive* or *constructive* [emphasis added] activities is the center of correlation. . . . They are not special studies which are to be introduced over and above a lot of others in the way of relaxation or relief, or as additional accomplishments. I believe rather that they represent, as types, fundamental forms of social activity . . . [85].

If indeed this mandate from Dewey's Pedagogic Creed applies to the education of occupational therapists, then engagement in activities characterized by *constructing* (i.e., building) and *expressing* (i.e., revealing) is essential to the learning process. Thus, students are required to plan and carry out a so-called "*constructive*" project and an "*expressive*" project, which will be described later on.

If desired, the Constructive Project may be assigned with more explicit guidelines—soft versus hard materials, time allotted for completion of the project, unfamiliar versus familiar activities, projects predesigned versus those designed by the student—to illustrate only some of the requirements that can be made explicit if the instructor or student group so chooses. All students are encouraged to make use of the many resources available for instruction and assistance; the student-led Teaching Labs (see Assignment 2), outside resource people, instructor, books, instructional videotapes, and magazines are among the many viable options. Thus, students learn how to assume responsibility for the shaping of their own learning experiences—how to seek out and use the methods of instruction that are most compatible with their learning needs and styles.

Crafts have been linked with occupational therapy since its inception. The learning of craft activities has traditionally been the focus of activities coursework in occupational therapy curricula, usually in the form of "studio" courses in arts and crafts. The approach to learning about arts and crafts is fundamentally different in this educational model, in both its format and emphasis. *Like all of the other activities explored, arts and crafts are experienced and examined with an emphasis on the natural contexts in which they usually take place.*

Craft and art activities can fit into an individual's activities configuration in a variety of ways. For most, these activities are hobbies or occasional leisure pursuits; for others, they are a means of livelihood. The characteristics of these two very different contexts make for activity experiences that are qualitatively different from one another. It is the examination of such overt and subtle distinctions that this type of study emphasizes. The Constructive Project is designed to encourage the exploration of art and craft activities as natural human phenomena.

After the activity has been learned and the project planned, the student becomes engaged in doing. For the activity to be experienced and examined in its natural context, students are encouraged to do the activities where and when they are usually done, whenever possible (see Chapter 7, The Natural Field of Action). Sewing on the living room floor on a Saturday afternoon, making papier-mâché sculptures on the kitchen table with the help of the children, and making wreaths on the front porch on a crisp fall morning all illustrate the intimate connections that exist between activities and the times and places in which they are done in everyday living. A journal is used as a tool for reflecting on the activity experience and bringing to conscious awareness the many ways in which the individual and the environment become intertwined through activities, in the rhythm of daily life.

Once a project has been completed, the final stage of this assignment is the students' sharing of their skills with others. In this case, the students are asked to teach an activity in a more structured situation than that of the Teaching Lab. This process, which is more formal, is a closer approximation of the activities experiences that take place in clinical settings; the hours and number of participants are specified ahead of time, and the setting is a classroom rather than the natural environment.

The teaching component of the Constructive Project requires that the students experiment with ways in which they can set up the field of action in laboratory-like environment that will create an atmosphere compatible with the activity. Students are encouraged to give careful consideration to the placement of objects (both human and nonhuman), as well as the incorporation of implicit and explicit rules that will influence the learners. In addition, the student-instructor must grapple with decisions regarding how best to use a limited time period to introduce participants effectively to the activity, and how to select instructional techniques (e.g., demonstration, doing, visual aids) that will be most effective. Students become aware of the need to develop objectves that are realistic given the time and resources available and a viable plan that will support their attainment. These skills are much needed by the practicing occupational therapist; in effect, they underlie the planning and implementation of occupational therapy programs in clinical practice.

Summary

Assignment as means of: experiencing and reflecting on all aspects of doing; developing planning, teaching, and problem-solving skills in relation to an activities experience.

End products: activities skills and expansion of repertoire (through participation in both Constructive Project and labs of other students).

Criteria for evaluation: end product evaluated in terms of its function, design, and craftsmanship, all in relation to the student's level of experience with the activity; constructive activity teaching session is evaluated for preparation (i.e., setting, timing), content (i.e., appropriate, clear, concise), finishing (i.e., clean-up, timing), and overall impression.

Method of evaluation: written evaluation by instructor and informal verbal feedback by peers. (Criteria for evaluation are specified before assignment is carried out.)

Constructive Project: Pillow Making

JOURNAL EXCERPTS*

. . . It began in late summer, actually, this feeling of creative inadequacy in the area of craftwork. . . . Fine motor skills, craftsy endeavors, etc. have never provided a rewarding outlet for the expression of my creativity. . . . So—here I am, frozen in blankness re: what I want to do with myself. In all honesty, nothing seems appealing. . . .

. . . With pillow-making, I can learn something I've never attempted before, but having seen homemade pillows many times, I feel familiar enough with the types of craftwork that can be applied, to give it a try. . . .

. . . I wanted to do something as non-academic as possible last night after the anatomy exam (ordeal?). . . . I pulled out the muslin, picked out a pattern, traced it, and commenced slowly with candlewicking . . . started on a cross-stitch pattern, but my eyes and neck began to feel the strain. . . .

. . . Found it relaxing, to just sit, abstractly listen to music, feel good about the finished products. . . . I have never been a patient person, especially with myself; when things are slow-going, I avoid them entirely. This time I had no choice, really—and I discovered when I give something like this a chance, it's not that bad, in fact, it's pretty satisfying.

* From the journal of a student who wished to remain anonymous.

Constructive Project: Grapevine Wreaths

JOURNAL EXCERPTS*

. . . My thoughts turned to something that would be an enjoyable leisure-time activity, but would also serve a purpose. The idea of grapevine wreaths for housewarming gifts popped into my mind. I made my decision by asking myself these questions: Could I complete them in the next two weeks? Did I want to give them as gifts? I answered yes and was very pleased. . . .

. . . Today my husband and I went out to collect grape vines. . . . It thrills me to take something from nature that you don't have to pay for and make something out of it. . . .

. . . Looking back on the process of making the wreaths, the effect of the project was one of relaxation. It allowed me to put my energy into something that was aesthetically pleasing. . . .

* From the journal of Darlene Halvorsen Sarchino, Columbia University, class of '90.

Constructive Project: A Crocheted Yarmulke*

JOURNAL EXCERPTS†

. . . I have known how to make a yarmulke for eleven years, even though I haven't made one in a while. . . .

I worked on the yarmulke from 4:00 P.M. to 6:10 P.M. while alone in my room and managed to complete most of the base. At 7:00 P.M., I was on dorm duty in the lobby. Many people passed by, came to visit, or asked questions, so it was hard to concentrate. . . . This time I am working with 25 colors; the most I have ever used before is 11. Since I used four shades of six different colors, I kept confusing the proper order of the shades. . . . I was so annoyed I almost decided to make a design with two colors. . . .

Today I managed to complete putting the colors in and completed the third row. Then I did it on the train from 1:00 to 2:00 . . . later from 8:00 until midnight while talking on the phone and visiting with friends. . . . Even though my hands were tired, I was very anxious to see it completed, so after I made the last border row, I washed it in Woolite, shaped it on my head, and let it dry until morning on a flat surface. . . .

* Skullcap worn by Orthodox and Conservative Jewish males.
† From the journal of a student who wished to remain anonymous.

Constructive Project: A Pinata*

JOURNAL EXCERPTS†

. . . Making this pinata was a great idea. I feel as though I'm back in art school . . . those were the best hours—just creating and letting it flow. . . . I'm just going to let this happen. I'll try to find odd things around my apartment and use them. . . .

. . . A project I can do while watching TV! Balloons, newspaper and glue, and I can create something that can be used as a gift for my godchild. . . .

I'm glad I can use my art knowledge with this project. The theories of colors, textures, light, and dark are all coming back. . . .

Well, time for the painting . . . first pop the balloons (strange sound they make when they peel off the inside of the newspaper) . . . so far, so good . . . it's like a 3-D collage. . . . I'm pleased with the final product. . . .

* In Mexico and Central America, a gaily decorated papier-mâché figure or container filled with toys, candy, and so on and suspended overhead, so that blindfolded children (mostly) can break it open or knock it down and release the contents.
† From the journal of Rozanne Pelosi, Columbia University, class of '88.

Other Constructive Project Ideas

Embroidery
pillow, wall hanging, sampler, stool, cover, pillow case

Stenciling
table mats, valentines, breakfast tray, stationery

Sewing
curtains, dress, Halloween costume, stuffed animal, potpourri sachets

Needlepoint
wallhanging, pillow, table runner, seat cover, bookmarks, eyeglass case

Basketry
rattan mats, purses, baskets

Artificial flower making
silk, ribbon, leather

Weaving
wall hanging, scarf, stole, belt, purse, evening bag

Leather
belt, bookmark, purse, key chain

Quilting
pillow cover, pot holder

Macrame
belt, Christmas ornaments, plant hanger, bracelets, wall hanging

Miscellaneous
collage, mobile with found objects, fabric picture frame, evergreen wreaths, rug hooking, bread dough sculpture, slab and coil pottery

ASSIGNMENT 4: THE EXPRESSIVE PROJECT

A. Choose an activity through which you can share an aspect of yourself. The activity should be one that lends itself to a presentation of approximately 30 minutes. The preparation time allotted is 12 hours.

B. The method of presentation is up to you—the sky's the limit! It is your responsibility to arrange for any special space, equipment, or materials that you need, making use of available resources.

C. Keep an ongoing journal throughout the development of your project. Record your experiences as they occur—the ups, the downs, the obstacles, the triumphs. (Be sure to keep your log as these experiences occur; our retrospective memories are prone to distortions!)

Each of us engages in activities that express our uniqueness, communicating to others something of who we are as individuals. As Dewey [185] has stated, involvement in *expressive activities* helps us learn about the world around us. Contrary to what many people realize initially, each of us, from the most to the least artistically gifted, is *expressive* nevertheless. While some individuals possess great talents in the fine arts, most express their individuality in much humbler ways. Cake decorating, karate, party giving, gift wrapping, pasta making, fashion styling, poetry reading, and snapshot taking are some of the everyday activities that can be vehicles for self-expression—communications of who we are and how we see the world.

This assignment is designed to provide the student with the opportunity to experience, reflect on, and share with others something of themselves through activities. The instructor may encourage students to engage in this assignment on an individual basis; in other cases students may be steered toward working in small groups on a collaborative project.

Once the activity has been selected, the planning and preparation of the project can begin. As in the Constructive Project, the students are encouraged to do activities in the context of natural fields of action whenever possible. Here again, doing activities where and when they are usually done provides students with opportunities to experience the "spirit" and "feel" of the activities, as they exist in natural, everyday contexts.

Engagement in the Expressive Project also helps the student learn to plan an activity experience from beginning to end (Objective 5). The ability to use time effectively, negotiate for necessary space and materials, and organize an activities-centered presentation are essential competencies for occupational therapists, who in clinical practice are required to engage in such problem-solving on a daily basis.

Involvement in expressive activities inevitably elicits emotional responses along the way. The journal is a useful tool for the processing of these feelings; the joys, the frustrations, associations with the past, and connections with significant people are all potential sources of personal feelings and reactions that can surface. Such first-hand experiences are later useful to practicing therapists who find that activities can similarly evoke strong feelings in their patients/clients at times.

The Expressive Project culminates in the students' presentations. Each student is allotted a specific time period for their presentation; 30 minutes is generally sufficient for most, and not so lengthy that it might be overwhelming. If a different time frame is needed for the presentation, it is up to the student to negotiate with both instructor and classmates.

The method of presentation that can be used is only limited by the student's imagination. Some may choose to engage their audience in the activities themselves; others may decide to present in the form of a performance; still others may use a combination of methods. As in the teaching component of the Constructive Project, it is suggested that presenters create a field of action that places their chosen activity in a fitting context—a poetry reading amidst the inspirational presence of one's collection of poetry classics, artwork displayed in a gallery-like setting with a wine and cheese "opening," a "chocolate lovers' experience" presented amidst an array of chocolate delights and related souvenirs, a flute recital presented with a background of the sun setting over the Hudson River (Expressive Project: A Flute Recital for description) are a few such examples. Thus, the critical importance of the field of action is reinforced in the presentation of these assignments, as students share their expressive activities with one another.

It is important to remain sensitive to the sometimes threatening nature of this assignment. It is personal (although to varying degrees), and all participants uncover at least a small part of themselves in the course of class presentations. A supportive environment is therefore essential to the success of the assignment.

Summary

Assignment as means of: becoming aware of the expressive potential of selected activities; monitoring and reflecting on an expressive activities process; learning to plan and problem-solve in relation to an activities experience.

End products: expanded activities repertoire, derived from own Expressive Project and sharing of projects through class presentations; negotiating skills (e.g., space, time, materials with instructor, peers, others); problem-solving and communication skills.

Criteria for evaluation: quality of presentation, (based on organization, use of time, use of field of action), overall impression; degree to which log reflects the ongoing activities process.

Method of evaluation: informal peer feedback; written evaluation by instructor. (Criteria for evaluation are specified before assignment is carried out.)

Expressive Project: A Painted Heart

THE PRESENTATION*

If you can, for a minute, close your eyes and try to imagine what a Swedish winter is like. There is snow piled several feet high on the ground, and all is very dark and quiet. The sun rises at 10 o'clock and sets at two in the afternoon, spreading a pale light against the frozen land. Families are gathered inside, around the fireplace, engaging in various games and crafts. A candle is burning and the house is filled with the smell of freshly baked bread. . . .

. . . In my mother's house, every corner is filled with pieces of handcrafted material—napkins, tablecloths, pillows, wall hangings, and rugs. Knitting, needlepoint, and woodworking have occupied the hands of my family members for generations. This is where I have gotten my love for crafts; they always remind me of peaceful days in Sweden. . . .

. . . The heart is a popular folk symbol in Sweden, and it is an important symbol in my life. To me, it symbolizes love, family, unity, happiness, warmth, and friendship. As an expression of myself, I made this heart to show to you. This heart has a history all its own. I found this rough hewn piece of wood in a wreckage pile, in an abandoned mining town in the San Juan mountain range of Colorado, when I was camping with my family for two weeks. The piece was from a broken rocking chair. . . . For many years now, it has sat in my room unchanged, but I have always wanted to make something of it. . . . What I have done is to sand it down by hand until it is silky smooth to the touch and pleasing to the eye. I painted it red as it is traditionally seen in Sweden. The design I have painted on it is from a paper cutting my father gave to my mother years ago. It symbolizes the strength and unity of the family to me. It also symbolizes my upbringing and many of my values. I see this as the tree of life— my family tree, with a strong heart at its roots. I have been free to grow and explore in whatever direction I have wished, with the knowledge that my parents are always supporting my upward reaching limbs. . . .

* From the presentation of Jennifer Winsor, Columbia University, class of '88.

Expressive Project: Stage Make-up
THE PROCESS*

Make-up has been used theatrically for centuries. Body markings of all kinds are found in virtually every culture. Clowns and actors in our own culture explore emotions, characters, and different stages of life through the use of make-up.

I find age make-up especially intriguing. As we age, our skin loses some of its tone, forming characteristic hollows, skin folds, and bony prominences. It is the careful sculpting of these shadows and highlights that can age a youthful face. I use a variety of shades and colors to bring out an aged effect. A pancake base evens out the skin tone, then greasepaints in brown,

* From presentation of Diane Heimer, Columbia University, class of '86.

"Make-up changes the way others look at me and the way I look at myself."

"It can be used to explore universal human emotions or the uniqueness of an individual. It can run the clock forward.

"My face is my canvas, and every little stroke (a brush, a sponge) comes between me and it."

"Wrinkles are sculpted by the movement of my face—if I laugh, so will my wrinkles."

white, red, and even yellow and lavender accentuate and recess particular features. Each new face therefore presents a challenge to depict not only the age but also the essence of the character.

The process of making up is not only fun, but meditative as well. One cannot help but contemplate and come to terms with the character evolving on one's face. This not only brings to greater awareness the assumed character, but must also bring greater awareness of oneself—one's reactions, fears, hopes, etc., are drawn out with each dab of shadow or brush of highlight. Thus the process moves beyond simple technique and can provide a powerful medium for self-exploration.

"I write my future by the way I live now; my past will be read in the lines of my face. The outer self will reveal the inner."

"As I paint my wrinkles, my smiles, and experience (and not stereotypic old woman frown lines), I realize I'll like the me I'll become."

"Making up is like spending time with a good friend."

"Next time, in real time, we'll be old friends, my face and I."

Expressive Project: A Flute Recital*

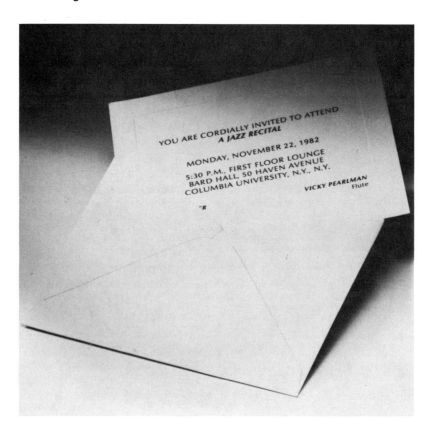

YOU ARE CORDIALLY INVITED TO ATTEND
A JAZZ RECITAL

MONDAY, NOVEMBER 22, 1982
5:30 P.M., FIRST FLOOR LOUNGE
BARD HALL, 50 HAVEN AVENUE
COLUMBIA UNIVERSITY, N.Y., N.Y.

VICKY PEARLMAN
Flute

DESCRIPTION

This invitation, sent out ahead of time to classmates and faculty, fulfilled its promise of an hour of music of near-professional caliber, in a large, comfortable lounge with a sunset river view. Not only was the performance satisfying, but the pleasure was enhanced by the transformation of the soloist from a jeans-clad student to a formally dressed performer in long skirt and festive blouse. Her accompanist at the grand piano was also formally dressed. Behind this seemingly effortless presentation was a great deal of preparation, including (1) Choice of program; (2) Enlistment of accompanist; (3) Negotiation for appropriate time slot (end of day for sunset, last expressive activity of the day to be presented by student group); (4) Negotiation for jealously-guarded space in student residence hall lounge with piano and comfortable seating; (5) Design, printing, and distribution of invitation; (6) Rehearsal of recital pieces; and (7) Planning of wardrobe.

* Project of Vicky Pearlman, Columbia University, class of '84.

Other Expressive Project Ideas

Not all expressive projects reach, or need to reach, a near-professional level such as the preceding examples. The range of expressive activities is as wide as the number of individuals who present them, from the seemingly "humblest" of offerings, as viewed by the young man who chose basic juggling as his expressive project, through the list that follows:

an Autumn picnic . . . holidays from different cultures . . . game playing . . . ethnic-cookie making . . . slide show of favorite art works from museums around the word . . . puppet making . . . aerobics demonstration . . . Jewish symbols . . . Oktober-fest party . . . toy making . . . gift wrapping . . . pasta making . . . cake decorating . . . clogging . . . karate demonstration . . . favorite classical guitar selections . . . ceramics . . . singing . . . sweater design . . . personal history through photographs . . . painting to music . . . poetry reading . . . international cooking . . . Halloween party . . . culture shock and a camera—learning to know the neighbors in a new and different environment . . . flower arranging . . . how we got to the United States—the travels of a family divided by war—maps, models, and narration . . . traveling the Yellow Brick Road . . . so you want to play the Autoharp! . . . ballroom dancing . . . batik . . . pasta making . . . French for travelers . . . tennis techniques . . . T'ai Chi . . . calligraphy . . . belly dancing . . . Polish paper cutting . . . acting exercises . . . baton twirling . . . collage . . . pie making . . . cornhusk dolls . . . soft sculpture

ASSIGNMENT 5: HOBBIES AND PASTIMES

Choose a hobby in which you have been involved, either currently or in the past. Write a paper that focuses on these questions: How did you get started? What kept you going? What interfered with your continuing this hobby? How much time do you (or did you) spend on it? Why do you think it appeals to you? What are the advantages? Disadvantages? What feelings are elicited? What other kinds of individuals might enjoy your hobby?

Hobby has been defined as "an activity or interest pursued for pleasure or relaxation" (*Random House Dictionary*, 1987). Unlike those activities that are necessary for survival, a hobby is by definition an activity of one's choice, indicative of one's personal preference. The range of choices is infinite—collecting (stamps, bottles, shells, postcards, maps), listening to or playing music (one particular composer or type of music perhaps), bird-watching, mountain climbing, doll dressing, cake decorating, photography, model plane or matchstick toy making, and puppetry represent only a few of the infinite possibilities. This assignment is designed to promote the student's examination of this category of activities as a facet of everyday living.

Once again, the emphasis is on the activity within its natural context and the way in which the hobby meets (or has met) personal needs. The assignment also provides the opportunity to examine an activity from a longitudinal perspective; tracing the historical development of the hobby in the life of the student adds yet another dimension to activities analysis.

Summary

Assignment as means of: developing awareness of the development of an activity over time in one's own life and the ways in which hobbies can fulfill personal needs.

End products: knowledge about hobbies as natural human phenomena.

Criteria for evaluation: awareness of the meaning and relevance of this activity to oneself over time and the ability to articulate this understanding clearly and concisely in written form.

Method of evaluation: written evaluation by the instructor.

Hobbies and Other Pastimes: Student Excerpts

PLAYING THE GUITAR

. . . During my third year in high school, I found out about a place where I could take lessons, so I signed up and bought a guitar the next week. I was so excited that I was actually going to learn how to manipulate those six strings so that music would result. . . . I quit my lessons when I went to college, and subsequently I didn't practice very much. . . . Two years later, I began lessons again. This time I learned how to play classical music; I really enjoyed playing because the music was new, a challenge, and very beautiful. . . . Lately, I've played once or twice a week because I've been busy with school. . . . I usually play at night as a break between my studies or just before I go to bed. . . . I really like to play because I can be expressive. . . .

PHOTOGRAPHY

. . . I started photography when I was fourteen. I joined the photography club at my high school. There we were taught the principles of using a 35-mm single reflex camera, and black and white film development. My mother gave me a camera to practice with, and I loved it. Every afternoon, I would take a walk and take pictures of the shadows created by sunlight streaming through the trees. . . . Throughout college I lived with it (my camera), taking pictures of my friends, at parties, at sports events, and around campus. Each event comes to life as I look back through my albums and these memories fill me with warmth and happiness. Though my friends may be miles away, they are always with me in my pictures. . . .

EXPLORING

. . . As a child living in the "house in the orchard," I wandered orchard lanes, dusty drives, and trails through the woods, I looked for gifts, clues, and landmarks. Gifts appeared in the form of ripe Rome Beauty apples, sheaves of wheat, sassafras roots, and the rarest glimpse of a fawn with her mother. I carefully deciphered the clues provided by broken twigs and animal tracks in accordance with my current imagined adventure. The landmarks of my imagination led me past witches' cottages, Indian encampments, animal homes, and dangerous abysses. . . . In those scrubby woods and fields my self was found and nurtured and grew. There I lived parts of my self and emotions that needed to be hidden elsewhere. . . . In the last twelve years my life has somewhat limited my rambling walks, but I still find ways to include long walks in my life. . . . Weekends there are walks in the park. . . .

CROSSWORD PUZZLES

The way in which a puzzle doer approaches a puzzle is another area of versatility, individuality, creativity—all the ups . . . all the downs . . . top left corner first . . . a random onslaught . . . odd numbers . . . last questions first . . . does one complete the puzzle all at once? pick it up whenever? do as much as possible and throw it away? whenever in lecture class? one question a minute?. . . . A crossword puzzle can be done by one's self (BEWARE: some puzzle doers are very possessive about their puzzles!) and for those more socially inclined, with the help of others, be it solicited or voluntary. . . .

CROSS-COUNTRY SKIING

. . . My interest in cross-country skiing began with a cross-country skiing clinic sponsored by the Outing Club at my high school. . . . Over the years I became addicted to the rhythmic, graceful movement of the sport as well as the silent beauty of the winter wilderness. To glide silently through a forest blanketed in a fresh powder snowfall is my idea of heaven. . . . The silence and the solitude gave me the opportunity to be contemplative and introspective. . . . However, I could choose to push thoughts from my mind by concentrating on the synchronous movement of my arms and legs and drinking in the beauty around me. . . . Obviously, I cannot engage in this sport as much in the city, and this is very frustrating to me. . . . I have had people stop me in the parks to ask what I was doing, as if they've never seen anything like it. . . .

CARING FOR PLANTS

Household plant care appeals to me partially due to my love of nature and the outdoors and also because of the feeling of a sense of accomplishment when the plants I care for have grown and look green and healthy. . . . In transplanting, it is gratifying to give renewed life to a previously droopy, lifeless plant. . . . I also enjoy the creativity plants allow when I can personally choose a decorative ceramic pot in which to place it. . . .

BICYCLING

. . . I rode places with friends in my elementary school years. In high school I rode alone, disdaining over-reliance on the gasoline engine. . . . [Years later,] I bought a 10-speed Peugeot from a friend . . . the Peugeot gave me great mobility as I moved further from town and work. In the summer of 1979, I measured my development by my gradual but eventual conquering (biking to the top and over without demounting) Lake Hill on my way home. I'd also use my bike for errands, for visiting, for fun. Gear or groceries were carried in a homemade backpack. Sometimes I'd go to Mount Tremper and stop at the State Park for a refreshing swim on the way home. . . . Now, my bike stands in the hall, a reminder of the life I miss. I want the bike here. I want to have leisure to ride it in areas I feel are safe and pleasurable, but schoolwork is very demanding. . . .

Summary Notes

These excerpts from student's descriptions of their hobbies and pastimes illustrate the following about activities as natural human phenomena:

The activity in relation to the individual's developmental stage	Guitar playing Photography Cross-country skiing Bicycling
The activity as a means of satisfying specific needs	All
The activity in a family context	Photography
The activity and friends	Photography Bicycle riding
The activity as a means of self-expression	Guitar playing Exploring Cross-country skiing Caring for plants
Idiosyncratic style	Exploring Doing crossword puzzles Caring for plants
Meaning of objects	Exploring Cross-country skiing Caring for plants Bicycling
Relation to other activities done concurrently or in sequence	Guitar playing Bicycling
Competence	All
Commonalities with others—other people to whom hobby might appeal	Crossword puzzles

ASSIGNMENT 6: THE ACTIVITIES GENOGRAM

A. Construct a genogram according to the following instructions, for three or more generations, in as much detail as you are able to provide:

1. Each family member is represented by a box or circle according to his or her gender. First names are indicated.

Male   Female

2. For a person who is dead, an X is placed inside the figure. Birth and death dates are indicated to the left and right above the figure.

3. Figures representing family members are connected by lines that indicate their biological and legal relationships:
   a. Marriage is depicted by lines down and across; m. followed by date indicates when couple was married.
      Example:

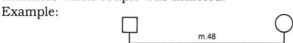

   b. Separation or divorce is indicated by one slash for separation and two for divorce.
      Example:

   c. A couple living together but not legally married is illustrated like marriage, but with a dotted line instead. The date when they met or started living together is noted.
      Example:

4. If a couple has children, then each child's figure hangs down from the line that connects the couple. Children are drawn left to right going from the oldest to youngest.
   Example:

B. Using the genogram and your activities configuration as points of departure, select at least two activities from your configuration that have been woven into your family history. Trace their development, focusing both on activities that you have learned from others and on those shared with others. In your discussion, relate your findings to what you have learned about activities as natural human phenomena.

Note: Because of its personal nature, handing in the genogram is optional. If you choose to, it is suggested that you use symbols to illustrate the activities that are woven into the family system.

Genogram is defined as "a format for drawing a family tree that records information about family members and their relationships over at least three generations" [58]. This assignment focuses on the ways in which activities patterns are influenced by family relationships throughout the life span.

Virtually all people have been influenced to some extent by family members or guardians in their doing of everyday activities. To examine this phenomenon, a tool can be borrowed from the field of family therapy—the genogram, which is a graphic representation of the family system. For the purpose of this assignment, a simplified version of the genogram is used to explore how family influences have contributed components of one's idiosyncratic activities configuration.

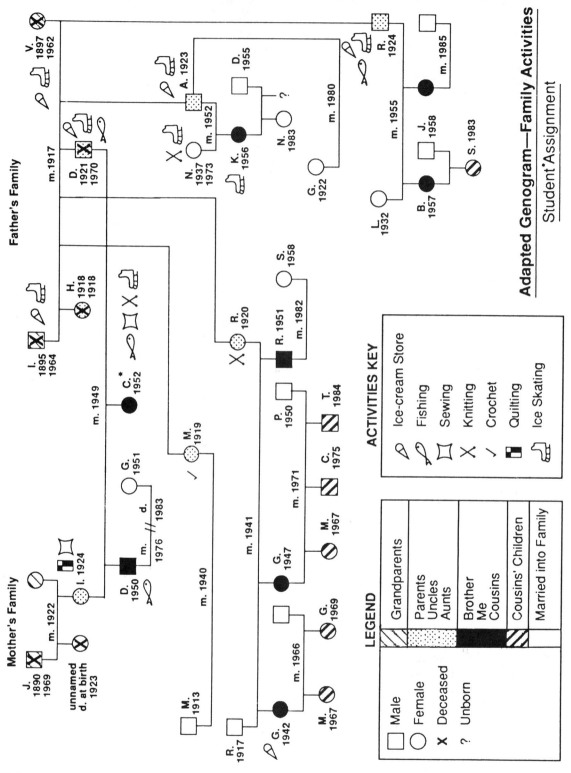

Adapted Genogram—Family Activities

Student Assignment

Thus, this assignment focuses on the family as a source of sociocultural influences in the student's activities life. Once again, Jerome Bruner's [15] notion of "reciprocity" is illustrated—that is, the "deep human need to respond to others and operate jointly with them towards an objective"—this time, within the specific context of the family.

Summary

Assignment as means of: exploring the ways in which one's family has provided opportunities to acquire and share activities skills; developing an awareness of the ways in which family influences impact on one's activities configuration.

End products: the ability to construct and interpret an activities-centered genogram; knowledge about the impact of the family on the doing of everyday activities.

Criteria for evaluation: understanding of the relationships between activities and the family, and ability to describe them in written form.

Method of evaluation: written evaluation by the instructor.

An Activities Genogram: Some Excerpts

. . . As a young child growing up in a small town, I was impressed by the fact that I was part of a very close extended family. Many of my friends had few of their relatives living nearby, but all of mine lived in my hometown or within an eight-mile radius of it. . . . My paternal grandparents owned a small ice-cream store and grocery, and it was a focal point of our family. My father, and sometimes his two brothers, helped out in the evenings dipping ice-cream cones, and my oldest cousin worked there during the summers when she was in high school. I eagerly anticipated my turn behind the ice-cream counter, but both of my grandparents died before I was old enough to work there, and the business was dissolved in the early 1960s. . . .

. . . My father's youngest brother and his wife built a house in the country just outside of our town, and their home became the field of action for many family get-togethers. They had a large basement where we gathered for holiday dinners and also a huge yard for picnics and outdoor games and sports. A special attraction was a large pond just below the hill from their house. . . . In the summers we would swim and row around in the boat that was docked there. My father and Uncle Rob would fish from the shore, and both my brother and I learned to fly-cast under my father's tutelage. . . . But probably the best time of year to meet at the pond was in the winter. We would anxiously wait for the weeks of cold weather to make it sufficiently frozen and safe to approach. The day that the snowplow could drive across and clear the ice was a day to rejoice. It was time for ice skating! This was probably the only activity that my whole family joined in together—men, women, and children alike. It was an implicit rule in the family that we would all get together at my aunt and uncle's place on Sundays for ice skating parties. We would skate the whole afternoon until dusk, when it was almost impossible to see any longer (there were no street lights out there at the time). After a day of good physical activity, we trekked back to the house with big appetites and had an impromptu dinner put together by the aunts who had contributed their specialties. . . .

As I approached my teen years and all my older cousins went off to college, the service, or to get married, the family became somewhat diffuse. Gone were the family dinners and weekly visits. . . . It was during this time that I began to concentrate on sewing, knitting, and other handcrafts and began to develop my own individual pursuits. I also became more aligned with my aunts than with my cousins, a point that I have noticed has persisted to this day. . . . My mother, my four aunts, and my great aunt decided to start a "sewing club," complete with weekly dues that would go toward financing some little trips in the summer. As I was seriously involved in perfecting my own needle arts, I joined their group for the weekly meetings, which rotated from house to house. This was strictly a women's activity, with my uncles nowhere in sight! . . . My Aunt Fran had never done any type of handwork, but she learned to knit through the instructions of my Aunt Sally and me. I had my own unique way of knitting, which was sort of a combination of the "European" technique taught to me by my mother and the method shown in most American knitting instruction books. . . . My particular contribution to the group, was to help them to read and interpret the patterns that they were working on. This was a special knack that I had, being rather adept at figuring out directions and problem-solving. Several of these women also got together one winter for quilting bees, working on each other's quilts in my Aunt Mary's basement on a quilting frame built by my father. Today, my mother is the only one who has continued to quilt. . . . As the family has matured, some moved away from the area, and we have grown further apart. These group activities have ceased to exist, and the bonds that once held the family together remain bittersweet memories of my past. It is a sad, but often inevitable fact, that you really "can't go home again."

ASSIGNMENT 7: A WORK ANALYSIS

    A. Do one of the following:
        1. Interview a working person whose sociocultural background is different from your own, and construct an activities pattern that reflects his or her typical workweek. Using the guidelines that appear in Appendix H, conduct a work-centered interview.
        2. Describe the characteristics of one of your own work experiences that has lasted for at least one year. Complete an activities pattern based on what you recall of your life-style at that time.
    B. From the information that you have gathered about a work experience of your own or someone else, write a paper that focuses on the following:
        1. Field of action (detailed)
        2. Time dimensions—duration and frequency of specific activities
        3. Routines and discontinuities
        4. Interpersonal relationships
        5. Meaning and relevance
        6. Rewards and sanctions
        7. Skills and levels of function required
    C. Prepare a 10- to 15-minute presentation of your work analysis, to be presented to other class members.

This assignment is designed to serve as a transition from the study of activities as natural human phenomena (the first part) to the second part, which is devoted to the investigation of the therapeutic potential of activities. As in clinical assessment, the assignment consists of a guided exploration of the individual in relation to his or her involvement in activities, in this case specifically those relating to work. The outline provided focuses both on a description of the work itself (i.e., skills required, field of action, routines and discontinuities, interpersonal relationshps, time dimensions), and the individual's reactions to the work experience (i.e., meaning and relevance, rewards and sanctions). The use of the activities pattern, which by its nature encompasses both work and non-work activities, ensures that work is viewed within the context of other kinds of activities that are part of everyday living.

The work interview represents one of the many means that are available for eliciting the qualitative and quantitative information that transforms an individual's activities pattern into a configuration (see pp. 16–17). In the second part, the student will have additional opportunities to investigate the everyday activities of various individuals, both without and with clinical dysfunctions. Clearly, an approach similar to the work analysis that focuses in particular detail on a specific aspect of everyday living can eventually be used in clinical practice to elicit information about any particular category of activities that requires in-depth examination.

The presentation of the work analysis to the class provides the student with an introduction to verbal reporting to develop skills that will ultimately be needed for collaboration with other professionals. The student is required to select and organize pertinent data that can result in an effective, yet concise description of an individual's life-style. There will be further opportunities to practice and improve on these skills in other assignments to follow.

Summary

Assignment as means of: developing interviewing skills; learning to develop an activities configuration from a pattern, with a specific emphasis on one activities category; learning to organize, document, and present information about an individual's activities configuration.

End products: knowledge about a variety of jobs and their characteristics, acquired through class presentations.

Criteria for evaluation: degree to which the paper and presentation accurately describe the individual and his/her work, covering the characteristics outlined.

Method of evaluation: written evaluation by the instructor, and informal feedback from peers.

Work Analyses: Student Excerpts

FROM "WORK IN A PRINTSHOP"*

FIELD OF ACTION

. . . The darkroom itself is a fascinating place. When I started this job, the previous cameraperson had already light-proofed the room with light-stripping around the doors and the camera frame. The walls and ceiling were painted black, and the cement floor was painted gray to absorb light. Red lights were placed in strategic places over the developer tray, the inspection table, and the camera back. When one works under red light, everything red appears white. One's eyes grow accustomed to working in the eerie, reddish darkness, and I used to feel like a mole when I emerged into sunlight at mid-day. I could hear the rhythmic chugging of the presses through the darkroom wall. It is axiomatic that a pressperson has radios going all the time, and if I heard that they were tuned into a song that was popular to all of us, I would tune mine into the same station. There were outbreaks of craziness when all the production workers had their radios going full volume, playing and singing the same song. Normally, however, the darkroom was a quiet place, insulated from the full racket of presses, cutters, folders, and the cursing of machine operators in the next room.

* From the paper of Susanna Cobb, Columbia University, class of '85.

Other than the radio, there were no personal amenities in the room. Everything in the room served the purpose of making negatives; the stacks of film and screens on shelves built over the film—cutting table, the drying lines, the inspection table, and, of course, the gigantic copy camera. The elongated sink was set up along one wall, with shelves for the five-gallon bottles of chemicals above. One of my strongest memories is that of the smell of the chemicals just mixed in the tray. The smell of the mixture would get more acid as the chemicals were "used up" in the developing process, and some days the smell would stay with me for several hours after I left work.

The room was free of clutter in order to minimize confusion when working in the dark. I kept the room very clean, since the slightest speck of dust could ruin a negative. . . .

TIME DIMENSIONS

. . . Since the first step in the production of an offset printing job is making the negatives, it is natural that the bulk of the camera work is done in the morning. This fitted in well with my needs as a part-time working mother. I wanted to be at home in the afternoon with my children after they had been in nursery school. I punched in at the timeclock by 9:30 each morning and punched out at 1:00 P.M. I rarely took the state-mandated break because of pressures to get the work done in the allotted time and pressures to get home to my children. . . .

. . . There is a premium on getting the most done in the least amount of time, and I took great pride in being able to get as much done in my three and a half hours as I figured it would have taken a full-time worker to do in five hours. For instance, I learned how to "gang" halftones in the developer tray, doing up to three at a time and still producing high-quality work. . . .

. . . There are "fast" and "slow" seasons in the printing business. During the slow months, like January and April, I was often asked to cut back my hours. Christmas is a fast season in every print shop, and during that period and other rush periods, there is a premium on keeping the work flowing evenly to the stripper, who then keeps the presses humming at a steady pace. . . .

. . . Working in the dark for long periods of time in the daytime can distort one's sense of time. I used to concentrate on the one-, two-, or three-minute intervals for exposure and development, then fail to realize when twenty minutes had passed. I learned to compensate for the lack of cues from changes in natural lighting by internalizing how long certain routines took. A radio helped, and I almost always had one going.

FROM "A 'PICKLES' EXPERIENCE—WORKING IN A DELICATESSEN"*

ROUTINES AND DISCONTINUITIES

. . . We opened at 7:00 A.M. and closed at 7:00 P.M. every day of the year with the exception of Thanksgiving (closed at 2:00 P.M), Christmas Eve (closed at 4:30 P.M.), and Christmas Day. I regularly worked Monday through Thursday, from 7:30 A.M. to 7:30 P.M. with an hour lunch break after the "rush," beginning between 2:00 and 2:30 P.M. Due to illness or an extra heavy work load (e.g., 60 sandwiches to be picked up at 10:00 A.M.), my schedule was subject to change; flexibility was very important. Work schedules were individually tailored, and by giving ample warning and a tentative substitute, changes could be made within reason. . . .

. . . Each day there was a general routine as to what had to be done, but when and how much varied—a supply and demand situation. Morning business involved many pots of coffee and the sale of breakfast items—muffins, bagels, croissants, and perhaps a few sandwiches for school or work lunchboxes. After the breakfast and coffee-break rushes, there

* From the paper of Kate Jacob McKay, Columbia University, class of '87.

was a slight lull in customer population, and we prepared for the lunch rush. "Prep to the max" is the Pickles' motto. Throughout the day, things are done for the day at hand as well as preparing ahead. In the morning, the day's immediate "to do's" were attended to—the final touches (e.g., making and garnishing salads and wrapping meats for display), as well as the more time-consuming and preparatory work (e.g., cooking and prepping soups, picking and chopping chicken, slicing onions or cabbage for cole slaw to be). Afternoons were devoted to restocking, clean-up (general and specific), and what had yet to be crossed off the "to do" list, and adding to the next day's "to do's." (The "to do" list was a perpetual process.)

On an average, the busiest times of the day were 7:15 to 8:45 A.M. and 11:30 A.M. to 2:00 P.M., with a steady flow of customers as well as "to do's." Summer weekends were particularly busy; since the deli is located in a town on the water, people would get off their boats and walk right into town. . . .

INTERPERSONAL RELATIONSHIPS

. . . In general, there was a good rapport between co-workers and with the customers. We (workers) got along with one another and worked together well, which was very important in working long and constantly busy days. We frequently went out together, but also respected the need to be and do on our own. Most of our customers were regulars (and characters at that), and for the most part, they were a pleasure to wait on. Some, however, left a lot to be desired. . . .

FROM "A JOB IN AN AWNING COMPANY"*

MEANING AND RELEVANCE

. . . This job was very important to me because it taught me not only the skills I acquired on the job, but immensely more about myself. I learned I needed a job that had more contact with people and that allowed me to be more creative in solving problems. It also helped me to clarify my values about balancing the need for money with the need for leisure time. It was through a co-worker at this job that I first heard about job opportunities at the psychiatric hospital where I am now employed. I reached a point where it was difficult to get out of bed in the morning to go to work, and this unhappiness prompted me to return to school for my degree in special education. I realize now I was depressed because I had no goals and was not fulfilling my potential. The job gave me the ability to understand the inactivity of the depressed who must meet a similar struggle when facing the prospect of getting out of bed to face another day. . . .

REWARDS AND SANCTIONS

. . . Because I worked a great deal of overtime, the money was quite good. I considered the opportunity to drive around the Connecticut countryside ablaze with autumn color an intrinsic reward of the job, as was seeing how the very wealthy lived. Facing a layoff in winter was the biggest sanction. It was demoralizing to stand in unemployment lines, although now I feel richer for the experience. I can empathize with the unemployed and poor, since I have experienced the blows to self-esteem being "on the dole" entails. . . .

* From the paper of Peter Ruopp, Columbia University, class of '89.

FROM "A JOB AS A FOOD SERVICES WORKER"*
SKILLS AND LEVELS OF FUNCTION REQUIRED

. . . The person requires different skills depending on the particular job. A server must basically have the cognitive ability to understand what a customer wants, memory to retrieve the order, fine and gross motor ability to gather an order, visual ability to fill the order, and interpersonal skills to interact with customers. A dishroom worker, a holder of a more highly skilled job, must have an understanding of how to operate the dishwashing machine, manual dexterity, adequate vision, and interpersonal skills if working with others. A checker must have counting ability, cash register skills, fine and gross motor skills, and adequate vision. A salad bar runner must have physical strength and endurance, ability to recognize what food item is needed or has run out, ability to prepare food, good vision, and an intact memory. A crew chief must have leadership qualities, clear verbal skills, knowledge of all service jobs, good vision, and good interpersonal skills. . . .

ASSIGNMENT 8: THE RESOURCE BOOK

> Construct a resource book that represents activities as natural human phenomena. It can contain information about any or all of the activities to which you were exposed during the course, in addition to any others that you choose to add. Together, they should represent a broad view of human activities, including all categories of everyday living. In addition, it is expected that the resource book will include information relating to the meaning and relevance of activities to groups and individuals (e.g., current attitudes, value of end products and processes, popularity, community interest). Resources and references may also be included if you wish.

Throughout this learning experience, students are exposed to dozens of activities from many aspects of living, some of which are familiar and some of which are new. As students become enlightened about activities as natural human phenomena, they develop insight into the relationship between activities and health. This assignment is designed to help the students integrate what has been learned so far—to reflect on and depict in the form of a resource book their understanding of the elements that together constitute healthy patterns of everyday living. Once again, integration is encouraged through doing—the students choose and make use of tools and materials that will best represent their understanding of activities as natural human phenomena. Later on, the resource book can be used as a clinical tool, as both a vehicle for discussion with clients about activities and health and a resource for activities ideas.

* From the paper of Rhonda Fisher, Columbia University, class of '87.

Summary

Assignment as means of: integrating learning thus far, developing the ability to represent activities as natural human phenomena.

End product: resource book representing activities as natural human phenomena, which can later be used as clinical tool.

Criteria for evaluation: the degree to which the resource book is representative of activities as natural human phenomena, depicting a variety of activities from all categories of everyday living; durability; neatness; creativity; overall impression.

Method of evaluation: written evaluation by the instructor.

CHAPTER 9

Activities as Natural Human Phenomena: Therapeutic Potential

Approaching the Study of Therapeutic Potential

As mentioned previously, it is suggested that you review the objectives listed in Chapter 7 under The Course Objectives before reading further about the methods that are used to achieve them. As you can see, this phase of the educational process is designed so that the student is guided through a transition from the examination of activities as natural human phenomena to the study of the potential of activities as therapeutic means toward a state of *activities health*. The pivotal point from which the student begins to look toward the therapeutic application of knowledge about everyday human activities is *activities health*, defined and described in Chapter 3.

The transition from the study of activities as natural human phenomena to the exploration of the therapeutic potential of activities presents an educational challenge, since it has frequently been observed that once the subject of clinical application is introduced, students tend to direct their efforts toward the reduction of symptoms. Our aim is to help the students develop a professional identity in which they conceptualize the role of occupational therapy in terms of the enhancement of the patient/client's quality of life, rather than simply the amelioration of symptoms, goals more appropriately adopted by other health care providers.

How can the therapeutic use of activities be studied in the framework of *activities health*? Given the student's propensity to adopt an almost exclusive focus on pathology at this critical educational juncture, it is important to design assignments in such a way that the emphasis on *health* is maintained. *When using an activities health approach, clinical conditions are considered within the context of an assessment of the obstacles that preclude the individual's attainment of activities health.* Educational methods are selected that promote the acquisition of skills that enable the occupational therapist to *assess* an individual's state of *activities health,* to *plan treatment* aimed at achieving a greater degree of *activities health,* to *implement* the plan, and to *assess the effectiveness* of interventions from an *activities health* perspective.

DIFFERENCES BETWEEN STUDYING PRODUCTS AND PROCESSES AND THERAPEUTIC POTENTIAL

Before the methods that are used to promote the attainment of the course objectives are discussed, a few distinct differences in format and structure between the first part, Products and Processes, and the second part, Therapeutic Potential, require specific mention. First, there is a transition from the use of an explicit contract between student and instructor in Products and Processes (see Chapter 7, The Learning Contract) to the use of an implicit contract between these parties in Therapeutic Potential. You will recall that the purpose of the written contract is to underscore the responsibility of both student and instructor for shaping learning experiences and to teach negotiation skills that are necessary in a number of different ways in the course of clinical practice and professional development in general. It is expected that by the beginning of the second part, the student will have internalized this sense of responsibility and so be able to use negotiation skills in a less formal manner. Therefore, while negotiation is clearly encouraged throughout the educational sequence, it is expected to occur more naturally and spontaneously as the coursework progresses.

A second significant difference is the incorporation of a "studio" approach to the learning of arts and crafts, which represents a kind of setting available in most communities for the learning of new activities. In a mini-course devoted to an introduction to woodworking (or other art or craft activity if deemed more valuable), students are exposed to the process of learning activities skills from an individual outside of the field of occupational therapy with a specific area of expertise. A "studio" situation is thus introduced as one of many potential resources for learning new activities. Such learning experiences are also examined from a perspective of *activities health;* whether the instructor is one who engages in woodworking as an occupation or a hobby, he or she represents a member of society for whom woodworking has become part of everyday living. In an effort to help students integrate this kind of "studio" arts and crafts learning with the practice of occupational therapy, mechanisms for linking the doing component with clinical reasoning skills are provided. Students are asked to analyze their own activities experience with woodworking (see Assignment 2b) and also to explore how woodworking skills can be used for the design and construction of adaptive equipment. At the same time, each student personally participates in an activity-sharing experience that can later be replicated in clinical practice—the collaboration between an occupational therapist and activity expert from outside the field—a kind of partnership that can generate exciting therapeutic possibilities.

THE LEARNING METHODS

The skills that underlie the use of activities as therapeutic means for the purpose of helping the individual to attain a greater degree of *activities health* fall within the domain of clinical reasoning. These skills are learned through the use of assignments designed to guide the student through a problem-solving process that underlies the assessment of patient/client needs, selection and structuring of therapeutic activities, and reassessment of *activities health* at appropriate intervals.

In keeping with the principles regarding the learning sequence (see pp. 94–95), students begin this phase of learning by examining their own *activities health*. Through self-assessment, the definition of *activities health* can be understood and integrated, thus preparing the students for their introduction to the process of clinical reasoning within a framework of *activities health*.

Given the nature of the objectives, the exploration of the therapeutic potential of activities lends itself to the use of three sets of methods described below, each of which plays a part in occupational therapy practice:

1. *Cognitively-oriented methods:* Since clinical reasoning is by definition a largely cognitive process, assignments are developed that require the student to *gather and sort information, engage in problem-solving, integrate knowledge,* and *analyze information,* first in relation to oneself, and then in relation to others— first without and then with clinically labeled dysfunction. Students are also required to participate in *planning* activity programs, as well as in *group problem-solving* aimed at the development of skills needed for collaboration with colleagues in clinical practice.

2. *Experiential methods:* In addition to the cognitively-based methods described above, the process of learning through *engagement* in activities continues. In keeping with the need to maintain a constant, conscious connection between activities as natural human phenomena and activities as therapeutic tools, experiences that involve *doing* and *reflecting* continue throughout the study of therapeutic potential, thereby reinforcing the value of learning through doing, as well as increasing the student's familiarity with a wide range of activities from all aspects of everyday living.

   The use of *videotaping* as an educational tool is of particular value and is therefore deserving of specific mention. Videotaping can greatly enhance the process of activities analysis and provides a number of opportunities for self-assessment and exchanges of feedback among students and instructor.

3. *Methods promoting integration and application of knowledge:* Learning experiences are designed to help the student "put it all together"—that is, to promote the integration of a varied body of knowledge and skills and to apply understanding of the process to assess patient/client needs, plan and carry out treatment, and reassess the client's functional status, all within a framework of *activities health*. Through the use of *simulated* and *actual clinical situations*, the students are required to make use of understanding of and appreciation for activities as natural human phenomena, understanding of the concept of *activities health*, knowledge of human physiological and psychological

systems and the problems that affect them, activities repertoire, understanding of the clinical reasoning process, and knowledge of theories and techniques for managing dysfunction.

In summary, it is evident that while there are many similarities in the methods used in both parts of this learning experience, there are also distinct differences. Clearly, the emphasis on learning through doing involves the methods used in the study of Products and Processes: *doing, reflecting, observing, sharing, writing, reading,* and *negotiating.* In addition, the study of therapeutic potential also calls for opportunities to *try out* and *practice* the *problem-solving* skills that are required for *clinical reasoning* and the collaborative skills needed for building effective working relationships with colleagues. Through the use of case examples—both simulated and real—the *integration* of knowledge and skills about activities and their therapeutic potential is facilitated. All of these methods are ultimately directed toward the development of the student's understanding of and appreciation for the central importance of activities of everyday living in the practice of occupational therapy and the acquisition of knowledge and skills needed for the use of clinical strategies incorporating activities as means and ends.

The Assignments

The assignments that follow make use of various combinations of methods described above. Whenever possible, they are sequenced in the order in which they actually occur in the clinical reasoning process. In this section, examples of assignments are presented and discussed. As in the study of products and processes, the description of each assignment is followed by a summary section, containing a description of (1) the *assignment as a means of* achieving specific objectives, (2) the *end products* (i.e., products, skills, and knowledge that result), (3) the *criteria for evaluation,* and (4) the *method of evaluation.* Examples of student work also appear for those assignments that call for illustration.

Some of the assignments described in this section can be done in laboratory sessions; others are more effectively done outside of class. Each is designed to focus on the following steps of clinical problem-solving all within a framework of *activities health,* as represented in Figure 9-1.

1. *Activities health* assessment, culminating in the determination of needs
2. Activities analysis
3. Identification of resources and constraints in the clinical setting
4. Identification of occupational therapy goals
5. Selection of activities as therapeutic means toward *activities health*
6. Selection of relevant theories and strategies for managing dysfunction
7. Structuring of activities experiences
8. Discharge planning
9. *Activities health* reassessment (at appropriate intervals)

Although these steps are listed in a rather neat sequence, it is important to note that in clinical practice, it is frequently necessary to alter the order in which they

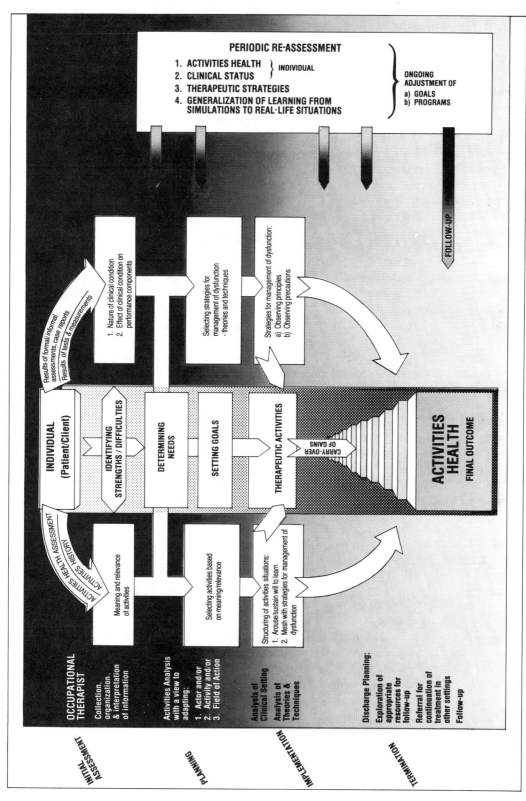

FIGURE 9-1. An *activities health* approach to clinical problem-solving.

occur. The clinician may need to backtrack and repeat previous steps in certain situations; although less frequent, there are also occasions in which steps are skipped or otherwise differently ordered. In particular, it is crucial that reassessment is perceived as an ongoing process that occurs at appropriate intervals throughout the entire clinical reasoning sequence (see Figure 9-1). As long as the students are made aware that clinical practice will ultimately require flexibility in problem-solving, the use of an explicitly outlined, step-by-step sequence for purposes of education helps build a foundation for understanding and appreciating clinical reasoning as a logical, systematic process. (See pp. 201–203 for further discussion.)

STEP 1: ACTIVITIES HEALTH ASSESSMENT

The assessment of *activities health* is the starting point for the clinical reasoning process. Given its degree of complexity, an introduction to *activities health* assessment is best accomplished in a gradual, stepwise manner. In keeping with the principles regarding the learning sequence (see pp. 94–95), the assessment of *activities health* begins with the student's self-assessment. This is followed by the assessment of an individual who seems to be in a state of *activities health* despite a clinically labeled condition. Then the same process is used with case examples and/or actual patients/clients that require the consideration of an additional factor—activities dysfunction resulting from a clinical condition.

Clinical assessment is approached through the use of the *Activities Health Assessment* (see Chapter 6), in combination with assessment methods used to examine functional performance and other available information. Regardless of the specific sources from which information is gathered about the patient/client's everyday functioning, a central principle regarding the *interpretation* of such information must be highlighted and reinforced: *The clinical condition is relevant to activities health assessment only insofar as it interferes with the individual's ability to engage in everyday activities in ways that are comfortable, satisfying, and socioculturally acceptable.*

Assignment 1a: The Activities Health Self-Assessment*

A. Using the guidelines that appear in the first four parts of Appendix A, complete an idiosyncratic activities configuration for yourself.
B. Use the 9-point scale below to indicate your degree of overall satisfaction, comfort, and feeling of "fitting in" with your sociocultural group(s) (see Chapter 3, Indicators of Activities Health, for definitions of each):
   1. Degree of overall satisfaction (as in Chapter 3 under Satisfaction):

* This assignment is a brief adaptation of the Idiosyncratic Activities Configuration (Appendix A), abbreviated because of time considerations. A more expanded version is preferable if time permits.

2. Degree of overall comfort (as defined in Chapter 3 under Comfort):

3. Overall feeling of "fitting in" (or appropriateness) with your sociocultural group(s) (as defined in Chapter 3 under Appropriateness):

C. What changes in your present activities configuration, if any, would be needed for you to attain an ideal state of activities health?
D. Based on the above information, estimate your own degree of activities health, based on the criteria discussed in Chapter 3.

We return to the *idosyncratic activities configuration*, first introduced at the very beginning of this educational process (see Chapter 8, Assignment 1, The Configuration). This time, the activities configuration is used as the point of departure from which students approach an assessment of *activities health*. Through a more structured exploration of the idiosyncratic activities configuration, students are able to discover the kinds of information that an assessment of *activities health* yields, while also personally experiencing the feelings and thoughts that are elicited. The self-assessment, in which students are asked a series of questions designed to assess their own state of *activities health*, provides a starting point from which qualitative statements about the idiosyncratic activities configuration can be made, which is expanded on in Assignments 1b through 1d.

The student's *activities health* self-assessment is followed by a discussion with other class members. Through sharing both satisfactions and dissatisfactions, students are likely to become aware that physical and psychological health do not necessarily result in *activities health*. Thus, the notion of *activities health* as a state of being not necessarily dependent on the presence or absence of a clinical condition is illustrated.

SUMMARY

Assignment as means of: understanding the definition of *activities health*, introducing the *activities health* assessment process; developing an introductory understanding of *activities health* in relationship to the presence or absence of a clinical condition.

End products: student's personal awareness of his or her own relative state of *activities health*; introductory skills in *activities health* assessment.

Criteria for evaluation: degree to which student uses guidelines provided to complete self-assessment.

Method of evaluation: self-assessment, with verbal or written feedback from the instructor.

Assignment 1b: An Activities Health Interview

Invite an individual to class whom you consider to be in a state of activities health despite the presence of a clinical condition. In a seminar forum, discuss with this person the ways in which everyday activities are performed, including in particular the following questions:

A. Which activities do you do by compensating for absent or impaired function?
B. Do you use any adaptive equipment? If so, how do you feel about these devices? Are there any that have been suggested to you that you chose not to use? If so, why not? Have you devised any for yourself?
C. For those activities that you cannot or choose not to do independently, how do you feel about receiving assistance?
D. When interacting with nondisabled people, what do you find to be helpful? not helpful?

The discussion of these and other related issues provides students with a realistic, personal introduction to an individual with clinical symptoms who is nevertheless in a state of *activities health*. When comparing their personal experience to that of the guest interviewee, students frequently become aware that while there are distinct variations in the particular ways in which some activities are performed, there are many commonalities found in what kinds of activities are routine and the needs and purposes they fulfill. Just as the self-assessment leads students to the discovery that the absence of a clinical condition does not necessarily result in *activities health*, they learn that the reverse is also true—*that the presence of symptoms does not necessarily prevent the individual from attaining a state of activities health* (see pp. 35–36 and Chapter 12, From "Coming Home to Die" to Activities Health, for illustrations).

Personal considerations regarding the use of adaptive equipment are also discussed, thus dispelling commonly held preconceptions that such devices possess nearly magical properties. The interview is likely to illustrate the reality that adaptive devices are merely assistive options, which will only be used if they are found to be personally satisfying, comfortable to use, and acceptable within one's sociocultural environment. *Similarly, the myth of complete independence in all activities as the desired end goal for all people can be dispelled, for virtually all people, both with and without diagnosed conditions, choose to seek assistance in some activities due to personal dislike, limitations in ability, or insufficient time and energy to perform them.*

In summary, the interview offers the students a chance to discuss such issues in a relatively nonthreatening environment, not hypothetically, but with the presence of an individual who has encountered activities obstacles on a daily basis. The discussion provides an excellent transition to the next phase of learning about the assessment of *activities health*—the examination of an individual in a state of clinical dysfunction referred for occupational therapy services.

SUMMARY

Assignment as means of: continuing to develop an awareness of *activities health* as a state of being that is not necessarily dependent on the presence or absence of a clinical condition; developing an understanding of factors that influence personal choices regarding the use of adaptive equipment and assistance from others; developing interviewing skills.

End products: knowledge and skills listed above.

Criteria for evaluation: degree to which the discussion addresses pertinent issues.

Method of evaluation: informal assessment by student group.

Assignment 1c: Case Study 1—A Preliminary Exercise in Activities Health Assessment

Choose a case example from Part III that describes a patient/client referred for occupational therapy services.

A. Construct an activities pattern as if you were the patient/client at the time of referral, following steps 1–4 of the procedure in the *Activities Health Assessment* found in Chapter 6. Fill in case details as needed. Using the pattern as a basis and the Interview Guidelines in Chapter 6 as a point of departure, describe the patient/client's current idiosyncratic activities configuration.

B. Based on what you know (or have inferred) about the patient/client's activities history, personal values, preferences, desires, and the norms, expectations, and values related to the sociocultural environment, what would an optimal state of activities health consist of for this individual? Construct a hypothetical activities pattern that reflects the patient/client's activities health ideal.

C. What is the patient/client's clinical condition(s)?

D. Compare the two patterns from steps A and B of this assignment and comment on how the presence of the clinical condition has affected the patient/client's ability to attain his or her optimal state of activities health.

E. What does the patient/client need to achieve activities health?

This case study provides a preliminary introduction to the examination of the *activities health* of an individual with clinical dysfunction; the more formal process of *activities health assessment* in a clinical situation is introduced in the next assignment, only after the student has learned to sort through activities-related and clinical information to answer the preceding set of questions. The current idiosyncratic activities configuration is used once again as a basis for the examination of *activities health*, this time of an individual with clinical dysfunction. Through an exploration of the patient/client's life-style, values, priorities, and preferences, the student is subsequently asked to construct a composite picture of the individual's unique profile of ideal *activities health*. It is only following this determination that the student is guided toward the investigation of the nature of the patient/client's clinical condition, and a subsequent analysis of the ways in which the condition is interfering with the attainment of *activities health*.

This assignment represents the student's first attempt to apply knowledge about activities as natural human phenomena to a clinical situation. The process is introduced in sequential steps for purposes of clarity, focusing on (1) the individual's current idiosyncratic activities configuration, (2) the description of optimal *activities health* as perceived by this particular individual, (3) the description of the clinical condition, and (4) ways in which the clinical condition interferes with the attainment of a state of *activities health*. This assignment culminates in the identification of patient/client needs, which are ultimately used to establish treatment goals in a subsequent step of the clinical reasoning process.

SUMMARY

Assignment as means of: beginning to apply an understanding of *activities health* to a clinical situation; acquiring preliminary clinical reasoning skills and knowledge related to the assessment of *activities health*.

End products: prerequisite skills for using an *activities health* approach to clinical assessment.

Criteria for evaluation: ability to identify optimal *activities health* in terms of the individual patient/client; ability to identify needs in relation to the patient/client's uniquely defined state of *activities health*.

Method of evaluation: written evaluation by the instructor.

Assignment 1d: Case Study 2—Introduction to Activities Health Assesment of the Patient/Client

A. Use the *Activities Health Assessment* found in Chapter 6 with a patient/client in your fieldwork setting. Review your findings along with the results of functional assessments used in the clinical setting and other relevant information. Use all of the available information to make an assessment of the patient/client's degree of activities health. Summarize your conclusions.

B. Identify and list what the patient/client needs to attain activities health.

Note: If it is not possible to use this assessment with an actual patient/client at this point, one of the case studies found in Part III can be used as the basis for this assignment. Students role-play an assessment session, improvising as necessary to fill in where information is not specifically provided.

Once the students have achieved the theoretical foundation needed to use an *activities health* approach to occupational therapy assessment, they are given the opportunity to try out the process in a clinical setting. The assessment of *activities health* requires the use of the *Activities Health Assessment* in conjunction with other evaluation methods that are designed to assess the patient/client's functional performance through techniques designed for this purpose (e.g., measurement of muscle strength and joint range of motion, simulations of selected activities). The use of such methods in combination with the Activities Health Assessment (and any other sources of information about the patient/client's everyday living) enables the occupational therapist to determine the degree to which the clinical problems interfere with the performance of activities that are meaningful to the patient/client and relevant in the context of everyday living.

This assignment completes the student's introduction to the first step of the clinical reasoning process—*activities health assessment*, accomplished through the use of the *Activities Health Assessment* in combination with other evaluation tools and methods. Subsequent opportunities for practice—with patients/clients of a variety of age groups and sociocultural backgrounds and with a diversity of clinical conditions—serve to further develop assessment skills and illustrate the general applicability of an *activities health* approach to occupational therapy assessment.

SUMMARY

Assignment as means of: becoming familiar with the administration of the clinical assessment tool, the *Activities Health Assessment*, and the interpretation of results in combination with other assessment findings.

End products: skills needed for *activities health* assessment.

Criteria for evaluation: ability to use the *Activities Health Assessment* and other evaluation methods for gathering necessary information, interpreting results, and presenting them clearly and concisely.

Method of evaluation: written evaluation by the instructor.

An Activities Health Assessment: Student Example*

Ms. J. was seen by an occupational therapist a few days after admission, and an *Activities Health Assessment* was administered. Ms. J.'s activities configuration revealed that her weekly schedule prior to hospitalization revolved around work and sleep and that she lacked leisure activities (alone or with others). Ms. J. left the spaces for the weeknights and weekend afternoons in the activities schedule blank. This was addressed during the interview, and she responded by saying, "I don't know how to categorize the activities I did during those times. I watch T.V. sometimes with my family, read in my bed after work, and on weekends I go food shopping, to the laundromat, help cook dinner, and occasionally go to the movies with my mother. They aren't important anyway." After discussing why she left the spaces blank on her pattern, she then filled them in. Ms. J. also states that she did not have any friends her age but that she did talk to one or two co-workers at the gift-wrapping counter. Ms. J. revealed that she was afraid to engage in conversations but that she would like to make friends.

After looking at the completed activities pattern, Ms. J. stated that she was not satisfied with how she spent her time and that she would like to do other activities such as sewing, knitting, or baking, rather than spending her time reading or watching T.V. Although Ms. J. was dissatisfied with how she spent her leisure time alone and with others, she was very satisfied with her job as a gift wrapper at the department store. At work, Ms. J. says she is neat and accurate and has excellent manual skills.

Overall, Ms. J. feels that there is an imbalance between her work and leisure time (alone

* Based on brief case history from Part III, p. 265. From paper of Monica Huang, Columbia University, class of '89.

and with others). On the rating scale of 0–9, Ms. J. indicated a "5" for both degree of overall satisfaction and overall comfort. She said, "I had to give both of them a "5" because I am happy and feel comfortable at work, but I am frustrated with how I spend my leisure time. I would like to learn new activities so that I can have opportunities to do different activities, to make some friends, to return to my job, and perhaps to move into community housing in the near future." Ms. J. indicated that she does not "fit in" because she is not allowed to go out in her neighborhood because it is considered to be unsafe.

In summary, the assessment of Ms. J.'s *activities health* reveals that Ms. J. is not in a state of *activities health* and that she would particularly like to improve how she spends her leisure time. For Ms. J. to attain a state of *activities health*, she needs to (1) learn new activities that she can engage in during her leisure time; (2) increase her socialization skills and opportunities for socialization; (3) spend more time outside of the home; (4) return to work; (5) explore the possibility of living independently.

STEP 2: ACTIVITIES ANALYSIS

As we make our way through the clinical problem-solving process, we temporarily shift our attention away from the examination of the individual to the analysis of activities. The ability to analyze activities is essential to the practice of occupational therapy, as it ultimately enables the student to (1) select meaningful and relevant activities to be used as therapeutic means and subsidiary ends toward the overall end goal of *activities health* and (2) structure and modify activities components (including environments) as necessary in order to promote the attainment of greater *activities health*. (See Figure 9-1 for an illustration of how activities analysis is incorporated into clinical reasoning.)

In keeping with the objectives and principles for sequencing, activities are first examined as they occur in the lives of individuals and groups without clinical problems, within their natural fields of action and actual time dimensions. Students learn how to analyze activities from three perspectives, each focused on one of the components present in all activities: (1) the activity itself, (2) the actor, and (3) the field of action. Each approach uses different methods, tools, and sources of information and yields results useful for a specific set of clinical purposes, which will be described in the discussion of subsequent steps of clinical reasoning. However, because these approaches to activities analysis are merely "ad hoc" tools designed to provide structure for a complex process, it is expected that there will be overlap in the information included. (See Chapter 4 [The Field of Action, The Actor, The Activity] for further discussion of activities analysis.)

Note: This set of assignments provides yet another opportunity for the student to explore a range of activities representing various aspects of everyday living. The students can be guided toward the selection of activities not yet examined in other parts of this coursework. While the choices are infinite, it is useful to select some that are routine and even mundane, along with others that are more unusual and individually distinctive.

An Activity-Centered Approach to Activities Analysis

An *activity-centered approach* to activity analysis can be used to describe the activity in terms of its

1. *Basic definition and inherent properties*—that is, the activity in its purest, most basic form. What are the essential properties and characteristics that are *intrinsic* to the activity, always present, in spite of individual differences in the way the activity is performed?
2. *Acquired characteristics*—which come from variations among individuals and groups in the ways they perceive, associate to, and carry out the activity. What are the many ways in which this activity takes place in everyday living? What are some of the fields of action in which the activity takes place? What variations exist among people of different backgrounds and personal styles, in relation to time? tools and materials? meaning and relevance?

Through the use of an activity-centered approach, the occupational therapist develops a comprehensive description of those features of the activity that make it what it is, and the many variations existing among individuals and groups in the way the activity is perceived and carried out. The boundaries of what is considered to be within the range of acceptable performance of the activity (without distorting its nature) are outlined.

This kind of analysis lends itself to working in small groups, so that the experiences of various individuals and groups doing the same activity can be compared. The assignment culminates in each group's presentation of their analysis, in a format of their own design; the use of creativity in planning the presentation is encouraged. This provides students with additional practice in the structuring of activities experiences that promote interest and learning. The use of groups and encouragement of creativity foster positive attitudes toward activities analysis, which is usually regarded as a mechanical and laborious procedure.

ASSIGNMENT 2a: THE CHORE ANALYSIS——AN ACTIVITY-CENTERED APPROACH

Students are divided into small groups and given the following instructions: Choose one chore that is done on a regular basis by all group members. Use your group members as primary sources of normative information and as secondary sources through their own investigations and knowledge of how this activity is done by others. Using the outline found in Appendix I, complete an activity-centered analysis. Present your analysis to other members of your class. Your creativity in presentation is encouraged; remember to modify your field of action to facilitate the learning of your participants!

Summary

Assignment as means of: developing skills needed for an activities-centered approach to activity analysis; developing the ability to convey knowledge about activities, designing the field of action to facilitate learning.

End products: the availability of several activity-centered activities analyses of a variety of chore activities, later to be used to assess a given patient/client's ability to perform the activity in accordance with accepted standards and norms; skills necessary for an activity-centered approach to activity analysis.

Criteria for evaluation: ability to analyze accurately a chore activity from an activity-centered perspective; ability to create a field of action that promotes interest and learning.

Method of evaluation: informal feedback from peers; written evaluation by the instructor.

AN EXAMPLE OF AN ACTIVITY-CENTERED ANALYSIS: TAKING OUT THE GARBAGE*

Martian professor (dressed as an "alien" being from another time and place): "Good morning, class. As you know, my name is Professor Martin Naitram, and I have called a special meeting of the students of Mars, specializing in other world behaviors today, to report on my research and recent return from the planet Earth. My present research is on the humanoids of planet Earth and specific behaviors and activities of theirs that are unusual and interesting to us. Our studies of intergalactic life, specifically those of normal daily activities, use of time passage, and energy, can continue to help us appreciate and understand the process and direction of species-specific evolution, especially those forms of life more primitive than ourselves. Humanoids serve to remind us how life once was, for us too, eons ago, and we may watch them solve their inherent evolutionary problems and issues, such as planetary waste disposal. My specific topic of research, on this interstellar mission, is the activity (translated by experts of language decoding from planet Gamma Gamma K) colloquially called 'taking out the garbage.' Most of you have no familiarity with this human activity since we, long ago, evolved the ability to neutralize and digest all self-created and planetary wastes, with subsequent transformation into pure E use.

"By definition, taking out the garbage translates to the removal of collected, discarded inorganic and organic (in humanoid terms) materials that by them are considered waste items. Examples of such Earth materials are empty food and beverage containers, food, paper, and cleaning wastes; materials are collected together and taken away from the place of residence. We, of course, ingest our corporal needs in tabular form.

"The inherent purpose of their activity is to maintain the aesthetic, spatial, and sanitary qualities of their environment. Unfortunately, humanoids are still land dwellers and suffer, as a result, from attack by other parasitic land dwellers such as vermin and rodents and micro-invaders such as bacteria and odors, a sensorium we lost long ago due to disuse.

"Inherent stages and sequences involve a specific site and container for collection, conscious discarding of undesired materials at this site (at regular and irregular time intervals), a reason for removal of collected materials, and lastly, a physical displacement of the container and unloading of collected materials to a specific area outside of the home dwelling.

"Essential tools and materials include collected waste items, collection container for wastes, and site out of the home area for unloading or release of wastes.

"This activity is connected to many other Earth functions or, as they say, activities and occurs as a result of conscious removal of undesired, undigested materials at specific and nonspecific time intervals. Common antecedents resulting in the production of collected wastes are typically preparation and eating of meals (humans still use a great deal of energy in the manufacturing, preparation, digestion, and excretion of food to release energy for work). Others are cleaning their dwelling and leaving and reentering their dwelling in response to the arrival or departure of guests, as part of a daily responsibility, or in response to a scheduled 'pick up' time, for further processing of removed wastes.

"Common consequences are cleaning and relining collection container and other activities concerning removal of collected wastes, such as burial into the earth's surface, burning, driving a land-based machine to a dumpsite (unload site), or releasing into the sea. Humanoids are still so inefficient in the use of wastes in the manufacturing of potential fuel.

* From presentation of Joan Augustine (class of '89), Robin Reece (class of '89), Darlene Halvorsen Sarchino (class of '90), and Nadia Shivak (class of '89), Columbia University.

"Space requirements can be quite small (by Earth standards). Because they are bound to land and sea, they collect their undigestible, discarded wastes in containers or capsules, as small as the average house robot (in human terms, 1 foot by 8 inches), and remove them from their home dwelling, to a possible location just as small.

"Time factors follow a solar passage of time they call day and night (day is the period of time the sun shines light upon part of the Earth). A light/dark or day/night period is divided into typical units of 24 hours, into smaller units of 1,440 minutes and further into 8,643 seconds. Collection occurs from once a day to 15 times a day, while the actual period for placement to site outside the residence ranges from 3 times a day to once a month and takes anywhere from 30 seconds to 1 hour (i.e., driving land machine to dumpsite). So much variation in individuals seems to occur . . . they are a very sensitive, distractable species indeed! Delays can be due to distraction or lack of motivation and responsibility, the container may break or rip, and the humanoid, who is fragile as a species, may suffer injury and need repair to finish the task.

"In speaking of the process, I observed that it does shift and change in predictability. This may be due to a change in the environment (leave for a period of play humanoids call vacation), the 'home-stay' intervals called weekends, and other varied human activities that alter the collection load or buildup of wastes.

"Force required for this activity must be understood in Earth terms—their gravitational and biological requirements are different. This activity engages the humanoid physique in a range from minimum to moderate output of kinetic or movement energy—specifically human muscular tension/output. Only one of the species, at a minimum, is required for both collection and removal.

"Please look at the viewing panel. You will see I have recorded the information brought back to you. I know most of you have seen this species before, but take note: Notice how large and cumbersome they are, how much water they contain and must carry about. We too once carried it in order to survive, though our gravitational field never was so great, influencing our smaller, lighter, more efficient shapes. I chose three subjects for you—also students who show quite a variety in energy use, emotion content, life-styles, and physique, within a culture from part of the Earth called Western. You may or may not have noticed, but the female of the species seems to predominate in this area of study, curiously enough. I intend to look into that on my next mission."

(Subjects shake and show garbage during narrations.)

"Watch our subjects for sensory input (as humans know it). This activity involves bland colors of gray and brown; many textures such as smooth sensations from papers, plastics, and bags (made from the tree, a large source for respiration), wet, slimy, soggy, sharp, and lumpy; and different weight sensations. Sounds such as those of breaking (i.e., glass), splashing, slapping, spilling, dumping, rustling, and crackling are also heard. Odors for humanoids range from putrid and foul (rotting organic matter) to benign and odorless. Temperatures (much cooler than ours) vary from that of inside the dwelling to the seasonal atmospheric temperature immediately surrounding these life forms.

"Take note of the kinematics." (Subjects silently carry out the motions during the narration). "Essential human motions required are those of stooping, bending, lifting, walking, carrying, releasing, and letting down loads of varying gravitational pulls. Cognitive skills required are simple and concrete, for humanoids of course, involving a minimum level of memory retention, some cortical processing or, as they say; learning, and a fairly high degree of problem-solving and decision-making (the attack of microparasites in their summer season requires an increase in the frequency of this activity). Cognitive motor skills require a degree of visual-limb coordination (eye-hand) to enable accurate discarding of wastes into the container and physical removal of it. I have observed potential that varies among individuals in creative thinking, planning, type, size, color of container, and carriage of container. The peculiar act of 'whistling,' a newly-documented behavior on the Martian horizon, was encountered during this task.

"The second part of my discussion focuses on variations—use their limbs to collect and move discarded, collected wastes out of their dwelling, use of energy, availability of resources (as you know, they still use money to barter with), and composition and amount of discarded materials. Some humanoids are far more advanced and ingenious than others in terms of altering and reusing the energy released from these materials they call waste. You may not know it, but humans still raise their children, for the most part, in separated dwellings, by a single male and female of the species. This leads to idiosyncracies in performing this chore among individuals and groups. Also, there is still, in humans, quite a difference in size and strength between the female and the male, with the female usually caring for the young. This shows a gradual trend toward equalizing.

"Class, again please address your attention to the viewing monitors, where you will meet the human called Robin, a student living in a student group dwelling away from her primary caretakers. Then there are the one called Darlene, a mother of two offspring, in a family unit of four, and the female who calls herself Joan, a single dweller who lives in a multiple housing unit.

"In the dramas that will take place, notice the wonderful variations within the species in the following areas: field of action, frequency and duration, distractability, energy usage, status, male and female roles, family life, time of day, collection site and container style, carrying style, religious implications, personal meaning and relevance, input from past experiences, habits, emotions, and more."

DRAMATIZATION 1

Robin (talking out loud to herself): "I can't believe it's only Monday, and I have a whole week to be in this dorm. I wish the weekend were here again so that I could leave the dorm and have less work to do. I've already made such a mess, and it's only the beginning of the week. I guess I should take the garbage out, but I don't feel like it. I'm ready to get into bed, and I don't feel like going into the hall. I wish my roommate was here, because I'd probably be able to convince her to take the garbage out. Better yet, I wish it was Saturday because on Saturday, for religious reasons, I *can't* take the garbage out, and that way I don't feel guilty about not wanting to. Well, I guess taking the garbage out about once every day or so isn't so bad . . . I guess I'll go out now.

"Well, at least in the dorm I can take the garbage out at any hour of the day or night. At home, the garbage is usually taken out when all activities for the day are completed, usually around 11:00 P.M. Since there are only females in my house, my mom usually takes the garbage, while my sister or I stand near the door just to keep an eye out. At least in the dorm, one person is enough.

"Anyway, I'm glad I took the garbage out. It makes me feel that my room is clean, neat, and orderly. This way, especially in the dorm, hopefully we can avoid the mice and cockroaches that have made their way into other rooms.

"Anyway, now that the garbage is out, and my room is clean, I guess its time for bed . . ."

DRAMATIZATION 2

Darlene (cleaning up coffee spilled by garbage): "Good morning, Joe, there is coffee made if you want some. I spilled coffee grinds all over the floor when I was throwing them in the garbage. At least I like the smell of coffee, unlike some other smells that I'd gag over.

"Speaking of garbage, today is garbage day. I have to remind the kids to bring down the garbage from their rooms. I think Robby has been practicing his basketball shot with his garbage. Last I looked, he had more papers on the floor *around* the can than he did *in* the can. Kate is funny—she thinks we should have a cleaning lady come in, like her friend Susie's family has, but I think it's important for them to have the responsibility. I'm happy with our decision to have them take the main garbage from the kitchen outside to the can, now that they are 10. I'm sure that for a while I'll have to remind them so it goes out with the pickup! Remember what a pain it was when we were in Vermont at your boss's house, and we had to drive the garbage to the dump? Thank goodness, we don't have to do that here.

(Yells upstairs). "Robby, Kate, hurry up, the bus will be here soon. Remember to bring down your garbage from your rooms—it's Tuesday. Wow, Kate, what did you do—leave rotten banana peels in that thing? Whose week is it to take out the garbage? On garbage days I'd like to have it taken out before you go to school so it goes out with the pickup. On the other days you can do it whenever you want—just so you do it before it spills over.

(Phone rings). "Oh, that phone again. Hello, oh hi, Debbie, how are you? Could you hold a minute? Kids, there is the bus—you'd better hustle—have a good day. Hi, oh no, I hear the garbage truck down the street, and the kids didn't remember to take it out. I'm going to have to call you back later." (Runs out with garbage).

"Oh, so many distractions. Well, I do feel better now that I've cleaned the refrigerator and the place is neat and clean.

"Chores like this bring back memories of how my parents made my brother take out the garbage and sweep the stairs—"typical men's work" as they believed—and we girls had to do the dishes. I swore I wouldn't teach my kids to be sexist like that. Boy, do I feel better that times have changed and we are bringing up our kids in a more equal way.

"Well, now that all that's done, I think I'll call Debbie back real quick before I go to work."

DRAMATIZATION 3

(Phone rings). Joan: "Hi, Mona" (while tying up bag of garbage). "Oh, I'm just throwing out another bag of garbage, and it's only Sunday. It's so nice during the week because I eat out so often, and as a result I hardly ever have garbage. I do have to admit, it would be nice to share the chore with someone else, so that the responsibility of remembering to throw it out isn't always left up to me. You're lucky to have a husband to help you take care of it.

"It's funny how my perspective on garbage has shifted throughout my lifetime. When I was a child living in an apartment with a dumbwaiter in the kitchen, taking out the garbage was more of a social affair and an adventure than a drudgery. All the neighbors would open their doors and talk with each other, and from a kid's point of view, some of the items thrown out were great—comic books, toys. Then when I got my first apartment, taking out the garbage had another meaning. I gained so much autonomy; I could use any type of container, throw it out at different times, without having to consult with another person. Unfortunately, after taking care of this chore alone for the past 7 years, it has lost some of its prestige. Most times I view it as a nuisance, I forget it even when I leave it at my front door to pick up on my way out. You'd think that with my ability to run a department at work, I could remember to throw out my own garbage! But I do have to admit, it still makes me feel as if I've accomplished something when I remove from my home all that stuff that I don't want. My home feels and even looks cleaner. Well listen, Mona, I've talked enough about my garbage. Now let me do something about it and throw it away while it is in my head . . ."

An Actor-Centered Approach to Activities Analysis

An *actor-centered approach* to activities analysis provides the occupational therapist with an understanding of one person's unique activities experience. In clinical practice, an actor-centered approach is used in conjunction with the activity-centered approach to determine, (among other things) the degree to which the patient/client's activities performance adheres to sociocultural standards and norms, an individual's idiosyncratic approach to the activity, and the specific performance components that a particular actor uses to carry out the activity.

Once again, students are introduced to this approach through the analysis of an activity in which they are personally engaged; this can be followed by a similar assignment focusing on another individual, first one without dysfunction, and then another with dysfunction. The development of observation skills is promoted, as well as an appreciation for the ways in which idiosyncratic and sociocultural values, preferences, and practices have an impact on the ways activities are performed and their meaning and relevance to each person.

ASSIGNMENT 2b: THE WOODWORKING ANALYSIS

Examine your own performance of the woodworking activity in which you are involved, using the outline found in Appendix J. For section II.B of the outline, your description should be limited to any single step of the activity that you have selected and identified.

Summary

Assignment as means of: developing skills needed for an actor-centered approach to activities analysis; developing the ability to determine the degree to which an individual's activity performance falls within the limits of acceptable standards and norms.

End products: skills necessary for an actor-centered approach to activities analysis.

Criteria for evaluation: accuracy of analysis, and ability to document findings clearly and concisely.

Method of evaluation: written evaluation by the instructor.

WOODWORKING ANALYSES: STUDENT EXCERPTS

Excerpt 1*

HISTORICAL TRENDS/ATTITUDES

. . . Woodworking has traditionally been a male activity. This is illustrated by the vast number of male craftsmen and furniture makers of the 16th, 17th, and 18th centuries. These attitudes are changing. . . .

(INDIVIDUAL) HISTORICAL RELEVANCE

. . . This project was done with leftover pieces of wood from a sculpture I had done. I had previous experience working with tools and a variety of materials. . . .

SYMBOLIC MEANING

. . . I associate this project with my college days when I had access to studio space and tools. Recently, I was in Vermont browsing through craft shops and saw several shelves similar to the pattern I had copied. It makes me long for the time and space I had in college. . . .

IDIOSYNCRATIC PERSONAL STYLE

. . . Although I followed a pattern, I felt each cut was made in my own fashion, as was the sanding. The varnish particularly went on in my painterly style, which was thick! It took forever to dry. . . .

---

* From the paper of Julie Lowy, Columbia University, class of '89.

Excerpt 2 ("Sawing One Side of a Stool Leg)*

MOVEMENTS INVOLVED

Starting position: standing with head and trunk bent, right hand gripping handle of saw, left hand holding piece of clamped wood, right leg weight-bearing and 6 inches behind left leg.

Joints and motions: neck, trunk, hips, knees, left wrist, elbows and fingers flexed. Both ankles dorsiflexed. Right wrist extended and shoulder flexed, adducted and internally rotated. Left shoulder protracted and left arm slightly externally rotated and supinated. Right shoulder alternated flexion and extension; thumb in extension and MCPs and PIPs [metacarpal phalangeal and proximal interphalangeal joints] of four digits in flexion. . . .

PERCEPTUAL MOTOR SKILLS

. . . A degree of eye-hand coordination was needed when sawing to avoid cutting anything other than the correct mark. Hammering also required coordination in holding each leg at the correct angle on the seat and hitting nails, not fingers. Painting required eye-hand coordination to cover the entire surface neatly. The use of the plane was beyond my scope—I was not able to coordinate its use to do what I intended despite several demonstrations and tries to imitate the instructor. Alignment of the legs required the cooperation of eyes and hands . . . .

HISTORICAL TRENDS/ATTITUDES

. . . the Women's Movement helped change the rigid idea that woodworking is solely a male activity. In my all-girls' junior high school there was no wood shop so we made wooden muffins in the school kitchen. My daughters made almost identical wooden name plates (same type of wood and incised letters) in 8th grade. . . . In their high school girls are invited to take "shop," but very few do. . . .

FEELINGS

. . . I associate fine woodworking with a friend who is a self-taught carpenter. Last year I spent time in his shop and wish I'd paid more attention to how he was finishing a box. . . . I also recall going to a Shaker furniture show at the Whitney [Museum] with an aunt I rarely see. Both of us loved the beautiful, simple pieces, and I connect that experience with my warm feelings for her . . . .

PERSONAL STYLE

. . . I thought of not painting the edges of the stool's legs because I liked the look of the sandwiched wood. I like irregularity better than symmetry, and mistakes can look more interesting than perfection. . . .

A Field of Action—Centered Approach to Activities Analysis

In Chapter 4, the elements of the field of action and its impact on activities experiences was discussed. A *field of action—centered approach* to activity analysis is used for the examination of the spatial/locational context in which activities are performed, leading to an understanding of the ways in which the objects (human

* From the paper of Helen Fogarty, Columbia University, class of '89.

and nonhuman) and implicit and explicit rules in the environment influence the performance, as well as the meaning and relevance of activities.

In the first assignment, students observe and analyze an activity connected with the observance of Thanksgiving, a uniquely American observance, focusing specifically on the field of action. This holiday is one familiar to virtually all Americans, but observed in unique ways by various individuals and groups. As the many varied Thanksgiving celebrations are described, students often become more conscious of the overt and subtle ways in which the arrangements of people and objects, and environmental rules (both explicit and implicit), influence the way in which the holiday activity described is carried out, perceived, and experienced. Because many of the students' previous and current celebrations center around their families and other significant people in their lives, discussion often focuses on the rules that govern such traditional activities and rituals and historical changes that affect them over time.

In the second assignment, students are asked to look outside of their own sociocultural group and to observe and analyze a characteristic game, with an emphasis on the field of action. Games provide a rich opportunity for this kind of investigation, as they generally have a set of explicit and implicit rules that govern the playing of the game. The arrangements of people and objects are inextricably woven into the existing rules and, to the outside observer, frequently appear to be choreographed according to a set of established practices. In many cases, the analysis of the field of action points toward elements that are characteristic of the sociocultural group of the participants, much like that observed in the Thanksgiving activity analysis. Students are asked to consider the ways in which the field of action and/or game reflects the values and life-styles of the players.

ASSIGNMENT 2c: AN ANALYSIS OF A THANKSGIVING CELEBRATION

Observe one activity that is part of the Thanksgiving celebration in which you participate, focusing in particular on the field of action. Identify the following elements:

A. The human and nonhuman objects
B. The implicit and explicit rules

What does this field of action tell you about the participants in this traditional holiday activity?

ASSIGNMENT 2d: AN ANALYSIS OF A GAME

Observe a game played by individuals of any age from a sociocultural group other than your own. Identify the components of the field of action as listed in Assignment 2a. In your opinion, is this game and its field of action reflective of the culture of its participants? If so, how?

Summary (for Both Thanksgiving and Game Analyses)

Assignment as means of: developing the ability to analyze elements of the field of action and assess their impact on activities performance; developing the ability to speculate about the ways in which one's sociocultural surroundings influence activities.

End products: Increased familiarity with a variety of holiday rituals and games, and knowledge of the ways in which they may reflect the sociocultural values and traditional practices of the players.

Criteria for evaluation: Ability to accurately analyze elements of the field of action and to document these findings clearly and concisely.

Method of evaluation: written evaluation by the instructor.

THANKSGIVING CELEBRATION ANALYSES: STUDENT EXCERPTS

Meal Preparation*

. . . Perhaps hundreds of individuals worked to provide this meal—farmers, truckers, packaging and fertilizer manufacturers, food processors, food scientists, advertising folks, supermarket owners and employees, inventors, refiners, and producers of kitchen equipment. . . .

. . . In New Jersey, the Garden State, the carrots came from Canada, the onions from Pennsylvania, the yams from New York. Asked the origin of the celery spinning in the Cuisinart, the homemaker replies, "It came from the supermarket." The eggs from the market come from a warehouse from "farms" where chickens never see daylight, unable to turn around in their box-like roosts. . . .

. . . The pie is made from canned pumpkin, sugar substitute and pasteurized, homogenized, milk in plastic-coated cardboard containers. . . .

. . . The meal is prepared almost single-handedly by the homemaker, who refuses offered assistance. She began making lists of chores last week, drove often to various markets to accumulate raw materials. She follows recipes from trendy books and allows her mother to provide her de rigeur Jello mold. When the meal is successfully served and appreciated, the homemaker feels satisfaction, pride, and relief. . . .

Playing "UNO" on Thanksgiving†

. . . An activity I engaged in as a participant-observer was that of a group game, UNO. This card game is characteristic of Thanksgiving in my family. . . .

. . . The field of action for the card game was as follows: It took place at the dining room table in my mother's apartment. . . . Lights were bright, and the overhead fan generated a light, comfortable breeze. The table was scattered with coffee mugs, napkins, and the remains of several desserts. The decor consisted of light beige print wallpaper with a pastel earthtone picture on the wall. This added to the calmness of the room. The dining room looks on to the living room, where two people were watching T.V. The rest of the group were seated at the table as participants (seven) and observers (three). The activity took place from about 8:15 P.M. to 9:15 P.M., about two hours after dinner. . . .

---

* From the paper of a student who wishes to remain anonymous. (Note emphasis on history of objects.)
† From the paper of Melanie Klein, Columbia University, Class of '87.

GAMES ANALYSES: STUDENT EXCERPTS

Surfing*

. . . The sport of surfing will be described as seen in the small town of Monmouth Beach, New Jersey. . . .

. . . The equipment needed for surfing is neither fancy nor expensive. The major equipment needed is the surfboard, which is a 5 by 10 foot long and 1.5 foot wide fiberglass board. . . . Every board has some kind of design on the top. Some can be quite attractive, and others simple. Besides the board, the only things needed to surf is the ocean with waves and a wetsuit if the water is cold. Once one has a board, the surfing is free and can be done any time of day and any season of the year, as long as there are waves at least a foothigh. . . .

. . . The sport is inexpensive and, for this reason, characteristic of the Monmouth Beach community. It is a community of people who don't spend much money. They lead simple lives. . . . Weekends are usually spent on the beach. . . .

. . . The method for surfing is as follows: Before entering the water, the top of the board (opposite of fin side), must be rubbed with wax to prevent the surfer from slipping. The surfer straps the cord to his/her ankle, walks with board under arm about 20 feet into the water, then puts the board down and lays prone on it. The surfer paddles with arms away from the shore until he/she is past the point where the waves break. . . . The surfer then sits upright on the board while waiting for a wave. If a wave forms, a prone position is resumed with stronger and quicker paddling toward shore and in front of the wave. The wave will continue to push the surfer toward the shore, and this time the surfer pushes him/herself onto his/her feet and stands sideways on the board. Arms are usually abducted from body. Knees are always bent. The wave is surfed until it is too small to move the surfer forward. At this time, the surfer paddles away from shore and repeats the process. . . .

. . . This is characteristic of the community in that there are many hard workers who look forward to the weekend on the beach. They work hard all day during the week, and then go to the ocean. . . . Those who participate are mainly young males. It is a solitary sport—the less number of surfers the better, they say, because there is more room. . . .

. . . Implicit rules of surfing: The board should only be stood on while in the water, not on the sand; surfing is done in the ocean, not in the river or lake; the fin side of the board goes down (into water); if a surfer is in front of you and surfing, then he should not be cut off. . . . An explicit rule comes from the lifeguards: Surfing should only be done in the roped off area adjacent to the swimmers. . . .

"The Game of Color"†

. . . The (Japanese) 10-year-olds I spoke with demonstrated Ero Oni, the Game of Color, and told me that this was a game for younger children. . . . Ten children are involved, standing in a circle. One volunteers to be "It," remaining in the circle and naming a color. "It," with hands over eyes, counts to 10, while other players are expected to find and be touching an object of that color at "10." Anyone unable to find the identified color is then chased by "It" in a tag-like game. If "It" succeeds in tapping the colorless fugitive, that player becomes the new "It." If the chased returns to his/her area of the circle without being tagged, the game resumes with the original "It." The game continues until members grow tired. . . .

. . . As noted above, this game was chosen by the players who felt it was indicative of Japanese life because it 'isn't played in America' and is not violent. I feel another component of the game that can be found in aspects of Japanese culture is its simplicity. . . . Sports are valued in Japan and children are allowed time to play. Clear-cut roles, present in the family and society, are mimicked in Ero Oni, with "It" as a directive authority figure. The

---

* From the paper of Lisa Aikins, Columbia University, class of '87.
† From the paper of a student who wishes to remain anonymous.

fact that children's roles as players are reinforced in Japan is evidenced by national holidays honoring kids—Dolls' and Boys' Festivals. . . .

A "Shoe Race"*

. . . They call it a 'shoe race.' It is an ingenious adaptation of a typical running race. The children discovered that the [apartment building] hallway wasn't long enough to get up speed for a satisfying running race so they created a game that requires more skill than speed. In the 'shoe race,' the contestants take off their shoes and stand on top of them. When a referee says, 'Go,' they take off, sliding down the hall on the tops of their shoes as fast as they can without sliding off their shoes. When they reach the end of the hall (my apartment door), they touch the wall, turn around, and slide back again to the finish line. No more than three children can participate at one time due to the width of the hallway. . . .

. . . Not only were these children working within the limitations of their environment to devise a feasible, challenging game, but they have been developing mastery over time by perfecting their skills. . . . The first three children to think of the game have been inviting other children in the building to come up and race them. . . . This is an excellent game for this community because it doesn't require any fancy, specialized equipment. No one need be excluded from this game because they can't afford the necessary equipment. . . . Even though structured games and sports allow room for self-expression, the creativity shown by these children in devising this game is a positive sign of adaptive behavior. . . .

STEP 3: IDENTIFYING RESOURCES AND CONSTRAINTS IN THE CLINICAL SETTING

Once the individual's needs have been determined and the components of their everyday activities analyzed, we move to the next step in the clinical problem-solving process—the assessment of resources and constraints that are present in the treatment setting. How are services delivered in this particular setting? What is the usual length of stay? How much treatment time is allotted to each patient/client? What does the physical treatment environment look like, and what tools and materials are available for use? What opportunities exist for treatment to take place in the patient/client's natural environment? This information is needed for treatment planning, as it enables the therapist to identify goals and choose methods that are realistic given what is available in the facility (see p. 155).

Assignment 3: Identifying Resources and Constraints

In your fieldwork setting, obtain information regarding available resources as listed below:

A. Time: What is the duration of the patient/clients' stay, and what is the frequency and length of treatment sessions? To what extent does the setting allow for the needs of patients/clients that call for the modification of the standard length of stay or the standard frequency or length of treatment sessions?

B. Space: What space is available for occupational therapy treatment? Given facility policies and legal restrictions, what opportunities exist to engage

* From the paper of Lauren Robertson, Columbia University, class of '87.

in activities outside of the usual treatment environment within the facility in the community or in the patient/client's home?
C. Tools and materials: What tools and materials are readily available? How are tools and materials obtained that are not on hand? What restrictions exist regarding the use of specific tools and materials and cost of tools and materials?

Through this assignment, the student learns to identify the resources and constraints that exist in a given clinical setting and that affect the practice of occupational therapy. This includes the determination of the amount of time that can be realistically allowed for each patient/client's treatment and exploration of the availability of space, tools, and materials and restrictions regarding their use. As part of the assessment, students examine the nature of the space designated by the facility for occupational therapy sessions and possibilities for and constraints affecting the use of other, more realistic environments that are located outside of the usual occupational therapy area. Thus, students are encouraged to identify the characteristics of the clinical setting prior to the development of the treatment plan, so that goals can be identified and activities, fields of action, and therapeutic strategies selected that are both appropriate and realistic.

SUMMARY

Assignment as means of: learning how to identify the resources and constraints of a clinical setting; becoming aware of some of the many potential treatment environments outside of the space designated for the practice of occupational therapy; becoming aware of the ways in which facility policies and procedures affect clinical practice.
End Products: skills needed for identification of resources and constraints in the clinical setting; creative ideas for the use of environments outside of the designated occupational therapy treatment area for therapeutic purposes.
Criteria for evaluation: ability to obtain such information; ability to use creative problem-solving for the identification of means by which treatment can be carried out in more realistic settings, within the guidelines set by the facility.
Method of evaluation: informal feedback from peers and the instructor.

STEP 4: THE BEGINNING OF TREATMENT PLANNING— SETTING OCCUPATIONAL THERAPY GOALS

This step in the clinical problem-solving process represents the first stage in the development of the occupational therapy treatment plan. At this juncture, the student is required to identify, *in collaboration with the patient/client,* goals that emanate from the needs determined through the *activities health* assessment. The setting of goals also requires that the students take into account the resources and constraints existing in the clinical setting. Once they have become knowledgeable about the time, space, tools, and materials that can be used for treatment purposes, goals can be identified that are realistic and appropriate.

Development of a comprehensive treatment plan often includes the identification of long-term goals beyond the scope of what can be realistically achieved in a given clinical setting. When this is the case, the role of the occupational therapist in discharge planning is an important one, which will be discussed more fully in Step 8 of the clinical reasoning process.

Assignment 4: Setting Goals

A. Using the case example from Assignment 1d, list the long-term goals that will promote the attainment of a greater degree of *activities health* in order of priority. (The needs identified in Assignment 1d will serve as a basis.) All long-term goals are to be included, even if they will most likely be addressed within the context of follow-up treatment in another clinical setting.

B. For each of the long-term goals, set at least one short-term goal that will lead toward its attainment. The short-term goals identified are expected to be realistic considering the resources and constraints of the current treatment setting.

C. Considering what you know about this patient/client, think about how you as the therapist would present the goals identified. Would you discuss the complete set of goals or address them more gradually? What role would the patient/client play in deciding the order in which goals are addressed? Role-play a session with the patient/client in which the goals are discussed.

In this assignment, the student is asked to work together with the patient/client to identify goals aimed at the improvement of the patient/client's state of *activities health* and to determine their order of priority. The establishment of long-term goals requires that the student consider the ways in which the presence of clinical symptoms is interfering with the attainment of a state of *activities health*; these long-term goals are identified in terms of the overall needs of the individual. In addition, the identification of long-term goals requires that the student begin thinking early on about the patient/client's future need for subsequent follow-up services.

Once long-term goals have been articulated, the student is asked to identify one or more of the short-term goals that will lead to their achievement. The selection of specific short-term goals to be initially addressed requires that the student take into account the resources immediately available as determined in Step 3 and the priorities identified by the patient/client and therapist.

Finally, the student is asked to think about the way in which the goals that have been outlined will be presented to the patient/client. This assignment serves to highlight the individualized needs of each client/patient in this regard. For some, it is crucial that they be aware of the plan in its entirety from early on; for others, it is more beneficial if such information is shared in a more gradual manner. By taking the time to consider the appropriate way to engage each patient/client in a discussion about goals, students are helped to realize that the way in which the resulting therapeutic contract is established can have a profound impact on the patients/clients' attitudes and feelings about their treatment. Developing sensitivity to the existence of varying degrees of readiness on the part of patients/clients to discuss the treatment plan as a whole is important in the establishment of strong therapeutic alliances in future clinical practice.

SUMMARY

Assignment as means of: developing the ability to set long- and short-term goals within a framework of *activities health* in collaboration with the patient/client; developing the ability to begin anticipating discharge needs from early on in the occupational therapy process; developing the ability to make a sound decision regarding the way in which goals are to be presented to the patient/client.

End products: skills needed for setting short- and long-term occupational therapy goals that relate to the patient/client's *activities health* and for discussing goals in a manner appropriate to each patient/client.

Criteria for evaluation: ability to identify and document long- and short-term goals that accurately reflect the individuals needs in relation to *activities health*; ability to involve the patient/client in the determination and prioritizing of goals in ways that are individually appropriate.

Method of evaluation: written evaluation by the instructor regarding goals; verbal or written feedback about role play from both peers and the instructor.

Setting Goals: Student Excerpts*
GOALS

1. *Long-term*: to help Ms. J. return to previous job.
   Short-term: to evaluate Ms. J.'s readiness through participation in simulated work activities.
2. *Long-term*: to learn a number of new activities in which Ms. J. can engage during her leisure time.
   Short-term: to learn specific activities such as knitting, sewing, and baking.
3. *Long-term*: to increase Ms. J.'s socialization skills and opportunities for socializing, so that she will be able to develop friendships outside the hospital.
   Short-term: to learn how to initiate a conversation, first with the therapist, and then with other patients.
4. *Long-term*: to help Ms. J. spend more time outside of her home.
   Short-term: to plan outings with family members when out on passes.
5. *Long-term*: to help Ms. J. become ready to live independently.
   Short-term: To evaluate Ms. J.'s ability to perform necessary household chores independently.

STEP 5: SELECTING ACTIVITIES TO BE USED FOR THERAPEUTIC PURPOSES

In the fifth step of the clinical problem-solving process, activities are selected that can be used for therapeutic purposes. As discussed at length in Chapter 5, activities can serve as therapeutic *means*. As means, the activities themselves or represen-

* As derived from needs identified in Assignment 1d. From the paper of Monica Huang, Columbia University, class of '89.

tations of them, are used to promote the achievement of goals articulated in the treatment plan. As *subsidiary ends,* specific activities are gradually incorporated into everyday living, in movement toward the ultimate end—*activities health.* Thus the therapist must address the questions of when, where, and how these activities will be introduced or reintroduced into the patient/client's activities configuration (see Chapter 5).

To choose specific activities that can be used as both means and ends toward greater *activities health,* the therapist can look to the following sources of information: (1) short- and long-term goals identified in Step 4; (2) the patient/client's idiosyncratic activities pattern and configuration; and (3) information obtained through activities analysis. The ways in which each of these sources of data is relevant to the selection of therapeutic activities are summarized below. It should be noted that each of these sources yields overlapping information in many instances:

1. *Short- and long-term goals:* When goals are developed within a framework of *activities health,* they identify specific activities of everyday living that are in need of occupational therapy intervention. The very same activities can be used in the therapeutic situation for the purpose of preparing for their integration or reintegration into the individual's activities configuration.

2. *Idiosyncratic activities pattern and configuration:* Activities identified during the assessment as part of the current or past life-style of the individual can be used for therapeutic purposes. The configuration depicts activities that are currently routine, as well as those done regularly in the past. In some circumstances, activities previously done competently can be sources of motivation and confidence, enabling the therapist to draw upon strengths to help the patient/client acquire other related skills. When such activities are resumed as part of everyday living, they can sometimes enhance the patient/client's overall sense of satisfaction with his or her activities configuration. One should be aware, however, that for some patients/clients, the introduction of familiar activities into the treatment situation may elicit negative reactions in the patient/client; for such patients/clients, attempting to do activities done competently in the past can trigger an increased awareness of the ways in which the clinical condition is interfering with everyday living. Therefore, it is important to take into account the patient/client's subjective reactions to such activities, as elicited in the *Activities Health Assessment,* before they are incorporated into the treatment plan.

3. *Activities analysis:* The use of each of the approaches to activities analysis provides the therapist with knowledge about the nature of the activities that are part of the patient/client's regular routine. Identifying performance components of these activities, learning about the patient/client's everyday surroundings, and understanding the meaning and relevance that specific activities hold for the patient/client and his or her sociocultural group are all useful in the selection of meaningful and relevant therapeutic activities. The actor-centered approach can be used to point out specific activities with which the patient/client is having difficulty due to clinical problems; the activity-centered approach can assist the

therapist in choosing activities that can be adapted while also maintaining their intrinsic characteristics; the field of action–centered approach can be used to guide the therapist in the selection of activities that are realistic given the patient/client's natural environment.

As in the determination of goals, the patient/client assumes an important role in the activities selection process. Through participation in decision-making, the patient/client's sense of control and shared responsibility for planning treatment are reinforced, thereby strengthening the partnership between therapist and patient/client.

Assignment 5a: A Work Sample

To be done in an activities lab setting: Review the work analysis done in Assignment 7 of Chapter 8. Imagine that a patient/client has been referred to you who held the same job that you have analyzed in your work analysis. Within the next 20 minutes, construct a work sample that represents an essential component of this job, to be used as part of an assessment of the patient/client's readiness to return to this type of work. Structure the field of action as you would for an actual evaluation session.

The practice of occupational therapy requires that the therapist design simulated activities within a limited amount of time. In actual clinical practice, the process of activities analysis generally takes place spontaneously, in the form of a quick "thinking through" of those steps outlined in detail for educational purposes in the preceding assignments focusing on activities analysis. This assignment is structured to illustrate one of the ways in which activities analysis is used in clinical practice—the selection and design of simulated activities and fields of action. The assignment requires quick thinking and creativity, both of which can be adversely affected by time pressures and limitations in available resources.

Following this laboratory assignment, students are asked to share their reactions. Responses are likely to focus on the anxiety that the constraints on time and materials generate. However, participants are often pleasantly surprised by their own ability to arrive at innovative solutions despite the presence of external pressures.

The students can then be encouraged to exchange informal critiques of the work samples themselves. They are asked to comment on the degree to which each work sample is representative of a given job. Also addressed are the ways in which commonly found features of the work-oriented field of action (i.e., time pressures, evaluation by the boss, noise and other distractions, cramped space,) can be simulated in clinical settings. Students benefit from sharing ideas with one another about creating work samples and fields of action that are representative of the jobs and workplaces analyzed.

Thus, this assignment is directed toward the further development of the student's ability to select activities and design relevant therapeutic fields of action so that they reflect the activities in their natural forms and contexts. In addition, students are asked to think about the conclusions that can and cannot be drawn from watching a given patient/client complete a work sample. What does this form of assessment tell the therapist about the patient/client's ability to perform a specific type of job? What conclusions can be drawn from this type of assessment? Which cannot be drawn? The consideration of these questions helps the student become aware that a single observation of a patient/client carrying out one of the many activities that characterize a job is valuable as part of a complete assessment but cannot be used by itself for the definitive determination of the individual's ability to perform the job in its entirety. The necessity for understanding single activities as part of a "chain" of other related activities (see Chapter 5, Activities as Means), rather than as isolated events, is thereby emphasized.

SUMMARY

Assignment as means of: developing the ability to create simulated activities experiences to be used for evaluative purposes (and potentially for treatment purposes); ability to use creative problem-solving skills, even with pressures like constraints on time and materials; developing awareness of the conclusions that can and cannot be drawn from such an assessment.

End products: a repertoire of ideas for job samples related to specific types of work, through exposure to a variety of simulated activities experiences; skills needed to develop simulated activities experiences.

Criteria for evaluation: the ability to accomplish the above to create relevant assessment and treatment experiences.

Method of evaluation: informal feedback provided by peers and the instructor.

Assignment 5b: Selecting Activities as Therapeutic Means and Ends

Using the case example from Assignment 1d and 4:

1. List in the first column one short-term goal for each of the long-term goals identified (under the heading *Goal*).
2. For each of these short-term goals, list in the second column those activities that can be presented to the patient/client as options to be used as therapeutic means to greater *activities health* (under the heading *Activity Selected as Means*).
3. In the third column, describe where the activity will ultimately fit into the patient/client's idiosyncratic activities configuration (under the heading *Activity Addressed as Ends*).

This assignment is designed to provide the student with practice in the selection of activities as therapeutic means and their incorporation into everyday living (as ends). It can be done within the context of a laboratory session with the use of small groups or as a written assignment done independently. The identification of activities to be used therapeutically necessitates that the student make use of (1) knowledge of the everyday activities that are characteristic of the patient/client's life-style, (2) awareness of which of these activities are presenting difficulties for the patient/client, (3) the ability to examine the same activities through activities analysis, and (4) the ability to explain clearly the reasons for the choice.

Even though it is not until Step 6 of the clinical problem-solving process that the students specifically address the carry-over of functional gains from the clinical setting to everyday living, it is important that from the start they begin to envision the eventual place of each activity in the patient/client's activities configuration.

SUMMARY

Assignment as means of: developing the ability to choose therapeutic activities that have meaning and relevance to the patient/client and to explain reasons for the choice; reinforcing the student's awareness of the value of choosing therapeutic activities that are relevant both as therapeutic means and as ends contributing to greater *activities health.*

End products: skills necessary for choosing activities as therapeutic means, that can ultimately be incorporated as ends into the patient/client's activities configuration.

Criteria for evaluation: the ability to accomplish the steps of the assignment and explain the underlying rationale.

Method of evaluation: if done in a lab session, evaluation can be through informal feedback; if done in written form, written evaluation is provided by the instructor.

STEP 6: THE SELECTION OF RELEVANT THEORIES AND STRATEGIES FOR MANAGING DYSFUNCTION

An *activities health* approach to occupational therapy practice is designed to be used in combination with other theories and therapeutic approaches. Before planning the students' introduction to the integrated use of an *activities health* approach with other appropriate frames of reference, it is important to take into consideration the degree to which students have completed coursework where such frames of reference are studied. When circumstances are ideal, the students are introduced to this step of clinical problem-solving *after* they have acquired a working knowledge of the theories and therapeutic approaches that are widely used in the practice of occupational therapy. Under such conditions, the students are equipped to examine the relationship between an *activities health* approach and other frames of reference.

When the sequencing of coursework makes this prerequisite learning unrealistic, it is suggested that this step of the clinical reasoning process be initially presented in concept only, with examples provided to illustrate how an occupational therapist using an *activities health* approach can also make use of other theories and approaches. Even though this set of circumstances prevents the students from practicing this step on their own right away, opportunities to apply the information can be built into assignments later on in the program, in keeping with the growth of their knowledge base.

Even though the selection of meaningful and relevant therapeutic activities is of central importance in an *activities health* approach to clinical reasoning, activities per se have no properties that can lead us to assume that the patient/client will attain a greater measure of *activities health* simply through doing them. As discussed in Chapter 12, for activities to be therapeutic, they must be structured according to a set of therapeutic principles. The media that are part of the occupational therapist's instrumental supports help the therapist decide how the activities can be structured to help the patient/client attain the goals that have been identified. The Activities Health Model (Figure 5-1) illustrates the connections between activities and those instrumental supports that help to make them therapeutic in serving as means and ends toward *activities health*. The Clinical Problem-Solving Model (Figure 9-1) shows clearly that treatment planning includes both the selection and structuring of therapeutic activities and the selection of appropriate strategies that will be used to address the difficulties that the patient/client encounters when performing everyday activities. In particular, it is important to include in the treatment plan strategies to be used to help the patient/client carry over the gains made in occupational therapy into everyday living.

Assignment 6a: Selecting Relevant Theories and Strategies

Once again, return to the case example from Assignments 1d, 4, and 5b:

1. List the long-term goals that you have established.
2. List the short-term goals that will lead to the attainment of the long-term goals.
3. Identify the theories and techniques that you believe could be used to help the patient/client attain a more desired state of activities health.
4. For those activities that you selected as therapeutic ends and means in Assignment 5b, how would you incorporate the theories and techniques that you have selected?

The assignment is directed toward helping the student to understand how an *activities health* approach can be used in combination with a variety of therapeutic strategies, thereby clarifying where in the clinical problem-solving process these occupational therapy theories and techniques fit in. The students integrate their existing knowledge about treatment principles and techniques with their understanding of an *activities health* approach to clinical reasoning. Subsequent and further learning about theories and techniques can then be similarly integrated.

SUMMARY

Assignment as means of: developing an understanding of the ways in which an *activities health* approach can be used in conjunction with other relevant theories and strategies; developing skills in the selection of appropriate theories and strategies to address stated goals.

End products: skills needed for using an *activities health* approach in combination with other relevant theories and strategies.

Criteria for evaluation: ability to explain the reasons for one's choice of specific theories and strategies; ability to articulate how they will be applied in practice.

Method of evaluation: written evaluation by the instructor.

Assignment 6b: Helping the Patient/Client to Carry Over Functional Gains into Everyday Living

Returning to the case example in Assignment 6a, identify the techniques that can be used to help the patient carry over into everyday living the improvements (or in some cases maintenance) in functioning observed in the therapeutic situation.

Throughout this book, the patient/client's attainment of the greatest possible degree of *activities health* has been presented as the ultimate goal of occupational therapy. How do the functional abilities gained or maintained throughout the course of therapy become integrated into the patient/client's activities configuration? Experienced practitioners frequently struggle with this dilemma, which is difficult to address, given many of the constraints that exist in the health care facilities in which many occupational therapists practice.

This assignment is designed to facilitate the student's exploration of ways in which the patient/client can be helped to apply what has been gained to everyday living. Interventions such as "homework" assignments, home visits, and follow-up group and individual sessions are presented as some of the techniques available for helping the patients/clients explore ways of incorporating what has been learned in the clinical situation into their daily routines.

SUMMARY

Assignment as means of: exploring ways in which the patient can be helped to apply functional gains to everyday living.

End products: knowledge about some of the potential means available for helping the patient/client apply functional gains to everyday living.

Criteria for evaluation: ability to identify some of the realistic and appropriate methods that can be used to help the patient/client incorporate learning into everyday living.

Method of evaluation: writen evaluation by the instructor if assignment is written; if done in a laboratory session, informal feedback among peers and the instructor is used.

STEP 7: IMPLEMENTATION—THE STRUCTURING OF THERAPEUTIC ACTIVITIES EXPERIENCES

Once the therapeutic activities and the strategies for managing dysfunction have been selected, we approach the *implementation* of the occupational therapy treatment plan. As one would expect, the implementation of the plan involves carrying out the specific activities identified in Step 5, according to the theories and strategies selected in Step 6. In addition to the implementation of these essential elements of the treatment plan, this step of the clinical problem-solving process also involves the use of therapeutic intervention strategies aimed at (1) modification of the activity, (2) modification of the environment, and/or (3) changes in the actor—all directed toward the attainment of a more desirable state of *activities health*. Students explore the ways in which each component of an activity experience (i.e., actor, activity, and field of action) can be structured or modified to promote the patient/client's mastery of activities that are part of his or her desired life-style. Thus, the potential for modification and adaptation is added as yet another purpose served by activities analysis. Since in practice the structuring of therapeutic activities experiences often encompasses interventions directed at the actor, activity, and field of action simultaneously, the delineation of three approaches to activities analysis and adaptation is to be regarded as a heuristic device only that orders and simplifies the processing of a great deal of information for purposes of investigation.

Assignment 7a: Modifying the Activity

Review your activity-centered analysis of a chore. With other members of your class, think about the clinical conditions that are likely to interfere with the individual's performance of this activity. How might the activity be modified so that it can be successfully done even in the presence of the clinical conditions identified, while preserving its purpose and other intrinsic properties? Experiment with these modifications through role play. How do these methods compare with the range of what is considered to be acceptable performance of this activity?

This assignment provides opportunities for brainstorming, experimentation, and practice in the modification of activities elements that will support the performance of the actor, illustrating one of the ways in which an activity-centered approach to activities analysis can be used in clinical practice. The students' knowledge of the intrinsic properties of activities and the range of acceptable variations that exist among individuals and groups helps the student modify elements in ways that promote the patient/client's competence, while maintaining the intrinsic purposes and characteristics of the activity itself.

SUMMARY

Assignment as means of: developing skills in the modification of activities components to meet stated goals.

End products: practical ideas for the modificiation of activities, which can be applied to clients with similar functional difficulties; skills needed for the modification of activities components.

Criteria for evaluation: degree to which modifications enhance performance of activities described while also preserving their purposes and other intrinsic properties.

Method of evaluation: informal feedback among peers and the instructor.

Assignment 7b: Analyzing and Modifying the Clinical Field of Action

1. Draw a schematic diagram of the space designated for occupational therapy in the setting in which you are involved in fieldwork.

2. Identify all objects, both human and nonhuman.
3. What are the explicit and implicit rules?
4. What feelings does the environment elicit in you?
5. Draw another diagram, this time indicating how the field of action might be rearranged so that it represents an office environment; a small, eat-in kitchen: an informal social hour; and a restaurant.

This assignment focuses on one of the ways in which information obtained through a field of action–centered approach to activity analysis can be applied. In this assignment, the student is faced with a dilemma commonly encountered in the practice of occupational therapy—how artificial environments can be adapted in such a way that they are more representative of real-life fields of action. The use of creativity and problem-solving are encouraged to generate ideas regarding the creation of simulated fields of action. Through designing activities simulations, students become aware of the process by which adjustments in the physical environment can result in a new set of environmental rules and thus potentially elicit changes in the patient/client's behavior.

SUMMARY

Assignment as means of: developing an awareness of the ways in which the clinical field of action influences the activities process and the potential for altering the clinical field of action so that it is more representative of the natural environment.

End products: creative problem-solving skills that can be used in modifying the clinical field of action.

Criteria for evaluation: degree to which the modifications of the field of action have resulted in more accurate representations of the natural fields of action identified.

Method of evaluation: informal feedback among peers and the instructor.

Assignment 7c: Modifying the Natural Field of Action

Choose one of the case studies in Part III that describes a patient/client who can benefit from the modifications of specific elements in his or her living or work environment to attain a greater degree of activities health.

1. What modification(s) would you suggest?
2. How do you think the patient/client would react to the change(s)?
3. How would you help the patient/client adjust to the change(s)?
4. How do you expect these changes would affect the other people in the environment?
5. How do you think the change(s) would affect the patient/client's feelings of overall satisfaction, comfort, and sense of fitting in with one's sociocultural group in the doing of everyday activities?

This assignment illustrates yet another application of a field of action–centered approach to activities analysis. One possible means of helping the patient/client attain a greater measure of *activities health* lies in the modification of the natural field of action. However, these environmental changes have ramifications, both for the patient/client and the other people who share the field of action. In addition, these changes often produce subsequent changes in the patient/client's perception of the environment itself and in the relationship of the patient/client to the people who are part of the immediate surroundings. This assignment helps the student to anticipate the consequences of such changes, both positive and negative, so that they can be addressed as part of treatment. Ultimately, the student is asked to assess the effectiveness of modification(s) by exploring with the patient/client how the change(s) have altered his or her degree of overall satisfaction, comfort, and sense of "fitting" in relation to the performance of everyday activities.

SUMMARY

Assignment as means of: developing skills in the modification of everyday activities environments; developing awareness of the ways in which these changes affect the patient/client, others in the environment, and the relationships between them.

End products: skills needed for the modification of the patient/client's natural environment.

Criteria for evaluation: the degree to which modifications in the environment will enhance the performance of everyday activities; the incorporation of appropriate methods to help the individual adjust to these changes; the awareness of possible ramifications of environmental modifications.

Method of evaluation: written evaluation by instructor if assignment is written; if done in a laboratory session, informal feedback among peers and instructor is used.

Assignment 7d: Interventions Directed Toward Changes in the Actor

Choose one of the case studies in Part III that describes a patient/client who is likely to benefit from interventions focused on changing the way in which he or she characteristically performs an activity. Consider clients who are apt to be more successful in the performance of everyday activities if interventions are directed toward changes in behavior, positioning, movement, cognitive performance, and so on.

In the practice of occupational therapy, interventions are frequently directed toward changes in the actor in an effort to enhance the quality of performance of everyday activities. Depending on the nature of the patient/client's clinical condition(s), and the ways the condition(s) affects the attainment of *activities health*, these interventions are specifically directed toward changes in the patient/client's management of performance components, such as social behavior, movement, or cognitive requirements. Actor-directed interventions include the use of splints, adaptive equipment, positioning, neurophysiological and behavioral approaches, and many other tools and techniques, all of which represent therapeutic strategies that will promote the client's ability to perform activities with greater satisfaction and comfort, in socioculturally acceptable ways.

SUMMARY

Activity as means of: exploring the use of theories, tools, and techniques specifically aimed at changes in the actor; understanding how adaptive equipment, splints, and other such tools and techniques can be incorporated into an *activities health* approach.

End products: skills needed for the use of interventions directed toward changes in the actor in the doing of everyday activities.

Criteria for evaluation: degree to which interventions directed toward changes in the actor can help the patient/client develop greater competence in everyday activities.

Method of evaluation: if done in written form, written evaluation by the instructor is used; if done in a laboratory, feedback among peers and the instructor is used.

Assignment 7e: Analyzing Interventions

To be done in small groups: Think of an intervention that you have made or observed in your fieldwork setting that was directed toward facilitating successful performance of an activity. Discuss with the members of your group the following, in relation to each intervention described:

1. Was the intervention directed toward change in the actor, activity, field of action, or a combination of these?
2. How does change in one of these three components affect the others?

Most occupational therapy interventions are directed at changes in more than one of the three essential components identified (the activity, field of action, and actor). To highlight this phenomenon, the assignment is designed so that students can examine how therapeutic approaches, separated out for educational purposes in Assignments 7a–d, are applied in combination with one another in actual practice. In addition, the assignment promotes the consideration of the impact that change elicited in one activities component can have on the others. Even though there is frequently overlap in the way in which interventions are targeted, it is important that the student know how to ascertain which component(s) are being addressed, so that if one approach proves to be unsuccessful, alternatives can be systematically explored.

SUMMARY

Assignment as means of: developing awareness of the rationale for choosing intervention strategies aimed at the actor, field of action, or activity; developing an awareness of the ways in which change in one activities component can result in change(s) in the others.

End products: skills needed for the use of a systematic approach to choosing alternative interventions when a given strategy is not successful.

Criteria for evaluation: ability to analyze and understand the way(s) in which therapeutic interventions are directed; degree to which there is an awareness of the possible effects of interventions on all activities components.

Method of evaluation: informal feedback among students and the instructor.

STEP 8: DISCHARGE PLANNING

The attainment of long-term occupational therapy goals frequently requires referral for additional services following discharge from a given facility. It is the responsibility of the occupational therapist to assess whether continued therapy is needed, and if so, the nature and frequency of such services must be considered. In clinical settings that use an interdisciplinary approach, discharge planning is most often done in collaboration with other members of the treatment team. In some facilities, a specific discipline has designated responsibility for referrals; in others, each discipline is expected to make appropriate follow-up referrals within their domain of concern. Whether or not the occupational therapist assumes total responsibility for referrals to other facilities, input regarding the functional status of the patient and the implications for the patient's needs upon discharge is of critical importance.

Assignment 8: Making Recommendations for Discharge Planning and Planning for the Termination of Treatment

Using the case example from Assignment 1d, 4, and 5b, review the long-term goals. Given the availability of resources in the immediate clinical setting determined in Step 3, think about the follow-up services that you anticipate may be necessary for the achievement of long-term goals. Answer the following:

1. What would be your recommendation for follow-up?
2. How would you facilitate a smooth transition for the patient/client?
3. What information would you include in the referral for follow-up?
4. How would you plan to help your patient/client terminate from the current stage of treatment?

This assignment is designed to acquaint the student with the role of the occupational therapist in the discharge planning process and brings to light some of the issues that often arise during the patient's termination from a given treatment situation. Through consideration of the questions posed in the assignment instructions, students are given a preliminary introduction to the kinds of issues that arise when planning for discharge. Students are guided toward the awareness that the patient/client's progress toward *activities health* can be a long-term undertaking, during which treatment may take place in more than one setting. Students are introduced to the occupational therapist's role in investigating options available to the patient/client for further services, when it has been determined that there is potential for further progress in functioning after discharge. They are also asked to consider strategies that can be used to prepare for a smooth transition for the patient/client. Although problems unavoidable in our health care system today make it difficult to achieve at times, a smooth transition from one clinical setting to the next is introduced to the student as an important goal. The importance of addressing both the patient/client's termination and subsequent transition as part of treatment is thereby illustrated and can later be reinforced when the student participates in discharge planning in a clinical setting.

SUMMARY

Assignment as means of: becoming familiar with some of the issues to be considered by the occupational therapist in relation to discharge planning, the client's termination, and transition to a subsequent treatment setting.

End products: skills necessary for participation in discharge planning and helping the patient/client to prepare for termination and transition to a subsequent treatment setting.

Criteria for evaluation: the degree to which discharge recommendations support the attainment of long-term goals; the degree to which the patient/client's termination and transition are addressed in the plan; the selection of pertinent information to be included in referral.

Method of evaluation: written evaluation by the instructor.

STEP 9: ACTIVITIES HEALTH REASSESSMENT

This final step of the clinical problem-solving process can only be presented conceptually as part of an introductory course in the study of activities. To acquire actual experience in reassessment, the students need to have access to a patient/ client who can be followed from the initial stages of treatment until follow-up. In most cases, this is not feasible until students are involved in full-time fieldwork. Carrying out Assignment 9 in the student's fieldwork setting provides a bridge from what has been learned in class to a clinical situation.

As stated in the introduction to Chapter 9 and illustrated in the Clinical Problem-Solving Model (Figure 9-1) an *activities health* approach to occupational therapy (like many others) calls for reassessment at the following points in the treatment process: (1) periodically during the implementation of the treatment plan, (2) at the termination of therapy, and (3) at a point (or more than one point) in time deemed appropriate for follow-up. At each juncture, the *Activities Health Assessment* can be readministered (in either complete or abbreviated form) to determine the degree to which the patient/client's participation in occupational therapy has resulted in desired changes.

Assignment 9: Occupational Therapy Reassessment

In your fieldwork, select a patient/client who can be followed from the point of referral to discharge and, if possible, to follow-up. Compare the patient/

client's idiosyncratic activities configuration prior to occupational therapy with the configuration immediately after termination. If possible, obtain a third configuration after a period of time has passed since discharge from occupational therapy. Be sure to include an assessment of the patient/client's feelings of overall satisfaction, comfort, and sense of fitting in with his or her sociocultural group(s).

1. What similarities do you see? What differences?
2. How does the most recent configuration compare with the long-term goals set at the beginning of treatment planning?
3. What further recommendations can be made at this time?

Through this assignment, the student has the opportunity to follow a patient/ client from the time of referral to follow-up. This time, the *Activities Health Assessment* is used to assess the degree to which previously stated goals have been achieved.

Through seeking answers to the series of questions that appear in the assignment, students may discover that in comparison to the more dramatic changes observed in the clinical setting, the patient/client's life-style is often slower to change. It is important that students develop an appreciation for the many obstacles that the patient/client may encounter when attempting to incorporate changes into everyday living. This awareness can help the eager new therapist to monitor the common impulse to encourge too many changes at once in the patient/client's life-style, which can potentially be overwhelming.

Finally, through participating in reassessment, students may discover a secondary benefit; at times, patients/clients previously resistant to further treatment are more open to recommendations for further services after they have adjusted to discharge. As addressed in the final component of the assignment, the follow-up reassessment provides an additional opportunity to reinforce or modify recommendtions for further treatment after the initial transition has been made.

SUMMARY

Assignment as means of: developing the ability to conduct a reassessment to obtain a longitudinal view of a patient from the point of referral, through treatment, to follow-up and to gain an understanding and appreciation for the obstacles that can be encountered by the patient/client as changes are incorporated.
End products: skills needed for *activities health* reassessment.
Criteria for evaluation: degree to which the reassessment accurately reflects the patient/client's degree of *activities health*; ability to recognize when additional discharge planning efforts are needed.
Method of evaluation: written evaluation by the instructor.

PUTTING IT ALL TOGETHER—STREAMLINING THE PROCESS

As the reader can see, the second part of this educational model, which addresses the therapeutic potential of activities, is designed so that the student is introduced to each step of the clinical problem-solving process in the order in which it occurs in clinical practice. For purposes of education, the introduction to an an *activities health* approach to clinical reasoning is presented over an extended period of time. However, once the sequence of steps has been introduced, it is also necessary that the students become aquainted with the way in which clinical problem-solving is streamlined in practice.

The first of the assignments is designed to elicit the student's spontaneous responses when asked to develop a treatment plan during a limited period of time. Afterwards, the students are asked to critique the way in which clinical problem-solving was approached. In the second assignment, students are required to administer an *Activities Health Assessment*, identify occupational therapy goals, and plan a simulated session, which is then presented in class. Such assignments can be used to assess the degree to which the student can "put it all together"—that is, to make use of the skills and knowledge that have been introduced throughout the learning process. In addition to the assignments that appear, the *Program of Instruction for Clinical Problem-Solving* in Chapter 12 can be used for illustration and practice of the clinical reasoning process from beginning to end, especially as the students' knowledge of theories, therapeutic strategies, and clinical conditions grows. Figure 5-1 and Figure 9-1 also provide a means for understanding how the many aspects of the student's learning fit together into a framework for occupational therapy practice.

For logistical reasons already discussed, it is unlikely that the final assignments can include all steps of clinical reasoning. The place of the coursework in the occupational therapy curriculum may preclude opportunities to practice the identification of appropriate strategies for the management of dysfunction or possibilities for trying out an *activities health* reassessment with an actual patient/client. Further opportunities to apply clinical reasoning skills as the students build on their knowledge base can be provided at appropriate intervals.

A Critique of Clinical Reasoning

To be done in groups of three students, after distributing one of the cases from Part III to two members in each group: Two members of the group who have been given this case are to review it together and develop a treatment plan within 45 minutes. Identify the following:

1. Short- and long-term goals
2. Activities to be used for therapeutic purposes
3. Theories and techniques to be used

The third member of the group will be designated as the observer and clinical reasoning "analyst." The observer will not participate in the development of the treatment plan but will listen carefully and take note of the process by which the plan is determined. The observer can ask questions of the other group members only to elicit information about how decisions are made (e.g., What made you come to that conclusion?) but is instructed not to comment on the decisions themselves.

The assignment is followed by a discussion of the process by which decisions were made by the treatment planners. Observers are first asked to share their accounts of the clinical problem-solving process, after which the two treatment planners share their thoughts and reactions. Through critiquing their own clinical reasoning patterns, students develop an awareness of the many factors that affect the making of clinical decisions. The following tendencies, some of which are known to be shared by many practicing therapists [75], are common:

1. Decisions are made almost automatically, based on previous experiences with similar patients/clients or on preconceptions about the functional ramifications of specific diagnoses.
2. When time is limited, the focus tends to be on problems, with little or no attention paid to *activities health*.
3. Methods are discussed before goals are identified.
4. When questioned, treatment planners find it difficult to articulate their rationale for decisions.

It may seem ironic that this assignment, which is among the last in the entire sequence, frequently elicits information indicating a lack of adherence to the approach explicity outlined in the course of study. This can be a sobering experience for students and instructors alike. However, as stated by Rogers and Masagatini [75], these tendencies are not unique to any one profession but are shared by professionals of other disciplines. Surfacing these potential pitfalls with students, even if initially disheartening, is ultimately constructive. The development of awareness of these natural tendencies is useful in helping students avoid them and follow more closely a reasoned approach to clinical problem-solving.

SUMMARY

Assignment as means of: developing the ability to critique the clinical reasoning patterns of others and oneself; developing an awareness of the potential pitfalls in the clincial reasoning process.

End products: the ability to critique clinical reasoning patterns; knowledge about one's own characteristic tendencies while engaging in clinical reasoning.

Criteria for evaluation: degree to which an *activities health* approach to clinical reasoning is used.

Method of evaluation: formal and informal peer assessment.

Final Project

To be done in pairs:

1. Choose a patient/client from one of the brief cases studies in Part III, or select a patient/client whom you have met in your fieldwork.
2. With your partner, engage in role play, videotaping if possible, in which one of you is the patient/client and the other a therapist, and administer the Activities Health Assessment according to the protocol (see Chapter

6). The student playing the patient/client should use the case information as the basis for the assessment, improvising additional information as necessary.

3. Both of you will then assume a therapist role and write your own summary of the results, including introductory data, assessment findings, and the identification of long- and short-term goals.
4. Your presentation (approximately 15 minutes long) will be a joint effort, consisting of the following:
   a. A presentation of assessment findings.
   b. A videotaped or live presentation of a simulated portion of an occupational therapy session, in which one of you plays the patient/client and the other the therapist, requiring that you
      1. Select one of the goals that will be addressed.
      2. Select an appropriate therapeutic activity.
      3. Structure the activity and field of action so that they support the achievement of stated goals.

This assignment represents the culmination of the study of activities as natural human phenomena and an *activities health* approach to clinical reasoning. The end products, which consist of both a written assessment and presentation, reveal the degree to which students have integrated the learning experience as a whole. The use of videotape provides the opportunity for students to be their own critics and to consider ways in which their efforts could be improved.

Listening to the presentations of others repeatedly reinforces the students' learning and provides the opportunity for both instructor and students to recall and highlight various aspects of learning as they are illustrated by the end products. For example, some of the same activities listed at the start of Chapter 8 in the students' cumulative activities repertoire and those presented in the Construction and Expressive Projects of Chapter 8 find their way into a therapeutic situation in the final assignment. In addition, the simulated occupational therapy sessions presented in class involve the making of clinical decisions and solving of problems, processes practiced repeatedly throughout the coursework. Thus, during the presentations, the students and instructor can reflect on the learning process in its entirety and view what has been gained as a foundation on which future learning can be built.

SUMMARY

Assignment as means of: assessing the student's ability to engage in several steps of the clinical reasoning process; reinforcing the need to structure therapeutic activities according to the goals identified; continuing to develop skills necessary for using an *activities health* approach to occupational therapy practice.

End products: skills and knowledge that underlie an *activities health* approach to clinical reasoning.

Criteria for evaluation: degree to which the assessment reflects the patient/client's degree of *activities health*; the student's ability to present assessment findings clearly and concisely; the degree to which the simulated occupational therapy session addresses goals identified; the student's ability to design a field of action that reflects the patient/client's natural field of action.

Method of evaluation: informal feedback among peers and the instructor, in addition to written evaluation by the instructor.

Final Paper: Student Illustration*

Mr. R., a 68-year-old man, was hospitalized for a cardiac condition 20 years ago, and has been stabilized through medications since that time. Mr. R. retired from his job at the post office 5 years ago and is currently living at home with his wife. Mr. R.'s wife is very concerned about his physical and psychological well-being; thus, she has assumed all household responsibilities since his first cardiac hospitalization. Additional support for Mr. R. is provided through the close relationships he maintains with his two sons and his younger brother. Mr. R.'s interests include fishing, traveling in and around the city, and attending church services.

Through an *Activities Health Assessment*, it was determined that Mr. R.'s current activities schedule is unsatisfying and uncomfortable for him. Thus, at the present time, Mr. R. is not in a state of *activities health*. This was evident when Mr. R. was filling out his activities configuration. He had difficulty categorizing the few activities he recorded and was indifferent when doing so. This was especially noted when discussing leisure activities. His decision that watching television was a leisure activity was arrived at by stating that "it's not work, a chore, or self-care, so I guess it's leisure if it has to be something." This indifferent attitude was also evident in his resistance to filling out the entire configuration. In reference to the blank spaces, he stated that he does nothing and stares at nothing and therefore refuses to categorize "nothing."

According to Mr. R., his activities schedule is the result of the limitations imposed on him by his cardiac condition and his enormous amount of free time since retirement. When he was questioned about his overall feeling of fitting in with his sociocultural group, he rated this feeling as "six," and stated that his configuration is "typical of what retired and sick people do."

Additionally, when asked about future configurations, Mr. R. expressed the desire to increase his leisure activities and to help himself and others as he used to do. However, Mr. R. stated that he was unsure of his ability to achieve these goals in view of his physical limitations.

Mr. R.'s prior hospitalization and recent retirement seem to have unnecessarily (since he is stabilized and no severe risk is evident) interfered with his activities of everyday living. He seems to believe that these factors render him incapable of doing many desired activities. Additionally, his wife's apparent overextension of herself by assuming all household responsibilities adds to this belief and decreases the amount of control he is able to exert over his environment.

Thus, in review of these findings, *activities health* for Mr. R. consists of a balance of activities that are personally satisfying and meet his needs for enjoyment, self-worth, and control. These activities would include fishing, traveling, attending church services, helping with chores in the house, and engaging in leisure activities with significant others (i.e., wife, brother, sons). To help Mr. R. achieve an ideal state of *activities helath*, the following goals will be addressed:

GOALS

1. *Long-term:* To increase his understanding of his cardiac condition and necessary precautions to decrease his anxiety about participating in desired activities.

* From the paper of Karen van den Heuvel, Columbia University, class of '89.

Short-term: To contact the physician for a consultation about his cardiac condition to determine limitations and possibilities regarding safe activities.

2. *Long-term:* To add leisure activities to his configuration to increase satisfaction.
   Short-term: To add at least one leisure activity to his configuration.

3. *Long-term:* To add household chores to his configuration to increase his feelings of self-worth and control over his environment (i.e., satisfaction and sociocultural fit).
   Short-term: To add at least one household chore to his configuration.

4. *Long-term:* To add one full day of volunteer church work per week to his configuration to increase his feelings of self-worth and control over his environment (i.e., satisfaction and sociocultural fit).
   Short-term: To add 2 hours of volunteer church work per week to his configuration.

DESCRIPTION OF SIMULATED OCCUPATIONAL THERAPY SESSION

In the simulated occupational therapy session, the therapist took Mr. R. on a fishing trip with the intention that Mr. R. would teach her how to fish. Mr. R. and the therapist both came dressed for the occasion, even down to Mr. R.'s well-weathered fishing cap. They were equipped with homemade fishing "rod," "bait", and "fish." The simulated session was held on the rooftop patio of the student dormitory, and the therapist and Mr. R. "fished" over the roof's edge. The therapist, who had little knowledge of fishing, relied on her patient for direction. As a result, Mr. R. became quite animated and offered a great deal of assistance and information as they went along, exemplified in particular when the therapist became squeamish and sought Mr. R.'s assistance when baiting the hook and taking the fish off after it was caught. During the more tranquil time, while waiting for fish to bite, the therapist was able to engage Mr. R. in a discussion about his fishing experiences, during which he shared several anecdotes. The therapist also used this as an opportunity to discuss the possibility of Mr. R.'s resuming fishing as a hobby in the future.

Postscript to the Educational Model: Challenge and Change

One of the greatest challenges encountered in introducing this educational model has been our intent to describe it in enough detail to clarify the conceptual framework on which it is founded, while also preserving the leeway the instructor needs to mold the coursework according to the unique characteristics of each curriculum and its students. The art of using this model lies in its application and suitable adaptation to a specific curriculum, with a distinctive group of students and instructor(s). To reiterate, this model presents a *conceptual* basis for an approach to the study of activities and their place in occupational therapy; it is not meant to be used only as a prescribed series of assignments.

The educational model can also easily be adapted for continuing education for practicing therapists. Regardless of the length of one's professional career, the world of human activities is most effectively examined by first reflecting on activities in one's own life, then in the lives of others around us, and finally as means and ends to greater *activities health*. Although the knowledge and experience of the practicing therapist are greater than those of the student, the process of learning about activities and occupational therapy in the context of *activities health* is in other respects somewhat similar. Also in the clinical setting, student fieldwork seminars can make use of appropriate sections of the educational model, thus encouraging supervisor and student to develop an appreciation for and understanding of activities as the heart of occupational therapy practice.

In the educational setting, a course devoted to the study of activities as natural human phenomena is the most logical place to begin, with links to other coursework along the way whenever possible. The use of the same assignment for more than one course can help the student make connections with other areas of study. An analysis of movements involved in the performance of a specific activity links the study of activities with kinesiology; the use of the *Activities Health Assessment* and clinically-based assignments in fieldwork settings link the study of activities with the study of theories, therapeutic strategies, and frames of reference. A graphic illustration of the integration of activities with other coursework comes from an occupational therapy program* where all instructors (even those teaching the basic science courses) were asked to teach an activity, which was often directly related to the course content. One of the many end products was the student's creation of a three-dimensional model of the fiber tracts in the human nervous system as part of a course in neurophysiology, thus highlighting the fact that activities are part of every aspect of daily living, while also reinforcing the power of learning through doing.

The development of this model has occurred over a period of several years. As one would expect, its evolution has included a number of changes and an equal number of exciting developments, resulting largely from the actions and reactions of participating students. Their provocative and challenging questions and suggestions have helped to clarify concepts, shape assignments, amend sequences, and expand methodological tools and evaluation procedures. It is hoped that each instructor exploring the use of this model will similarly be encouraged to take the plunge and then be guided toward enrichment of the learning experience along the way.

We have yet formally to assess the ways in which participation in these kinds of learning experiences has influenced the clinical practice of occupational therapists. But it is our belief that this educational model can, over time, serve as a unifying framework for the frequently fragmented, and seemingly disparate, foci of study that are incorporated into the coursework of the typical occupational therapy curriculum. It is striking that each area of learning defined as part of the American Occupational Therapy Association's "Educational Essentials" [3] fits very neatly into the *Activities Health Model* (Figure 5-1). The study of activities as natural human phenomena and their potential as agents of growth and change can provide means for connecting education with practice and serve as the link for "putting it all together" in the development of the occupational therapist.

* University of Florida at Gainesville, Florida, 1983.

PART THREE

Activities in Practice: The Promise of the Profession

CHAPTER 10

Enlisting Instrumental Supports for Activities as Means

From the concepts, connections, and conclusions presented in Part I, it is evident that the effective incorporation of activities as *means* toward a state of *activities health* depends on a therapeutic program in which carefully selected *media* (activities) are integrated by systematic *methods* with the aid of appropriate *tools* and *techniques*. Each of these four instrumental supports, enlisted in varying combinations in the process of tailoring activities to fit the special needs of each individual, will now be defined and discussed in detail.

MEDIA (ACTIVITIES)

It is quite apparent from previous discussions that the primary media of occupational therapy are activities. The conditions under which activities become therapeutic for the individual have already been set out in detail in Chapter 5. Other considerations, however, that relate to external circumstances also affect the incorporation of activities into therapeutic programs. No matter in which setting occupational therapy is practiced—clinic, hospital, nursing home, school, community center, prison, or the patient/client's home—a number of constraints are imposed on programs by environmental conditions, external rules, regulations, and policies, and the implicit but nonetheless pervasive value system operating in the setting. One such situation not uncommonly encountered is the limited space allocated for occupational therapy in plans for new hospital departments, regardless of the numbers of patients and the kinds of equipment needed. In many instances, particularly where treatment of physical disabilities is concerned, this reflects a value system that gives a low priority to a discipline dealing with quality of life, because such a discipline is neither essential in a lifesaving sense nor "scientific" in a technological sense.

Activities and External Constraints

To meet patient/client needs within the limitations imposed by external conditions requires that activities be appropriate, practical, versatile, and adaptable.

APPROPRIATENESS

Activities need to be appropriate not only in terms of meaning and relevance to the patient/client but also to the setting in which the activities programs are applied. It might be ideal, for instance, to install power tools for woodworking in a clinic treating a large number of injured workmen, but the physical structure of the clinic and its staffing patterns may preclude constant supervision, or more of a problem still, the structure of the building may not meet required safety standards.

PRACTICALITY

Activities need to be practical, in the sense that they can be administered quickly and easily without laborious preparation, they can be completed within the time frames imposed by the setting, and they fit within budgetary restrictions.

VERSATILITY

Activities need to lend themselves, by virtue of their properties and characteristics, to a variety of processes, end products, and situations. A broad appeal, often related to current fad and fancy, across cultural, age, sex, and other differences also adds to the versatility of an activity.

An example of a very versatile activity, already used as a telling example because of the importance with which it is invested (particularly in this day and age in our society), is cooking. The processes and end products are endless in their variety, ranging from the utilitarian fixing of a sandwich and the routines of preparing a family meal to the highest flights of haute cuisine, from pasting recipes in a scrapbook to the production of a cookbook with an exotic theme. The versatility of cooking is further compounded by the fact that it takes place in the activities configurations of individuals in a number of different guises and can thus be structured, according to the needs of the individual, to serve as a hobby, a work activity, or an activity relating to care of self and environment.

A most creative activity project at the tasting end was conceived by a group of young adults who needed to develop interpersonal and decision-making skills prior to returning to jobs in the community. In twos, they explored restaurants in the community serviced by the hospital and wrote their own version of a restaurant guide, having developed criteria and procedures for evaluation by group consensus. They also designed and produced a printed version, cover and all, allocating and organizing tasks with minimal direction from the therapist.

ADAPTABILITY

Activities need to lend themselves to adaptation to the individual and thus differing patient needs. The adaptable elements in activities are their *properties* and *characteristics* and the *field of action*.

The game of *marabaraba* (see pp. 55–56), for instance, and indeed any game played with a board and checkers, lends itself to adaptation in many ways. In the case of the patient referred to in Chapter 5, the game was adapted to incorporate lower limb motion by the use of greatly enlarged pieces, the introduction of wire hoops, an expanded area for the board, and location on the ground instead of a tabletop. Many other physical adaptations are possible. For the individual lying flat in bed, this type of game can be played overhead with pieces (felt, Velcro-backed, or magnetic) that cling to the board, which is clamped in place to ensure correct positioning. The game may be placed vertically on an easel to ensure standing balance and shoulder and elbow motions. The pieces can be shaped in a number of ways to ensure particular kinds of finger function, or they can be weighted for resistive motion. (See numerous articles and pictures in current and back issues of the *American Journal of Occupational Therapy* that describe other adapted activities.)

The field of action can also be modified in a number of ways. The setting may range from clinic, dayroom, or bedside to outdoors in the hospital grounds, from a quiet corner of a library to a recreation hall in which the game is set up in tournament style and rules are added for a laddering system that advances the ultimate winner to the top. The number of people can be varied from an intensely involved and isolated dyad through numerous combinations of persons to a large and vociferous group encompassing players and spectators. Adaptation of the explicit rules of the game is also possible. The game may end for one session when a specified number of pieces are captured, thus shortening and simplifying the process; the interaction between players may be prolonged by a challenge to a return match; or a win may be determined by the best of a prearranged total of games.

Actual and Simulated Situations

Activities in their fields of action are quite literally rehearsals for everyday living. Therefore the more closely activities situations in the clinical setting resemble the activities patterns in the real world, the better. In many instances, activities can be readily introduced into the patient/client's day in patterns that approximate those that are socioculturally designed and approved. Daily living skills such as eating and dressing can be practiced in most settings at relatively appropriate times in relatively real situations (even though institutional hours scarcely coincide with those of the real world). Similarly, leisure activities (among which are arts and crafts) and other hobbies selected for individual pleasure and gratification lend themselves to structuring in close approximation to actual situations.

However, because of the great range of patient/client needs, the variations in individual and sociocultural activities configurations, and the constraints inherent in the settings in which occupational therapy is practiced, activities most often serve only as simulations of situations encountered in the real world. It is for this reason that the criteria of versatility and adaptability are so important. It also has much to do with why arts and crafts, which fulfill these criteria more fully than most other kinds of activities, have played a dominant role in occupational therapy programs. It is necessary to examine only one craft—pottery—to realize the potential for an infinite number of structural variations designed to meet a number of different needs.

Imagine now an individual crouched in solitary absorption, raising a pot on a wheel. Inherent in this situation is intense involvement, self-expression, a creative outlet, satisfaction, and ultimately approval by others of a beautiful, tangible object. In another setting, four individuals sit around a table, each place neatly set out with appropriate materials, with a number of tools in the center for all to share. They concentrate intently on the therapist, who demonstrates step-by-step how to measure and cut off a ceramic tile—the setting and rules designed to facilitate interpersonal communication, which will in turn lead to completion of a set task. An attenuated assembly line—simulating conditions in the world of work—occupies a long room. Individuals work in clusters, each cluster being responsible for one stage in the process of manufacturing molded ceramic coffee mugs—pouring slip, unmolding, trimming, sanding, decorating, stacking the kiln. All clear away and clean up. A foreman allocates the jobs, checks on punctuality, and supervises the workers, while a general supervisor plans the overall project and checks on the quality and quantity of productions. There are sanctions for nonadherence to rules and material rewards for compliance (for example, tokens, credits toward a weekend pass, a movie, or dining out with the group). The therapist watches and intercedes only when necessary. Some individuals lead; most individuals follow but have room for upward mobility as a reward for good performance. The end products are sold, and the profits are contributed to the patient government committee. In yet another situation, a young man with a splint on his hand rolls out and pinches clay into the shape of an ashtray as the therapist watches closely for substitute motions and signs of fatigue.

Needless to say, arts and crafts can be integrated into actual situations as well. An excellent example of how this can be done is an aftercare plan for a group of adolescent girls who were to live in a house in the community. The house needed extensive repair and redecoration, and the activities program encompassed painting, woodworking, sewing, decorative needlework, macrame, lampshade-making, furniture refinishing, upholstery, textile design, linoprinting, and tile setting. There were also heated discussions about themes, color schemes, styles, and designs for living. In this instance, the arts and crafts program not only cut across the boundaries of work, chore, leisure, social, and recreational activities but transcended them as a total experience in communal living.

The use of simulated situations is justified by the underlying assumption that learning can be transferred from one situation to another by generalization. It is therefore imperative that the occupational therapist, when designing simulations, constantly checks, by referring back to the idiosyncratic activities configuration (as revealed by the *Activities Health Assessment*) of each individual, whether these simulations in fact have connections to the total context of the everyday activities life of that individual. Moreover, it is important to bear in mind that arts and crafts, games, or any other kinds of activities serving as vehicles for simulation will be effective only if

1. They have meaning and relevance to the patient/client.

2. Their purpose is clear and acceptable to the patient/client either as part of a transition in the movement toward *activities health* or as practice situations that parallel those in the real world.
3. There are enough elements of similarity between simulated and actual situations to make transfer of learning likely, whether it be to increasingly complex situations or to parallel situations in the real world.

The assumption that generalization of learning is possible, while a valid one, does not guarantee that the patient/client will automatically be able to bridge the gap between simulation and reality. Ideally, in any activities program, provision is made for periodic assessment of whether transfer of learning to actual situations has indeed taken place, by giving appropriate activities assignments and/or following up on patient/client performance in real-life situations (see Educational Model, Part II).

It goes almost without saying, for instance, that for a housewife with cardiac failure, no amount of practice of energy-saving techniques in the simulated kitchen of the occupational therapy clinic will suffice if she does not adapt her newly acquired skills to the kitchen in her own home, carry them through to other household activities, and incorporate them into her habitual activities life, as revealed in her idiosyncratic activities configuration. And unless she is made aware of the need for such transfer of learning and helped to adapt as needed, it is unlikely that she will return to a desirable state of *activities health*.

There is no question, of course, that the more closely the therapeutic activities situations approximate the real-life activities situations of the individual, the less complicated is the process of ensuring that the transfer of learning takes place. And there may be many more actual situations available in most clinical setting than at first meet the eye (see Assignment 4). Of necessity, simulations have their place, but artifice can be taken to ludicrous extremes, as evidenced by the prevalent use of a plastic material as a substitute for meat when practice is needed in cutting with a knife. The color and texture of the plastic not only bear no resemblance to any known food, but also are an assault to the senses. And the danger of overdoing the arts and crafts is highlighted by the remark of one bright young student dependent on a wheelchair for mobility. As a member of a panel discussing how rehabilitation helps that patient, he said of occupational therapy: "The underlying idea is great. But you people missed the boat when you gave us macrame belts to knot instead of a chance to make hamburgers in the kitchen!" Once again, the possibilities for the "real thing" may sometimes be more readily available than is at first apparent if the patient/client's real-life activities needs are first explicitly articulated and realistically established through the *Activities Health Assessment*.

METHODS

Methods are the procedures and processes by which activities are designed, structured, and integrated into treatment as means toward attainment of a state of *activities health*. These procedures and processes include selection, structuring, scheduling, and interaction.

Selection

Activities are selected on the basis of patient/client needs within the resources available and the realistic constraints of the particular setting in which the program takes place. Needs are established by the collection and interpretation of data obtained from functional evaluations, case records, the *Activities Health Assessment*, and other activities histories; knowledge of individual and sociocultural activities configurations; and the resources and constraints of the setting in which the program takes place. Alternative selections are an important part of the process, to allow for unexpected situational contingencies and changes in the patient/client's status.

Structuring

The activities selected are structured in ways that make them therapeutic. These include (1) designing the context of each activity so that it has meaning and relevance to the patient/client (all or some of the elements of the field of action may have to be adjusted or modified) and fulfills the requirements for arousing and sustaining the will to learn; (2) breaking down each activity into manageable steps; (3) integration with a systematic approach to management of dysfunction; (4) decisions about number and sequencing of activities to be incorporated into the program, with provision for making changes as the patient/client moves toward function; (5) inclusion of visible means of checking progress; and, when necessary, (6) adaptation or modification of activities and their fields of action, the introduction of assistive devices, or both.

Scheduling

Each activity has to be integrated into the patient/client's daily schedule; one activity is dovetailed with another, time periods are allocated for each activity, and frequence and duration of each activities session are determined.

Interaction

The interaction between the occupational therapist and the patient/client is the cornerstone of the therapeutic process. The contract for interaction, whether implicit or explicit, requires that the occupational therapist serve as a *competence model* (see p. 58) with whom the patient/client can interact in these activities situations, which by their structure call forth the will to learn on the part of the patient/client. But the occupational therapist also acts outside these activities situations to plan, organize, evaluate progress, serve as an advocate for the patient/client with professional colleagues and agencies or as a counselor with the family, and engage in a number of transactions with the patient/client in ways that are designed, step-by-step, to guide the individual toward *activities health*. Because patient/client functioning includes not only activities performance per se but also the ability to plan, solve problems, make decisions, initiate action, and carry over skills to a number of different situations, the occupational therapist intervenes less and less as the patient/client does more and more with increasing confidence and a growing sense of competence.

Within each activities situation, the interaction between occupational therapist and patient/client varies with the individual's needs and the context in which each activity takes place. Thus for the patient withdrawn into a schizophrenic world, an intense one-to-one relationship—the therapist a nurturing figure, recognizing and responding to the patient's dependency needs—may be the most effective beginning. On the other hand, for an office worker, whose activities routine includes typing for strengthening and coordination of fingers and wrist, the occupational therapist is a matter-of-fact but eagle-eyed supervisor who checks periodically to ensure correct positioning, watches the time carefully, evaluates progress at the end of the session, and, in addition, encourages the intelligent, well-motivated individual to work on creative solutions for coping with daily chores at home. At the other extreme, the occupational therapist, having set up the activities situation, may remain at the periphery, delegating a number of leadership tasks to the patient/client and intervening only under predetermined conditions. This kind of interaction is apparent in the description of the ceramic assembly line under Actual and Simulated Situations.

Determination of the patient/client's readiness for the acceptance of increasing responsibility is not simple. In our present state of knowledge, there are too few systematic links between behavior and performance to provide predictive criteria on which to base decisions. An illustration is provided in the case of Mrs. C, who played an unusually accurate game of tennis, was a productive member of the library committee, dressed with meticulous neatness, and was a superb craftswoman. During a particularly busy crafts session, the therapist suggested that she look for another length of leather lacing in the cabinet, to join to the piece that had run out while she was assembling a wallet. Half an hour later, when the bustle in the craft room had died down, the therapist found Mrs. C transfixed at the cupboard, face furrowed with anxiety, unable to decide which of two almost identical lengths would most closely match the one that needed joining.

In this instance, the underlying symptomatology had been glossed over by a deceptive competence. On the other hand, neither preconceptions based on clinical labeling nor a direct correlation between one kind of performance and another will serve any more accurately in the judgment of levels of functioning. The story of S. emphasizes this point well.

S., a beautifully dressed, delicate 12-year-old, was brought to the prevocational evaluation unit by her distraught parents. Both successful professionals, they were still unable to accept that their only child had been labeled severely mentally retarded and therefore ineducable. S., neat as a pin, liked nothing better than to clean and tidy up and, in the course of so doing, became acquainted with the old, creaky mimeograph machine. Her interest in the stencils, as she removed them carefully and efficiently for cleaning, prompted the occupational therapist to wonder whether she could learn to fasten them into place correctly. After painstaking, step-by-step practice, she succeeded—upside down, reverse, and all. So adept did she become that one day the occupational therapist called from across the other end of the room: "S., when you have the stencil in place, roll off 100 copies." The occupational therapist looked up and caught the expression on her face—like a puppy that had been scolded. Then it dawned on the occupational therapist—S. could operate the machine, but the concept of "100" completely eluded her because she could count only to 10. This particular story has a happy ending. When the occupational therapist told her that "100" meant one, zero, zero side-by-side, she set the dial correctly and finished the job.

By the same token, underestimation of the patient/client's capabilities and potential for change is equally undesirable. As was established in Chapter 5, the will to learn is elicited when effort is required. It is a matter of common observation that individuals tend to rise to the occasion, reinforcing Bruner's (15) contention that situations have their own demand value. This is perhaps most vividly illustrated by the behavior of a group of patients in one of the back wards of a psychiatric hospital. When a group of fashionably dressed occupational therapy students visited, it was remarkable how many of the shrunken, unkempt, empty-eyed old men automatically straightened up, made ineffectual dabs at their uncombed hair, and tugged at nonexistent collars and ties.

In the reciprocity of the interaction, the perceptions, attitudes, and reactions of the occupational therapist can either facilitate or hold back progress toward independence in functioning for the patient/client. One of the most prevalent expectations—that the patient/client's progress will follow a neat sequence of orderly steps provided that certain formulas for action are followed—paves the way for frustration and disappointment on both sides. *The development of healthy functioning takes for the most part an uneven course, marked occasionally by encouraging leaps, with plateaus of quiescence and even with regression (perhaps when expectations are too high or when achievement arouses anxiety about inability to respond to higher expectations).* This recognition is the first step in establishing realistic guideposts for progress. The road to patient/client independence may also be blocked, all too often quite unwittingly, by the occupational therapist's personal needs, one of which is to retain the kind of control that is sanctioned under the guise of "helping."

Modes of interaction involve both verbal and nonverbal communication. Since much of the occupational therapy emphasis is on "doing," a large and significant part of the interaction between therapist and patient/client is nonverbal. However, with the high value placed on verbal facility as an interpersonal skill in our society, all too often many of the nuances of nonverbal communication are lost in an overlay of conversational gambits that are at times irrelevant and even countertherapeutic. The concrete evidence of achievement inherent in the activities situation may be far more telling than a number of mechanical phrases (such as "That's nice," "Very good," "Fine") that frequently accompany every action in an effort to provide encouragement, whether the results are good, bad, or simply neutral.

It is in the area of interaction that the clinical skills of the occupational therapist are called into play, skills that are more than the sum of knowledge of theoretical concepts and the ability to select and organize appropriate activities. These clinical skills require sensitivity to and awareness of patient/client needs, a fine attunement to the subtlest cues provided by the patient/client, ability to interpret these cues accurately, and a wholesome respect both for the uniqueness of each individual and for the shared human potential for change. Therapeutic communication is a study in itself. Hein [43] and Ruesch and Bateson [78] offer valuable guidelines for the helping professional.

TOOLS

Tools are defined, in Bruner's [14] sense, as *amplifiers of human action* and therefore include but also encompass far more than conventional artifacts. These conventional artifacts may be equated with *equipment*, but *environments* and *time*, as we shall see from further discussion, can also serve as amplifiers of human action.

Equipment

Equipment includes specially designed apparatus and devices that assist function or compensate for absent function and labor-saving and convenience gadgets obtainable as standard merchandise. Examples of equipment range from wheelchairs, splints, protheses, Braille watches, bathroom rails, and pocket calculators to universal cuffs, rocker knives, jar openers, long-handled reachers, and graphic memory aids. Some of the most efficient items of equipment are homemade devices of astonishing simplicity, such as a length of wood set with four nails hammered halfway in at one end to lock over an old-fashioned faucet—a boon to a housewife with early-morning stiffness in her arthritic wrists and fingers, who can now lever the faucet open with shoulder abduction and elbow flexion. Another example is even more ingenious—the use of texture-matched tags stapled like laundry labels in an inconspicuous but accessible spot, to coordinate outfits for a blind business executive living alone. Other items of equipment are designed and constructed by the occupational therapist and include splints and devices to aid function, such as cuffs to hold writing and eating utensils. Equipment may be applied or attached to

1. The patient/client—splints, slings, prostheses, weighted cuffs, functional devices.
2. Objects in the environment—bath rails, jar opener attached to kitchen shelf, armrests for chair, medication chart on refrigerator door.
3. Activities apparatus—padded grip for printing press lever or toothbrush, easel for checkerboard, pulley and weight for vertical sanding block, colored indicators for hot/cold faucets.

Environments

Environments consist of physical settings, people, and objects.

SETTINGS

Occupational therapy is carried out in a variety of settings but need not be confined to the space formally allocated to its operations. The game of marabaraba (see Chapter 5) is moved to a path outside the tiny occupational therapy department. An unfrequented corner of a pediatric floor is an area admirably suited to a game of sedentary balloon volleyball for a group of children recovering from extensive burns. The dayroom of a unit is a good place to practice social skills with coffee, cake, and a demonstration of beauty products for a group of women for whom the institution is home, while the gymnasium, preempted for an hour, becomes a ballroom for elderly men and women with Parkinson's disease. In good weather, the hospital grounds, with their lawns and trees, are the best possible setting for the intricate needlework project that is the means of communication between a therapist and a withdrawn young mother. The gift shop run by the women's auxiliary offers a practical and realistic way to help an uncoordinated adolescent cope with the hazards of shopping—communicating his needs to the salesperson, negotiating the narrow aisles cluttered with merchandise projecting from the shelves, selecting and carrying an item to the cash desk, taking money from a purse, and gathering up change and package.

PEOPLE

The *interpersonal environment* with its rules for interaction can be varied as much as the physical setting. At one extreme the occupational therapist and patient/client may be isolated in a secluded area from which extraneous stimuli have been deliberately excluded, while at the other extreme the patient/client may be at the center of a large and vociferous group (e.g., the marabaraba game again).

OBJECTS

The objects in the environment encompass (1) those that may be peripheral to the activities situation—such as the furnishings of a room—and (2) those that are deliberately incorporated into the field of action—such as activities equipment, a special arrangement of chairs, or the merchandise in the hospital gift shop.

In most cases, environments are preselected and structured, but there are instances, given the appropriate milieu, where the selection of environment and indeed an activities "happening" can occur quite spontaneously, as the following vignette provided by an occupational therapist illustrates:

It has been more than usually hectic in the occupational therapy department. Walking along the glassed-in corridor I glimpse the inner court, enticingly empty—a good place to munch apple and cheese and unwind from the morning's tensions. I enjoy the coolness of the stone bench and the marvelous patterns formed by the multicolored pebbles on the ground. In wanders R., fair hair disheveled, pale eyes dreamy and distant. Diffidently, he asks if he may join me. A social overture from R.—usually so withdrawn, beset with his inner demons—how can I refuse? He crouches down beside the bench, poking among the pebbles with a stick. We sit in companionable silence for a while. Then, "Look at the colors"— his eyes still fixed on the pebbles—"lovely swirly patterns—just stones—and these tiny plants coming up between them—and they're alive." "Yes," I say, "isn't it incredible? Pushing up for survival among the stones, tiny as they are." He looks up at that, dreamy film gone, and smiles. We talk on, about the trees fringing the courtyard, the number of birds that come to visit, growing plants as a hobby, bird-watching. Several other young people have drifted in, and we are now deeply into environment, pollution, and ecology; some are professorial like R., others contribute their opinions in the pithy language of the streets. "Hey, man," says S., "we could make our own ecology group! That __ pile in back of the OT could be cleared up for a start." The lunch break has moved fast. In trots B., cute face plastered with rouge, deep blue eyes fringed with improbable spikes, platform shoes clattering on the pebbles. She looks at me anxiously. "Is this a special group?" (We use group activities a great deal in the hospital.) "Yes, it's a special group for special people. Come join us for the time we have left."

Time

Time amplifies human action in that a number of repetitions over time are required to ensure that

1. Learning is integrated enough to promote carry-over to appropriate situations.
2. Physical changes, such as building up of endurance, can take place.
3. Interpersonal relationships can be established and developed.
4. Newly acquired skills can be applied and tested in a variety of situations.

As has been discussed at length in Chapter 2, *time* is an important tool for the organization of activities in socioculturally acceptable patterns, thus reflecting an integral aspect of reality. In many instances, an individual's chief problem may be, for a variety of clinical reasons, inability to make use of time effectively. This includes not only underactivity but also the kind of overactivity that can turn a period of free time into a fearsome experience for an anxiety-ridden or hyperactive individual.

A device that serves as the framework for the Idiosyncratic Activities Configuration (as well as, of course, the *Activities Health Assessment*) is the weekly printed schedule. It is useful simply as a tool for organization, but it may also require of the individual an increasing assumption of responsibility, such as in making selections from a repertoire of choices, solving problems of clashes and conflicts, and budgeting time realistically. The "musts" and electives as well as free periods, meal breaks, and the unwritten time to be allocated for preparation, travel, and other contingencies apply as much to general activities patterns as to those more overtly familiar, such as the student schedule.

TECHNIQUES

Techniques are those procedures that are derived from theoretical propositions or are based on an empirical approach. As indicated in Chapter 5 (under Management of Dysfunction), there are numerous theories about human function and dysfunction and numerous treatment approaches arising from them. To be incorporated into occupational therapy programs, it is important that such procedures

1. Relate to the physical and psychological needs of the individual.
2. "Make sense" in an activities-related system of intervention.
3. Dovetail with those activities, procedures, and situations that can sucessfully be administered within the constraints of a particular setting.

For the occupational therapist to select the most appropriate technique requires sufficient knowledge of the theoretical concepts and, in many cases where applicable, the methods advocated to answer the following questions:

1. What does the proponent have to say about the nature of the human condition?
2. How does the proponent differentiate a functional from a dysfunctional individual?
3. What are the stages of development leading to function or dysfunction?

4. By what mechanisms does change from dysfunction toward function take place?
5. In what time period is change expected to take place?

(A worksheet for this kind of analytical look at theoretical approaches will be found in Appendix E. See also Assignment 4 at the end of Chapter 5.)

An example of a carefully documented, step-by-step treatment method based on empirical observation and a theoretical rationale is that advanced by Brunnstrom [17]. Her fundamental premise is that recovery from hemiplegia in adults follows a sequence that parallels the ontogenetic development of neuromuscular control—from a preponderance of reflex activity, through linked patterns of movement, toward ultimate dissociation from synergies, and finally voluntary control. At the basis of treatment are two assumptions: (1) that sensory input can influence motor input and (2) that recovery can be hastened by first harnessing the mechanisms present in the existing level of function/dysfunction (e.g., reflex activity) and then incorporating them with sensory input and feedback into a series of facilitation techniques, which lead toward the next stage of recovery.

The techniques for evaluating level of function/dysfunction and for facilitating change in the direction from dysfunction toward function are precisely and clearly described by Brunnstrom. It is for the occupational therapist to examine the method and ask if it meshes appropriately with an *activities health approach*. One of the crucial determinations to be made, assuming that Brunnstrom's propositions "make sense," is at which stage of recovery it is possible to begin occupational therapy. Is Stage 1, flaccidity, the point at which the needs of the patient can be met by incorporation of an activities program? Perhaps—if the unaffected side is used to facilitate associated responses that will influence the development of tone in the muscles of the affected side. On the other hand, if occupational therapy incorporates bimanual activities when spasticity has developed, what then will be the effect on muscle tone? How does this consideration affect the planning, design, and administration of activities, when one bears in mind that these activities also must have meaning and relevance to the patient/client?

A combination of more than one theory is used in a psychiatric outpatient program, serving patients with chronic psychiatric illness and long-standing dysfunction. Erikson's [28] psychoanalytically based developmental theory, which is based on the assumption that "the human personality in principle develops according to steps predetermined in the growing person's readiness to be driven toward, to be aware of, and to interact with, a widening social readiness," is used to assess the patient/client's degree of psychological maturation and readiness to grapple with age-appropriate developmental tasks. However, since the patient/clients generally lack the ego strengths necessary for making use of treatment strategies that would assist them in progressing to subsequent developmental stages, and the length of stay is limited, other theories focusing on the acquisition of activities skills needed in the here and now are also incorporated. The Occupational Behavior Model guides the therapist in the identification of roles that the patient/client has assumed by choice or necessity, the assessment of performance skills necessary for carrying out these roles, and the patient/client's level of motivation and perception of his or her own level of competence.

Treatment goals are established that are consistent with the patient/client's degree of developmental readiness. They may include modifications of the roles assumed or desired by the patient/client to bring them into better alignment with their skills and psychological ability to carry them out; they also may address the improvement of performance skills necessary for carrying out the activities that are required of the patient/client.

The approach to treatment is a practical one, incorporating the kind of learning experiences that Bruner [15] describes. The therapist serves as a "competence model," from whom both the "techniques and rituals" of everyday living are learned "in context" to the degree possible, making use of everyday fields of action outside of the facility for therapeutic activities experiences.

At each stage of the clinical reasoning process, each of these theories is carefully selected and used to develop procedures for treatment (see Figure 9-1) within an *activities health* framework, which serves as a structure for organizing information and making an ordered series of clinical decisions. (See also the case of Mr. and Mrs. G. in Chapter 12 for another example of how theories lead to strategies for the management of dysfunction.)

Techniques, together with activities and the tools for amplifying human action, are the instruments by which the individual is helped to a state of *activities health*. The methods adopted by the occupational therapist ensure that those instruments are best suited to the psychological and physical needs of the individual and that they serve their purpose in a controlled progression on the way toward functional independence of the patient/client.

Assignment 1

In a clinic known to you, list the activities available that fulfill the criteria for defining activities as therapeutic. What other activities could you introduce to meet individual needs of patients/clients?

Assignment 2

List all the ways of adapting activities that you have observed or used. What other potential for adaptation—when you look at properties and characteristics of the activity and its field of action—do these activities have?

Assignment 3

A. Make four separate lists—each representing one patient/client—of activities that would have meaning and relevance for that patient/client (without considering external constraints). Each patient/client is to be selected from a different age group, socioeconomic status, and ethnic background, and each is to have different physical and/or psychosocial problems.

B. Reduce the list of activities in each of your lists to those that are also firstly *adaptable*, then *versatile*, and then *practical*.

C. Finally, list those activities for each person that have a combination of all the qualities needed to make them therapeutically useful.

Assignment 4

Whenever you have a chance to observe in a clinic, make notes of the potential for using environments other than the space formally assigned. Consider even long-distance therapeutic situations—for example, a phone call from a patient who in great trepidation had to negotiate a subway ride alone as his activity assignment and reported on his safe arrival at his destination; or little M., dying of a congenital and incurable cardiac condition, receiving a picture-letter from her vacationing occupational therapist, in which was enclosed a small bag of sand and tiny shells glued to the pages between funny sketches of fishermen and bathing beauties. Compare your list with those of your class-mates/colleagues.

CHAPTER 11

Incorporating Activities as Means and Ends: General Principles

A number of general principles follow from a point of view centered on activities both as therapeutic agents and as beacons of healthy functioning. These principles, which are applicable to any form of intervention for any patient/client, relate to the four stages that characterize the total occupational therapy process. These four stages are *Initial Assessment, Planning, Implementation,* and *Termination* (Figure 11-1). The Clinical Problem-Solving Model (Figure 9-1) illustrates the components of each of these steps.

Stage 1: Initial Assessment

Stage 1 is designed for two purposes: to establish patient/client needs and to establish whether occupational therapy can help meet these needs.

The processes and procedures used in the clinical assessment are directed toward answering the following questions:

Who is this individual who has come for help?

What is this individual's activities configuration in terms of past and present experiences and future wishes?

What are the physical, intellectual, emotional, and interpersonal skills required to perform these activities in ways that are individually satsifying and socioculturally acceptable?

Which of these skills does the individual have?

Which of these skills have never been developed?

Which of these skills has the individual lost, temporarily or permanently?

How long have these skills been lost or unavailable?

Time Frame	Principles	Interaction	
		Therapist	Patient/ Client
1 day to 1 week	Stage I. Initial Assessment		
	1. Begin all programs with initial assessment	F	M–F
	2. Select suitable data-gathering methods	F	
	3. Correlate all data and interpret	F	
	4. Determine patient/client's needs	F	
	Initial assessment consists of:		
	Data collection	F	M–F
	Interpretation of data	F	M
Variable	Stage II. Planning		
	1. Establish goals, both long-term and short-term	F	M–F
	2. Select activities on the basis of established criteria	F	M–F
	3. Structure activities in a field of action	F	F
	4. Incorporate adaptations and equipment with discrimination and restraint	F	M–F
	5. Schedule according to criteria that will assure therapeutic administration	F	M–F
	6. Establish conditions for interaction	F	
	Planning consists of:		
	Definition of goals	F	M–F
	Establishment of priorities	F	M–F
	Design of a program	F	M–F
Variable	Stage III. Implementation		
	1. Prepare activities situation as determined in plan	F	M–F
	2. Instruct according to a methodical sequence of steps	F	
	3. Check correct positioning and standard of performance periodically	F	
	4. Graduate amount of supervision and interaction	M–F	
	5. Follow conditions for interaction as determined in plan	F	M–F
	6. Incorporate a means for checking progress	F	
	7. Prepare patient/client for each required step	F	M–F
	Implementation consists of:		
	Structuring of activities situations	F	M–F
	Instruction in activities procedures	F	M–F
	Interaction with patient/client	M–F	M–F
	Observation of precautions	F	
	Observation of patient/client performance and attendant behaviors	F	
	Evaluation of progress	F	M–F
Variable	Stage IV. Termination		
	1. Prepare patient/client for termination	F	F
	2. Establish links with family, other individuals, and community agencies	F	M–F
	3. Prepare activities plan for daily living at home	M	F
	4. Arrange for follow-up	F	F
	Termination consists of:		
	Tapering off program for ultimate independent or near-independent functioning in home and community	M	F
	Follow-up	F	F

Figure 11-1. Summary of the occupational therapy process, highlighting the relationship between the occupational therapist and the patient/client. (M = minimal participation; F = full participation; M–F = minimal to full shared participation.)

What are the possibilities for (1) regaining lost skills, (2) compensating or substituting for lost skills, and (3) achieving new skills?

What are the probabilities, given realistic constraints, of regaining these skills?

To answer these questions, it is clear that the occupational therapist requires special assessment tools as well as special emphases in assembling data gathered from other sources, whether it be by the use of tools borrowed from other disciplines (e.g., goniometry from physical therapy, or genogram from social work) or by incorporating reports from other disciplines. Also, further instruments for exploration of the activities life of the individual are directed to selected aspects of an activities history. In the context of an already existing activities situation or carefully designed and controlled simulations of activities situations, it is possible for observations to be made of the level of functioning in any one or combination of performance areas as diverse, for example, as leadership skills or thumb to finger prehension (see Fidler [31]). This kind of ad hoc assessment adds descriptive detail that is useful in helping to make determinations of the extent to which dysfunction in performance components affects the ability to carry out essential activities of everyday living with satisfaction and comfort. In the realm of physical dysfunction, a functional evaluation—that is, an assessment of the basic patterns of motion required for functioning in day-to-day living—is much more to the point for occupational therapy than measurement of isolated ranges of joint motion and strength of individual muscles. Indeed, goniometry and muscle testing are useful only insofar as they can be directly correlated with an assessment of functional level in the skills necessary for performance of activities. Likewise with psychological testing—results of cognitive evaluations are relevant to occupational therapy insofar as they relate to the doing of everyday activities. However, for every kind of clinical dysfunction, guarding against indiscriminate use of evaluation tools and overzealous accumulation of data is important for effective and efficient assessment. Often reports from other disciplines, such as physical therapy, social work, or psychology, suffice for background information, without the need to subject the patient/client to similar routines of investigation in occupational therapy.

Since prognosis and projections have to be made, it is necessary not only to gather data but also to interpret them. An interpretation that leads to determination of patient/client needs based on strengths and liabilities, general life-style, and wishes and desires also permits the decision to be made as to whether occupational therapy is able to provide assistance in meeting those needs. The principles of occupational therapy emerge as follows:

1. Begin every occupational therapy program with an initial assessment.
2. Select carefully from existing data or methods of obtaining data to ensure that information about the activities needs of the patient/client will be obtained in the most economical and effective way.
3. Correlate and interpret data in terms of patient/client strengths and liabilities as they relate to skills needed for activities functioning.
4. Determine, in the light of assessment of patient/client needs, whether occupational therapy is able to assist in meeting those needs.

Stage 2: Planning

Stage 2 involves defining goals for meeting patient/client needs, establishing priorities in the case of multiple goals, and designing a program that will lead the patient/client, step-by-step, toward attainment of the goals.

The design of the program encompasses selection of activities and their fields of action, selection of appropriate tools and techniques, breakdown of activities processes into manageable steps, adaptation of activities (if necessary), and scheduling, not only for activities per se but also for sessions directed to evaluating progress toward *activities health*, checking on meaning and relevance and transfer of learning. Into the design is built provision for changes in program, either because of changes in the patient/client's condition or because of changes in external circumstances. The establishment of realistic goals requires that the occupational therapist predict in some measure the results of following an advocated method and the length of time required for these results to occur. Principles for planning include the following:

1. Establish goals that not only meet patient/client needs but also can realistically be carried out within the resources and constraints of the therapeutic situation.
2. Establish both long-range overall goals and short-term goals as attainable steps toward reaching the long-term goals.
3. Select activities for each short-term goal that have meaning and relevance for the patient/client.
4. Select activities as alternatives to be held in reserve in case of changes.
5. Structure activities situations in ways that arouse and harness the will to learn.
6. Select and schedule activities situations that are as close as possible to situations in the real world.
7. Incorporate the simplest and the least number of adaptations possible to ensure maximal function.
8. Use the simplest and the least amount of equipment possible to effect maximal function.
9. Schedule activities with sufficient frequency of repetition and duration to promote integration of learning.
10. Schedule specific periods for evaluation of progress and subsequent adjustment or modification of program.
11. Establish conditions for interaction with the patient/client, including frequency of instruction, kinds of intervention (directive or nondirective), degree of closeness, ways of reinforcing desired behaviors, ways of evaluating progress, delegation of parts of the program to others, and incorporation of others into the program, as in group activities with family.

Stage 3: Implementation

Implementation is the carrying out of the occupational therapy plan, which includes structuring of activities situations, instruction in activities procedures, interaction with patient/client, observation of precautions, observation of patient/client performance and attendant behaviors, and evaluation of progress. The plan is adjusted according to patient/client responses and modified according to step-by-step progress toward attainment of goals. Principles for implementation are as follows:

1. Design the activities situation ahead of time to ensure that (a) the conditions for arousing and sustaining the will to learn are fulfilled; (b) the physical setting and the activities in their fields of action are arranged and structured as predetermined in the plan and that extraneous objects, people, and external stimuli do not obtrude; and (c) all necessary precautions have been taken for the comfort and safety of the patient/client.
2. Whenever necessary, break the activities down into manageable steps, making explicit the relationship of one step to another.
3. When instructing, explain in ways comprehensible to the patient/client, checking to see that each step has been mastered before proceeding to the next.
4. When demonstrating, make sure your starting position is the same as the patient/client's (sit when the patient/client is sitting; stand when it is desired that the patient/client stand; face the same way as the patient/client).
5. Check, at appropriate intervals, to ensure maintenance of correct positioning and standard of performance.
6. Watch for signs of fatigue or stress or unusual behaviors and respond accordingly, either suspending activity or adjusting the situation as required.
7. Graduate amount of support and assistance given according to the patient/client's responses.
8. Follow conditions for interaction established in the plan.
9. Incorporate a visible means for checking progress (e.g., score in a game, recording of time taken to perform, number of knots achieved toward completion in a macrame belt, completion of an end product, number of pounds of weight lifted, tokens earned) in the steps of each activity.
10. Prepare the patient/client for continuity of the program by outlining a plan for the following session or soliciting suggestions from the patient/client, when ready to contribute.
11. At appropriate intervals, design activities assignments to check whether transfer of learning from simulated to actual activities situations has taken place.

Stage 4: Termination

Tapering off and ending a patient/client program in preparation for indepedent carry-over of newly acquired skills into the real world of day-to-day living is of such crucial importance that *termination* is designated as a separate stage.

Under ideal conditions, goals are reached in a predictable period of time, so that termination plans can be incorporated in advance, including preparation of the patient/client for separation by an increasing number of assignments at home and in the community. Unfortunately, particularly in institutional settings, a number of externally imposed conditions often preclude such planning, much less follow-up of patient/client progress after termination. Sometimes the occupational therapist may be able to "buy time" for the patient/client, by proposing a plan for further treatment or referral to another agency for the period of transition. But in all events, if occupational therapy is to fulfill its promise for the patient/client, the stage of termination, and the principles that apply, must be considered as an integral part of the occupational therapy process, even if the patient will never be able to return to the world outside or will have to undergo repeated hospitalizations for a progresssively worsening condition. The principles for termination are as follows:

1. Prepare the patient/client for termination of the program by indicating a possible termination date (in consultation with the therapeutic team when appropriate), acknowledging and dealing with feelings about separation as needed.
2. Assign as many activities requiring near-independent or independent functioning as possible, preferably in the home or community.
3. Establish links with the family and other individuals important to the patient/client to ensure support for carry-over of activities into the home.
4. Establish links with agencies in the community that can be of assistance to the patient/client.
5. Prepare with the patient/client, family, and other individuals a plan for a day-to-day activities program that will be personally satisfying as well as socioculturally acceptable.
6. Arrange for follow-up reports, or other contacts to review functioning, at regular intervals.

An alternative to steps 3, 4, and 5 would be to refer the patient/client, with a proposed activities plan, to a community agency or a community or home-care therapist for furtherance of independent functioning in the home and community.

Integrating Specific Principles

Besides these general principles, which serve as a framework of operation for all patients/clients, there are specific principles that arise out of each special situation, requiring selected theoretical approaches relating both to management of dysfunction and to the relationship between the individual and activities. These specific principles have to be integrated and meshed with the principles for incorporating activities as means and ends. The patient/client participates in each stage as fully as physical, emotional, and intellectual capacities allow. Figure 9-1 summarizes the stages of the occupational therapy process, the principles that apply to each, and the points at which activities participation by the patient/client, ranging from minimal contributions to complete independence from the occupational therapist, is possible.

Assignment 1

Teach yourself a skill that is currently in style from written instructions. Record you responses and reactions as you go through the learning process and the time taken to learn the skill. Note the modifications you would make in recommending this method of learning to another individual. Now that you have mastered the skill, analyze step-by-step the procedure you would use to impart it to other individuals in age groups, in sociocultural groups, and at levels of intelligence different from your own. Check in each case whether you have introduced any elements that arouse and sustain the will to learn.

Assignment 2

Practice teaching a fellow student or colleague a skill that is familiar to you but that you do not particularly enjoy. Ask for comments and suggestions from your learner at the end of the teaching session. This may also be done with the addition of a group of observers who contribute their comments at the end of the session.

Assignment 3

Try out a number of different ways of introducing yourself and an activity to an individual who

A. Is considerably older than you.
B. Is much younger than you.
C. Finds it difficult to communicate verbally.
D. Has some form of sensory deprivation.
E. Appears to you to be superior (indicate in what ways).

Videotaping would be most appropriate for this assignment and also useful for Assignment 2.

PUTTING IT ALL TOGETHER: CLINICAL PROBLEM-SOLVING

To arrive at a workable plan of clinical intervention that (1) is designed to meet the needs of one individual, (2) balances the constraints of the clinical setting with the fulfillment of principles for the incorporation of activities as means and ends, (3) integrates the principles for the incorporation of activities as means and ends with the principles for the management of dysfunction, (4) incorporates means for the periodic reassessment of progress, including checking on transfer of learning to real-life situations, and (5) incorporates provisions for continuity and follow-up until the individual's needs are met requires a complex problem-solving process that is generally referred to as clinical reasoning. This process is by no means confined to the planning stage of the clinical program. In the day-to-day events of implementation, on-the-spot "problem-solving" (often intuitive) tends to replace deliberative reasoning in response to patient/client reactions and unexpected but inevitable situational disruptions. But the deliberative process has to continue, both in retrospectively assessing the appropriateness of the intuitive response and in making decisions relating to reassessment and adjustment at predetermined intervals.

In the Educational Model (Part II), the clinical reasoning process has been broken down into manageable steps (much as activities are broken down for the patient/ client) to facilitate learning. As with all learning of complicated procedures, clinical problem-solving begins as a slow and laborious process, which, with practice, finally becomes integrated as a special skill applied to solving problems in a systematic manner within a reasonably short time. In the press of the clinical situation—and indeed in the health care environment as a whole—where time is at a premium, even a "reasonably short time" may tend to be compressed or curtailed in favor of producing immediate "treatment." But without the proper weight attached to careful thinking through of plans and strategies designed to meet the particular needs of each individual, activities do not, and cannot, fulfill their promise as means toward *activities health*. (See Parham [66] on the reflective therapist.)

The steps in the clinical problem-solving process, as they appear in the Educational Model, with accompanying explanations (pp. 136–171) are

1. The assessment of *activities health*—through the use of the *Activities Health Assessment*, other evaluation tools, and sources of information for (a) establishing needs and (b) setting goals.
2. Analysis of activities—selected on the basis of interpretation of information.
3. Analyzing available resources in the clinical field of action, which includes (a) identifying available resources and the constraints that may impinge on implementation and (b) uncovering untapped resources.
4. Treatment planning—setting occupational therapy goals on the basis of (a) determination of individual needs and (b) consideration of realistic constraints.
5. Selecting activities to be used for therapeutic purposes—including instrumental supports.
6. Selecting relevant theories and strategies for managing dysfunction.
7. Implementation—structuring therapeutic activities experiences on the basis of needs, resources available/constraints, which includes modifications of actor/activities/field of action as needed.
8. Discharge planning—making provisions for transfer of learning, continuity of program, follow-up, and/or appropriate termination of program.

The following two parts of the process are each of a different order from the preceding steps:

9. Reassessment, which is interwoven throughout the treatment process, occurring at selected intervals. Determination of when it is appropriate to pause for formal reassessment and what adjustments are to be made on the basis of that reassessment is part of the clinical reasoning process.
10. "Putting it all together"—combines all the steps into an integrated procedure for clinical problem-solving. (See also Chapter 9, A Critique of Clinical Reasoning.)

Chapter 12 takes the practice of clinical reasoning a step further—by application to real people, whose cases represent a wide range of individuals (age, gender, sociocultural, and regional differences) in different clinical situations, with a wide variety of clinical dysfunctions.

Assignment

Following each of the explanations in the Educational Model are assignments that provide a number of opportunities to practice, in sequence, the procedures relating to each step of the clinical problem-solving process. The two final assignments are directed to the integration of many of these steps into a continuous process.

CHAPTER 12

Application to Specific Instances: Making Use of Case Material

The individuals selected for the case histories in this chapter highlight an *activities health* approach to clinical problem-solving. They not only are representative of the age, cultural, and socioeconomic groups encountered in our complex society but also have experiences uniquely their own. Their problems result from dysfunction. Our proposed solutions look toward function. Although the cases reflect problems that are representative of those commonly found in practice, the procedures that are advocated, if tried and true, should be just as applicable to the different, the unusual, and the more complex.

The Ideal Case: Mr. and Mrs. G.

We begin with an "ideal" case, presented in its entirety, complete with intervention strategies, activities programs, outcomes, and follow-up. This case serves as a lode-stone that guides our efforts, even though we know that in the real world of health care we seldom find such a felicitous match among the couple who have come for help, the clinical situation that is conducive to immediate application of intervention strategies to the real world and allows for attainment of outcomes perceptibly related to these strategies, and an occupational therapist who is skilled in "putting it all together."

Program of Instruction for Clinical Problem-Solving

A sequence of procedural steps, following the principles in Chapter 11, guides the processing of information for purposes of clinical problem-solving, which ultimately leads to the incorporation of activities as means toward *activities health*.

The specifics of Mrs. B.'s case (to follow) serve as a concrete example for illustration. The program of instruction is applicable to each and every case that follows—and indeed, *any other case*, including those presented in briefer form (see Brief Case Histories on pp. 256–265).

Mrs. B.

The second very detailed case serves to introduce Mrs. B. She is more "typical" in that she suffers from a widely prevalent clinical condition, hemiplegia, and is being treated, in common with many others who suffer from the same condition, in a rehabilitation center. Because of the organizational constraints—rules, regulations, policies, and the structure of the clinical setting in which Mrs. B. finds herself—she is, of necessity, removed from her everyday activities environment, even though provision is made for practice of daily living skills by means of simulations, which to some extent resemble conditions in the real world.

For Mrs. B. and *all other individuals* who, like her, are being treated where activities simulations have to be used, it is necessary to make provisions for facilitating the transfer of learning to real-life situations. (See Actual and Simulated Situations in Chapter 10.)

Mr. S.; P.; M.; and Mr. D.

Four other detailed case histories follow—a 35-year-old man in a psychiatric facility, with a history of delusions, heavy drinking, and homicidal tendencies; a nearly 7-year-old first-grader with learning disabilities treated by an occupational therapist in private practice; a 7-year-old girl with multiple psychosocial problems on an inpatient child psychiatry unit; and a 66-year-old man with a severe hand and forearm injury treated in a private hand rehabilitation center.

The Activities Health Assessment

The *Activities Health Assessment* has been used as a primary instrument for obtaining information about the activities life of Mr. and Mrs. G., Mr. D., and Mrs. N. For the other detailed cases, activities information was collected in less structured ways, such as informal interview, history-taking, observation, and reports from other sources. However, steps in the program of instruction allow for information gathered in these ways to be processed *as if* the *Activities Health Assessment* had been used. It is inevitable that there will be some gaps in the information collected from a number of diverse and diffuse sources as contrasted with the special focus and systematic method of a formal instrument such as the *Activities Health Assessment*, which also serves to direct and bring into focus a collection of information from secondary sources. Thus some inferences will have to be made (and clearly recognized as such) to bridge the gaps and continue with the clinical problem-solving process in the ensuing steps. The program of instruction makes provision for such eventualities by means of leading questions and helpful cues.

Brief Case Histories

The brief case histories give some indication of the scope of practice of occupational therapy. Included are settings, like the nursing home for Mr. D. and the institution for developmental disabilities for Mr. L., that become home for the individual unable or unwilling to cope in the outside world or that are transitional but increasingly necessary sources of support for those like D., suffering from AIDS. Not included are many other specific clinical conditions that always have been and are still encountered by the occupational therapist in the course of daily practice, some of the special problems that have come to the fore in recent years (e.g., Alzheimer's disease), or the newer settings that have been entered (e.g., the prison, the hospice, and the streets where the homeless wander). As mentioned earlier, the program of instruction for clinical problem-solving applies as appropriately to the briefer cases as to the more detailed ones. However, because the information given is less comprehensive, it becomes necessary in each case

1. To make inferences, from the information given, about the ways in which the clinical condition affects the performance components required for carrying out the activities of everyday living. (For students still unacquainted with clinical conditions, this information can be provided by the instructor in summary form, which is enough to help with subsequent problem-solving.) This part of the clinical problem-solving process may also serve as a class assignment, with appropriate selections from the briefer histories, for courses presenting clinical conditions in terms of medical description or application to the practice of occupational therapy.
2. To make inferences about the state of *activities health* of the individual, clearly indicating the reasons for these conclusions. (Group discussion is very valuable here).

From "Coming Home To Die" To Activities Health: The Case of Mrs. N.

The case presentations end with a narrative entitled "From 'Coming Home to Die' to *Activities Health*." In this detailed description of how Mrs. N. moved from an almost hopeless situation toward *activities health*, it is possible to detect

1. Strengths and liabilities—both in Mrs. N. and her family situation.
2. The deficits in *activities health* that were present at the time of referral, because of her clinical problems.
3. The state of *activities health* Mrs. N. attained (check for *overall satisfaction, comfort, fit with sociocultural group, variety,* and *balance* in activities patterns).
4. The conditions under which Mrs. N. attained a state of *activities health*:
   a. Arousing and sustaining the *will to learn.*
   b. Incorporating activities that have *meaning* and *relevance* to Mrs. N. as therapeutic *means.*

      c. Incorporating *strategies for management of dysfunction* based on a theoretical rationale or empirical observation.
      d. Using appropriate *instrumental supports* for incorporating activities as therapeutic *media.*

The case of Mrs. N. serves as (1) an aid for review of the concepts, connections, and conclusions of Part I as applied to a specific instance; (2) a reiteration of the statement that *activities health* can be attained *despite* clinically labeled signs and symptoms, because often the most effective human action is of a "substitute or compensatory nature"; and (3) a confirmation of the effectiveness of activities in their total context (a) when they serve as means toward the attainment of a state of *activities health* and (b) when the occupational therapist "puts it all together"—assessment, reassessment, implementation, and conclusion.

AN "IDEAL" CASE: MR. AND MRS. G.—GERONTIC OCCUPATIONAL THERAPY IN PRIVATE PRACTICE

Patricia A. Miller

The following case study illustrates the multidimensional approach used by the gerontic occupational therapist. Psychological, physical, social, and environmental parameters are integral to assessment and treatment. The means to achieving a state of well-being for the older person is the development of new or modified roles and activities patterns, valued by the individual and his/her significant others.

The capacity to make a positive adjustment to retirement is based on multiple variables. Was the individual's retirement voluntary or mandatory? How much of a person's identity or self-esteem was based on the work role? Have there been activities performed outside the work role that have been meaningful to the individual? Do the person's leisure or other interests include a spouse or friends? If the answer is "no" to one or more of the above questions, does the person have the mental and cathectic flexibility to be able to develop new activities and relationships? Does the person's state of health facilitate or impede pursuit of varied, valued activities? These are just a few of the issues addressed by an occupational therapist when referred a client who is depressed following retirement.

Referral Information

A married couple was seen for consultation by this occupational therapist. The referring psychiatrist stated, "I understand you're an expert in helping older people find new interests after retirement." He went on to say that the husband of the couple came to see him at his wife's request, but he saw the two of them together for just two visits. "Although Mr. G. is the 'identified patient,' they are both depressed and need help," he explained.

Identifying and Background Information

Client: Mr. S. G.

Age: 81 years.

Diagnoses: Depression, post-retirement (2 years); emphysema, peripheral vascular disease (aneurysm surgically removed from right leg, 1986, one is being monitored in left leg); two transient ischemic attacks in 3 years.

Concurrent treatment: Mr. G. is seen regularly by an internist and neurologist. Medications include theophylline, Ventolin, Persantine, and Disalcid.

Occupation: Electrical engineer (retired 2 years); consultant engineer (part-time) for 6 months post-retirement. Since retirement, Mr. G. tried two volunteer positions, one in a hospital and the other in a nursing home. He described the former as "demeaning" and the latter "depressing."

Social data: Mr. G. and his wife have an apartment in Manhattan, a country home in Connecticut, and 3 to 4 months of every winter are spent in Florida. They do not have children but derive great pleasure from their 6-year-old cocker spaniel. Mr. G.'s three siblings are deceased. At present, he spends much of his time in bed.

Client: Mrs. A. G.

Age: 63 years.

Diagnosis: Adjustment disorder, mild depression.

Concurrent treatment: None. Mrs. G. is in good health. She goes to an internist for annual checkups.

Occupation: Executive secretary of large law firm (retired, 1 year).

Social data: Mrs. G.'s parents are deceased. She has one older sister and a brother-in-law, who live in Rhode Island. Because of their three homes, Mrs. G. states that it is difficult to pursue friendships, and socializing in recent years has been minimal. She and her husband always had many interests in common in the past. However, she states, "Now all we have in common is mutual lethargy!"

Initial Evaluation

ORIENTING THE CLIENT TO GERONTIC OCCUPATIONAL THERAPY

In language understandable to the layperson, the occupational therapist oriented Mr. and Mrs. G. to the purpose of therapy. "As you know, retirement is a difficult adjustment. You have gone from being very productive and recognized for your contributions in your work lives to having lots of free time and feeling dissatisfied with your activities of everyday living. The 'lethargy' you describe becomes a vicious cycle—the less you do that's satisfying, the less you feel like doing, and the less initiative you take, the worse you feel about yourselves. The purpose of occupational therapy will be to pool your resources in order for you to regain *activities health*, that is, to improve the quality of your lives."

Although Mr. G. was presented by the referring psychiatrist as the person who was suffering, the therapist pointed out that "the suffering of one affects the other in a two-person household. Being human, Mrs. G. may also be having difficulties that, in part, may be a reaction to Mr. G.'s mood, but may be related to individual concerns as well." Mr. and Mrs. G. were each asked to describe their reasons for coming for assistance (felt need) and willingness (motivation) to do something about their needs. The therapist made an assessment (objective need) that was shared with Mr. and Mrs. G. In this participative mode, the therapist and clients "put their heads together" to determine needs, to set goals, and to modify activities and activities patterns to reduce dysfunction and promote *activities health*.

GATHERING DATA

While Mr. and Mrs. G. were getting their bearings in the new surroundings, the occupational therapist requested identifying and background information (see p. 209) from each of them. Collection of this information also served as an informal cognitive assessment, as the therapist carefully noted the accuracy and appropriateness of response to questions.

EXPLORING NEEDS

A semi-structured interview followed to create a relaxed and nonthreatening atmosphere. Open-ended questions included: "What brought you here? Are there any other difficulties you'd like me to know about? Tell me something about how you spend your days? What do you enjoy doing—alone? together? How frequently do you do the things you enjoy? Are there many activities you do just because you feel you have to do them?"

SETTING GOALS

"What do you want to change?" and "How would you like to see your lives differently?" are necessary questions to be asked before setting goals. They were asked in an unhurried, nonjudgmental manner to avoid having Mr. or Mrs. G. feel defensive or tested. Explicitly telling Mr. and Mrs. G. to take their time between questions and answers and allowing silences enabled them to be introspective and to respond with answers reflective of their true feelings.

The First Visit

Mrs. G. drove to the occupational therapist's office with Mr. G. in the passenger seat. Both ambulated without difficulty, with Mr. G. using a cane.

Mr. G. appeared alert and is a good-looking, well-built man. A mild hearing impairment (hearing aid in right ear) caused Mr. G. to ask unself-consciously for things to be repeated when he missed something. Mr. G. stated his chief complaint: "I've had nothing important to do since retirement." He also spoke (slowly with a flat affect) about not being able to do some of the things he used to be able to do because of his illnesses. He no longer felt safe rowing in the pond on their country property or dancing, both activities Mr. and Mrs. G. enjoyed together, because of shortness of breath and poor balance. He stated, "I'm disgusted with my situation."

Mrs. G., an attractive, articulate woman stated that she enjoyed her position as an executive secretary. "I enjoy relating to people, but I'm glad to be relieved of the responsibility." When Mr. and Mrs. G. go to Florida, she works part-time as a hotel desk clerk and likes the opportunity to talk with different people. However, Mrs. G. stated that she feels guilty doing this, because Mr. G. spends most of the day in bed when she is away. As a result, most of Mrs. G.'s activities involve taking care of both of their self-care needs and their three homes. "It is time-consuming and draining," Mrs. G. explains. When asked what other difficulties she might want to mention, Mrs. G. stated that she and Mr. G. were having trouble relating to each other. Mr. G. was surprised by this statement, which prompted a dialogue between them. Both admitted to being more "short-tempered" and "less fun" than they used to be. The therapist then ascertained what activities they used to enjoy together that they were no longer pursuing, and what activities they were continuing to carry out.

ACTIVITIES ENJOYED TOGETHER	CONTINUED	REDUCED	STOPPED
Concert-going		X	
Theater-going		X	
Watching spectator sports (e.g., T.V. baseball)	X		
Fishing			X
Rowboating			X
Walking		X	
Dancing			X
Vegetable gardening			X

The following *goals of treatment* were delineated in the evaluation meeting:

Goals: Mr. G.   1. Develop new, valued activities and roles.
2. Compensate for physical losses with safe, gratifying activities.
3. Increase respiratory capacity and tolerance for physical activity with an occupational therapy–prescribed exercise regime.*
4. Renew interest in joint activities with Mrs. G.
5. Relieve depression through involvement in program staged above

Goals: Mrs. G.   1. Find individual interests that give pleasure.
2. Renew support network of friends and family.
3. Renew interests in joint activities with Mr. G.
4. Remove "inertia" through program stated above.

At the conclusion of the first evaluation session, Mr. and Mrs. G. were each asked to maintain a record of the activities they were involved in every day until their next therapy session. They were each given a blank Activities Schedule (part of the *Activities Health Assessment*—see Chapter 6) and asked to bring it to their next session as a basis for beginning a discussion regarding the degree to which they were satisfied or dissatisfied with their present life-styles (Figures 12-1 and 12-2).

Theoretical Rationale Guiding Assessment and Treatment†

Three major paradigms guide this occupational therapist's practice in work with older adults: *developmental, psychodynamic,* and *activities health.*

---

* Therapist received authorization from Mr. G. to contact his internist about an exercise program for him. The internist approved the exercise regimen developed by this therapist.
† References in this section appear in Suggested Readings.

	Monday	Tuesday	Wednesday	Thursday	Friday	Saturday	Sunday
Morning				Read paper. Crushed grapes. Collected fireplace wood.			
Early Afternoon				Lunch. Repaired tree wound. Spread soil for fertilizer and grass seed.			
Late Afternoon				Watched plumber repair shower.			
Early Evening				Happy Hour. Watched news on TV. Had dinner.			
Late Evening							

Figure 12-1. Mr. G.'s activities in week 1.

	Monday	Tuesday	Wednesday	Thursday	Friday	Saturday	Sunday
Morning 7 A.M.–12 P.M.*	Up at 7. Fed dog. Ate breakfast. Listened to news and read paper. Called plumber. Woke Sid and served breakfast. Drove to town to have set of keys made and buy newspaper.	Up at 8. Follow-up calls to plumber, refrigerator serviceman.	Up at 8. Listened to news during breakfast. Read newspaper.	Up at 8. Called plumber. Listened to news. Read paper. Breakfast ordered. Mark calendars. House cleaning.	Up at 7. Prepared grape juice in preparation for making jelly. Cleaned	Tidied house. Prepared breakfast food for Sid for Sat. and Sun. Bus to	Visit to cemetery with sister. Supermarket shopping with brother.
Early Afternoon 12–3 P.M.	Drove to consultation.		Call to plumber.		house; got laundry together. Packed for return to New York. Drove	Providence. Read 2 newspapers, bulletins from health org., social activities org., and AARP†	Lunch with family: sister and brother-in-law, niece, 2 nephews and wife and baby.
Late Afternoon 3–5 P.M.	Two-hour consultation. Feed & walk the dog.	Made mint jelly. Telephone conversation with friend and neighbor—local gossip, sighting of crane, health problems, tenant problems. Feed & walk the dog.	Chimney sweep. Grocery shopping. Feed & walk the dog.	Feed & walk the dog.	back to New York. Shopped for groceries. Feed & walk dog.	Met at bus by sister.	Bus ride back to New York. Read novel during trip.
Early Evening 5–8 P.M.		Drove to New York. Dinner with friend.	Prepared dinner. Watched TV news, Mets game.			Dinner with whole family.	
Late Evening	Call from friend: 1 hour conversation; discussed recent news—CBS, etc.	Returned at 10:30. Watched TV news. Crossword puzzle.	Dinner. Call and long conversation with Sid's niece.			Attended Klezmer‡ concert with niece.	Returned home. Upset that Sid took only a couple of pills; unshaven, unkempt.

* Mrs. G added her own bands of time
† American Association of Retired Persons
‡ Jewish folk musicians

Figure 12-2. Mrs. G.'s activities in week 1.

DEVELOPMENTAL

Peck expanded on Erikson's developmental tasks of later life. Peck delineated three developmental subsets of later life conflict: (1) ego differentiation versus work role preoccupation, (2) body transcendence versus body preoccupation, and (3) ego transcendence versus ego preoccupation. According to Miller, "Successful adaptation to old age, in Peck's view, may require the establishment of a variety of valued activities and new roles."

In the second subset, the elderly person needs a perspective that focuses on remaining strengths, while deemphasizing physical frailties and limitations. Assisting the older person to place a value on living generously and unselfishly corresponds with the last subset Peck delineated.

PSYCHODYNAMIC

Miller described a model for understanding depression in the elderly as follows:

In the 1950's Edward Bibring, a psychoanalyst, described the mechanism of depression differently from Freud, and his contribution has been widely recognized. Bibring formulated the mechanism of depression as the individual's shocking awareness of real or imaginary helplessness, which is accompanied by a loss of self-esteem. The depressed person sees himself as unable to live up to highly-valued (narcissistic) aspirations such as the wish to be worthy and appreciated; to be strong, superior and secure; and to be good and loving. . . . This model seems well suited to the elderly person who does not necessarily reduce his standards in keeping with decreasing capacities, and, thus, becomes depressed. Assessment and treatment approaches appropriate to this model include:

1. determining the conditions causing feelings of helplessness and hopelessness. To what extent are these feelings real or imaginery?
2. aiding the client in seeing his strengths and limitations in perspective, and
3. encouraging participation in meaningful activities in which strengths can be supported and enhanced, thereby increasing self-esteem.

ACTIVITIES HEALTH

There are aspects of an *activities health* approach that are implicit in the developmental and psychodynamic models described. The occupational therapist's major focus of promoting change from dysfunction to function through activities is demonstrated in this case description. Selecting activities that lead to increased competence serves to break the inactivity cycle, reverse negative activities patterns, and lead to *activities health* (see Chapter 3 under Indicators of Activities Health for discussion).

Treatment Program

INDIVIDUAL TREATMENT: MR. G.

In the early occupational therapy sessions, Mr. G. was given the opportunity to talk about his life prior to retirement. His mask-like expression lifted as he discussed his earlier accomplishments, status, and power. He only filled in one day of the activities schedule because he was "too tired to do anything." The occupational therapist reviewed his one day of activity charting and discovered that he enjoys repairing things, especially because he is working with his hands. This led to questions related to how these interests and skills originated. He talked about his vocational schooling prior to becoming an engineer. "Drafting, drawing, woodworking are lifelong interests," he stated, "but I'm too weak, too tired to do them now." The occupational therapist talked about the strong relationship between one's physical health and general state of well-being. Mr. G. was receptive to beginning an exercise program to increase respiratory capacity and endurance for increased activities. These 15 minutes of exercise were practiced in the therapist's office each week. It took 1 month for Mr. G. to initiate the exercises without the therapist in his own home.

Further exploration of interests continued with Mr. G. expressing ambivalence about using any of his interests and skills with children in a volunteer capacity. Gentle probing revealed, "I love kids," but he admitted to a fear of failure. "I haven't done these things in a long time," he stated. The therapist then took out some drawing paper and asked Mr. G. to sketch something in her office. Mr. G.'s demeanor changed from a droopy posture and sad expression to an alert, artist's stance. The rendition of the therapist's desk and objects on the desk was clearly that of an experienced draftsman. He was very pleased, smiling broadly. Mr. G. wondered if he could still work in an industrial arts program, assisting in a woodworking class. The occupational therapist proceeded to ask Mr. G. some questions to ascertain his abstract thinking ability. For example, "If a student wanted to make a walnut and birch lamp, how would he/she go about laminating the wood together?" Mr. G. was unable to answer questions of this nature and did not feel comfortable exploring possibilities in these areas. The therapist decided to steer the client toward the possibility of work with younger children in school or afterschool programs. Sketching, reading, and assisting with simple mathematics were realistic, given his apparent strengths and limitations. It was vital that Mr. G.'s volunteer experience be a successful one.

The concept of wanting to do something "really important" was a recurrent theme. Philosophical discussions about "What is important? What is meaningful? How does one make a contribution to one's loved ones and society at different stages of life?" occurred frequently. Helping Mr. G. to recognize the value of each individual, for example, his relationship with his wife (a microcosmic rather than a macrocosmic perspective), was a frequent approach of this therapist. Mr. G. remarked on several occasions to the therapist, "I'm amazed by your optimism and confidence in me." As a depressed man, he needed help to stop thinking that if he wasn't an engineer, he wasn't anything or anyone.

Eventually, Mr. G. accepted the occupational therapist's recommendation to visit the director of the Retired Senior Volunteer Program (RSVP), which his therapist arranged. He appeared unshaven for the interview and was confronted by the director. "Why didn't you shave?" he was asked. Mr. G. responded, "This is only an interview for a volunteer position, so why should I?" The director of RSVP then explained the responsibile role volunteers play in a variety of positions, assisting people of all ages. Mr. G. never left his home unshaven after that day (eliminating a frequent complaint of his wife and demonstrating a positive turning point in his dysfunction/function continuum). He explored several preschool programs before leaving for Florida. None of them seemed quite right, but he was beginning to regain confidence in expressing his interests and describing his skills, and he was no longer spending most of the day in bed.

The concept of helping his wife with her daily chores required exploration in individual therapy and together. One of the wife's responsibilities, which she seemed happy to relinquish to her husband, was walking the dog. This was built into Mr. G.'s exercise program, and he began to joke about how much more exercise the dog was getting. In addition, a major chore that Mr. G. had resisted doing for several months was accomplished before Mr. and Mrs. G. left for Florida. Mr. G. made extensive drawings of their plumbing system with Mrs. G.'s help, so that Mrs. G. would know what to do in an emergency. Mr. G. was tremendously gratified with this accomplishment and began to show signs of being more open and expressive in therapy and, more importantly, with his wife at home. At the end of his last session before leaving for Florida, Mr. G. stated, with a twinkle in his eye, "Perhaps we should discuss our sex life with you, although we're doing somewhat better now." The therapist replied encouragingly, "I'd be happy to discuss your sex life with you and Mrs. G. It's another activity in which you can give each other pleasure."

INDIVIDUAL TREATMENT: MRS. G.

In the initial visits with Mrs. G., there was much discussion about her activities schedule and all the "shoulds, musts, and oughts" that motivated her daily activities. In one of the occupational therapy sessions, Mrs. G. made a list of the activities she would like to do, and discussion followed regarding their feasibility and frequency. She was encouraged to continue the list at home and to consider the kinds of satisfactions each of the activities would provide. For example, Mrs. G. realized that reading fiction would "divert my mind from worries" and provide a "pleasurable, stimulating escape." At the same time, she realized that despite the fact that Mr. G. was at home, she often felt isolated. Therefore, calling old friends and making lunch dates would be an opportunity to "enjoy herself with other people." After very few therapy visits, Mrs. G. began to make positive changes toward achieving her first two goals: finding individual interests that could give pleasure and renewing a support network of friends and family. She seemed to be waiting for permission to individuate from her husband and to have a somewhat separate emotional and social life.

Mrs. G. stated that she did not like herself when she was with her husband. Instead of talking about mutual interests, as they did during most of their marriage, their communication deteriorated to "nagging," and "exploding" at each other. "This makes me feel like a bad person," she declared tearfully. Discussion ensued about the causes of the nagging and explosions. Mrs. G. said that Mr. G. forgot to take his medication, no longer walked the dog or helped around the house, and got "furious" whenever she reminded him or asked him to do things. At the same time, Mr. G. always criticized her driving and parking abilities. The therapist suggested that some of these issues could be brought up in their couple therapy sessions. Mrs. G. stated that she felt the joint sessions were "a charade—too polite." The therapist encouraged Mrs. G. to be more open in expressing herself with her husband.

Mrs. G. wondered whether Mr. G.'s forgetting to take his medication had to do with "not caring or real forgetfulness." "How much responsibility should I take for him?" she asked. The therapist and Mrs. G. talked about her anger, prompted by the reality that they were no longer "equal partners" because of his limitations from his several illnesses. Role-playing different styles of communicating without blaming or nagging was practiced. Gradually, as Mr. G. began to be more functional and less morose, Mrs. G. began to accept the "new Mr. G." and to appreciate his strengths. In the joint sessions, the therapist served as a competence model, supporting the building of Mr. G.'s confidence. Mrs. G. learned to use some of the same techniques, and her feelings toward Mr. G. became less negative. No longer feeling like a "bad person," her reactive depression lifted.

COUPLE THERAPY: MR. AND MRS. G.

The first sessions with Mr. and Mrs. G. were leader-dominated, and this therapist had difficulty getting Mr. and Mrs. G. to talk to each other about the issues that had arisen during the individual sessions. It became clear that Mr. and Mrs. G. would have their separate goals for the couple sessions. The therapist therefore defined the first goal for Mr. and Mrs. G., a goal that both would be likely to agree on without either feeling that the therapist had betrayed their confidence. This concrete suggestion broke the ice, and the following goals for Mr. and Mrs. G. were then developed by pooling their resources and those of the occupational therapist:

1. To discover activities that provide pleasure together.
2. To change behaviors from nagging and irritability to conversations about what would make the other feel better about everyday activities.
3. To recognize that each of them can have separate interests and activities and still care about the other.

The explicit goals that were reviewed in each session served as a catalyst toward improving communication and changing dysfunctional behaviors to more adaptive ones. One of the first complaints Mrs. G. made to Mr. G. was that they no longer had breakfast together because Mr. G. was not getting out of bed until late morning. Mr. G. was shocked that Mrs. G. wanted his company any more of the day. This gave Mrs. G. an opportunity to reminisce about pre-retirement days when Mr. G. always rose earlier than she and prepared coffee for both of them. Mr. G. stated that he did not want to have to get out of bed at 7:30 A.M. Mrs. G. stated that she would be willing to have breakfast at 8:30 A.M. if he would join her. Mr. G. agreed to get up for breakfast at 8:30 A.M. and seemed pleased that he was wanted. During the remaining 2½ months of treatment, he joined his wife for breakfast three to four times per week.

The therapist was able to point out to Mr. and Mrs. G. through this successful breakfast negotiation how open communication, which included listening to each other's wishes and compromising, can help to attain one of their primary goals—

being happier or more content while pursuing daily activities. Developing a weekly check-off chart that Mr. G. could use as a reminder to take his medications was something to help Mr. G. remember and also prevent Mrs. G. from nagging. They decided to keep the chart on the counter next to the kitchen sink, as Mr. G. always cleared the table after meals, and it would serve as a reminder he could not miss.

The therapist pointed out that they were affected by each other's moods and might want to think of ways they could lift each other's spirits. Mr. G. said that he would select theater tickets to please Mrs. G., whereupon he added, "There is no more wonderful woman in the world than my wife." Mrs. G. responded, "You haven't said anything like that in a long time." Mr. G. explained, "I didn't think I had to say these things—you know how I feel." Mrs. G. stated, "I didn't think you cared anymore because you're not happy when you're with me." Mr. G. explained, "You mean everything to me. I'm just disgusted with my situation." This exchange of caring feelings was an important turning point in the therapy for Mr. and Mrs. G. Both seemed less angry and readier for further change in their relationship and activities.

Mr. G. was especially interested in hearing about what went on in Mrs. G.'s individual sessions. "I hope you haven't accused me of anything," he murmured to his wife. This gave Mrs. G. an opportunity to mitigate his suspiciousness and talk about her personal needs. They each began to explain their need to have separate relationships and activities. At the therapist's suggestion, they decided to explore activities at a neighborhood senior center. Mrs. G. thought she might be interested in attending the weekly Yiddish class, and Mr. G. stated, "The Center isn't for me—so many old people— it's sad." Through the therapy, they were able to accept these differences in attitude and involvement.

Both Mr. and Mrs. G. made appointments with New York City's Organized School Volunteer Program. They each had separate interviews to discuss the various volunteer positions they could pursue in the spring when they returned from Florida. These goal-directed behaviors broke the pattern of inactivity and sleeping during the day for Mr. G. and gave Mr. and Mrs. G. something in common to talk about and look forward to after the winter. Mrs. G. became concerned about how they would feel and what they would do in Florida. "It would be terrible if we reverted back to the way we were last winter," Mrs. G. lamented. The therapist gave Mr. G. the telephone number of the director of RSVP in the Florida county in which they lived. Mrs. G. remarked that if Mr. G. volunteered part-time, she would consider working as a hotel desk clerk again. Lists of activities that they could pursue alone and together in Florida were written. Opportunities to socialize seemed greater, as relatives and friends enjoyed visiting them in the winter, in part to get away from the cold. Mr. G. expressed hesitation about having "too many visitors," while Mrs. G. said that "visitors would decrease my loneliness."

The therapist speculated that Mr. G. might not like the company because he is hard of hearing, causing him to lose the conversation when several people are together. Mr. G. acknowledged that this was true, and Mrs. G. stated that sometimes Mr. G. interrupted conversations with a different topic and embarrassed everyone, including himself. Since the therapist observed this in the couple sessions as well, she moved the chairs around in the office and asked Mr. G. to sit in the seat where he could best observe people talking. It was suggested that he get in the habit of looking around at people's lips to see who was talking before he spoke in a group. Mr. G. acknowledged that this was helpful in the office, but he was hesitant to do it at home. Mrs. G. said they had a lightweight chair that would not be too hard to move. The therapist also pointed out that this would be a worthwhile habit to develop, as it would be advantageous in his volunteer work as well as his social life. Mr. G. said, "I'll try."

Summary

Mr. and Mrs. G. were seen once a week both individually and as a couple for 3 months. Initially, Mr. G. was moderately depressed, having lost interest in almost all activities, spending most of his days in bed. Grieving about physical losses compounded the magnitude of his worker role loss to the extent that his view of himself and his future was extremely negative. His depression interfered with his use of the activities configuration as a home assignment in once-a-week therapy. Mr. G. could not take the initiative to pursue activities without a great deal of regular encouragement. The family dynamic involving his wife's nagging needed to be broken, so the only home assignment for several weeks was the exercise regime. However, weekly written goals and the activities configuration were used on a regular basis in Mr. G.'s individual sessions. Depression and a mild cognitive impairment made it necessary for the therapist to state the purpose of therapy repeatedly and to suggest very concrete methods to attain his goals. Mr. G. made slow, but consistent progress in his view of himself and his world view. By the end of the 3 months, he was spending most of his day out of bed—having breakfast with his wife, walking the dog, exercising a few times per week, pursuing volunteer work leads, enjoying occasional dinners out with his wife, assuming selected household responsibilities regularly (such as clearing the table), and performing self-care (shaving, bathing, taking medications). Finding "important" volunteer positions in Florida and New York was not achieved.

Initially, Mrs. G. was mildly depressed, expressing "lethargy" about pursuing anything pleasurable for herself, and resentful of her huge responsibilities for her husband and three homes. She is a warm, intelligent woman who was very motivated to change her activities patterns and improve the quality of her life. Mrs. G. responded positively to reexamining her activities configuration three different times during the course of treatment. She was excited about the degree of control she had in switching the valence from unsatisfying to satisfying activities. Patience with her husband grew as she recognized his efforts to please her and do more for himself. She was helped to see his strengths and limitations in a more realistic perspective and therefore could be less demanding and more accepting. This had a positive affect on both Mr. and Mrs. G.'s self-esteem.

Together, Mr. and Mrs. G. were able to learn that open, caring communication was a vital activity to pursue at this stage of their lives. During the 3 months, it became somewhat easier for Mr. and Mrs. G. to express their needs and wishes in such a way as to change the patterns of their daily lives.

Three months after Mr. and Mrs. G. were discharged from occupational therapy, this therapist received a note from Mrs. G., who was in Florida by that time. She said that Mr. G. was working in an elementary school three mornings a week, "reading to the children and helping with their numbers. The children love him and he enjoys going." Mrs. G. said that she had her hotel desk clerk job again and that her nieces had just visited. "We all had a hectic but good time together," she went on to say.

This therapist believes that the successful outcome of this course of therapy derived importantly from the application of the clinical problem-solving described and the decision of this therapist to use Mrs. G. as an adjunct therapist in working with her husband at times, while also meeting her own needs simultaneously. Mrs. G. was well-suited for this role, while Mr. G. had just enough mental and cathectic flexibility to compensate for losses and adapt to new, valued roles and activities.

PROGRAM OF INSTRUCTION FOR CLINICAL PROBLEM-SOLVING

The reader will find the Assignments in the Educational Model (Chapter 9) helpful for practice of the clinical problem-solving process before using this more complex program. Similarly, the reader is urged to refer to Figure 9-1 (on the activities health approach to clinical problem-solving), which helps to clarify the complete process while working with the stages and steps of this program. Mrs. B.'s case history (pp. 237–240) is used for illustration.

Stage I: Initial Assessment

PROCEDURES	Resources	Content	Cues	Mrs. B.
Step 1: <u>Collect information</u> 1. Collect information from patient/client as far as possible, supplementing with information from other sources as necessary. 2. Adjust pace of information-gathering in the needs of the patient/client. 3. Record results, including descriptive information where necessary.	• Activities Health Assessment	• Information about patterns and configurations • Indexes of satisfaction, comfort, and sense of overall sociocultural "fit" relating to activities	• Review principles for initial assessment (pp. 195–197). • Activities health assessment will be found on pp. 67–77.	• Activities Health Assessment not used as formal instrument for collection of information, but activities health frame of reference influences emphases in the case history (pp. 237–238).
	• Activities histories: Informal/formal interviews about life-style Reports from others (e.g., family, friends) about life-style Records and reports from other disciplines about life-style Observations in controlled activities situations	• In-depth probing of: Specific activities components in configuration Ways of interacting during course of everyday activities Characteristic styles of coping	• See pp. 40, 55 for discussion of activities histories and other ways of obtaining information about activities. • See case histories for examples of how life-style information is collected and recorded.	• See pp. 237, 240 of case history for other kinds of information about activities.
	• Tests and measurements for assessment of specific areas of function/dysfunction Functional assessments • Interdisciplinary reports and results of tests and measurements	• Information about clinical condition and its effects on the patient/clients performance, now and in future.	• See case histories for examples of the kinds of information obtained about clinical conditions and how they affect the patient/client.	• See pp. 238–240 of case history for information about clinical condition.

(continued)

Stage I: Initial Assessment (*continued*)

PROCEDURES	Resources	Content	Cues	Mrs. B.
				• Judging from Mrs. B.'s case history, in what ways would you need to adjust the pace of information-gathering for her? • Consider: Physical condition Emotional state Endurance Integrated functioning
Step 2: <u>Organize information</u> 1. From the Activities Health Assessment, list the activities that the patient/client: a. Carries out daily. b. Carries out less frequently (less than daily but more than once weekly). c. Engages in occasionally.	• Frame of reference: Activities health	• Activities pattern: Specific components Sequences Time allocations Duration Categories	• Add information about activities that you have obtained from other sources to help in establishing the importance of the activities (as they appear in the configuration) to the patient/client	• To process the activities information in the case history (pp. 237–238) as if the Activities Health Assessment had been used, follow step 1 (Procedures) • It will be necessary to make inferences to fill in some gaps in information, e.g., Mrs. B.'s perception of which activities are essential, optional, or barely noticed in the daily routine. • Read Mrs. B.'s opinions and activities history carefully for clues.

2. Using the weekly activities schedule as a guide, list the activities the patient/client perceives as: a. Essential but not necessarily enjoyable. b. Optional. c. Essential and enjoyable. d. Enjoyable but not particularly important. e. So much a part of routine that they are practically unnoticed.	• Activities configurations: Frequency Ordering of importance Feelings History of acquisition Future projections Typical day With whom, where activities are done			
3. From the information gathered about the extent to which the clinical condition affects the patient/client, make a list of the performance components that are impaired.	• Theories of function/dysfunction	• Listing—the effects of clinical condition on the performance of activities • Listing—specific performance components affected by the clinical condition	• Review pp. 43–44 for discussion of performance components.	• Performance components: Neuromuscular function Spasticity Synergies Slow, laborious movements Slight limp Sensory integration Neglect of affected side (upper limb) Difficulty correcting errors Slight aphasia Psychological function Depression Some emotional lability? Social interaction Slight aphasia (communication) Tendency to be solitary

(continued)

Stage I: Initial Assessment (continued)

PROCEDURES	Resources	Content	Cues	Mrs. B.
				• Effect of frail physical condition • See pp. 238–240 of case history for description of clinical condition
	• Other frames of reference, e.g.: Human occupation model [45], which emphasizes occupational (or activities) choices relating to social roles			
	• The patient/client		• Especially for Procedures 2 and 3.	
Step 3: Interpret information. 1. List all activities, in order of priority, that you consider to be essential if the patient/client is to continue with everyday activities in a way of life that is personally satisfying, comfortable, and socioculturally acceptable.	• Frames of reference see Step 2. • Organization of information (result of Step 2). • The patient/client	• See Step 2. • Thoughts • Feelings • Reactions • Opinions • Suggestions • Additional contributions	• Reread Chapter 3. • Check Activities Health Assessment for patient/client's self rating of: Overall satisfaction Overall comfort Sociocultural "fit" • Compare patient/client's rating with information from other sources. (Con-	• Consider Mrs. B.'s possible thoughts and feelings about your list (see clues in case history, pp. 237, 238, 240).

2. From the assessment of the patient/client's integrative functioning and the performance components involved, list: a. The *difficulties* that are likely to be encountered in the performance of the activities listed.	Clinical reasoning skills of occupational therapist	Weighing and sorting information for setting goals in treatment planning	Besides performance components (Step 2) affected, consider: The patient/client's home and community environment including field of action for activities Behavior habitat (e.g., traveling hazards, time requirements, performance requirements)	sult your listings in Step 2) • What are the patient/client's thoughts and feelings about this list? • Consider possible modifications • Consider: Home environment (need more information on physical layout and possible architectural barriers) Solitary periods at home Fourth-floor walk-up!
b. The *strengths* that will enable the patient/client to overcome or compensate for these difficulties.			• Consider: Habitual ways of coping Problem-solving skills Motivations Will to learn Home and community supports Residual capacities in terms of performance components	• Consider: Positive attitude Motivation to get better Residual physical capacities Positive aspects of home and community, e.g., Helpful husband Light homemaking responsibilities for lengthy periods Young friend Church activities
c. The *new skills or methods* that the patient/client might have to acquire in order to			• Consider: Interests Successful learning habits (learning history)	• Consider: Expansion of environment and interests Acquisition of compensatory skills, e.g.,

(continued)

Stage I: Initial Assessment (*continued*)

PROCEDURES	Resources	Content	Cues	Mrs. B.
cope with, or compensate for these difficulties.			Will to learn Meaning and relevance of activities Course and prognosis of clinical condition • Consider: Actor Activity Field of action • Reread Chapter 4	one-handed activities by: Improving dexterity of unaffected upper limb and learning new ways of doing things. Modifying field of action. e.g., stabilizers for kitchen equipment such as mixing bowls or changing arrangement of pots and pans so that they are more easily reached.
3. Separate using the list of activities arrived at in Step 1, those that: a. Are unaffected by the clinical condition. b. Can be performed with adaptations or modifications. c. Cannot be performed.			• Consider "real-life" situations in which these activities are carried out • In looking at the activities, remember antecedent and consequent activities as well (Chapter 5, pp. 52–54).	• Fourth-floor walk-up Many hours of being alone Homemaker role, which entails a number of specific activities: Meal preparation Housecleaning Bed-making Shopping for supplies Church activities Getting to these places Communicating Use of telephone to keep in touch with family

Stage II: Treatment Planning

PROCEDURES	Resources	Content	Cues	Mrs. B.

Step 1: Set goals.
 	
1. List the overall goals of occupational therapy for the patient/client in the light of the activities configuration and difficulties and strengths that have been identified (long-range goals).
	• Information gathered, organized, and interpreted in initial assessment	• See Stage I.	• Review principles of planning (p. 198).
			• State goals in relation to skills and behaviors that will indicate patient/client has attained maximal activities health.
			• Reread definition of activities health (pp. 27–33).
				• One pointer to activities health is Mrs. B.'s pride in keeping her home neat and clean. This necessitates a network of activities that contribute to the end results:
				  Vacuuming
				  Dusting
				  Tidying
				  Laundry
				  Bed-making
				  Shopping for cleaning supplies
				• Think also of:
				  Church activities
				  Communication with children
				  Reading
				• Index of satisfaction is high, even though she does not particularly like some of what she is doing (see pp. 237–238, 240).
				• Index of comfort may be low (consider clinical conditions).

(continued)

Stage II: Treatment Planning (*continued*)

PROCEDURES	Resources	Content	Cues	Mrs. B.
2. List the attainable steps (short-term goals) by which the ultimate goals may be reached: a. In order of priority b. In a realistically determined period of time	• The occupational therapist • The patient/client	• Setting priorities • Offering creative ideas for selection and structuring of activities situations	• Consider: Time constraints Periods available for occupational therapy Expected length of stay in clinical settings Course and prognosis of clinical condition	• Analyze each of these activities from an actor-centered (Mrs. B.) point of view, obtaining as much information as possible from Mrs. B, about her characteristic ways of doing these activities and the field of action in which they are done. (See Appendix J). • Daily half-hour periods for morning and afternoon (Monday to Friday) are available for occupational therapy. • Maximum stay—3 months. • Some return of function in upper limb expected.
Step 2: <u>Identify resources/constraints.</u> 1. Identify resources in clinical/therapeutic setting that would be helpful in structuring appropriate therapeutic activities/situations.	• The occupational therapist • The patient/client and family/friends	• Identifying resources in the clinical setting	• Consider resources available in the clinical situation: Space available for patient/client needs Equipment available for patient/client needs People helpful to patient/client	• Consider: Two separate rooms—one for general activities and the other set up for homemaking. Variety of adaptive equipment and craft materials. Besides occupational therapist, bioengineer

			and COTA is available. Daily half-hour periods (Monday to Friday) are available.
2. Identify constraints in the clinical setting that have to be taken into consideration in structuring appropriate therapeutic activities/situations.	• Identifying and coping with realistic constraints in clinical setting and possibly patient/client's home	• Consider constraints in clinical situation: Fields of action that do not lend themselves easily to adaptation for patient/client needs. Limited space Limited equipment or limited budget Rules and regulations that conflict with those of the "real world" to which the patient/client has to return (see pp. 181–183). Length of stay affected by payments for treatment	• Clinic rooms crowded with equipment, mostly sedentary activities • No budget for additional equipment • No weekend O.T. or evening activities • Institutional hours for meals • Only half-hour sessions for activities • Limited stay (3 months) because of third-party payments. Timetables cannot be adhered to strictly because of porter lateness, schedules for medical tests, etc.
3. Identify other resources previously untapped that might be helpful in structuring appropriate therapeutic activities/situations.	• Finding untapped resources in, connected with, or outside the clinical setting	• Consider alternative untapped resources: Ways of "buying time" Environments beyond the confines of the space allocated for occupational therapy People to be introduced into the patient/client's program who are part of the patient's home/community environment or who can serve as "competence models"	• Consider: Other environments Cafeteria Library Gift shop Long, seldom frequented corridors in a research wing Busy streets and stores outside Other people to be introduced in program: Groups—patient/clients Husband (occasionally)

(continued)

Stage II: Treatment Planning (*continued*)

PROCEDURES	Resources	Content	Cues	Mrs. B.
			Activities that can be introduced from the patient/client's own repertoire Activities that do not need special funding	16-year-old friend Contacts from church Remember that duration of clinic stay is dependent on third-party payments, but extension can be obtained if patient's condition warrants it. • Consider Mrs. B.'s ideas about: Coping with or compensating for dysfunction Her activities choices
Step 3: <u>Design therapeutic activities situations.</u> 1. Select appropriate activities in the light of goals set and resources/constraints identified.	• Listing of goals • Identification of resources/constraints • Patient/client	• See steps 1 and 2. • Suggestions for activities that have meaning and relevance	• Use principles of planning as a guide (p. 198). • Check that activities selected: Have meaning and relevance to patient/client Are acceptable to the patient/client, either as stages toward the attainment of activities health or as parallels to those in the real world	• With each selection check: Meaning and relevance Fulfilling conditions for arousing and sustaining the will to learn Arousing curiosity Desire to emulate a model Reciprocity Desire for competence A known beginning and end

Are congruent with the goals set in Step 1.
- Decide on number of activities to be done at one time.
- Select alternatives for unexpected contingencies and change in patient/client status.
- Consider patient/client's wishes as well as needs.
- The will to learn (pp. 57–58)
- Management of dysfunction (see pp. 59–63, 191–192)
- Consider, where necessary, adaptation/modification of:
  Activity
  Field of action
  Actor

Built-in ways of checking progress
Requiring the exercise of effort
Socioculturally approved
Following a systematic approach to management of dysfunction
Broken down into manageable steps
- Some suggestions for now and as Mrs. B. progresses:
  Homemaking tasks
  Dusting and polishing
  Bed-making
  Knotting macrame straps and shoulder sling for book holder
  Helping in library, e.g., sorting books, stacking from a wheeled cart
  Presenting a story to a group of youngsters, including selecting, summarizing, writing, (or typing) notes
- Select surface for dusting and/or polishing that allows Mrs. B. to move out of flexion synergy by degrees while:
  Sitting
  Standing (balance).

(continued)

Stage II: Treatment Planning (*continued*)

PROCEDURES	Resources	Content	Cues	Mrs. B.
				• For macrame, use specially adapted frame, ensuring that Mrs. B. incorporates correct movement patterns as she makes each knot (see Figure 12-3). • In both these instances, the theoretical approach to management of dysfunction is that advocated by Brunnstrom [17]. See p. 192. Figure out why the other activities have been selected. Add your own suggestions
2. Structure activities in the field of action so that they: a. Fulfill conditions for arousing and sustaining the will to learn b. Are integrated with a systematic approach to management of dysfunction c. Are broken down into manageable steps	• Occupational therapist	• Ideas for appropriate activities—meeting patient/client needs within the constraints of the clinical setting • Clinical problem-solving—for selection, structuring, scheduling, and establishing contract for interaction		
3. Schedule activities so that they are:			• Coordinate with other members of therapeu-	• Coordinate times with:

a. Integrated into patient/client's total schedule b. Dovetailed with other activities in timing, frequency, and duration		• Coordinate with clinic routines. • "Buy time" if necessary, e.g., two patient/clients whose needs mesh, for 1 hour, instead of one for half an hour each. • Negotiate for activities times that approximate those of the patient/client's configuration as closely as possible.	tic team Physical therapist Speech therapist (if necessary) Other members of treatment team • Negotiate for times of day and days of week when activities are usually done by Mrs. B. • When Mrs. B. is ready, prepare assignments for weekend. • Schedule macrame and dusting for same days (A.M. and P.M.) to ensure carry-over from simulation to "real" activity.
4. Establish conditions for interaction between patient/client and occupational therapist		• Outline patient/client responsibilities for participation (see Figure 11-1). • Outline occupational therapist's role in the therapeutic relationship.	• Consider: Mrs. B.'s initiative and creativity in solving problems related to coping with tasks one-handed Ability to communicate Difficulty in dealing with son's death Tendency to drive herself beyond physical limitations Intelligence and educational level
5. List precautions that will have to be observed.		• Consider: Effects of clinical condition Level of patient/client functioning Environmental hazards	• Minimize neglect of upper limb • Give constant encouragement to keep limb in view during activities. • Watch for associated

(continued)

Stage II: Treatment Planning (continued)

PROCEDURES	Resources	Content	Cues	Mrs. B.
				reactions in affected limb (increase in spasticity, with force-ful movements of un-affected limb)
				Frame for macrame ensures incorpora-tion of affected upper limb in sym-metrical, bilateral movements to pre-vent neglect of limb and to reeducate patterns of move-ment.
				• Do not use special equipment if Mrs. B. can manage without in comfort and safety.
				• Consider incorporat-ing reflex-inhibiting postures while one-sided activities are being carried out [11].

- Remember fatigue—physical condition plus some depression.
  Do not allow overexertion.
- Watch for correct position of head, neck, trunk, upper and lower limbs in all activities.
- Watch for:
  Objects or situations that have become hazards because of unilateral neglect
  Loss of kinesthetic awareness in elbow and shulders
  Slowness of motion around, e.g., hot stove
  Projections on which affected limb can catch
  Disturbance of body balance while reaching over furniture, stove, or sink

Stage III: Implementation

Without an actual patient who responds and reacts, Mrs. B.'s program from here on becomes purely hypothetical. There are, however, ways to practice the general principles of implementation. Some are presented here. Others will most certainly occur to you.

1. Set up the macrame project as depicted in Figure 12-3. Explain its purpose to an individual who is playing the role of the patient (a fellow student, colleague, or captive friend). Teach the activity to the patient, making sure you have broken it down into manageable steps. At the end of the session (half an hour, as in the clinic), mark progress and prepare "patient" for the next step.

   Try to observe a patient (or better still, patients) whose physical functioning approximates that of Mrs. B. How do you think they could cope with the activity as you taught it to your substitute patient? If you have the chance, try it out with a patient. Many patients, like Mrs. B, are intrigued and stimulated by taking part in a new project; others may find the situation too threatening.

   Note: Watch positioning throughout the activity and check pacing. Check that the "patient" has mastered what you have taught.
2. Set up any other activity in a field of action that you have included in your plan for Mrs. B. Test it out with a substitute patient or, if you can do so appropriately, with a real patient.
3. Consider the following questions, which materially affect implementation:
   a. How would you introduce the program and the very first activity to Mrs. B.? (Practice different approaches. Exchange ideas with fellow students or your supervisor or colleagues.)
   b. What signal behaviors would tell you that it is an appropriate time to introduce changes in the program?
   c. What kind of a contract for interaction would you set up with Mrs. B., bearing in mind her difficulties, strengths, and striving toward independence? How would you specifically carry out this contract in terms of the goals that have been set and the timetable you have drawn up? What modes of interaction would you favor?

Stage IV: Termination

Assuming that Mrs. B., within 2 weeks of her announced discharge date, has in the $3\frac{1}{2}$ months of her stay attained all but the final steps that you have determined as important:

1. Write a discharge plan that follows the principles set out in Chapter 11, pp. 199–200.
2. Evaluate her total program. What would you have added, omitted, changed? Why?

DETAILED CASE HISTORIES

Mrs. B.

APPEARANCE AT FIRST INTERVIEW

Mrs. B. is a tiny, trim 58-year-old housewife. She looks younger than her years, despite streaks of gray in her dark hair, which is drawn back into a neat bun. Even with obvious spasticity in her right upper limb and a slight limp, she moves with an unusually erect carriage. Her eyes are large and brilliant; her face is unlined, but there is a perceptible droop at the corner of her mouth. While she is conversing the droop is accentuated, particularly during times when she struggles for an elusive word, frowning intently and testing several introductory syllables before finding the right one. Speech is thick but quite intelligible. Movements are slow and laborious. Her impatience shows occasionally as she playfully slaps her right hand, which does not perform as quickly and deftly as she would like.

Mrs. B. was transferred from a general hospital to a rehabilitation center 4 months after the onset of a stroke, which has left her with right residual hemiplegia. Besides occupational therapy, she was referred for physical therapy and speech therapy.

BACKGROUND DATA

Mrs. B. lives in a third-floor walk-up, four-room apartment in an old house in a predominantly black neighborhood with her husband, age 56, who is a truck driver. They have two children, a daughter and a son. The daughter, age 24, is a college graduate, is married, has one child, and lives in the South. The son, who has just completed college at 22, has a job as a reporter for a small-town newspaper. He is unmarried and lives about 40 miles away from his parents' home. The youngest, a son age 19, was killed in cross fire from a gang fight two weeks before Mrs. B. had the stroke.

GENERAL STYLE OF LIVING

Mrs. B. is what might be termed a reluctant housewife. She is not particularly interested in household activities, including cooking, but has always kept her home "nice and clean; you can eat off the floor." She cuts cooking to a minimum. When her husband is away, she eats very little. Breakfast out of a cereal box, lunch a simple sandwich, and a TV dinner are more the rule than the exception. Her husband, however, is a hearty eater and she feels it incumbent on her to take more interest in food preparation when he is at home. She considers it fortunate that her husband helps a great deal with the cooking and other household chores. Her chief tasks are bedmaking, washing dishes, setting the table, doing the laundry, dusting, and light cleaning for daily maintenance of the apartment.

Her own person is meticulously neat. She dresses simply and uses no make-up. She likes to get up early, shower and dress immediately, and get household chores over with as soon as possible. She says she has been brought up in the tradition of a middle-class, black Baptist family to "do her duty" properly without complaining, even if she does not like what she does. Her father was a minister, and both she and her husband are regular churchgoers. They also participate in the social life emanating from the church, which has included group outings, picnics, travel, lectures, and Bible classes, mostly on weekends.

Her husband is a long-distance truck driver, so he is away from home at intervals, with as much as a week off between trips. She says, not without a twist of humor, that he gets "under her feet" when he is around, but he also helps with shopping, carrying heavy packages of household supplies upstairs for her, and cooking, which he greatly enjoys. He also enjoys watching TV variety and talk shows and boxing and basketball matches, and occasionally he takes a turn at the basketball court at the park a few blocks away. They both go to bed early—10:30 P.M.—unless they are going to a church social.

Mr. B. earns a "decent" salary, which enables them to live comfortably though simply. Both living children got through college with scholarships and part-time work. Their youngest son had been a promising athlete but had not accepted any of the several scholarships available to him. He had been working as a guitarist in a rock band at the time of his death.

The children and grandchild occasionally visit, but the family communicate mainly by telephone, regularly on the part of the daughter, less frequently on the part of the son. The youngest son lived at home, but apparently because of his erratic hours, he participated little in daily family life. (Mrs. B. is still very emotional about her son's death, so questioning has been kept to a minimum.) Mrs. B. has few friends other than the families she is acquainted with through church activities. A neighbor's daughter, age 16, pops in several times a week to chat, especially when Mrs. B. is alone. Mrs. B. feels that she lives a quiet life, "where nothing much happens," except for the daily fear that she may be the next victim of a mugging, or worse.

ACTIVITIES HISTORY

Mrs. B. states that she was always a quiet and obedient child, unlike her two younger sisters, who were "regular tomboys." She never liked to get her pretty clothes dirty and was not interested in games involving physical activity. She cannot remember any favorite playthings, even dolls, and never wanted particularly to have a pet animal. All she has loved, and still does, are "books, books, and more books." Her face lights up as she recounts that she was a top pupil in English, and she says that she will read anything, from stories of true romance to the Bible. Her scholastic record was so good that she obtained a Merit scholarship for college; however, her father died when she was in her second year, leaving her mother and two young sisters penniless. So she went to work as a packer in a perfume factory and stayed for 13 years, even after her sisters had begun working to support themselves and their mother. Besides work, her activities consisted of help with household chores, churchgoing, teaching at Sunday school, and reading. At the age of 32, shortly after her mother's death, she married, somewhat "beneath her," she considers, because her husband barely managed to complete high school and is not interested in anything to do with "brain work."

Mrs. B. continues her lifelong involvement in reading. She states that she borrows books, mostly romantic novels, from the bookmobile of the public library, which parks at the nearby school once a week. Sometimes while shopping at the supermarket she will stop at nearby thrift shops and browse among the paperbacks, and she also picks up bargains at garage sales and fund-raising events at the church.

PHYSICAL ASSESSMENT
General Functioning

Mrs. B. moves slowly and laboriously, but her sitting and standing balance is good. She walks with a slight limp, dragging her right foot. As she walks, the right upper limb is maintained in a position of flexion and adduction of the shoulder, partial flexion of the elbow, partial pronation of the forearm, and flexion of the wrist and fingers. She has some voluntary motion of the right upper limb but can use it only as a gross assist, because movements are linked in synergies. Hand function consists of voluntary mass grasp, which she is able to release voluntarily by concentrating very hard. Her right side is dominant, but she has good coordination and dexterity on the left. Erect posture is well maintained; her head is held in midline.

Motor Assessment

Right upper limb motions are locked in flexion and extension synergies when voluntary motion is attempted. In both synergies, wrist and fingers are flexed.

Passive range of motion is minimally limited in shoulder flexion, abduction, and external rotation, with pain in the final degrees of motion.

Active range of motion is as follows:

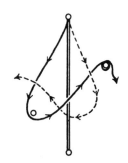

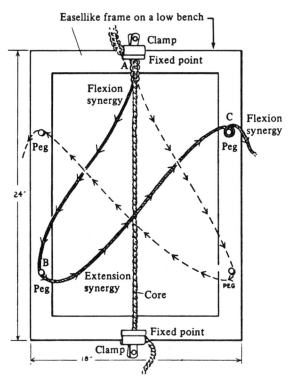

Figure 12-3. Macramé adapted as a therapeutic activity for Mrs. B., a patient with right hemiplegia.

	Flexion Synergy	**Extension Synergy**
Shoulder girdle	Partial elevation	—
Shoulder	Full retraction	—
Shoulder	Full hyperextension	Full adduction
Shoulder	Partial abduction	Full flexion
Shoulder	Partial external rotation	—
Elbow	Full flexion	Partial extension
Forearm	Partial supination	Partial pronation

Spasticity is present in elbow, wrist, and finger flexors.

No spasticity is detected for the head, neck, and trunk. There is full, active range of motion in neck and trunk rotation and trunk and neck foward flexion and extension. Ranges of motion of lateral flexion of the neck and trunk are a few degrees short of full.

Sensory Assessment

Position sense and kinesthetic awareness are absent in the shoulder and elbow. Tactile sensation is intact for the right upper limb.

Ocular pursuit is within normal limits. Visual scanning is slow but accurate. There is no field neglect.

INTEGRATED FUNCTIONING

Mrs. B. is cooperative and anxious to do well. She has a tendency to drive herself beyond her physical limitations. She shows signs of fatigue long before she admits she is tired but is relieved when the therapist calls the activity to a halt. She concentrates well and grasps instructions quickly. At times she has difficulty in correcting errors, even when she has recognized them herself. Memory appears to be unaffected.

She has a mild expressive aphasia. Any reference to her deceased son produces a marked emotional reaction—her eyes fill with tears, and her voice trembles. Since her admission to the hospital, she has cut herself off from current events, keeping away from newspapers and news broadcasts. She is independent in all self-care activities, maintaining an exquisitely neat appearance, and she has shown initiative and creativity in solving problems related to coping with tasks one-handed. In her eagerness to perform well and quickly, she tends to neglect her affected side. As she says: "I forget all about it!"

M., Age 7 Years

The case of M. illustrates through a painfully dramatic case the convergence and interweaving of psychological, physical, and social factors in a picture of extreme dysfunction. In the occupational therapist's summary of the case, a process of strong interdisciplinary collaboration is evident. The case also serves as an example of the way in which information obtained from professionals of other disciplines is incorporated into the assessment of a patient's everyday functioning. Thus, the case of M. provides us with a model for the role of the occupational therapist as a member of an interdisciplinary treatment team, who is relied on to provide ongoing assessment and treatment surrounding the doing of everyday activities that have meaning to the patient and sociocultural relevance.

INTRODUCTION AND PRESENTING PROBLEMS (AS PROVIDED BY PSYCHIATRIST)

M. is a 7-year, 4-month-old girl who was admitted to a psychiatric unit for increasing hyperactitivity and extremely disruptive behavior at school and at home. M. had been living with Mrs. H., an adoptive grandmother who has been her legal guardian since she was $2\frac{1}{2}$ years old, until a month ago, when Mrs. H. became too physically ill with cancer to handle M. At that time, M. moved in with her biological mother, B., who was living in a single-room-occupancy hotel.

M. attended a special education class. Her teacher, Ms. C., has been concerned about M. for the past few months, as her functioning has been deteriorating; she and the guidance counselor insisted that M. be brought for emergency screening and psychiatric evaluation, after which she was referred for hospitalization.

TEACHER'S REPORT (AS PROVIDED BY SOCIAL WORKER)

M.'s teacher and guidance counselor report that M. has become increasingly unable to attend to any schoolwork even with individual instruction. In class, she has been found eating chalk, crayons, glue, and garbage and sitting on the floor of the class, chewing on her chair. She has been rocking constantly, singing or talking to herself. Ms. C. noted that M. was the youngest and most disturbed child in the class, causing her peers to treat her like a baby, rather than to pick on her.

Ms. C. reports that on the day of admission, M. came to school with eyes glassy; she was mumbling and incoherent all day long. The teachers suspected that M. had accidentally taken some drugs in the house. When she asked M. about it, M. told her she had been kicked and beaten by her mother.

MOTHER'S REPORT (AS PROVIDED BY SOCIAL WORKER)

In the screening interview, M.'s mother stated that M. has been out of control—unable to listen or sit still; her mother has been afraid that M. was going to hurt her physically. She admitted openly that she did not like M. and that it was her daughter's fault that she had started drinking again.

M.'s mother dates the beginning of her current problems back to the previous summer, when her adopted grandmother became ill and could not care as well for M. M.'s father also failed to show up during the same summer when he had said he would pick her up for the weekend. When he did take M. to visit with him, he would frequently drop her off at various relatives' houses for days at a time.

DEVELOPMENTAL HISTORY (FIG. 12-4) (AS PROVIDED BY PSYCHIATRIST, SOCIAL WORKER, AND OCCUPATIONAL THERAPIST)

M. was an unwanted pregnancy (which she has repeatedly been told); she was born full-term at a city hospital. M. was small for gestational age at 4 pounds 9 ounces. Her mother's pregnancy was marked by cocaine use during the first trimester, methadone daily throughout the pregnancy, 4 quarts of malt liquor and 2½ packs of cigarettes daily. Her mother was also treated for syphilis in her sixth month of pregnancy at which time she tried unsuccessfully to stop taking drugs. No Apgar score was noted; M. remained in the special nursery for 18 days to be withdrawn from methadone, after which she went home with her parents.

One year prior to M.'s birth, her mother had a baby boy, who reportedly died of crib death at 2 months. M.'s mother reported that the father was reluctant to touch M. as a result and barely paid any attention to her. M.'s mother reports that M. was a "good baby and hardly ever cried until she was 8 to 9 months old." She was bottle-fed and had a good appetite; she sat at 6 months without support. At 8 to 9 months, M. became increasingly restless and more difficult to comfort. Her parents, who also had frequent bitter and violent fights, frequently controlled M.'s behavior through hitting with a belt or other physical punishment.

When M. was 2 years old, her parents separated, and she remained living with her mother for a few months. M.'s mother had a great deal of difficulty toilet training her. When M. was 2½ years, Mrs. H., who was like a mother to M.'s mother, took over the care of M., taking her faithfully to health centers and to a Head Start program. M. was visited often by her mother and extended family members.

At age 3, teachers in the Head Start program reported that M. was hyperactive and disruptive in the class, and recommendations were made at that time for a psychiatric evaluation. Neither Mrs. H. nor M.'s mother followed through on the recommendation. At home, Mrs. H. found M. to be a very active child, but she only found her to be "frantic and unmanageable" when the child's mother was visiting.

In kindergarten, M.'s teacher reported that she was hyperactive and disruptive and had difficulty concentrating. Around that time, M.'s mother moved in with Mrs. H. and M.; she began to use heroin and consume large amounts of alcohol. The teacher and guidance counselor noticed a severe deterioration of M.'s behavior in school, describing her as "overanxious, jumpy, and super-frantic." M. and her mother were interviewed by the school psychologist, at which time the mother admitted that she was on the verge of physically hurting M. An

Gestation—mother was taking cocaine during first trimester, drinking 4–5 quarts of beer daily for all 9 months, smoking 2½ packs of cigarettes daily, taking methadone for 9 months, and was treated for syphilis in sixth month.

9/6/77	M. born full-term, 4 lb., 9 oz.
	18 days in nursery for methadone withdrawal; returned home to live with parents.
3/78	6 months—sat without support.
9/78	12 months—spoke first words, and Mrs. H. is diagnosed with cancer.
10/78	13 months—walking.
11/78	14 months—M. hospitalized for stomach virus.
9/79	Parents separate, M. remains living with mother.
3/80	2½ years—toilet training difficult. Goes to live with Mrs. H.
9/80	Headstart program—M. hyperactive and disruptive in class.
9/81	Headstart program—M. recommended for psychiatric evaluation for hyperactivity. Not pursued by Mrs. H. or mother.
9/82	Kindergarten—very hyperactive in school and home.
1/83	Mother moves in with M. and Mrs. H. M.'s behavior worsens; mother starts heroin and heavy drinking again.
3/83	M. referred emergency screening—psychiatric clinic.
4/83	Crisis disposition—M. spends 3 days in hospital; mother has voluntary psychiatric hospitalization and then detoxification at a second facility; M. returns to live with Mrs. H., and Mrs. H becomes legal guardian.
6/83	Bureau of Child Welfare requests that Mrs. H. bring M. for appointments with psychiatrist; M. diagnosed with Attention Deficit Disorder with hyperactivity—Ritalin recommended, but family refused; M. diagnosed by pediatrician with Fetal Alcohol Syndrome.
4/84	Mrs. H. stops bringing M. in for appointments.
8/84	Mrs. H. brings M. on vacation to Barbados; M. displays dangerous behavior toward other children.
9/84	M. begins special education class; teacher reports that M. cannot attend to schoolwork, chewing furniture, eating crayons and chalk, talking and singing to herself.
11/84	Mrs. H. meets with teacher/guidance counselor; Mrs. H. sick with pneumonia and swollen kidney, regular appointments for follow-up re: tumor. Can no longer manage M.
11/84	Emergency psychiatric screening; mother cannot handle M.; mother starts to drink again even though she is in an alcoholism treatment program.
12/84	Screening/admission to inpatient child psychiatry unit.

Figure 12-4. Developmental life event chart for M.

emergency referral was made; M. was hospitalized for 3 days and then returned to Mrs. H.'s home. M.'s mother had moved out of the house by the time of M.'s discharge.

At the time of her discharge, the Bureau of Child Welfare insisted that Mrs. H. bring M. in for regular visits with the psychiatrist; she was seen once weekly for 9 months. M. had been diagnosed with attention deficit disorder with hyperactivity, and Ritalin was recommended which her family refused. She was also diagnosed with fetal alcohol syndrome.

PSYCHOLOGICAL EVALUATION

When M. was 6, she was referred to a special class for the emotionally handicapped. She was tested by the school psychologist, who reported the following results: M. scored in the average intellectual range, but with indicators of a higher potential. Visual motor development was slightly delayed, but it was felt that impulsivity and attention difficulties strongly interfered with her performance on the tests. Rorschach tests showed that M. had poor judgment and impulse control and that she viewed her environment as dangerous and threatening.

At the time of this hospital admission, M. scored in the low-average range on an intelligence test and was one year behind in her reading, spelling, and arithmetic.

OTHER OCCUPATIONAL THERAPY ASSESSMENT FINDINGS (BASED ON OBSERVATIONS IN THE MILIEU)

From the time of admission, M.'s appearance was disheveled, and she often smelled of body odor. She required assistance with her grooming; when left on her own, she was careless in showering, brushing teeth, and combing her hair, rushing through each step, with minimal attention to what she was doing. M. generally awoke in a foul mood and would begin whining when staff insisted that she shower and get ready in the morning. When dressing herself, she was poorly coordinated and easily frustrated with tasks such as buttoning her shirt and tying her shoes.

M. had difficulty being in the company of other children. She would "accidentally" bump into walls and objects in the room, "playing drunk," as she called it. M. provoked other patients by taking away their toys, causing them to become angry and tease her.

M. stated that she has had no friends but described an imaginary friend named Martinique. She said that she has no toys to play with at home, so she spent most of her time watching TV. She stated that when she lived with Mrs. H., she enjoyed being read stories and playing cards with her. In an initial interview, she expressed interest in animals, games, video games, and art projects, although her experiences have been extremely limited.

In occupational therapy, it was apparent that M. had little familiarity with the toys and games that are commonly played with by others her age. She was enchanted with such activities when they were initially presented to her but obviously had little idea of how to play with the toys and games, which would frequently cause her to become frustrated and angry. Once she became better acquainted with the activities, her concentration and frustration tolerance while engaging in them markedly improved.

FAMILY HISTORY (AS PROVIDED BY SOCIAL WORKER)

In M.'s family, there is a three-generation history of substance abuse and violent behavior. M.'s mother has supported her drug habit by shoplifting and prostitution; over a 10-year period she has been arrested numerous times. M.'s mother has an older child, who was born heroin-addicted and was placed by the Bureau of Child Welfare in foster care. She is autistic and lives with foster parents, attending a special day-school program. As mentioned earlier, M.'s mother had a second child, who died of crib death at 2 months.

M.'s father is 33 years old and lives at various intervals either alone, with a girlfriend, or with his mother. His history of drug abuse is similar to that of M.'s mother. He made it clear from the interview that he was concerned but could in no way assume any responsibility for M.'s care. M.'s father did not show up for scheduled appointments after the first interview.

MENTAL STATUS ON ADMISSION (AS PROVIDED BY PSYCHIATRIST)

During the screening, M. initially was climbing all over the furniture, overturning objects, and saying that she wanted to kill her mother. She appeared disheveled, unable to sit still or attend to tasks. She had some facial abnormalities that are consistent with fetal alcohol syndrome. Her speech was pressured and rapid, but coherent. She at first was quite preoccupied and disorganized, refusing to interact with staff. She was oriented to time, place, and person and was alert, but seemed highly anxious and frightened.

HOSPITAL COURSE (AS DESCRIBED BY INTERDISCIPLINARY TEAM CONSISTING OF PSYCHIATRIST, PSYCHOLOGIST, SOCIAL WORKER, OCCUPATIONAL THERAPIST, NURSING STAFF, AND TEACHER)

M. adjusted quickly to the ward routine and was initially very cooperative, affectionate, and clingy to staff. She has been hyperactive since admission, often seen in constant motion, running down the hall during unstructured time. She verbalized clearly that she was sad and afraid that her mother had left her at the hospital and would never return because she had been "bad" at home and at school.

During the second week, M. became somewhat more oppositional, responding less to limit setting, and her hyperactivity increased. She was constantly hurting herself by standing and tumbling on furniture or pushing herself into other children and interrupting them. She needed assistance with self-care because she was so easily distracted by peers and environmental stimuli.

M. went on a pass for the Christmas holiday, which was unsuccessful. Mrs. H. reports that M. was unmanageable on pass and that the family felt that M. was worse since she had been hospitalized. Mrs. H. was very apprehensive about taking M. on the subway because she is so uncontrollable. (On short walks outside of the hospital, staff has also found that M. does not follow directions and tends to walk off from the others.) Since the holiday pass, Mrs. H.'s visiting has decreased, and she has refused to take M. on any more passes until her behavior changes. Mrs. H. continues to have medical problems and speaks of her fear that she is going to die.

In the special education class in the hospital, M. has been able to work for up to 20 minutes independently, which is remarkably different from what was reported by her teacher at time of admission. In the hospital school, she has not displayed any of the other behaviors that were reported by M.'s teachers in her community school. This suggests that there is an environmental component to her displaying these disorganized behaviors. M.'s academic skills fall into the kindergarten and first-grade range. In classes, she tends to tease and provoke her peers, who are then verbally abusive to her.

PSYCHOTHERAPY (AS PROVIDED BY PSYCHIATRIST)

Throughout her hospitalization, M. has used psychotherapy to verbalize her feelings about her parents and her hospitalization. The most prevalent issues are her somewhat realistic fear that her mother has left her and that she won't see her anymore because her mother feels she is "evil." She fluctuates between being afraid her mother will kill her and being afraid that she wants to kill her mother.

M. says she is afraid of "ghosts," who are always around and listening to everything she is saying, causing her to be afraid. At times, she pretends to use sign language.

M. has been started on Ritalin, resulting in a definite decrease in hyperactivity and improvement in concentration. Her behavior and sleep problems continue.

Mr. S., Age 35 Years

Mr. S. is a 35-year-old baker who was admitted to the hospital 2 weeks ago, after attacking his employer with a kitchen knife. The employer, Mr. V., was not hurt, but he claims that Mr. S. threatened him with violence on several occasions, shouting, "Why are you making me put poison in the bread?"

GENERAL APPEARANCE AND BEHAVIOR

Mr. S. walked into the occupational therapy department with a shuffling gait, head down. He is tall and very thin, with sunken cheeks accentuated by a dark stubble. His clothes are rumpled and his thick dark hair, which he wears rather long, is disheveled. His shoes are cracked and unpolished, and the loosely tied laces trail along the ground. Although it is chilly, he wears no socks and his open-necked shirt, with a top button missing, leaves his neck and upper chest exposed. His baggy sweater is stained. He smokes incessantly, and his fingers are stained with nicotine. His nails are bitten, though quite clean. In conversation he started by mumbling and avoided eye contact, but he became more relaxed and spoke more clearly as the session proceeded. He was at all times able to give coherent replies to questions and to initiate a few conversational gambits of his own. He concentrated hard on the questionnaires and forms he was asked to fill in and completed them rapidly.

BACKGROUND INFORMATION (FROM INTAKE NOTES)

Family History

Mr. S. was born in Greece but came to America with his parents when he was 3 years old. His father died of leukemia when he was 5. The father, 35 at the time of his death, had worked as a short-order cook in an uncle's restaurant, and his mother did "a little bit of dressmaking" for neighbors and relatives. Relatives had to help the struggling widow and her young child for 3 years. She refused to live with Mr. S.'s uncle and his children, claiming she had too much pride to live on the charity of her in-law family, but she had to accept their offers of financial help, which she regarded as a loan. Mr. S. remembers her "always dressed in black, never a smile, never a soft word, old before her time."

The mother remarried when Mr. S. was 8 years old. Mr. S.'s stepfather was an American of Italian-Greek parentage. A widower, 25 years older than his wife, with grown-up children from his first marriage, he adopted Mr. S., who took his stepfather's second name. According to Mr. S., he was "a kind man, always smiling, always wanting to be a nice guy, gave me a lot of presents, money—lots of things."

Mr. S. says he had a happy time at home until he was 17, when his stepfather "did a terrible thing." Mr. S. was unable to discuss this further, but relatives subsequently revealed that the stepfather had been convicted of embezzlement and sentenced to an 8-year prison term; he died of a heart attack a year later.

At the time of the "terrible thing," his mother went into a deep depression and attempted suicide. She was hospitalized in a state institution for about 3 months, given shock treatment, and sent home; there she "mooned around, hardly ever speaking, carried out her jobs at home all right, but did nothing else except to go to church and cry." After her return from the hospital, Mr. S. moved with his mother to a self-contained part of a house owned by his uncle. All his father's relatives were very helpful at this stage. On the other hand, the step-father's family withdrew completely after the "disgrace," and Mr. S. has had no further contact with them since.

These troubles affected Mr. S.'s schoolwork. He had been a hard-working student with average grades and was set on earning his high school diploma, despite the fact that he disliked school. However, he left school in the twelfth grade, having stayed away from classes on a number of occasions. He claimed that he could not concentrate and anyway had to go out and get work, because the stepfather had left them no money. Through the help of his uncle he was apprenticed as a baker to Mr. V., for whom he has worked ever since.

When Mr. S. was 22, his mother made a second attempt at suicide, taking an overdose of sleeping pills. She was in a coma for 4 months before she died. He continued to live at this uncle's house for 3 years; then he married, against the advice of his relatives, a "no-good" woman of 28. She had a 7-year-old son by a previous marriage that had ended in divorce after her husband, an alcoholic, had severely beaten her and the child. Apparently she had been "keeping company" with another man at the time. According to the relatives, she was a good-looking blonde who liked "high living."

The newly married couple moved into an apartment in a nice neighborhood, and Mr. S. had it "fixed up good." The wife started frequenting bars and "picking up" men early in the marriage. Their quarrels became frequent and violent, to the extent that the neighbors had to call the police on several occasions. Eventually, after a little more than a year the wife disappeared, taking a large sum of money with her but leaving the child with Mr. S. He was "so disgusted" that he had the child put in a foster home: "I never did like that kid—sniveling, lying little _____!" He obtained a divorce 5 years after his wife left.

Mr. S. moved back to the uncle's house when his wife left and has lived there ever since.

Medical History

Mr. S. had the usual childhood illnesses, mumps at 7, measles at 5, and occasional colds and sore throats. He now looks undernourished; he weighs 140 pounds and is 5 feet 11 inches tall. A thorough medical check-up, including neurological tests, shows no abnormalities. Mr. S. says he is "strong as a horse," has never missed a day's work because of illness, and has always eaten and slept well except for the past 8 months, when he has had "terrible nightmares." His relatives urged him to get help when they discovered his drinking problem, but he says no doctor has the power to stop "them" (the evil ones). By the time Mr. S. was admitted because of the attack on Mr. V., he was quite calm and rational, and there have been no signs of recurrence of violent behavior. He is receiving no medication and has made no mention of or indicated in other ways his need for alcohol.

GENERAL STYLE OF LIVING (FROM INTERVIEWS WITH MR. S., HIS RELATIVES, AND MR. V. BY OCCUPATIONAL THERAPIST AND SOCIAL WORKER)

Mr. S. lives in a large, comfortable three-story house owned by an uncle in a lower-middle-class neighborhood. He occupies a suite on the second floor, which consists of a large bed/sitting room and bathroom, comfortably furnished. Six days a week, he took his evening meals with the family. Besides Mr. S.'s uncle, a hale and hearty 76, and aunt age 69 ("a wonderful cook and housewife"), two married cousins and their wives—all in the family restaurant business—occupy portions of the house divided into separate duplex apartments with their children, a total of three boys and two girls, ranging in age from 4 to 16. Two other cousins are away at college. The extended family has strong bonds and everyone is very "emotional" and vociferous. All talk loudly and enthusiastically, and they "fight and love with gusto." Mr. S., though never overtalkative, was "one of them before his troubles." After that, he became morose and monosyllabic, although until his "breakdown" he showed his attachment to the family by a number of touching gestures—remembering birthdays with gifts of beautifully decorated cakes, offering to babysit for the little ones, mending a broken toy or household appliance, helping with household chores.

Before his "breakdown," Mr. S. got up at 4:30 A.M. six days a week and walked to work one mile from home. He started work at 5:30, took a quick breakfast—although he was allowed a 45-minute break when the first batches of rolls and Danish pastries were ready for the oven—and then worked until 1:30 P.M. He used to stroll to a nearby coffee shop for lunch, sit in the park reading a newspaper left lying around or "just watch," or play a game of bocce (an Italian version of bowling) with a group of old-timers. In bad weather he would go to the local bar, linger over a drink, and watch TV. He returned from his lunch break at 3:00 and worked until 5:00, preparing the dough for the early morning baking, except on Saturdays, when he finished work for the day at about 2:00.

About 8 months ago, he started going straight to the bar every day during his afternoon break, downing "quite a few drinks" before going back to work. Neither his punctuality nor the quality of his work seemed to suffer.

Mr. V. says that Mr. S. was a "fantastic" worker, very diligent and conscientious to the point where he refused to take time off due to him. He was careful and "artistic"; he decorated all the cakes, designing "from his head" as he went along. The bakery has an excellent reputation and is always crowded with customers. Mr. V. manages the tiny shop, while he let Mr. S. be "king" in the kitchen, lording it over the two helpers. This has been the only source of friction in the 15 years Mr. S. has been a master baker. He bullied his helpers, drove them hard, and complained all the time that the new generation does not know what hard work and quality mean. In the last 4 or 5 months, Mr. S. has become even more suspicious, bad-tempered, and demanding, and he has leveled accusations of poisoning attempts at Mr. V. three or four times. Nothing specific seemed to precipitate the outbursts of shouting, obscene language, threats, and finally the physical assault directed at Mr. V. Mr. S. says Mr. V. has been a fair and good boss, but the "devils" have got hold of Mr. V. and must be removed.

After work Mr. S., until recently, took the bus home, went up to his room, and took a nap until dinner time, which is punctually at 7:00. Generally the two or three adults working in the restaurant are absent from the family meal. Mr. S. participated very little in conversation at the table. He went back to his room immediately after dinner, watched TV, did a few chores like sewing on buttons, or played solitaire, and went to bed at 10:00. Occasionally he babysat, joined the children in a game of Monopoly, or helped them with crafts projects.

On Sunday the whole family gathers for an elaborate meal at noon that goes on for several hours. Until his strange behavior took over, Mr. S. always joined the family and sat in the living room reading the newspapers, mainly the sports and travel sections. He was without fail invited to family outings and celebrations but declined unless the gatherings took place at home. At these he was usually to be found playing cards with a group of men he had known for years. Mr. S. says he at one time enjoyed going down to the "club" (an informal gathering of men from the neighborhood in one of the old-fashioned food store-cum-cafes that are rarely found nowadays) to play cards, especially pinochle, drink wine or beer, and chat. For the rest of Sunday, he used to take a walk, watch TV, or help his uncle with a few maintenance chores around the house. For supper he would fix a sandwich and take it up to his room.

Since his "breakdown" he has gone up to his room after work and has refused to take evening meals with the family. His food, brought on a tray, is eaten very sparingly, but he drinks all evening until he falls asleep. On Sundays, until a few weeks before his attack on Mr. V., he made an effort to join the family at the noon meal, interacted with them to some extent as before, but went upstairs to his solitary drinking in the late afternoon.

According to his aunt, Mr. S. used to make his bed before going to work and leave his room clean and tidy. He dressed neatly and "quite elegantly" and was very particular to keep his hands clean. He always smoked heavily but aired his room and cleaned out the ashtrays before leaving for work. He did his own cleaning and mending of clothes. But a few months ago he began to look slovenly. He stopped going to the barber regularly every 2 weeks for a trim, and his clothes became creased and dirty. Instead of neatly making his bed, he pulled the cover over the tumbled bedclothes; he left his room messy, clothes tossed on chairs, ashtrays filled with cigarette butts, a dirty glass on the table. However, he always hid the empty bottles after his drinking bouts.

ACTIVITIES HISTORY (OCCUPATIONAL THERAPY)

Mr. S. filled in a questionnaire designed to provide information about his activities history and also a checklist for an interest inventory. The information obtained was discussed with Mr. S. at a subsequent interview. He left the answers blank for all questions that addressed his hopes and aspirations. For many of the questions dealing with the interpersonal relationships involved in activities, he wrote, "It's a lot of _____" or "More _____" or "Who cares?" The following is a summary of the information obtained from the questions he completed, the checklist he filled in, and the interview.

Mr. S. was an average student at public school, which he attended until he was 9 years old. He worked hard and passed all his subjects. He had no favorites but did well in mathematics and drawing. His worst subject was English. At school he felt "different," because all the other children had spending money and wore nice clothes. His mother considered pocket money an extravagance and saw no reason why he should not wear hand-me-downs from his cousins, which she remodeled for him. He cannot remember any teachers whom he particularly liked. He had one or two friends from class with whom he played a variety of ball games in the street after school.

His life changed in a number of ways when his mother remarried. He was sent to a parochial school with a fine reputation, but he disliked the "uppishness" of most of the teachers and the emphasis on academic excellence. By working very hard, he just managed to attain passing grades. The art teacher was the only one Mr. S. remembers with warmth. This was the person who encouraged Mr. S. to go on to get his high school diploma and continue with drawing and design, the one subject at which he excelled. Mr. S. disliked any group activities and got into trouble several times for cutting gym classes and team sports. Yet he enjoyed physical activities—walking, running, bicycling—that he could do on his own. His stepfather lavished gifts on him—books, records, expensive construction kits, musical instruments ("I've got no feel for music"), games, sports equipment, clothes. He tired very quickly of those objects, and he still felt "different" at school, despite the fact that he now had the "right" clothes and ample pocket money.

The childhood objects Mr. S. considered important and for which he felt affection were a model train set he received from his uncle for Christmas when he was 7 years old, a number of coloring books, and modeling clay, which he hoarded for a long time. The only object given to him by his stepfather that he still cherishes, and in fact has mounted on the wall of his room, is a fishing rod. His stepfather used to take him fishing at dawn on Sundays. His mother was too "cheap" to give him presents, even when her financial situation improved.

The objects that are important to Mr. S. now are his TV set, playing cards, his cake-decorating tools, and his baker's hat. His list of hobbies and interests encompasses work, especially cake-decorating and shaping rolls and cakes, watching TV, walking, fixing things (broken toys, toasters, and so on), and playing cards, especially solitaire.

Asked how he would sum up his general style of living before he "got sick," he said that he had been pretty comfortable. "No money problems, no women problems, no work problems except for those fresh kids—before people [not specified] started bugging me with their wrongdoing." He had always lived a clean, decent life, and "they" were out to spoil his record. Those "devils" all around were at work to make something terrible happen. To the question about what he most wanted to do with life, he replied, without any change of emotional tone, "To be left alone."

P., Age 6 Years

P. is 6 years and 9 months old. He is somewhat shorter than average, thin, and wiry, with a mop of red-gold curls and bright blue eyes. He is currently enrolled in a first-grade program at a public school. As part of his program at school, he attends a special physical education class once a week for children with learning disabilities, is enrolled in a program that deals with auditory discrimination for assistance with spelling, and is in a special reading class. He has been referred to occupational therapy because of a series of problems noted by his teachers.

GENERAL BACKGROUND AND FAMILY STYLE OF LIVING

In addition to 8 months of first grade, P.'s formal education has included 9 months of a half-day kindergarten program and 12 months of a daily preschool program. The family moved into the present school district at the beginning of the current school year. They reside in a three-bedroom apartment in a complex that has indoor and outdoor recreational facilities for children. P. is the oldest child and has a room of his own. His two younger siblings, both girls, are 4 years old and 18 months old. He does not have any close friends with whom to play, although there are many children available at the complex.

The father's work in sales requires him to travel during the week, but he is home for weekends. The mother works part-time as a secretary in an office and is away from home during the school hours. The two younger children attend a day-care center. The mother drives P. and his sisters to and from school or the day-care center.

FUNCTIONAL HISTORY

P.'s mother gives the following information. P. has difficulties in learning to read, print, and spell. His performance in mathematics and science is outstanding. During school hours he cannot sit still, talks aloud frequently, does not follow simple rules, and cries easily. He is apparently having difficulties with his peer group and is also difficult for the teachers to handle. On the playground P. does not join in group activities. He will "strike out" at other children and seems very "clumsy" in playground activities. P. hates school because the children tease him about his clumsiness and call him "Dum-dum." The teachers requested that P. be seen by a pediatrician to rule out physical causes for his school difficulties and to obtain advice about the proper kind of approach to P. Both the kindergarten and preschool teachers had reported and discussed difficulties similar to those that P. now has at school.

SCHOOL REPORTS

The teachers report that P. has been tested by the school psychologist and a speech pathologist. Tests administered by the school during the past few months have included the Wechsler Intelligence Scale for Children (WISC), the Bender-Gestalt Test, the Illinois Test of Psycholinguistic Abilities (ITPA), and the Frostig Developmental Test of Visual Perception. Results indicate that P. has above-average intellectual ability, the verbal subtests of the WISC being superior to the performance subtests. The Bender-Gestalt Test indicated possible organic causes for P.'s behavior and apparent visual-motor difficulties. There is evidence of both auditory and visual perceptual problems, relating to auditory discrimination and sequencing, visual form constancy, and figure-ground discrimination. Auditory and visual memory appears adequate. The specifics of these reports are not available because P.'s father refused to sign a release, demanding that no results appear as part of P.'s school records.

The teachers confirmed the description of P.'s behavior given by the mother and said that she is most cooperative in every way and tries to carry out their suggestions in the home. They feel that the current programs are helping P. and that it would be helpful for him to repeat first grade next year. P. has missed many days of school because of frequent falls, upper respiratory infections (URIs), and stomach problems. During school he falls frequently and has to visit the school nurse for minor care at least twice a week.

PEDIATRICIAN'S REPORT

The pediatrician reports that he has seen P. on three occasions. The last visit was requested by the teachers because of P.'s school problems. P. has a history of frequent URIs, allergies, the usual childhood diseases, and two arm fractures. His height, weight, and head circumference are within normal limits. Neurological screening indicates some soft neurological signs: P. cannot stand on one foot, is unable to hop or skip, and has difficulty with fast alternating movements of his upper extremities. There is a very mild intention tremor in the fingers, and muscles appear to be slightly hypotonic. P. has had examinations of both hearing and vision within the past 6 months. No complications were noted. No medication was prescribed.

PARENTAL ATTITUDES

P.'s mother is most cooperative, giving whatever information is requested, because she is so relieved that P. is getting help and that so many people are showing an interest in him.

She diligently carries through programs and regimens recommended and tries not to let her irritation with P. or frustration at being unable to get through to him at times force her into punitive action.

She receives very little support from her husband, who, she feels, laughs at her when she tries to approach the subject of P.'s difficulties. P.'s father refused to participate in a conference with the occupational therapist, even though a weekend time for meeting was suggested, and similarly refused to enter into a discussion by telephone. He denies that there is a problem, stating that P.'s mother and the teachers are making matters worse by interfering. He is certain that P. will "grow out of" his clumsiness and inability to spell and read, just as he himself did. The root of the matter, he feels, is that the schools do not enforce discipline and that the reason the teachers cannot control P. is that "he is too smart for them." He plans to send P. to a military prep school when the boy is 10 years old.

SENSORY INTEGRATIVE ASSESSMENT

The occupational therapy evaluation reveals sensory-motor integrative difficulties, which contribute to P.'s learning and behavior problems.

FUNCTIONAL ASSESSMENT (FROM OBSERVATION OF ACTIVITIES PERFORMANCE)

P. has immature equilibrium reactions with poor midline stability. His postural control is influenced by primitive righting reactions. Under stress or when fatigued, P. cannot differentiate head and trunk movements, so when he turns his head the entire trunk turns with it, affecting performance of the tasks to which he is attending.

Prehension patterns are immature. He begins an activity with full prehension, but as he fatigues he regresses to pincer or total grasp. He has an unusually tight grip. He seems to prefer to use his left hand but will switch when doing an activity.

As he works at desk activities, he loses control of posture and needs external props to maintain an erect sitting position. He has difficulty using scissors and substitutes for normal grasp with an immature palmar grasp and forearm pronation. He tends to abduct and hyperextend his fingers when releasing objects held in his hand. P. shows signs of tactile defensiveness. He is easily distracted, is in constant motion, and appears to be "driven" to move without apparent purpose.

P. is motivated to participate in the occupational therapy activities and seems pleased with whatever he accomplishes. He shows interest in the younger children around him. He seems to have some understanding of his problem. Once he told the therapist that he could not think about how to print letters and learn what they looked like because "my mind just won't let me do two things at a time."

DEVELOPMENTAL AND PLAY HISTORY (OBTAINED FROM MOTHER AND P.'S BABY BOOK)

Infancy

P. had URIs and some wheezing; he was allergic to milk and was put on a soybean formula diet. Infant feeding time was difficult; it was hard for P. to suck from the nipple of his bottle, and his mother had to cut larger holes for him to manage. P. was a "fussy" baby who never seemed to enjoy being held or rocked. He spent most of his first 6 months in his infant seat or on his back in the crib or on the floor. He liked watching mobiles, sucking on toys, or being talked or sung to. He would cry when placed on the floor on his tummy to play. He rolled over by himself at 6 months but never seemed to roll to reach objects or for other specific purposes. He sat alone at 7 months, crawled at 9 months, and took his first steps at 15 months. The mother does not remember when he stood alone. He continued to walk and run on the tips of his toes until he was 5 years old.

Toddler Stage

P.'s father liked to "roughhouse" with him, but the child seemed quite frightened and started to scream, particularly when he was tossed in the air. P. enjoyed playing with large wooden blocks, cars, and trucks for short periods. Play usually ended with P. becoming frustrated because he could not get the blocks or cars to do what he wanted. His favorite activities were playing in the sandbox and playing with boats in the bathtub. When P. was successful with an activity, his attention was "endless."

Motor Skills

P. rode a "kiddy car" when he was 2 years old but was unable to ride a tricycle when he was 3½. His father made attempts to play catch with P., but the game usually ended in frustration for both. P. accomplished climbing stairs at 4, after a great deal of difficulty, and climbed with alternating steps at 6. He still needs to use a handrail when descending.

P. seldom engaged in activities requiring fine motor skills. He refused to finger-paint, scribbled aimlessly with crayons, and still has difficulty handling crayons and pencils. He began to use scissors for cutting paper at 4 but is still unable to use them proficiently.

Self-Care

P. fed himself finger foods at 12 months and handled a training cup and a spoon at approximately 15 months. He still is a "messy" eater, and his poor table manners irritate his parents. They refuse to take him out to eat in public because he constantly spills food and drink.

P. started to undress himself at age 3 and to dress at 4. His biggest problem was differentiating top from bottom and inside from outside. He still buttons his shirts in a careless manner (third buttonhole matching first button). He can tie his shoes, slowly and with difficulty. He is encouraged to take care of his own dressing, but his mother reports that she usually ends up doing the task for him on school mornings, rather than trying to "push him along."

ACTIVITIES WITH PEERS

At home P. prefers to stay indoors and watch TV. While he is watching he frequently jumps from chair to chair, attempts to turn somersaults, and jumps up and down. At times he is so active that his mother makes him go to his room and get control of himself.

She often insists that he go outside to play, but within 10 minutes he comes in crying, saying that "the kids hit me." Mother reports that P. has never been able to play with other children without getting into fights. She has tried a variety of methods to improve the situation, from coaxing to forcing, but nothing seems to work.

Because of P.'s difficulties with peer relationships, the mother has sought out a variety of youth programs at the local YMCA. P. starts out pleased, but after three or four tries he wants to stop. Swimming has been the most successful activity. He is proud that he can jump off the diving board and swim to the edge of the pool. P.'s two greatest wishes are to be able to ride his bicycle without training wheels and to be able to bat a baseball when he plays with his father.

Mr. D., Age 66 Years

OCCUPATION

Mr. D. is a jeweler and second-hand business retailer. He owns and directs a home-based business selling fire equipment.

DIAGNOSIS

The diagnosis is severe angulation deformity and limitations in range of motion (ROM) and strength of left forearm, wrist, and fingers due to motor vehicle accident approximately 1 year ago.

MEDICAL HISTORY

Mr. D. sustained a severe crush injury to the left forearm and wrist during the automobile accident and has undergone a series of surgeries to correct the multiple problems that have occurred due to the injury. He sustained a severe comminution fracture of the radius and ulna, marked soft tissue loss, and lacerations of digital and thumb flexors and extensors and the median nerve. He has undergone debridement, skin grafting, and external and ultimately internal fixation of both the radius and the ulna. He developed a subsequent infection so that fixation had to be removed. Four months after his injury, Mr. D. had developed a nonunion of the radius and malpositioning of the ulna. He was admitted for further surgery—a distal radioulnar fusion with internal fixation to immobilize the fusion. He also underwent a tenolysis (scar removal) of the extensor tendons. During this time Mr. D. was receiving therapy at a local hospital to maintain passive range of motion to all finger joints and to maximize tendon gliding of the digital flexors and extensors through active extension.

One month later, Mr. D. began developing a recurrent angulation due to loosening of the screws and plate in the radius. Despite efforts to immobilize the reduction, it continued to angulate and protrude into the skin. At this point, a third surgeon was consulted. On his recommendation, Mr. D. underwent an osteotomy of the radius, a free bone graft, excision of the ulna, and removal of the plates and screws.

When proper healing had taken place (1 year after his accident), Mr. D. was referred to a hand rehabilitation center for a complete program to remobilize the left wrist and fingers prior to having further surgery (i.e., repair of the median nerve, tendon transposition to the thumb).

He presented with

Slightly limited supination (75 degrees).
Limited wrist extension/flexion (35 degrees/5 degrees), no radial deviation, and wrist held in ulnar deviated position.
A tightly adducted thumb with the metacarpal phalangeal (MP) joint contracted in 40 degrees.
Limited MP extension; limited proximal interphalangeal (PIP) and distal interphalangeal (DIP) flexion in adjacent digits (60-degree PIP flexion, 35-degree DIP flexion in middle, ring, and small finger).
Edema—moderate in palm and dorsum of hand.
Impaired sensation—insensate thumb/index and adjacent median nerve innervated digits.
Grip strength: left hand—no registration; right hand—60 pounds.
Lateral pinch strength: left hand—8 pounds; right hand—28 pounds.
Palmar pinch strength: left hand—9 pounds; right hand—18 pounds.

EFFECT OF CLINICAL DYSFUNCTION ON PERFORMANCE COMPONENTS

Because of limited range of motion in radioulnar joints, wrist, and hand, aggravated by sensory loss in thumb and lateral two fingers, Mr. D. reports that he uses his right, non-involved hand to perform most tasks. He requires assistance in managing bilateral self-care tasks such as knotting a tie and cutting food. He presently cannot manage the fine, bilateral tasks involved in the jewelry business: examining stones and settings, fastening watchbands and bracelets, handling jeweler's tweezers—all of which necessitate the use of his left hand. His limited motion interferes with his ability to play golf, which he states is his favorite sport. He does much computer work with his home-based business and currently can use only his right hand for this.

GENERAL LIFE-STYLE

Mr. D. lives in a comfortable ranch house with a "fair-sized" garden with his wife, to whom he has been married for 39 years. They have children, all married, and five grandchildren "divided among our two daughters; my son and his wife have decided they don't want children right now." All live many miles away, but the family meets at one of their homes for Easter, Thanksgiving, and Christmas. Mr. D. has always been very gregarious, and for the past 7 years he and his wife have been members of a nearby country club. They spend many of their weekend evenings and Sundays there, except in the winter, socializing with a number of friends at cocktail parties and dinners, as well as participating in the sports and recreational programs offered by the club. They also belong to a theater-going group. The D.'s are also very "neighborly"; Mrs. D. will keep an eye on the neighbors' house and garden while they are away, take in their mail and care for their pets, and Mr. D. is always ready to lend a hand when there is a fence to be repaired or leaves to be raked.

When the children were all at home, the D.'s house was a "bit of a tight squeeze," but now the son's room has become an office for Mr. D. for his home-based business. He still gets down to his jewelry business in the center of the city two or three times a week, being driven by a friend who commutes to work daily. An old and trusted employee "minds the store" for him, but Mr. D. likes to keep his "hand and nose in the business." He has always served on a number of committees, such as the country club's management board, and believes, like his wife, that you have to "give back a little in thanks for what you've got." Both work as volunteers—Big Sisters and Women's Hospital Auxiliary for Mrs. D., the Lion's Club and Police Athletic League for Mr. D.

Mrs. D., other than doing volunteer work and meeting her friends for their weekly "bridge club," is primarily "my caretaker," as Mr. D. puts it. She looks after the "inside of the house," except for repairs and taking out the garbage, which are Mr. D.'s jobs. He also looks after the garden and helps Mrs. D. with food shopping, if she has a big load to carry. She prepares "great food," including brown-bag lunches when he goes downtown. Mrs. D. helps him whenever he gets himself "into a knot" while trying to cope with some bilateral self-care tasks and often makes sensible suggestions for modification; for example, she concocts dishes that use bite-size ingredients but are "not mushy, invalid food" and has suggested that Mr. D. temporarily use snap-on ties. He is somewhat reluctant to do this, since he considers himself a "snappy dresser" and likes to have a range of ties available that "do something" for his outfits. Mr. D. dresses formally for his business and social engagements, even when an open-neck shirt would be quite acceptable.

Specific details about Mr. D.'s activities will be found with the *Activities Health Assessment* (Fig. 12-5).

ACTIVITIES HEALTH ASSESSMENT

Much of the summary/discussion of Mr. D.'s activities configuration [Fig. 12-5] took place as we completed the interview. Mr. D. is very open about discussing his life activities and demonstrates a consistent "gather ye rosebuds while ye may" attitude to his life throughout this evaluation. Mr. D. is also consistent in his philosophy that work is enjoyable; he perceives household repair tasks and committee work as "leisure." He distinguishes this type of "leisure" from "social leisure," as in sports and theater. Although his recent bout with cancer has made him rather philosophical about his serious hand injury, he expresses frustration at his limitations in fine bimanual tasks necessary for his work. He misses participating in golf and tennis and makes it clear that he is determined to return to these favorite leisure activities.

	MONDAY	TUESDAY	WEDNESDAY	THURSDAY	FRIDAY	SATURDAY	SUNDAY
12 Midnight to 1 A.M.	Sleep	Sleep				Sleep	Sleep
1 A.M.–2 A.M.							
2 A.M.–3 A.M.							
3 A.M.–4 A.M.							
4 A.M.–5 A.M.							
5 A.M.–6 A.M.							
6 A.M.–7 A.M.							
7 A.M.–8 A.M.	Self-care Washing up	Self-care Washing up				Self-care Washing up	Self-care Washing up
8 A.M.–9 A.M.	Breakfast	Commute to city					Reading, committee work
9 A.M.–10 A.M.	Household chores	Work				Commute to city	Golf or tennis
10 A.M.–11 A.M.	Occupational therapy	Jewelry and second-hand business				Jewelry business	
11 A.M.–12 Noon							
Noon–1 P.M.	Lunch on road						
1 P.M.–2 P.M.	Fire equipment and business operated from home Work on computer and other business tasks					Lunch	
2 P.M.–3 P.M.						Work	
3 P.M.–4 P.M.							
4 P.M.–5 P.M.							
5 P.M.–6 P.M.						Committee work	
6 P.M.–7 P.M.	Dinner	Dinner				Dinner	Dinner
7 P.M.–8 P.M.	Organizational work, reading	Work on computer				Theater, etc.	Socializing with friends
8 P.M.–9 P.M.							
9 P.M.–10 P.M.	Self-care Washing up	Self-care Washing up					
10 P.M.–11 P.M.	Organizational work	Reading					Self-care Washing up
11 P.M. to 12 Midnight							

Sleep   Chores   Leisure with others

Work   Leisure alone   Self care

Figure 12-5. The Activities Schedule for Mr. D.

INTERVIEW (AS RECORDED DURING INTERVIEW BY THERAPIST)

Part I

1. *What other activities that are part of your everyday life do not appear on this schedule?*
That covers it pretty well.

2. *Do you consider this to be a typical week for you?*
Yes.

3. *Which activities have you coded as chores? work? self-care? leisure?*
(After pointing out the categories on the schedule, Mr. D. comments:) Carpentry, cutting grass, painting—I call that leisure, but they are household chores.

4. *When you look at the completed schedule, does anything in particular strike you?*
No.

5. *Did you have any problems fitting your activities into categories in the code?*
I find my chores to be leisure. I like commuting . . . I ride with a friend and we talk. I have the tape recorder—I can play classical music, I can study (from tapes), I can do whatever I want.

6. *Which activities did you choose to do? Did you have to do? Why?*
(After discussing this aspect of his configuration at length, he comments:) I'd probably do more volunteer work if I had the time . . . the homeless, the uneducated.

7. *Feelings about specific activities: On a scale of 1–9, how do you like these activities?*
Sleep?
5.

Self-care?
Other people would care if I didn't wash—5.

Work/chores (carpentry, painting, grass cutting)?
Anything I do with my hands I enjoy—9.

Hand therapy? [*He attends occupational therapy three times weekly, Monday, Wednesday, Friday.*]
Hopefully I won't be doing it 5 years from now. It's a necessary evil, it is not something I enjoy. I enjoy the company—not the therapy.

Therapy tasks?
4–5.

Therapeutic milieu/social aspects?
9.

Therapist's note: At this point, an interesting interlude occurred. The other patients, now Mr. B.'s "pals," intervened . . . lots of laughing, joking at this point from the other patients, that ended up in a group discussion of what activities were meaningful to them, how people with varying disabilities (mental or physical) would be affected by not being able to do the activities that made their lives rich and meaningful. They also understood how doing activities that are a "1" or a "5" all the time can make one chronically unhappy. The patients were rapt and deeply interested in this whole activities theme—and completely understood the occupational therapist's view of how therapeutic activities, particularly work simulations, can help to lead them back towards Activities Health. Mr. D.'s rating of specific activities and categories of activities continued:

Work?
9 for both jobs—I enjoy work.

Leisure?
9—organizational work—I'm on the Board of various religious and social organizations.

Social leisure? [Mr. D. distinguishes between "social" and other types of leisure.]
Golf, tennis—9—I haven't been able to do this since the accident—I absolutely want to get back to them.

8. *From whom and how activities were learned?*
(Therapist decided that for Mr. D., this question was not relevant to the assessment, and could therefore be ommitted.)

9. *Frequency and duration of specific activities?*
(After reviewing the frequency of activities noted on the configuration, Mr. D. comments on the length of time he has been doing these activites:) More than 10 years for all activities.

10. *Comparison with past configurations?*
Same schedule—I had more time to work and less time in therapy (O.T.).

11. *Future projections?*
I probably won't be working in the city any more . . . I'll retire from the jewelry and second-hand business . . . decrease some of the Board work . . . I'll probably spend more time at home working—what I call leisure—gardening, etc.

Part II
1. *Sense of balance?*
Good balance.

2. *What changes would you like to see in your configuration in the future?*
Yes . . . to reduce my schedule . . . I've learned that you can't push. I spent 6 months in cancer therapy [2 years ago—lung cancer]—I've learned I have to slow down.
(When asked about his feeling about his bout with cancer:) If you're blessed enough to be fortunate—I've been free of cancer for 2 years—grab life while you can. . . . My friends are great—there hasn't been a day when I haven't been able to call a friend.

3. *Despite the fact that there are times when you wish you could do something different or differently, rate, on a scale of 0 to 9, to what degree your activities as a whole provide you with a sense of overall satisfaction.*
8 to 9.

4. *Despite problems (e.g., negative feelings, physical handicaps, general stress, aches and pains), rate, on a scale of 0 to 9, to what degree you feel able to cope with your activities of everyday living, that is, overall sense of comfort.*
There's a certain amount of frustration involved—I'm interested in getting back to my previous configuration—i.e., handling small metal watchbands for a customer—I can't do it now—playing golf and tennis—3.

5. *Overall, on a scale of 0 to 9, rate to what degree you feel that your activities are acceptable to the people in the groups to which you belong (e.g., family, friends, nationality, religion), that is, overall sense of sociocultural fit.*
9—no problem.

BRIEF CASE HISTORIES

Ms. R., Age 69 Years

Ms. R. is a retired post office clerk who was in fairly good health and active with her oil painting until 5 months ago when she began experiencing acute mental changes, problems in balance and mobilty, and general unsteadiness. She was hospitalized for 10 days, during which time she was diagnosed and treated for Parkinson's disease. When medically stabilized, she was sent home to her trailer and to the supervision and care of her married daughter. To aid her in the transition from hospital to home, Ms. R.'s doctor referred her to a home health care agency to assess her physical and social environment and her level of independent functioning in her own home and to provide a home therapy program if necessary.

Ms. R. lives alone in a trailer adjacent to a log home where her daughter and son-in-law live and farm the family land, several miles from the center of town. Now dependent on a wheelchair and crutches for locomotion, Ms. R. finds she is unable to get into and out of her trailer independently, as there are five steps up to the entrance. There is no railing for support. Her bed has been removed from her bedroom, and she now has a hospital bed with an overbed table as well as a commode. Her bedroom is at the end of the trailer, next to the bathroom, which she can get into only when helped in the transfer from her bed to her wheelchair. Since she needs help to use the toilet, she prefers to use a bedpan.

Ms. R. and her daughter and son-in-law get along well. Her daughter and son-in-law plan to build an addition onto their house for Ms. R., which will include wheelchair access. The addition will have a private entrance from outside and will consist of a bedroom, kitchen, bath, and living room. Ms. R. insists on her privacy, but her daughter is concerned about her safety due to her continually unpredictable judgment when moving from place to place.

F., Age 6 Years

F. is a 6-year-old girl diagnosed with cerebral palsy. She was referred for outpatient occupational therapy services by her school due to apparent problems in fine-motor, visual-perceptual skills and self-care. F. also receives outpatient physical therapy services at the local hospital. She is learning to ambulate with a walker, but in the meantime she uses her wheelchair or crawls on her own to get around.

F. lives with her mother, stepfather, older sister, and a new younger half-sister. She has her own bedroom, a converted large closet on the ground floor. She is an active, bright, inquisitive child, always smiling and willing to try most tasks given to her. Her favorite toys are Matchbox cars, Legos, and stuffed animals. She has an active imagination and always asks, "What new toys do you have today?"

An activities assessment reveals that F. is able to stand at the bathroom sink with support and can brush her teeth, although with difficulty, wash her hands and face, and hold a cup of water. She can don and doff her undershirt easily and, given time, can doff and don long-sleeved shirts. She is unable to dress when her lower extremities are involved. F. is independent in feeding and bed mobility. She can assume a cross-legged sitting position, go from prone to side-sit, and roll from side to side. Sitting balance is fair, although she does tend to fall forward when she tires.

F. will be attending first grade in the fall (6 months from now) and will be in school all day. She will have a classroom aide but hopes to become as independent as the other kids.

Mr. J., Age 49 Years

Mr. J. spent 11 days in a hospital and is now in a short-term skilled nursing facility for treatment of his third cerebrovascular accident (CVA). Mr. J. is a smiling, outgoing, slightly overweight man and at first appearance seems older than his 49 years, as he has a full head of white hair. His speech is difficult to understand at first, but when he tries again and speaks slowly, the words come easily.

BACKGROUND INFORMATION

Prior to his three CVAs, Mr. J. spent more time working than anything else. He had no hobbies; there was no time. He smoked two to three packs of cigarettes a day, "let my weight go," but did enjoy walking and said he often would walk up to 5 miles a day. "My biggest problem was that I just had to do everything right. If it wasn't done right, it wasn't any good. Even when I was a kid, my parents told me the same thing. I was scolded if I wasn't perfect."

Mr. J., his wife, and two daughters live in a neat, one-story ranch home about 4 miles from the center of town. Mr. J. has always enjoyed his vegetable garden, his indoor house-plants, and helping his wife with the household chores. Mr. J. and his wife are early risers, getting up at about 6 A.M.

ACTIVITIES HISTORY

Mr. J.'s activities configuration since his last stroke is considerably different from what he remembers as his life-style before the series of strokes. In the pre-stroke period, he spent most of his time working and practically no time relaxing. Before his last hospitalization, he divided his time among household chores, self-care, and relaxation. He worked in his vegetable garden and enjoyed outings on the weekends with his wife for breakfast, as well as social events at the Elk's Club and visiting relatives.

MEDICAL HISTORY

This is Mr. J.'s third stroke; the first was when he was approximately 37 years old, and the second shortly thereafter. The exact timing of the first two strokes is not clear, and Mr. J.'s memory is very spotty about this time period. The first stroke occurred while Mr. J. was out working in the yard. At first, it was thought that he had suffered from sun stroke, but his symptoms were those associated with aphasia—Mr. J. could not communicate verbally or in writing. He thinks the second stroke came very soon after the first. He had recovered "pretty well" after the first stroke, had continued speech therapy, and had returned to work. The second stroke affected his left side. The third stroke occurred at Christmas while Mr. J. and his wife were attending an Elk's Club Christmas party. While dancing, he all of a sudden froze and in his words, "keeled over."

Respiratory status: Decreased apical and lateral costal expansion on left, decreased respiration in both lower lungs.
Muscle tone: Within normal limits in neck, hypertonic trunk, combination extensor/flexor synergy, left upper extremity, and extensor spasticity in both lower extremities.
Orthopedic findings: Passive range of motion within normal limits, edema left foot.
Control of active movement: Left upper extremity combination flexor/extensor synergy, but able to break out of this; extensor tone dominating both lower extremities especially when supine, but breaks out of this distal to proximal, slowly.
Coordination: Not able to do rapid alternating movements; heel to shin is slow and only grossly accurate bilaterally.
Sensation: All areas of sensation impaired, proprioception severely.
Postural reactions: Slow righting reactions; response with head but not with lower extremities; arms respond but decreased rate of response.
Functional abilities: Can roll to either side but cannot accurately move bottom, and has difficulty with motor planning to move to edge of bed. Can go from supine to sitting with close supervision; bridging requires moderate assist; goes into extension, and from sitting to standing needs contact guard with moderate assist; from standing to sitting needs moderate assist.
Gait: Uses walker, contact guard; ambulates a maximum of 60 feet; tends to keep left lower extremity in extension and circumducts instead of using hip/knee flexion during standing phase; trunk tends to be flexed forward.

OCCUPATIONAL THERAPY ASSESSMENT

An initial occupational therapy assessment revealed the following: Mr. J. was able to communicate verbally with difficulty but was unable to write; hearing and orientation appeared within normal limits; vision was impaired. Depth perception and sensation were impaired, both without significant pattern, and proprioception was severely impaired. Futher perceptual evaluation is necessary. It should be noted that residual effects from the two previous strokes made evaluation difficult. Mr. J. needed assistance in all areas of self-care except eating. He exhibited severe apraxia and became confused when given verbal instructions that required awareness of spatial relations. When Mr. J. spontaneously initiated tasks such as getting a drink of water or using the toilet, he had no problems, but when given a verbal command to do the same thing, he was unable to follow through. He was aware of his dysfunction but was unable to correct himself mid-task.

CURRENT FUNCTIONING

Mr. J. still holds his life-long beliefs regarding work and perfection. When given any task during therapy, either he has to complete it perfectly or he blocks it out. When given activities to complete on his own, Mr. J. overdoes the activity and gets tired. When this behavior pattern is pointed out to him, he admits that it is a problem and wants to amend his life-style. When asked how he might change his activities configuration, Mr. J. said he would still be happy working at any one of his previous jobs but that he would try to work at only one job at a time, relax more, and spend more time with his family. He was appalled at the "imbalance" of his life before the strokes. His goals were to be able to walk well again, to be able to walk outside without fear so that he could be more independent; and to be of more help to his wife.

A., Age 25 Years

A. is an unemployed man, admitted to a hospital for drug addiction. His diagnosis is heroin abuse/dependence, continuous. He has a history of poly-drug abuse, including occasional alcohol and cocaine use and frequent intranasal heroin use. There is no history of intravenous drug use reported. Currently, A. uses approximately $20 to $50 worth of heroin a day.

PAST HOSPITALIZATIONS

A. was hospitalized 3 years ago for cocaine abuse. Approximately 1 year ago, A. voluntarily entered a residential therapeutic community, where he remained for several months. He left the residential community 6 months prior to this admission.

MEDICAL HISTORY

A.'s current mental status is within normal limits. He stated that he has been using drugs and drinking alcohol since age 12. He identified his drug abuse as "problematic" at age 20; his longest period of sobriety outside of an institutional setting in the past 5 years was about 1 week. A. currently describes his mood as "angry and lazy." He is otherwise in good health.

FAMILY INFORMATION

The second youngest of six siblings, A. was born and raised in a large city, where he has lived all his life. A.'s mother is 60 years old and in good health; his father is 65 years old and an active alcoholic. A. has three brothers; all are active alcoholics, and two also abuse drugs. His two sisters are both "social drinkers."

A. has been married for 5 years and has a 2½ year-old daughter. At the start of this most current relapse, his wife asked for a divorce.

WORK HISTORY

A. has a high school diploma. He has worked steadily since he graduated, at a variety of jobs, working as a custodian, mechanic, and security guard. Shortly before his admission, A. was fired from his job of 3 years as an elevator operator because of excessive tardiness.

OCCUPATIONAL THERAPY ASSESSMENT

A.'s expressed interests include swimming, card games, reading, listening to music, playing pool, sewing, going to the movies and parties, bowling, cooking, fixing things, window shopping, and watching TV—although judging from his activities pattern immediately prior to admission, most of his time has recently been occupied by getting high, hanging out with his friends, and watching TV. He does, however, attend to chores around the house and self-care activities like washing clothes and grooming; he takes pride in dressing stylishly.

A. is interested in getting back to work. He hopes that while he is in the hospital, he and his wife will be able to reconcile and have a "new start" on their marriage. After discharge, he plans to spend more time with his wife and child and also to attend adult education classes. He is also interested in doing some volunteer work in addition to his paying job at some time in the future.

STRENGTHS

1. High-school graduate with steady work history.
2. Family support (although limited).
3. Apparent willingness to examine his behavior and attempts to make changes in the past.
4. Wide range of leisure interests.

PROBLEMS

1. Lack of sober social supports.
2. Currently unemployed as a result of drug abuse and associated behaviors.
3. Separation and possible divorce from wife.
4. No significant history of sobriety in past 5 years.
5. Immature and impulsive behavior.

K., Age 16 Years

K. was out for a "night on the town" with his friend who had just gotten his driver's license. They were excited and were speeding down a familiar but dark and winding road when they suddenly missed a turn and crashed. Both were admitted to the hospital with serious injuries. K., a 16-year-old high-school junior, received a traumatic closed head injury, which resulted in significant brain damage. He was in a coma for his first 3 days of the 9-week stay in a large city hospital, 50 miles away from his home. His concerned family and friends visited often and were as glad as he when it came time to go home. But life had changed markedly for K. and his whole family.

Although his parents and sister were helpful, life was difficult with the changes that had to be made in the house to accommodate K.'s rented hospital bed, wheelchair, special tables, and standing frame. So much strange and complicated equipment to fit into a small house! K. arrived home totally dependent on others for his care. In the hospital, he had a gastrostomy and was therefore dependent on tube feedings alternated with oral feedings of pureed food when he could keep it down. He was learning to eat again but could not feed himself. K. had a catheter and a dependent bowel and required 24-hour nursing services for his continued medical and personal care.

K. was referred for home health services to receive physical and occupational therapy to assess functional deficits and strengths and to set up a daily program in K.'s home. Fortunately, K.'s mother was able to change her full-time job schedule to part-time, which enabled her to learn how to assist with her son's care on his return home. K. is the only one of the four siblings living at home now. However, one of his sisters lives across the street and is able to help, thanks to her training as a nurse's aide. His father has had difficulty handling the situation both physically and psychologically. K.'s father works around the house, however, and can be counted on for help with lifting or adjusting equipment. He seems mildly interested in what the trained caretakers are doing. K.'s father is usually working on the repair of old and antique cars he continually brings into the driveway. The yard and large shed joining the house are filled with car parts, materials, and tools.

The house K. lives in is small; his parents have set up his hospital bed in the living room of the first floor, adjacent to their room and across from the kitchen. A crude ramp has been built from the driveway up to the garage.

K. appears alert and generally interested in what is going on around him. Although he is unable to talk, he appears to understand what is said and responds nonverbally, using his eyes, facial expressions, or head movements. He laughs heartily, shows spotty factual recall, gives inconsistent responses to questions, and uses his index and middle fingers of his right hand to indicate "yes" and "no" by bending them or extending them. This too is inconsistent.

Functionally, K. is dependent in isolated and specific movements of all four extremities. Problem-solving ability is diminished; he has poor verbal communication and markedly limited verbal reception. He is unable to turn independently in bed, to transfer to and from his wheelchair, to use his upper extremities for self-care activities, and to verbalize his ideas. There is spasticity in all four extremities, more pronounced in the left arm and leg than in the right. Sensory perception and function are unreliable. Swelling and pain are evident in the upper extremities, and there is the presence of myositis ossificans, noticeable particularly in the left arm. Passive and active range of motion are markedly decreased. K. is right-handed and has maintained a functional prehension (pincer) grip with this hand, as well as a gross reach with shoulder flexion to approximately 60 degrees. As stated, he is able to isolate his index and middle fingers to a moderate degree for activity performance. Visually he is able to discriminate and identify letters and numbers. He has some figure-ground perception, color distinction, and stereognosis function. His functional problems are intensified by decreased mental and physical endurance, spasticity, poor coordination, and a tendency to wait for someone else to do things for him. He continues to have tube feeding and catheter care and is on medication for post-trauma seizures.

Before his accident, K. enjoyed cars and their repair, hunting, fishing, and having a good time. He wanted to finish school and get a job doing car repairs like his dad. He did not have much patience for school and had no interest in attending college. K. does not know whether he will be able to return to school in the fall to complete his senior year.

T., Age 33 Years

T. is a 33-year-old man who is attending a psychiatric day hospital in a large city. For the past 6 months, he has been living in an apartment about 15 miles away with his girlfriend, who was previously also a patient at the day hospital. Prior to that time, he had been living in a supportive apartment program for 18 months. T.'s diagnosis is bipolar affective disorder (axis I), chronic alcohol abuse in remission, and organic brain syndrome (axis II).

T. has had numerous psychiatric hospitalizations for alcohol detoxification, and both manic and depressive episodes. His most recent hospitalization was 9 months ago, after he experienced a blackout secondary to drinking and was arrested for disorderly conduct.

T. is the fourth of six children and was born in the inner city. Both of his parents were alcoholic, and his mother also had psychiatric problems. His mother died 10 years ago; his father died 2 years ago.

T. always had academic difficulties, and he dropped out of high school in the eleventh grade. He recalls having an active social life, enjoying friendships and dating until tenth grade, when he began abusing alcohol heavily. By the time he dropped out of high school, T.'s only remaining social contacts were his "drinking buddies." A few months after leaving school, he got a job as a stockboy in a supermarket, which went well for about 6 months, after which he became argumentative with his co-workers, which quickly escalated to the point that he was fired. The depression that followed severely affected his motivation to find another job and attend to his self-care needs. After months in which he rarely left the house, his family eventually persuaded him to see a psychiatrist, who admitted him to a psychiatric unit.

After his discharge from the hospital 3 months later, T. was referred to a vocational training program, where he studied air conditioner repair. He had difficulty learning what was expected but managed to earn his certificate. During his first job in the field, however, his boss was dissatisfied with T.'s work from the start, and he was fired soon after. Feeling defeated, he got a job as a cook's assistant, which lasted for a year. For the next 10 years, T. continued to live with his family and had numerous short-lived jobs as a handyman or stockboy. His drinking binges recurred intermittently; during these 10 years he had four hospitalizations for alcohol detoxification and the exacerbation of psychiatric symptoms. After each of the hospitalizations, T. consistently rejected discharge recommendations that he attend a day program after discharge, insisting he could return home and find a job.

By the time his father died 2 years ago, all of his siblings had moved out of the house on their own. He and his father had shared household chores; T. especially enjoyed fixing things around the house, shopping for groceries, and cooking for himself and his father. T. only occasionally went to family gatherings at his siblings' homes, although he would join the others when they came to his house. Otherwise, T.'s social life remained virtually nonexistent. During his free time, he went to a neighborhood bar, watched TV with his father or alone, and took long walks and bike rides, which would sometimes last for most of the day.

T.'s most recent hospitalization occurred soon after his father's death. Because he felt he had little choice, he accepted the staff's recommendation that he move into a supportive apartment program, which also involved a commitment to attend a day hospital program. Much to his surprise, he adjusted rather easily to both. In his apartment he had his own bedroom, and he and his two apartment-mates coexisted fairly comfortably. They all appreciated T.'s willingness to cook for them, and with the assistance of the apartment counselor, the other chores were divided among them all. In the day hospital, he enjoyed the groups in which he was able to make things with wood and participate in cooking activities. He was less interested in the groups that involved talking, and he sometimes grew tired of spending so much time with other people. When he first came to the day hospital he met E., a female patient who was discharged shortly after he arrived. After dating for about a year, they moved into an apartment together. He reports that everything is going very well at home.

During his stay at the day hospital, T. participated in the prevocational program. When initially evaluated, he was given the Revised Beta II Exam, a test that correlates with the subtests of the WAIS. His scores indicated minimal mental deficiency. A vocational interest test indicated the need for structure and inability to see himself as a worker, despite his expression of a strong desire to work. During the testing phase of the prevocational evaluation, he showed the ability to concentrate well with a great deal of structure. Following his initial evaluation, after great resistance, T. was placed as a volunteer kitchen helper in a shelter for the homeless. He helped with food preparation, cleaned the kitchen, and did other related jobs in the kitchen. Even though the job was going quite well, on one occasion T. went on a weekend drinking binge, after which he returned to the day hospital feeling demoralized. His spirits were temporarily lifted when the boss on his volunteer job offered him a full-time paying job. However, the day hospital staff felt that after his recent drinking binge, he was not yet ready for discharge, and so they could not support him in taking the job. He accepted their recommendation, but his performance in the volunteer job began to deteriorate; after a kitchen assistant was hired, he became increasingly critical of the way things were run. He eventually stopped attending the volunteer job.

T. was then referred to the Office of Vocational Rehabilitation (OVR) for a complete vocational assessment. He insisted that he wanted to go to electronics school and persisted with this desire despite the counselor's recommendation that he also explore other areas. She eventually agreed to allow him to take the entrance examination, on which he received a very low score. He rejected the other options that OVR offered and is now back in the day hospital full-time.

In the apartment, T. participates in shopping and cooking and especially enjoys fixing things in the apartment. He continues to attend Alcoholics Anonymous meetings almost every evening. On weekends, he and his girlfriend occasionally go to the movies or go to visit her family or his siblings.

The single goal that T. expresses is to get a job in electronics. He continues to refuse to consider other vocational options at this time.

D., Age 35 Years

D. is a 35-year-old man of Italian descent, with acquired immunodeficiency syndrome (AIDS), diagnosed 2 years ago. He is severely emaciated with peripheral neuropathy and is confined to a wheelchair. Because of generalized muscle weakness, he does not have the strength and endurance to attend to any of his self-care needs independently; he therefore requires a 24-hour home health aide. Although D. had been a successful stand-up comedian up to 4 years ago, he now stays home all day in his spacious apartment, watches TV, and is very depressed. He has been shunned by his family (parents and two married sisters) since they learned of his homosexuality shortly after he was diagnosed. Many of his friends are deceased because of AIDS. Regular social contact is currently limited to one longtime friend, who visits or calls him on a daily basis.

D. was an excellent student at school, with a special gift for creative writing. He also was an active member of his college's drama group, which won awards for a number of outstanding performances. D. dropped out of college after 3 years to travel around the world with his lover, an older man with wide business interests, who, on their return, sponsored his career in acting for the next 2 years. When D. was 23, this relationship came to an end. While he continued to pursue acting, D. worked as a waiter to earn a living, with occasional acting jobs in between. Finally, at 27, he developed a comic act that "took on," and he was invited to appear on the nightclub circuit all over the country. He also won particular acclaim in the gay community for a satirical revue that he wrote and in which he appeared as part of the cast.

Prior to his illness, D.'s leisure interests included contemporary music, ballet, and travel. He states that he no longer pursues any of these very much, aside from watching an occasional ballet on TV and listening to the radio.

E., Age 17 Years

E. is a 17-year-old girl who was admitted to an acute inpatient unit at a large metropolitan teaching hospital. She was admitted after taking an overdose of Valium, which she found in her mother's medicine cabinet after they had a major argument. Immediately after the overdose, she became frightened and told her mother, who took her to the emergency room. E. states that she really did not want to die and that she took the pills so that her mother would realize how depressed she is feeling.

E. is an only child. She has lived alone with her mother in a house in the suburbs for the past 5 years since her father left their home without warning and relocated to another city a thousand miles away. Prior to that time, E. states that she was "very close" to her father and "relied on him for everything." Her father has since remarried, and she sees him only once a year for 2 weeks in the summer. E.'s mother, who had been a housewife up until the time her husband left, went back to school a year later and complete her Master's degree in social work. Her mother now works full-time. Most recently, her mother began dating for the first time; she has also made many new friends at work and socializes with them often during the weekday evenings and on weekends as well. E. and her mother have historically had a strained relationship, which has intensified over the past 5 years, with intermittent explosive arguments like the one that preceded E.'s overdose.

E. attends a private high school, where she is a junior. She was recently suspended for truancy and increasing problems in getting in along with teachers. Until very recently, E. had been dating Tom for 6 months. Tom is a junior in a college out of town, which means that she sees him only during his monthly weekend visits home or school vacations. After her overdose, Tom told her that he did not think it was a good idea for them to see one another any longer.

ACTIVITIES HEALTH ASSESSMENT

E. found it difficult to fill out the weekly activities schedule "because my life changes so much." This was especially true when recording her weekends because her activities depend on whether her boyfriend is in town. With the exception of her part-time job on Saturdays, where she helps out in a program for 3 and 4 year olds, she spends as much time as possible with Tom.

E. was struck by the fact that in the past several months since she began dating Tom, she has become less interested in spending time with her girlfriends, who she finds to be "immature." The only extracurricular activity in which she has remained involved is the volleyball team, which she says feels like a chore this year because the team morale is so low. Prior to this year, E. enjoyed volleyball, especially because she "felt part of a group." Other activities previously pursued that she does no longer are drama, choir, and horseback riding. Now, with the exception of her time with Tom, she spends leisure time alone, "listending to music and just thinking."

E. states she hates school because she "can't relate" to the other kids and lacks interest in any subject. As a child, she was diagnosed as having dyslexia and states that although it is not as much of a problem as before, it takes her an inordinate amount of time to complete her reading. She does homework for 2 to 6 hours daily and is still struggling to pass her subjects. E. states that although she and her parents have always expected that she will attend college, she is "not so interested anymore." She describes her Saturday job as a positive experience because it makes her feel as if she is doing something "important."

E. states that since her mother started to work full-time, she is now expected to do additional chores around the house. She says that the chores are assigned to her by her mother when the need arises and that she's bothered by the fact that there's no set routine in the household in general. E. attributes her recent problems at school to an increase in responsibilities for chores that were previously done by her mother.

E. was unable to articulate any future plans or goals. She is extremely upset and preoccupied about her breakup with Tom and becomes tearful when she talks about their relationship. She is eager for discharge and states nonchalantly that she will probably resume therapy with her previous therapist after discharge.

L., Age 39 Years

L. has been in institutions for the mentally retarded since the age of 16. He lived with his grandmother before that; his mother abandoned him, and his father is unknown. When his grandmother died, he was sent to a state institution, where he remained until 3 months ago, when the institution was closed because of a public outcry. He was transferred to another state facility, which has a much better reputation. At the time he was referred to occupational therapy, he was confined to a cottage because of his repulsive personal habits. Although his personal hygiene and dressing are attended to by the nursing staff, he is unkempt, clothes unbuttoned and food-stained. He eats "like an animal," wolfing his food in great chunks, allowing it to dribble down his face and clothes, unable to use a knife and fork, and making loud, repellant noises when he drinks. He takes his meals alone because the residents refuse to have him around while they are eating. His greatest wish is to have coffee with the others in the dining room.

Mr. Y., Age 76 Years

Mr. Y. was admitted to a nursing home after hospitalization for a third transient ischemic attack in the last 7 years. He had lived alone in a room above the general store; there he helped with odd jobs, passed the time of day with the customers—to whom he was the town character—and kept a wary eye and ear open for intruders after hours. Now he has made a good physical recovery, but his memory has become affected. Memory for recent events is poor, and recollections of his past are confused. He is very lonely and depressed. His wife died 20 years ago, and one son, a merchant marine officer, has lived in Australia for many years. A daughter, an aspiring stage actress, visits him occasionally between marriages and acting engagements. Before his retirement at 65, Mr. Y. was a food inspector. His hobbies are gardening, collecting postcards from around the world, and reading adventure stories. He was also "quite a dancer" in his younger days. This particular "home" has a very caring staff and a varied activities program.

G., Age 22 Years

G. was knocked over by a car that mounted the sidewalk. She suffered a head injury, resulting in ataxia, severe intention tremor in the right upper limb, loss of memory, and thickness of speech. G. comes from a family of high achievers. Her parents are divorced; her father is a well-known businessman, and her mother is a very successful advertising executive. At the time of her accident, G. was a fourth-year student at a prestigious school of business administration. She was referred as an outpatient to the occupational therapy clinic 6 months after discharge from her initial hospitalization with the following problems: inability to concentrate, inability to write (because of intention tremor, unnoticeable until she begins a manual task), which provokes great anxiety about her ability to complete her studies; flashes of irritability and anger; fleeting lapses of consciousness; feeling unsteady on her feet. She has been going to typing classes in the hope of compensating for her inability to write and has been driving herself feverishly to get physically fit; she practices the exercises given to her on discharge and does yoga and typing exercises at home. She is independent in all self-care activities, including travel by subway. She manages steps, crowded trains, and streets but cannot run. Hobbies are reading—philosophy and modern novels—and table tennis. She likes going to parties and giving parties in the large home that she shares with her father.

J., Age 21 Years

J. is a sales assistant who was admitted to a psychiatric hospital with a diagnosis of acute schizophrenia—withdrawn, confused, flat affect, psychomotor retardation. She was put on medication and referred to occupational therapy a few days later. J. was able to give a history; she lives with her mother and a younger brother and sister in a city housing project, never had more than one or two friends, and is unable to socialize easily. She did not complete high school—school did not seem safe with assaults and muggings—although she received good grades. She found a job as a part-time helper in a department store at age 17 and was promoted to full-time gift wrapper at 18 because she was so neat and accurate. J. has no hobbies or special interests but would like to "learn" some. Her occupational therapy activities evaluation revealed an ability to follow directions (both written and oral) with facility, excellent manual skills, poor interpersonal skills, and good concentration; there was a flat affect throughout.

FROM "COMING HOME TO DIE" TO ACTIVITIES HEALTH: THE CASE OF MRS. N.

Anne Spencer

Mrs. N. is a tiny woman of 74 years. From her bed or her recliner she appears to be totally dependent in her functional performance. She greets the visiting therapist with a somewhat apprehensive smile of welcome, motioning weakly to a nearby chair. S., her daughter-in-law, is bustling about the room, shooing her two small children out of the way and putting the last-minute touches on the already tidy room she has fixed up for her husband's mother. Although Mrs. N. has been washed and dressed by the home health aide who comes every morning, she is still lying on her hospital bed in her makeshift room next to the living room on the first floor of her son's house where she is now living, taking a rest before getting up for the day.

BACKGROUND INFORMATION

Mrs. N. feels that her life revolves around her children and their children. A year ago her husband died suddenly, and soon after she lost her will to live. She had always worked hard, first as a child growing up among many siblings out in the country, and then as the wife of one of her father's farmhands. She and her husband had raised 10 children and had spent a hard life working on the farm. All but one child still live in nearby communities and come to visit often. Life on the farm was active and busy, with parental responsibilities, household chores, and farm duties in which all participated. There was little time for leisure activities except for the sewing and needlework she did for the family and for the grange. Her son, B., remembers his mother as a strong woman with lots of stamina and a positive attitude toward life. He is distressed to note her current lack of interest and activity and wants to help make her comfortable and happy.

MEDICAL HISTORY

For many years, Mrs. N. was in fairly good health. Within the past 6 years or so, she has developed cardiac problems, and she has continued to suffer persistent shortness of breath and a congested cough on strenuous activity. She has complained of intermittent pain and fatigue due to arthritis in her joints (she was told that her bones were osteoporotic). She has been developing contractures that hinder upper extremity functions. She has a volar splint on her right hand and wrist to keep fingers open and wrist extended to ensure both proper circulation and neurological function. Mrs. N. also has suffered several minor strokes, the most recent 1 month ago. Residual effects were noted in increasing hesitancy and slurring of speech, as well as decreased active range of motion and strength in both arms, more pronounced on the right side. She also has had difficulty in walking. After the death of her husband, Mrs. N.'s problems became overwhelming; she lost her motivation for independent activity and soon became bed-bound. Her medical problems eventually resulted in severe swallowing problems, for which she required pharyngeal suctioning and tube feeding. On discharge from the hosptial she was admitted to a nursing home. She became very depressed there, so she was brought home by her son "to die."

GENERAL STYLE OF LIVING

Mrs. N. lives a sedentary life, confined to her wheelchair or reclining chair in the living room. She is unable to transfer from place to place without the assistance of one or two persons; once she is placed in a specific location in the house, she remains there until it is time to go back to bed. She receives food through the feeding tube and is washed, bathed, and groomed by the aide from the agency who comes every morning for several hours. She is not required to move her limbs or to perform any activities of personal care and has become willing to be cared for, sitting and watching TV and dozing in her chair. Since the house is often filled with people, Mrs. N. gains some amusement and stimulation from the generations of relatives going in and out, but she does not participate with them in their activities unless they draw her into their conversations; they are usually "too much in a hurry." Summers are more lively than winters, which seem to progress slowly from day to day with little happening. Mrs. N. is unable to go outside, as there are four steps to go down and she is unable to use her walker. The house is on a hill, and the ground is rough near the house. She is no longer able to drive her car for jaunts in the country as she did many months ago, does not talk much, and generally lets life pass by her, sitting, snoozing, or daydreaming of better times in the past, smiling once in a while at a happy memory.

REFERRAL

A referral was made to the occupational therapist to assess Mrs. N.'s home situation and to find out if there is potential for increased functional activity. There was much concern on the part of her daughter-in-law that Mrs. N. was losing ground and was becoming more and more depressed due to her inactivity. A nurse and a physical therapist were also requested.

ASSESSMENT

The occupational therapist set up a schedule of sessions twice a week to begin the assessment process. The initial visit was made to Mrs. N.'s home in the morning. On arrival, the occupational therapist finds her already bathed and dressed and sitting in her recliner. She is propped up by many pillows (she tends to slide down because her feet do not touch the floor). She is wearing a volar cock-up splint, which extends distally to the metacarpophalangeal joints of her right hand. She smiles when greeted and says, "Hello." Mrs. N.'s daughter-in-law and the nurse's aide are curious to see the evaluation and are available should there be questions. The occupational therapist sits down near Mrs. N. and attempts to engage her in a conversation about how things have been and are now—what her major problems and concerns are and what she wants to do that she cannot. They discuss her hospitalization and time in the nursing home only briefly, as this arouses unpleasant associations. Mrs. N. speaks little; S. has to fill in, while Mrs. N. prefers to gaze off at the quiz show on the TV. During informal conversation, the occupational therapist evaluates Mrs. N.'s sitting position and makes notes of possibilities for improvement, planning a later discussion with Mrs. N., her son, and her daughter-in-law about this. Her son reports that Mrs. N. needs help with personal care—transfers from bed and chair, bathing, dressing, grooming, and eating. There is no sign of Mrs. N.'s interest during the subsequent discussion, and when asked about activities in general or constructive activities in particular, she is not responsive. However, she does say that she would like to "get up and walk again."

It is evident that Mrs. N. is able to see, hear, and understand and use speech for simple communication. She knows when the therapist changes the position of her extremities to check range of motion and sensation. She is able to detect and localize sensory stimuli to determine the shape of objects when the therapist puts them in her hand, and to identify them even with her eyes closed. She can sit balanced in the chair without a backrest, but her standing tolerance is poor and ambulation is laborious and painful. Mrs. N. can exert pressure on the therapist's hand with both hands in a gross grip but is unable to register any measurable grip strength on the dynamometer gauge. She has the functional ability to pick up small objects such as eating utensils, a hairbrush, and a washcloth with her left hand and is able to open her right dominant hand to achieve a space almost an inch between the tip of her thumb and the tip of her index finger, although her hand is markedly limited by flexion contractures.

Mrs. N.'s sitting position in the recliner is conducive to kyphosis and immobility of the extremities. She shows marked limitation of active and passive range of motion in her shoulders, and is able to flex to just within 90 degrees. She shows a 35-degree limitation of active elbow extension in the right arm and 10 degrees in the left. The recliner keeps her hips passively flexed at about 40 degrees and her knees bent at about 30 degrees. Her ankles are dropped in plantar flexion. Mrs. N. demonstrates that she is able to flex and extend her legs independently and alternately and to dorsiflex her ankles actively to achieve a functional standing position for walking. She complains of pain in her right hand due to her splint and general inability to use her hand, which appears to be due to flexion contractures of the metacarpophalangeal joints and extension contractures of the interphalangeal joints. She has, however, some active opposition of her thumb, sufficient to grasp small objects.

SUMMARY REPORT ON INITIAL INTERVIEW

Mrs. N. is performing no self-care activities, no manual activities, and no independent transfers. She is generally content to sit and watch TV. She complains of pain and weakness in all four extremities, is unable to stand and to walk, is unable to feed herself, and spends the day poorly positioned in her recliner. She is pleasant but shows little affect and appears to be unmotivated to move toward independence in any activities, other than expressing some interest in walking again. *Obviously she is not in a state of activities health.*

POTENTIAL

On evaluation, it appears that the home situation is supportive. Several items had been sent home with Mrs. N. from the hospital to aid her in regaining independent functioning, including a hospital bed with a trapeze and side rails, a commode, a walker, and a Hoyer lift to help the aide get her to and from bed. She has not used most of the equipment. Evaluation of the extremities reveals limited range of motion but intact sensation and potential for improving muscle strength, which is now affected by disuse. She seems to be "frozen" within her routine of dependency. There clearly appears to be potential for the development of a daily pattern of activities of everyday living, with the aid of therapeutic positioning and systematic exercise. The potential for such improvement was discussed with Mrs. N., her son, and her daughter-in-law, as well as the aide, the nurse, and the physical therapist.

TREATMENT PLAN

The treatment plan is to include

1. Continued assessment of functional capacity, deficits, and potential.
2. Daily activities program directed toward learning those activities routines appropriate in view of Mrs. N.'s limitations and her potential for active function.
3. Increase in range of motion—passive range of motion to both arms, followed by active range of motion through manual activities related to object handling and self-care.
4. Strengthening of upper extremity, using manual activities, self-care regimen, and wheelchair and walker propulsion.
5. Self-locomotion with wheelchair.
6. Increased general mobility, activity endurance, and functional independence through instruction to Mrs. N. and her caretakers regarding the program objectives and appropriate techniques for correct management of dysfunction.

In all areas, it was stressed to Mrs. N. and her family that the activities are to be done gradually and within Mrs. N.'s physical and mental tolerance.

Course of Treatment and Progress

The assessment itself was an ongoing process, incorporated into the treatment sessions. Occupational therapy continued twice a week over the course of 3 months. With the initial focus of therapy on self-care activities such as handling a cup, glass, fork, and spoon, Mrs. N. began to gain a sense of her potential to engage in activities independently. Swallowing improved to the point of readiness for self-feeding, so she was able to practice her manual skills as she gained strength and coordination. She enjoyed practicing writing by doing pencil puzzles and crayon drawings with her granddaughter. She began to participate in her bathing routine in bed, with the help of her aide, as well as dressing and grooming activities in both bed and wheelchair. She performed most unilateral activities using her left hand as dominant and practiced distinguishing small objects by feeling and handling bimanually with both hands, with her eyes closed. This also was fun to do with the younger children who came to visit often, as they loved playing with their grandmother. What was an exercise for her was fun for them; their joy was fun for her.

The splint was evaluated and eventually changed to provide ease in putting it on and comfort in wearing, while also providing assistance in passive functional placement of her thumb, fingers, and wrist for grasp. Although unable to put it on herself, Mrs. N. could remove it and massage her hand and wrist after wearing the splint to stimulate circulation. She began to use her right hand again in minimal activity. Pushing her wheelchair required a lot of strength, and the task was made more difficult because it was necessary for her to position her overly flexed fingers (from contractures) onto the wheelrims. She did not believe it when she was actually able to push herself across the living room rug, around the woodstove, and out into the kitchen for meals! She began to use both her arms and her legs more when struggling to put on her clothes. Although these morning activities tired her out for a while, they in fact gave her energy to do more during the rest of the day.

With her residual capabilities, Mrs. N. could hold the washcloth, move it over her body, dry herself, and brush her hair. Her slippery silky dresses with no fastenings were easy to put over her head and pull down, and she gained security in her sitting balance in the wheelchair. As time progressed, so did she. "I feel good!" she happily exclaimed one day. Mrs. N. was beginning to talk more, to laugh, and to joke with those around her. She learned to operate the locks on her wheelchair for increased safety and expressed an interest in returning to doing her needlework.

Mrs. N. was pleased that she was able to move her limbs more and to require less care from others, but she felt that self-care activities alone lacked the outlets for creativity she had previously found from her knitting and crocheting; she yearned for something she could do with her hands where she could again choose bright colors and make things others would enjoy. It had indeed been a long time! She could now feed herself and was helping a good deal with bathing and dressing; there was no longer the need for an aide. But her wheelchair prevented her from getting close enough to any table in the house for tabletop activities. Again her family got into the act. This time, her son, B., asked what he could do. Since he was an expert carpenter (in fact this was his trade), he designed a lapboard for his mother out of a piece of plywood and an old chair, which she could use and remove from the wheelchair. He made it "just the right height" so that she could work on the weaving in which she had previously expressed an interest. She found that her "magic" new table was also good for eating, dart games, manual activities, and even reading. It was so much better than the high table that she felt more like being up and doing.

One day, Mrs. N. decided it was time to get up and walk to the sink. She had been using the walker and practicing her transfers with the physical therapist for several weeks and felt she was getting stronger. She really wanted to get over to the sink and surprise her daughter-in-law by doing the lunch dishes. She "packed" her glasses, magazine, her hand splint, and her handkerchief in the "apron" a volunteer had made for her to tie onto her walker for carrying things, and with the help of the occupational therapist, she pulled herself up to the walker and struggled over to the sink. She reached the faucets, turned on the water, and filled the sink with the dishes. As she looked up, she saw a view she had missed for several months—the bird feeder and the field across to the neighbor's house. Oh, how she had missed those sights! And what a struggle it had been!

Pretty soon, using the walker became a routine. At first she had to use the forearm platform for her left hand and arm because it hurt to grab onto the walker. But, with the increase in active range of motion and strength, she was finally able to grasp both sides well and to use the walker for ambulation as well as standing. There was added motivation for this from her son, B., who, with the advice of the occupational therapist with regard to adequate slope and length, was building a ramp to cover the side-door steps so that Mrs. N. could go into the yard by using either her wheelchair or her walker. He almost had it done—right down to the nonslip paint, the safety edge guards, and the railings! What a joy it would be at last to go outside when she wanted to, not alone, of course . . . it was still important to be careful.

All of a sudden, it seemed, the days were not so long, and there were interesting things to do. Even her pain did not seem as noticeable, at least not as annoying. She had other things to think about. In spite of all the special equipment she had, she did not have to be totally dependent on her daughter and her family. Her physical endurance improved as well as her general outlook. She was pleased that her family had begun to include her more in their conversations and activities. It was like times she remembered, when they showed they wanted to be with her. She even felt she was worthwhile again. As Mrs. N. was well on her way to independent living within her limitations (a state of *activities health*), it was no longer necessary for her to receive skilled therapy services in her home, which meant she could be discharged to her own care.

Appendixes

APPENDIX A

Idiosyncratic Activities Configuration—Instructions and Questionnaire*

Instructions

1. Keep a small notebook and pencil with you at all times. Record everything you do every day for one week (Monday through Sunday), hour by hour.
2. Fill in the Activities Schedule on p. 276. If more than one activity is done at the same time (e.g., watching TV and sewing), bracket both in the same time slot. If any activity does not occupy the full hour, fill in all the activities that occupy the time slot in order (no further detail is necessary). [ACTIVITIES PATTERN]
3. Use the completed schedule to make a list of all the activities that you have done during the entire week.
4. Classify the activities and code them by color in the completed Activities Schedule. [CLASSIFICATION; ACTIVITIES PATTERN]
   Activities Schedule Coding Key:
   Sleep—green
   Work—red
   Chores—purple
   Leisure
      Alone—yellow
      With others—orange
   Self-care—blue
5. Answer the following Questionnaire.

---

* Capitalizations in brackets refer to themes appearing in the text of Chapter 2.

Questionnaire

I. Using the completed Activities Schedule and activities list:
   A. At which specific times (hour and day) is each activity done? [TIMING]
   B. For how long is each activity done? [DURATION]
   C. What activity comes before each activity? After each activity? [SEQUENTIAL ORDER]
   D. How often during the week do you do the same activity? [FREQUENCY]
   E. List the activities appearing in the completed schedule under the following headings:
      Number of times weekly
      Number of times daily

II. Using the list of activities only:
   A. For how long have you been doing each activity? [HISTORICAL DURATION]
      Tabulate under the following headings:
      Ever since I can remember
      More than 25 years
      15–25 years
      10–15 years
      5–10 years
      1–5 years
      Less than 1 year
   B. Where do you do each activity? [SPATIAL/LOCATIONAL] Tabulate under the following headings:
      Indoors
      Outdoors
      Special setting
      Same place always
      Variable (describe)
   C. With whom do you do each activity? [SOCIAL]
      1. Tabulate as follows:
         a. With others:
            1 person
            2–4 people
            Small group
            Large group
         b. Alone
      2. Code each activity as follows:
         F = friends
         R = family
         C = colleagues (co-workers, fellow students, committee members)
         X = other (specify)
   D. From whom did you learn each activity? [PERSONAL EQUATION] Code each activity as follows:
      P = from peers
      K = from family

T = from teachers
Z = from others (specify)
E. How do you feel about each activity? [PERSONAL EQUATION]
   1. Use the rating scale below to indicate a number for each activity that best indicates how you feel (1 = dislike, 5 = like, with gradations in between):

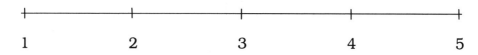

1   2   3   4   5

   2. Tabulate under the following headings:
      Like
      Dislike
      Neutral
      Variable (explain)
   3. List all your activities in order of preference (i.e., "most liked" first).
F. Which activities do you choose to do? Which activities do you have to do? [PERSONAL EQUATION] Tabulate as follows:
   Choose to do
   Have to do

ADDENDUM TO QUESTIONNAIRE

Using the completed Activities Schedule, answer the following questions:

1. How many hours per week do you spend at work?
2. How many hours per week do you spend in sleep?
3. How many hours per week do you spend with leisure activities?
4. How many hours per week do you spend on chores (taking care of self and environment, including others in it)?
5. What proportion of your weekly time do you spend on each of the above categories of activities?
6. What proportion of your weekly time do you spend:
   a. alone?
   b. with others?
7. What proportion of your weekly time do you spend:
   a. at home?
   b. away from home?
8. What proportion of your weekly time do you spend on activities you:
   a. dislike?
   b. like?
9. What proportion of your weekly time do you spend on activities you:
   a. choose to do?
   b. have to do?

	MONDAY	TUESDAY	WEDNESDAY	THURSDAY	FRIDAY	SATURDAY	SUNDAY
12 Midnight to 1 A.M.							
1 A.M.-2 A.M.							
2 A.M.-3 A.M.							
3 A.M.-4 A.M.							
4 A.M.-5 A.M.							
5 A.M.-6 A.M.							
6 A.M.-7 A.M.							
7 A.M.-8 A.M.							
8 A.M.-9 A.M.							
9 A.M.-10 A.M.							
10 A.M.-11 A.M.							
11 A.M.-12 Noon							
Noon-1 P.M.							
1 P.M.-2 P.M.							
2 P.M.-3 P.M.							
3 P.M.-4 P.M.							
4 P.M.-5 P.M.							
5 P.M.-6 P.M.							
6 P.M.-7 P.M.							
7 P.M.-8 P.M.							
8 P.M.-9 P.M.							
9 P.M.-10 P.M.							
10 P.M.-11 P.M.							
11 P.M. to 12 Midnight							

APPENDIX B

Framework for a Sociobiological Classification of Activities

Table B-1. Sociobiological Classification of Activities

Existence (individual)—Activities for meeting basic biological needs	*Coexistence (group)—Activities for meeting needs related to others*
1. Obtaining nourishment	1. Giving / Sharing / Taking → nourishment
2. Obtaining shelter	2. Giving / Sharing / Taking → shelter
3. Elimination	3. Observing measures for hygiene and sanitation
4. Reproduction	4. Participating in mating rituals, caring for offspring
5. Defense	5. Bonding together for support and strength—staking out territory
6. Sleep	6. Allocation of designated sleeping places

Table B-2. Examples of Activities Fitting into Table B-1

Existence (individual)	*Coexistence (group)*
Obtaining Nourishment	
1. *Related to getting nourishment:* Foraging → supermarket shopping for oneself	Hunting/gathering → shopping at farmer's market, being served by waiter (dining out), etc.
2. *Related to preparing nourishment:* Natural state (no preparation) → cooking over fire → gourmet cuisine in formal setting	Sharing meal preparation → home cooking, short-order cooking, restaurant cooking, preparing meals; see description of North American Indian life in Chapter 1 Offshoots: publishing/writing cookbooks; making pots; manufacturing cookware, silverware, utensils, stoves, etc.
3. *Related to taking in nourishment:* Eating/drinking (no rituals) → setting a beautiful table for one—complete 3-course meal	Sharing spoils → participating in feasts (celebrations/rituals) → simple snacks, full-course meals with accompanying wines Think of manners, appropriate use of eating utensils, decor, place-settings, fads in foods For a whole host of associated activities; see discussion on eating in Chapter 4
Obtaining Shelter	
Natural hollows, caves → putting up tent → building/owning home	Caves → group shelters → skyscrapers, etc. Offshoots and specialized roles (hence a network of activities): maintenance, landlords, decorators, house painters, realtors, furniture movers, architects, builders, gardeners

APPENDIX C

Framework for a Sociocultural Classification of Activities

Time (historical duration)	Sociocultural Influences	Examples of Activities	Specific Instances
Continuous			
Longitudinal threads from generation to generation; continuous through life span	Learning from generation to generation; emphasis on family as socializing influence; value placed on *tradition* and *ritual*	Annual religious ceremonies, national holidays, birthday celebrations, ceremonial feasts, family gatherings, preparing traditional meals, folk arts and crafts, customs, games	Christmas, Yom Kippur, Chinese New Year, Memorial Day picnic, Bastille Day, Mardi Gras, baking Scottish shortbread, horseshoe throwing, candlemaking, quilting, flower arranging, making painted heart (see Chap. 8), folk-dancing, visits to the zoo
Periodic			
Appear at different times in the life span; last for a variable but finite period	Prescriptions for activities suitable to developmental stages and transitional roles; latitude for personal choice within a prescribed framework	Rites of passage, developmental tasks, hobbies, sports, play, chores, work activities	Confirmation, wedding, baptism, Bar Mitzvah, tribal initiation rites, learning to drive, dating, starting school, preschool and school activities, household management, meal preparation, independence in personal hygiene, grooming, changes of work or career
Fleeting			
Fads and fancies— passing fancies of short duration	Latitude for personal choice within a framework that allows for novelty	Adhering to fashions in personal appearance, clothes, hairstyles, makeup; standards of grooming; music, dancing socializing, eating, games	Wearing leather jackets, adjusting hemlines, putting on heavy eye makeup, shopping for clothes, making or swapping macrame "friendship bracelets," eating out, going to discos and rock concerts, reading popular magazines

Comparison of Fields of Action: Eating Out

	Eating as Leisure—Family Picnic	*Eating as Work—Business Lunch*
Environment		
Physical setting	Outdoors—natural surroundings	Indoors—restaurant
	Large open space (specially designated for picnics or selected as suitable by participants)	Confined space
	Changing sets (free to move about to different sections of the environment, e.g., river, rocks, barbecue area)	Fixed set (stay in one place)—host orders, periodic interruptions by waiter or busperson for service
People	Many—all generations, friends/family	Host and guest—adults; waiters, buspersons, other diners in background
Objects	Natural objects (e.g., trees, rocks water)	Carefully arranged decor
	Household objects (e.g., food containers, plastic containers and utensils, paper towels, ground sheets)	Formal artifacts (silverware, china, flowers, carpets, curtains, tables, chairs)
	Items of food and drink—easy to eat, traditional	Elaborate food and drink; Formal menu
	Portable games (e.g., Frisbee, playing cards, soccer ball, children's toys)	

	Eating as Leisure—Family Picnic	*Eating as Work—Business Lunch*
Rules		
Explicit	Do not litter. Little ones: Do not stray too far. Everyone be back by specified departure time.	Come at prearranged time. Guest: Choose the restaurant.
Implicit	Be alone or join with others, as you wish. Forget about time. Relax and enjoy yourself. Eat how, when you want. Wear easy, comfortable clothes. Help clean up.	Host: Be punctual. Reserve table ahead of time. Defer to guest about menu and wine. Do not seem to be rushed. Introduce business talk at right time. Guest: Be punctual. You can choose even the most expensive items. You can choose time to finish. Both: Dress appropriately. Follow rules of etiquette for ordering and eating. Food will be served in orderly, carefully-timed sequence. Business talk will accompany eating.
Time frame	Loose, allowing a great deal of individual variation	Preset, constrained by external considerations, following a formal sequence.
Behavior habitat	Free, spontaneous personal transactions and interactions Potential conflicts among participants of different ages, family relationships, role perceptions, interpretations of implicit rules	Formal, prescribed, limited transactions and interactions between host and guest, and between host and guest with waiter.

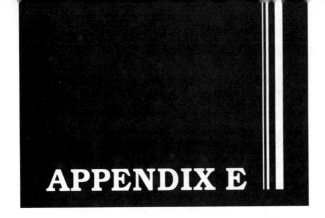

APPENDIX E

Worksheet for Summary of Approaches to Treatment of Dysfunction Based on a Theoretical Rationale

I. Theoretical approach or system of therapy (give full descriptive title):

II. Originator(s):

III. Followers:

IV. Techniques advocated (step-by-step description):

In the case of theories that do not explicitly indicate the techniques to be followed, use the underlying rationale for theory (see next section) to make your own inferences.

V. Underlying rationale:

   A. Theory
      1. Statements about the human condition
      2. Description of a functional individual
      3. Developmental stages by which functional condition is reached
   B. Therapeutic techniques
      1. Reasons for dysfunction
      2. Stages that lead to dysfunction
      3. Ways to reach function despite dysfunction
      4. Ways to reverse dysfunction
      5. Mechanisms by which change takes place
      6. Time period in which change takes place
   C. Occupational therapy

VI. Indications for clinical application (areas of dysfunction, age groups, individual patient/client considerations):

VII. Relationship to Activities Health frame of reference:

   A. Fits in with use of therapeutic activities (how?)
   B. Fits in with use of therapeutic activities with the following modifications or adjustments
   C. Does not fit in with use of therapeutic activities

Activities Lab Contract

Student's name _____

I would like to earn course credit for the following assignments (to total 200 points):

I. Constructive project
   A. Date due _____
   B. Specific project chosen (describe *process* and *end product*; see Chap. 8, Other Constructive Project Ideas for examples):

   _____

   _____

   C. Level of engagement (circle one):
   Level I   (80 points): Project can be completed in 8 hours.
   Level II (90 points): Project can be completed in 10 hours.
   Level III (100 points): Project can be completed in 12 hours.

II. Expressive project
   A. Date due: _____
   B. Specific project chosen: (describe specifics; see Chap. 8, Other Expressive Project Ideas for examples):

   _____

   _____

   III. Number of credits elected for teaching lab(s) (optional—maximum of 4 hours; may teach more than one lab; sessions may range from 1–4 hours each; see Chap. 8, Assignment 2 for explanation). Indicate the activity, number of hours, and credits for each lab you would like to teach:
   A. Activity 1: _____
      Number of hours: _____   Credits (@ 5 points per hour) _____
   B. Activity 2: _____
      Number of hours: _____   Credits (@ 5 points per hour) _____
   C. Activity 3: _____
      Number of hours: _____
      Credits (@ 5 points per hour; maximum of 20 points): _____
   D. Activity 4: _____
      Number of hours: _____   Credits (@ 5 points per hour) _____

   Total teaching credits _____

TOTAL CREDITS (should total 200 points)
   Constructive project: _____ points
   Expressive project: 100 points
   Teaching credits: _____ points
   TOTAL: 200 points

Student's signature _____

Instructor's signature _____
Date _____

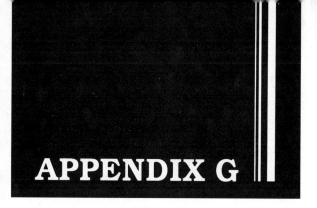

APPENDIX G

Plan for Teaching Lab

The plan for a teaching lab must include but need not be confined to the following information:

1. Name of student/leader
2. Title of class
3. Teaching/learning goals
4. Expected outcomes
5. Total number of hours; time of meeting; frequency of meeting
6. Meeting place
7. Program, hour by hour
8. Materials, equipment, tools required
9. Minimum and maximum enrollment
10. Special preliminary instructions to participants (e.g., specific attire to be worn)
11. Criteria and method(s) to be used for evaluating effectiveness of class

APPENDIX H

Guidelines for Work Interview*

1. Relevant background information about the individual interviewed: age, income (range), educational level, place of residence, family relationships, interests, hobbies, childhood working ideals (e.g., pilot, model, teacher), role models for work.
2. Work history: number of jobs; dates worked; brief description of work; information about employer; relationship to employer, fellow workers; reasons for leaving; how new job was acquired; feelings about jobs, likes/dislikes; problems, advantages, disadvantages.
3. View of self as worker (e.g., competent/not competent, appreciated/not appreciated, qualified/not qualified, interested/disinterested, permanently/temporarily employed.
4. Present job:
    a. How job was obtained
    b. Description of working environment—places, people, objects (in detail)
    c. Description (step-by-step) of job—a typical work week
    d. Hours worked—total per day; breaks (e.g., coffee, lunch); days off (e.g., vacation entitlement, sick and personal leave, holidays)
    e. Feelings about job—likes, dislikes, neutrals
    f. Training needed for job—type, duration, and cost of training
    g. Prospects for advancement
    h. Salary range for work
    i. Other jobs done concurrently
    j. Summary of job satisfactions/job problems
    k. Recognition of achievement
5. Place of work in a week's activities configuration—relationship to other activities. Use coding to distinguish work from leisure and chores in a weekly schedule.
6. Future plans: real or in fantasy; steps taken to attain goals, wishes, dreams.

* To be used in conjunction with activities pattern; see Appendix A for activities pattern instructions.

APPENDIX I

Activities Analysis Outline: Activity-Centered

I. Basic definition and description (*intrinsic properties*)—see Llorens [53] on inherent factors
   A. *Definition*: If you were observing this activity for the first time, how would you describe what it is?
      1. Intrinsic purpose
      2. Intrinsic stages and sequences
         a. Duration of each stage; total time required for entire activity
         b. Delays intrinsic to the process
         c. Is it a single process that is constant and predictable or one that has shifting, varied processes?
      3. Essential requirements
         a. Space—minimum required
         b. Tools
         c. Materials
      4. Antecedent and consequent activities that are essential to the activity (see Chapter 5, Activities as Means)
   B. Performance components entailed (based on Mosey's [62] categories and expanded; see Chapter 4, The Actor, for discussion of performance components, and note additional details included here): Describe by identifying the ways and degree to which the performance components are involved by virtue of the nature of the *activity*.*
      1. Sensory integration—processing of sensory stimuli during activity: Identify specific stimuli.
      2. Neuromuscular function
         a. Starting position* (e.g., sitting, standing, kneeling)

---

* It is intended that the performance components identified here will be compared with the description of the ways and degree to which performance components are involved when this activity is done *by a selected actor*, as identified in the actor-centered activities analysis (see Appendix J).

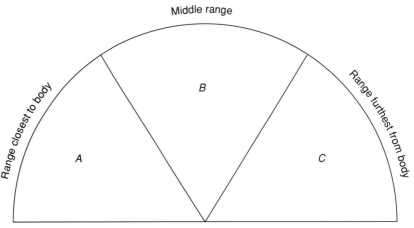

Figure I-1. Diagram showing range of motion. For simplicity, the inner range in this diagram always refers to that part of the range that is closest to the body.

    b. Joints involved and range of motion for each*: Use Figure I-1 to determine in which range movement is required: *A*, *B*, *C*, or a combination.

    c. Muscle groups involved*—see Rasch and Burke [69] on group action of muscles

    d. Coordination

        (1) Degree required (i.e., minimal, moderate, maximal)

        (2) Type (i.e., gross or fine motor, eye-hand)

    e. Strength and endurance

    f. Laterality—bilateral symmetrical (both sides involved equally), bilateral asymmetrical (dominant/assisting sides)

  3. Cognitive function

    a. Level of thinking (concrete/abstract, simple/complex)

    b. Memory required (e.g., semantic/episodic)—see Tulving [84]

    c. Degree of problem-solving and decision-making involved

  4. Social interaction

    a. Context (e.g., 1:1, group, teacher/learner, collaborative effort)

    b. Type (formal, informal)

    c. Amount

II. Variations in characteristics (*acquired characteristics*)

  A. Temporal characteristics—socioculturally determined variations in:

    1. Duration of activity

    2. Frequency of activity

---

* Note modification of outline for Assignment 2a in Chapter 9, where only a small segment of the activity is analyzed for purposes of illustration.

3. Time of day activity is done
4. Sequence
   a. How is the activity combined with other activities?
   b. What are the variations in sequencing of steps?
B. Field of action: In what kind of field of action can/does this activity take place?
C. Tools and materials: What kinds of variations are possible?
D. Performance components (see I.B): What variations are possible in relation to the actor's sociocultural context? To idiosyncratic style?
E. Meaning and relevance—socially and personally determined attributes of objects, actions, and interpersonal relationships involved in performing the activity.
   1. *Sociocultural meaning and relevance* based on how different groups perceive the activity from these perspectives:
      A. Notions of roles as they relate to age, sex, class, and status
      b. Religious and ethnic significance
      c. Historical trends and resulting attitudes
      d. Current concepts regarding work and leisure
   2. *Personal meaning and relevance* of the activity, based on how various individuals perceive the activity from these perspectives:
      a. Historical relevance—past experiences with the activity; resulting attitudes, feelings, and associations
      b. Symbolic meaning of the activity
      c. Affective feeling states generated
      d. Personal needs gratified
      e. Idiosyncratic personal style

APPENDIX J

Activities Analysis Outline: Actor-Centered

Consider the following in terms of one selected actor:

I. Basic description
   A. The purpose of the activity
   B. The steps of the activity in the sequence that they are done
   C. Tools and materials used
   D. Other activities with which it is connected (*antecedent* and *consequent activities*—see Chapter 5, Activities as Means)
   E. The field of action in which this activity takes place, including:
      1. Physical environment
      2. Human and nonhuman objects
      3. Implicit and explicit rules
   F. Time factors
      1. Duration of each stage, total time used
      2. Delays intrinsic to the process
II. Performance components (based on Mosey's [62] categories and expanded; see Chapter 4, The Actor, for discussion of performance components, and note additional details): Describe by identifying the ways and degree to which the performance components are involved by virtue of the nature of the *activity*.*
   A. Sensory integration—processing of sensory stimuli during activity: Identify specific stimuli.
   B. Neuromuscular function
      1. Starting position† (e.g., sitting, standing, kneeling)

---

* It is intended that the performance components identified here will be compared with the description of the ways and degree to which performance components are involved *by virtue of the nature of the activity alone*, as identified in the activity-centered activities analysis (see Appendix I).

† Note modification of outline for Assignment 2b in Chapter 9, where only a small segment of the activity is analyzed for purposes of illustration.

      2. Joints involved and range of motion for each*: Use Figure I-1 to determine range.
      3. Muscle groups involved*—see Rasch and Burke [69] on group action of muscles
      4. Coordination
         a. Degree required (i.e., minimal, moderate, maximal)
         b. Type (i.e., gross or fine motor, eye-hand)
      5. Strength and endurance
      6. Laterality—bilateral symmetrical (both sides involved equally), bilateral asymmetrical (dominant/assisting sides)
  C. Cognitive function
      1. Level of thinking (concrete/abstract, simple/complex)
      2. Memory required (e.g., semantic/episodic)—see Tulving [84]
      3. Degree of problem-solving and decision-making involved
  D. Social interaction
      1. Context (e.g., 1:1, group, teacher/learner, collaborative effort)
      2. Type (Formal, informal)
      3. Amount
III. Meaning and relevance to the individual
  A. Meaning and relevance as it is determined by the individual's sociocultural group, including:
      1. Notions of roles regarding the activity and age, sex, class, and status
      2. Religious and ethnic significance
      3. Historical trends and resulting attitudes
      4. Influence of current concepts regarding work and leisure
  B. Meaning and relevance as it is determined by the individual, including:
      1. Historical relevance—past experiences with the activity, resulting attitudes, feelings, and associations
      2. Symbolic meaning of the activity
      3. Affective feeling states generated
      4. Idiosyncratic personal style
  C. How the activity is integrated into the individual's past, present, and future activities configurations
      1. Time of day, day of week
      2. Frequency per week
      3. Historical duration
      4. Future projections

* See footnote † on p. 290.

References

1. Allen, C. K. *Occupational Therapy for Psychiatric Diseases: Measurement and Management of Cognitive Disabilities.* Boston: Little, Brown, 1985. Pp. 3–29.
2. Allen, C. K. Activity: Occupational therapy's treatment method—Eleanor Clarke Slagle Lecture. *Am. J. Occup. Ther.* 41:563, 1987.
3. American Occupational Therapy Association. *Essentials and Guidelines of an Accredited Educational Program for the Occupational Therapist.* Rockville, Md.: American Occupational Therapy Association, adopted 1935, revised 1983.
4. Anderson, J., Hinojosa, J., and Strauch, C. Integrating play in neurodevelopmental treatment. *Am. J. Occup. Ther.* 41:421, 1987.
5. Aristotle. *The Nicomachean Ethics II, I.* New York: Oxford University Press, 1980.
6. Asimov, I. Thinking and the Problem-Solving Process. In R. Bootain (Ed.), *Psychology Today* (5th ed.). New York: Random House, 1982.
7. Ayres, A. J. Ontogenetic Principles in the Development of Arm and Hand Function. In *The Development of Sensory Integrative Theory and Practice.* Dubuque, Iowa: Kendall/Hunt, 1974.
8. Ayres, A. J. *The Development of Sensory Integrative Theory and Practice.* Dubuque, Iowa: Kendall/Hunt, 1974.
9. Beck, A. T. *Cognitive Therapy and Emotional Disorders.* Madison, Ct.: International Universities Press, 1976.
10. Berne, Eric. *Transactional Analysis in Psychotherapy: A Systematic Individual and Social Psychiatry.* New York: Ballantine Books, 1978.
11. Bobath, K., and Bobath, B. The neurodevelopmental treatment of cerebral palsy. *Phys. Ther.* 47:1039, 1967.
12. Bronowski, J. *The Ascent of Man.* Boston: Little, Brown, 1974.
13. Browne, R. B. Popular culture as the new humanities. *J. Pop. Cult.* 17:1, 1984.
14. Bruner, J. S. A Retrospect on Making and Judging. In *Toward a Theory of Instruction.* Cambridge, Mass.: The Belknap Press of Harvard University Press, 1978.
15. Bruner, J. S. The Will to Learn. In *Toward a Theory of Instruction.* Cambridge, Mass.: The Belknap Press of Harvard University Press, 1978.
16. Brunnstrom, S. Motor behavior of adult hemiplegic patients. *Am. J. Occup. Ther.* 15:6, 1961.
17. Brunnstrom, S. *Movement Therapy in Hemiplegia.* New York: Harper & Row, 1970.
18. Buckminster Fuller, R. The Artist-Scientist-Inventor. In *The Arts and Man.* Englewood Cliffs, N.J.: Prentice-Hall, 1969.
19. Campbell, J. *Winston Churchill's Afternoon Nap.* New York: Simon & Schuster, 1986. Pp. 130–134, 149–154.
20. Curle, A. A theoretical approach to action research. *Hum. Relations* 2:271, 1949.
21. Currie, C. Evaluating function of mentally retarded children through the use of toys and play activities. *Am. J. Occup. Ther.* 23:35, 1969.

22. De Bono, E. *Lateral Thinking*. New York: Harper & Row, 1963.

23. Delind, L. B. The party behaviors of a small community. *J. Pop. Cult.* 17:85, 1983.

24. Delind, L. B. Bingo: The whys and wherefores of a popular pastime. *J. Pop. Cult.* 18:149, 1984.

25. Edlin, G., and Golanty, E. *Health and Wellness* (2nd ed.). Boston: Jones and Bartlett, 1985.

26. Erikson, E. H. Growth and Crisis in the Healthy Personality. In H. Chiang and A. Maslow (Eds.), *The Healthy Personality*. New York: Von Nostrand, Reinholt, 1969.

27. Erikson, E. H. *Childhood and Society* (35th anniversary ed.). New York: Norton, 1986.

28. Erikson, E. H. Eight Ages of Man. In *Childhood and Society* (35th anniversary ed.). New York: Norton, 1986.

29. Erwin, E. *Behavior Therapy: Scientific, Philosophical and Moral Foundation*. New York: Cambridge University Press, 1978.

30. Facklam, M., and Facklam, H. *The Brain: Magnificent Mind Machine*. New York/London: Harcourt Brace Jovanovich, 1982.

31. Fidler, G. S. The Activity Laboratory: A Structure for Observing and Assessing Perceptual, Integrative and Behavioral Strategies. In B. Hemphill (Ed.), *The Evaluation Process in Psychiatric Occupational Therapy*. Thorofare, N.J.: Slack, 1982.

32. Fidler, G. S., and Fidler, J. W. *Occupational Therapy: A Communication Process in Psychiatry*. New York: Macmillan, 1963.

33. Fidler, G. S., and Fidler, J. W. Doing and becoming: Purposeful action and self-actualization. *Am. J. Occup. Ther.* 32:305, 1978.

34. Fine, S. B. Nationally speaking—working the system: A perspective for managing change. *Am. J. Occup. Ther.* 42:417, 1988.

35. Florey, L. Studies of Play: Implications for growth, development and clinical practice. *Am. J. Occup. Ther.* 35:519, 1981.

36. Fox, S. *The Medieval Woman: An Illuminated Book of Days*. Boston: Little, Brown, 1985.

37. Frankl, V. E. *The Doctor and the Soul: From Psychotherapy to Logotherapy*. New York: Random House, 1986.

38. Freud, S. *Therapy and Technique*. New York: MacMillan, 1963.

39. Freud, S. *Introductory Lectures on Psychoanalysis: A General Introduction to Psychoanalysis*. New York: Livewright, 1977.

40. Fromm, E. *The Sane Society*. New York: Fawcett, 1977.

41. Goelet, R. Preface in R. White. *Dark Caves, Bright Visions: Life in Ice Age Europe*. New York/London: Norton, 1986.

42. Harlow, H. F. Behavior of Non-Human Primates. In A. M. Schrier and F. Stollnitz (Eds.), *Modern Research Trends*, Vol. 1 and 2. New York: Academic, 1965.

43. Hein, E. C. *Communication in Nursing Practice*. Boston: Little, Brown, 1973.

44. Kielhofner, G. Temporal adaptation: A conceptual framework for occupational therapy. *Am. J. Occup. Ther.* 31:235, 1977.

45. Kielhofner, G., and Burke, J. P. A model of human occupation: Part One. Conceptual framework and content. *Am. J. Occup. Ther.* 34:572, 1980.

46. Kluckhohn, C., and Murray, H. A. *Personality in Nature, Society and Culture* (2nd ed.). New York: Knopf, 1961.

47. Kneller, G. F. *Science as Human Endeavor*. New York: Columbia University Press, 1978.

48. Kolb, D. A. *Experiential Learning: Experience as the Source of Learning and Development*. Englewood Cliffs, N.J.: Prentice-Hall, 1984.

49. Krathwohl, D. R., Bloom, B. S., and Masia, B. B. *Taxonomy of Educational Objectives—Book 2: Affective Domain*. New York: Longman, 1964.

50. Kroeber, A. L. *Anthropology: Culture Patterns and Processes*. New York: Harcourt Brace Jovonavich, 1963.

51. Lifton, W. M. *Groups Facilitating Individual Growth and Social Change*. New York: Wiley, 1972.

52. Llorens, L. Facilitating growth and development: The promise of occupational therapy. *Am. J. Occup. Ther.* 24:93, 1967.

53. Llorens, L. Activity analysis for cognitive-perceptual-motor dysfunction. *Am. J. Occup. Ther.* 27:453, 1973.

54. Llorens, L. Activity analysis: Agreement among factors in a sensory processing model. *Am. J. Occup. Ther.* 40:103, 1986.

55. Lorant, S. *The New World: The First Pictures of America.* New York: Duell, Sloan & Peerce, 1946.

56. Maslow, A. H. *Toward a Psychology of Being* (2nd ed.). New York: Van Nostrand, Reinhold, 1968.

57. Matsutsuyu, J. S. The interest check list. *Am. J. Occup. Ther.* 23:323, 1969.

58. McGoldrick, M., and Gerson, R. Constructing Genograms. In *Genograms in Family Assessment.* New York: Norton, 1985.

59. Miller, B. R. J. What Is Theory and Why Does It Matter? In B. R. J. Miller et al. *Six Perspectives on Theory for the Practice of Occupational Therapy.* Rockville, Md.: Aspen, 1988.

60. Morehead, L. The occupational history. *Am. J. Occup. Ther.* 23:329, 1969.

61. Mosey, A. C. The concept and use of developmental groups. *Am. J. Occup. Ther.* 24:272, 1970.

62. Mosey, A. C. *Occupational Therapy: Configuration of a Profession.* New York: Raven, 1981. Pp. 75–76.

63. Nystrom, E. P. Activity patterns and leisure concepts among the elderly. *Am. J. Occup. Ther.* 28:337, 1976.

64. Opie, I., and Opie, P. *Children's Games in Street and Playground.* New York: Oxford University Press, 1985.

65. Pacey, P. Family art: Domestic and eternal bliss. *J. Pop. Cult.* 18:43, 1984.

66. Parham, D. Nationally speaking—towards professionalism: The reflective therapist. *Am. J. Occup. Ther.* 41:555, 1987.

67. Piaget, J., and Inhelder, B. *Psychology of the Child.* New York: Basic Books, 1969.

68. Price, J. A. Social science research on video games. *J. Pop. Cult.* 18:111, 1985.

69. Rasch, P. J., and Burke, R. K. *Kinesiology and Applied Anatomy: The Science of Human Movement* (6th ed.). Philadelphia: Lea & Febiger, 1978.

70. Reed, K. L. Tools of practice: Heritage or baggage?—1986 Eleanor Clarke Slagle Lecture. *Am. J. Occup. Ther.* 40:597, 1986.

71. Reilly, M. Occupational therapy can be one of the great ideas of twentieth century medicine—Eleanor Clarke Slagle Lecture. *Am. J. Occup. Ther.* 16:1, 1962.

72. Reilly, M. (Ed.). *Play as Exploratory Learning.* Beverly Hills, Calif.: Russell Sage, 1974.

73. Rogers, C. R. *Client-Centered Therapy.* Boston: Houghton-Mifflin, 1957.

74. Rogers, C. R. *Freedom to Learn.* Columbus, Ohio: Merrill, 1969.

75. Rogers, J., and Masagatini, G. Clinical reasoning of occupational therapists during the initial assessment of physically disabled patients. *Occup. Ther. J. Res.* 2:195, 1982.

76. Rood, M. S. Neurophysiological mechanisms utilized in treatment of neuromuscular dysfunction. *Am. J. Occup. Ther.* 4:220, 1956.

77. Rubin, K. Early Play Theories Revisited. In D. J. Pepler and K. H. Rubin (Eds.), *The Play of Children: Current Theory and Research.* New York: Karger, 1982.

78. Ruesch, J., and Bateson, G. *Communication: The Social Matrix of Psychiatry.* New York: Norton, 1987.

79. Sharrott, G. W. Occupational Therapy's Role in the Client's Creation and Affirmation of Reality. In G. Kielhofner (Ed.), *Health Through Occupation.* Philadelphia: Davis, 1983.

80. Smithsonian Institution. *Village Life* and *Children at Play*—17th century Chinese scrolls. Washington, D.C.: Collection of Freer Gallery of Art, exhibited January, 1983.

81. Szalai, A. Introduction: Concepts and Practice of Time-Budget Research. In A. Szalai (Ed.), *The Use of Time: Daily Activities of Urban and Suburban Populations in Twelve Countries.* The Hague: Mouton, 1972.

82. Takata, N. The play history. *Am. J. Occup. Ther.* 23:314, 1969.

83. Terkel, S. *Working.* New York: Ballantine Books, 1985.

84. Tulving, E. *Elements of Episodic Memory.* Oxford Psychology Series No. 2. Oxford, England: Oxford University Press, 1983.

85. Ulich, U. (Ed.). John Dewey. In *Three Thousand Years of Educational Wisdom: Selections from Great Documents.* Cambridge, Ma.: Harvard University Press, 1954.

86. Wagner, E. A. Baseball in Cuba. *J. Pop. Cult.* 18:113, 1984.

References

87. West, W. L. A reaffirmed philosophy and practice of occupational therapy for the 1980's. *Am. J. Occup. Ther.* 38:15, 1984.

88. White, R. *Dark Caves, Bright Visions: Life in Ice Age Europe.* New York/London: Norton, 1986.

89. White, R. W. Motivation Reconsidered: The Concept of Competence. In L. Y. Rabkin and J. E. Carr (Eds.), *Sourcebook of Abnormal Psychology.* Boston: Houghton Mifflin, 1967.

90. White, R. W. The urge toward competence. *Am. J. Occup. Ther.* 25:271, 1971.

91. Yerxa, E. J. Nationally speaking—research: The key to the development of occupational therapy as an academic discipline. *Am. J. Occup. Ther.* 41:415, 1987.

Suggested Reading

Abreu, B. C., and Toglia, J. P. Cognitive rehabilitation: A model for occupational therapy. *Am. J. Occup. Ther.* 41:439, 1987.

American Journal of Occupational Therapy. Special AOTA 60th Anniversary 1917–1977 Commemorative Issue: A retrospective and prospective view of occupational therapy. Vol. 31, November–December 1977.

Berger, M. M. *Working with People Called Patients.* New York: Bruner-Mazel, 1977.

Bibring, E. The Mechanism of Depression. In P. Greenacre (Ed.), *Affective Disorders: Psychoanalytic Contributions to Their Study.* New York: International University Press, 1961.

Breines, E. An attempt to define purposeful activity. *Am. J. Occup. Ther.* 38:543, 1984.

Breines, E. Pragmatism as a foundation for occupational therapy curricula. *Am. J. Occup. Ther.* 41:322, 1987.

Bronowski, J. *Science and Human Values.* New York: Harper & Row, 1972.

Chatthopadaya, K. The Crafts as an Embodiment of the Great Folk Tradition. In *The Arts and Man.* Englewood Cliffs, N.J.: Prentice-Hall, 1969.

Dasen, P. R. The value of play. *World Health,* Jan./Feb., 1984.

Diasio, K. Psychiatric occupational therapy: Search for a conceptual framework in light of psychoanalytic ego psychology and learning theory. *Am. J. Occup. Ther.* 22:400, 1968.

Erikson, E. H. *Childhood and Society.* New York: Norton, 1986.

Fidler, G. S. From crafts to competence. *Am. J. Occup. Ther.* 35:567, 1981.

Fidler, G. S. *Design of Rehabilitation Services in Psychiatric Settings.* Laurel, Md.: Ramsco, 1984.

Florey, L. L. Intrinsic motivation: The dynamics of occupational therapy theory. *Am. J. Occup. Ther.* 23:319, 1969.

Florey, L., and Michelman, S. Occupational role history: A screening tool for psychiatric occupational therapy. *Am. J. Occup. Ther.* 36:301, 1982.

Fogel, V., and Rosillo, R. Correlation of psychological variables and progress in physical rehabilitation. *Dis. Nerv. Syst.* 30:593, 1969.

Freud, S. *Civilization and Its Discontents.* Edited by J. Strachey. New York: Norton, 1984.

Greenberg, L., Fine, S., Cohen, C., et al. An interdisciplinary psychoeducation program for schizophrenic patients and their families in an acute care setting. *Hosp. Comm. Psychiatry* 39:277, 1988.

Hasselkus, B., and Safrit, M. J. Measurement in occupational therapy. *Am. J. Occup. Ther.* 30:429, 1976.

Heine, D. B. Daily living group: Focus on transition from hospital to community. *Am. J. Occup. Ther.* 29:628, 1975.

Hinojosa, J., Sabari, J., and Rosenfeld, M. Purposeful activities. *Am. J. Occup. Ther.* 37:805, 1983.

Holt, J. *How Children Learn* (rev. ed.). New York: Dell, 1986.

Hurlock, E. *The Psychology of Dress: An Analysis of Fashion and Its Motive.* Salem, N.H.: Ayer Co., Repr. of 1929.

Hurlock, E. B. *Developmental Psychology: A Life-Span Approach* (5th ed.). New York: McGraw-Hill, 1980.

Jones, M. *The Therapeutic Community.* New York: Basic Books, 1953.

Jones, M. *Beyond the Therapeutic Community.* New Haven, Conn.: Yale University Press, 1968.

Jung, C. *Man and His Symbols* (24th printing). New York: Laurel/Dell, 1984.

Kottak, C. P. *Cultural Anthropology* (4th ed.). New York: Knopf, 1986.

Levi-Strauss, C. *Tristes Tropiques* (rev. ed.). Evanston, Ill: Adler's Foreign Books, 1984.

Llorens, L. A. *Application of a Developmental Theory for Health and Rehabilitation.* Rockville, Md.: American Occupational Therapy Association, 1976.

Lyons, B. G. Purposeful versus human activity. *Am. J. Occup. Ther.* 37:493, 1983.

Marmo, N. A. Discovering the lifestyle of the physically disabled. *Am. J. Occup. Ther.* 29:475, 1975.

Matsutsuyu, J. Occupational behavior: A perspective on work and play. *Am. J. Occup. Ther.* 25:291, 1971.

Mechanic, D., Lewis, C., and Fein, R. The growth of bureaucratic medicine: An inquiry into the dynamics of patient behavior and the organization of medical care. *A Right to Health.* New York: Wiley, 1976.

Miller, P. Preventive Treatment Approaches. In L. Davis and M. Kirkland (Eds.), *ROTE: The Role of Occupational Therapy with the Elderly.* Rockville, Maryland: American Occupational Therapy Association, 1986. Pp. 227–235.

Miller, P. Models for Treatment of Depression. In E. Taira (Ed.), *Community Programs for the Depressed Elderly: A Rehabilitation Approach.* New York: Harworth, 1987. Pp. 3–11.

Miller, R. J. (Senior Author). *Six Perspectives on Theory for the Practice of Occupational Therapy.* Rockville, Md.: Aspen, 1988.

Mosey, A. C. *Psychosocial Components of Occupational Therapy.* New York: Raven, 1986.

Peck, R. Psychological Developments in the Second Half of Life. In B. L. Neugarten (Ed.), *Middle Age and Aging.* Chicago: University of Chicago Press, 1968. Pp. 88–92.

Pelland, M. J. A conceptual model for the instruction and supervision of treatment planning. *Am. J. Occup. Ther.* 41:351, 1987.

Rogers, J. D. Clinical reasoning: The ethics, science, and art—Eleanor Clarke Slagle Lecture. *Am. J. Occup. Ther.* 37:601, 1983.

Schwartzman, H. B. The anthropological study of children's play. *Annu. Rev. Anthro.* 5:289, 1976.

Wehman, P., and Abramson, M. Three theoretical approaches to play: Applications for exceptional children. *Am. J. Occup. Ther.* 30:551, 1976.

White, R. W. (Ed.). *Workbook in Personality.* Prospect Hghts., Ill.: Waveland, 1982.

Williamson, G. G. A heritage of activity: Development of theory. *Am. J. Occup. Ther.* 36:716, 1982.

World Federation of Occupational Therapists. *Cultural Patterns and Their Influence on Rehabilitation: Proceedings of Third International Congress.* Philadelphia: The Federation, 1962.

Worth, S., and Adair, J. Navajo filmmakers. *Am. Anthro.* 72:9, 1970.

Yerxa, E. Authentic occupational therapy. *Am. J. Occup. Ther.* 21:1, 1967.

Zimmerman, M. Devices: Development and direction—1960 Eleanor Clarke Slagle Lecture. *Am. J. Occup. Ther.*, AOTA Conference Issue, 1960.

Index